Lecture Notes of the Institute for Computer Sciences, Social Informatics and Telecommunications Engineering   104

Alessandro Puiatti   Tao Gu (Eds.)

Mobile and Ubiquitous Systems: Computing, Networking, and Services

8th International ICST Conference, MobiQuitous 2011
Copenhagen, Denmark, December 6–9, 2011
Revised Selected Papers

 Springer

Volume Editors

Alessandro Puiatti
Networking Lab - ISIN SUPSI-DTI
Centro Galleria 2
6928 Manno, Switzerland
E-mail: alessandro.puiatti@supsi.ch

Tao Gu
University of Southern Denmark
Department of Mathematics and Computer Science
Campusvej 55, Odense M., Denmark
E-mail: gu@imada.sdu.dk

ISSN 1867-8211   ISSN 1867-822X
ISBN 978-3-642-30972-4   ISBN 978-3-642-30973-1 (eBook)
DOI 10.1007/978-3-642-30973-1

Springer Heidelberg Dordrecht London New York

Library of Congress Control Number: 2012939380

CR Subject Classification (1998): C.2, H.4, I.2, H.3, D.2, H.5

Typesetting: Camera-ready by author, data conversion by Scientific Publishing Services, Chennai, India

Printed on acid-free paper

Springer is part of Springer Science+Business Media (www.springer.com)

Preface

This volume is the result of the 8th Annual International Conference on Mobile and Ubiquitous Systems: Computing, Networking and Services (MobiQuitous 2011), which was held in Copenhagen during December 6–9, 2011.

Copenhagen is the capital and largest city of Denmark, and one of the most beautiful cities of northern Europe. It is a major regional center of culture, business, media, and science, as indicated by several international surveys and rankings. Life science, information technology and shipping are important sectors, and research & development plays a major role in the city's economy. Its strategic location and excellent infrastructure, with the largest airport in Scandinavia located 14 minutes by train from the city center, have made it a regional hub and a popular location for regional headquarters and conventions.

MobiQuitous has a well-established reputation as a friendly and interactive forum for practitioners and researchers from diverse backgrounds, where they can interact and exchange experiences about the design and implementation of mobile and ubiquitous systems.

This year the main conference was complemented by an industry track, including contributions from industry researchers and from professionals in the field, and a poster and demo session. The program also featured two keynote speeches delivered by distinguished experts in the field. Sajal K. Das (Director of the Center of Research in Wireless Mobility and Networking, at the University of Texas at Arlington, USA), opened the first conference day with a speech on collaborative, distributed, and multi-modal sensing applications entitled "Collaborative Multi-modal Sensing: Challenges and Opportunities." The second day was opened by Andrew T. Campbell (Director of the Smartphone Sensing Group at the Dartmouth College, USA), who presented the potentialities and the challenges of the smartphone as a sensing devise in the speech entitled "Smartphone Sensing for the Masses." At the end of the conference two workshops covered emerging research areas in the field of wireless sensors networks, [The Second International Workshop on Advanced Applications in Sensor Networks (WAASN)], and in design, evaluation, optimization and testing of systems for context computing [Third Workshop on Context-Systems Design, Evaluation and Optimization (CoSDEO)].

This volume includes the revised versions of all papers, posters and demos presented at MobiQuitous 2011 in a single-track format, organized thematically in nine parts as indicated in the Table of Contents. We also had a dedicated session for papers that were competing for the "Best Paper Award," which was assigned to the paper entitled "What's Around Me? Spatialized Audio Augmented Reality for Blind Users with a Smartphone" (Jeffrey Blum, Mathieu Bouchard and Jeremy Cooperstock). We also assigned a "Best Paper Run-Up Award" to the second best paper: "Real-Time Detection of Anomalous Taxi

Trajectories from GPS Traces" (Chao Chen, Daqing Zhang, Pablo Samuel Castro, Nan Li, Lin Sun and Shijian Li).

Attendance increased this year considerably, laying the foundation for establishing MobiQuitous as a key annual conference in the calendar of researchers in this area. We are happy to announce that the ninth edition of MobiQuitous will be held in Beijing in December 2012.

We close this preface by acknowledging the vital role that the Technical Program Committee members and additional referees played during the review process. Their efforts ensured that all submitted papers received a proper evaluation. We thank EAI, and ICST for assisting with organization matters, and CREATE-NET, Nokia, and Technocell AG for technically co-sponsoring the event, and the University of Applied Sciences and Arts of Southern Switzerland (SUPSI), for supporting the organization of the event. We also thank the rest of the team that put together this year's event, in particular the Publicity Co-chairs Mikkel Baun Kjærgaard, Yunhuai Liu, and Qi Han, and the Web Chair Alan Ferrari. We particularly thank Elena J. Fezzardi who managed the financial issues, the publication process and the local organization in a very prompt and professional manner on behalf of EAI, and Imrich Chlamtac of CREATE-NET for his continuous support of the conference. Finally, we thank all participants for attending MobiQuitous 2011 and making it such a successful conference!

December 2011   Alessandro Puiatti
                                                              Tao Gu
                                                    Florian Michahelles
                                                          Marc Brogle
                                                      Emiliano Miluzzo

Organization

General Chair

Alessandro Puiatti
Networking Lab - ISIN
University of Applied Sciences and Arts of Southern Switzerland
Centro Galleria 2
6928 Manno
Switzerland

Technical Program Chair

Tao Gu
Department of Mathematics and Computer Science
University of Southern Denmark
Campusvej 55 DK-5230
Odense M
Denmark

Florian Michahelles
ETH Zurich
Scheuchzerstrasse 7
8092 Zürich
Switzerland

Publicity Co-chairs

Europe: Mikkel Baun Kjærgaard
Institut for Datalogi
Åbogade 34
bygning 5346, lokale 121
8200 Aarhus N
Denmark

Asia: Yunhuai Liu
Shenzhen Institute of Advanced Technology
1068 Xueyuan Avenue, Shenzhen University Town
Shenzhen
P.R. China

USA: Qi Han
Colorado School of Mines
1500 Illinois Street
Golden, CO 80401

Financial Chair

EAI
Elena J. Fezzardi
Via alla Cascata 56 C
Povo, Trento
Italy

Industry Track Chair

Marc Brogle
SAP Research Zürich
8008 Zürich
Switzerland

Demo and Poster Chair

Emiliano Miluzzo
AT&T Labs
180 Park Avenue
Florham Park, NJ, 07932
USA

Web Chair

Alan Ferrari
Networking Lab - ISIN
University of Applied Sciences and Arts of Southern Switzerland
Centro Galleria 2
6928 Manno
Switzerland

Table of Contents

Classification and Profiling

Industry Track

Poster and Demo

Wireless Communication and Routing

Context Awareness and Architecture

Location and Activity Recognition

Social Geoscape: Visualizing an Image of the City for Mobile UI Using User Generated Geo-Tagged Objects

Koh Sueda[1], Takashi Miyaki[2], and Jun Rekimoto[3]

[1] The Univesity of Tokyo/National University of Singapore
[2] Karlsruhe Institute of Technology
[3] The University of Tokyo/Sony CSL
21 Heng Mui Keng Terrace, Level 2 Singapore 119613
apochang.jp@gmail.com, {rekimoto,miyaki}@acm.org

Abstract. In this paper, we propose a people-powered location recognition application, Social Geoscape (SGS) that provides highly descriptive geographical information to mobile users. GPS provides the user with latitude and longitude values; however, these values are cumbersome for determining a precise location. A traditional reverse-geocoding database system (i.e., one that converts latitude and longitude values into street addresses) provides locative information based on administrative labeling, but people often do not recognize locations or their surrounding environs from street addresses alone. To address this problem with location recognition, we have created Social Geoscape, a reverse geocoding system that enhances locative data with user-generated information and provides assistance through a mobile interface.

Keywords: Social tagging, Visualization, Design, Urban sensing, Mobile interaction, Reverse geocoding, AR, Social Geoscape.

1 Introduction

In today's world, people often use GIS (geographic information systems) or GPS (global positioning systems) on mobile devices in their everyday lives. People have used these technologies based on latitude and longitude values for navigation and to record people's activities. The values of latitude and longitude are not easily understood by typical users, so several GIS technologies provide the corresponding street addresses using a reverse geocoding database (i.e., a database that converts latitude and longitude values into street addresses); however, users cannot always identify the spatial correlation between the street address and the user's location. Generally speaking, users define their spatial understanding from their memories and personal experiences [1]. Thus, their definition of a space is not the same as a street address defined by an administrative district. According to 'The Image of the City' written by Kevin Lynch [1], people define places by not only street addresses but also using other factors, including landmarks, nodes (e.g. waiting points, stations, intersections), rivers, nicknames of the places, and famous events that occur at a well-known locale. Lynch also pointed out that people build a "public image", which is the overlap of many individual definitions for the living environment. For example, people who live in Tokyo identify places as being "around Tokyo tower"

A. Puiatti et al. (Eds.): MobiQuitous 2011, LNICST 104, pp. 1–12, 2012.
© Institute for Computer Sciences, Social Informatics and Telecommunications Engineering 2012

(a landmark), "near Sumidagawa" (a river), or "at the front of Shibuya station" (a node), and these places are not defined by street addresses. In this study, we focused on user tags from geotagged photos on the Flickr (www.flickr.com) website. Users tag these photos with descriptions alluding to environments, situations, and interests that were relevant when the user took the photo. Many web services (including Flickr) can provide information that is easily understood by using the user tags as collective intelligence [2]. At present, there are already over one hundred million geotagged photos on Flickr, which include social tagging by their users. In this study, we utilize the user tags as collective intelligence to capture the public image from living environments. The aim of this study is to propose "Social Geoscape" that allows mobile users to provide their image of an environment. This is meant to encourage the retrieval of users' memories and stimulate discovery in their daily lives through use of geotagged objects such as photos and user tags on the Internet.

2   Visualizing "The Image of the City"

As mentioned above, people often do not recognize places or situations from the street address alone. Figure 1 is a plot of geotagged photos from Flickr that users tagged as 'Shibuya' (included in Japanese characters) in Shibuya-ward. In order to plot these images onto the maps we use statistical algorithms with R (a tool for statistical computing and graphics (www.r-project.org)).

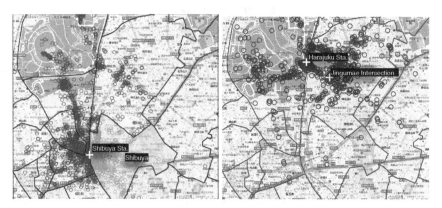

Fig. 1. The plot of photos tagged as 'Shibuya' (Blue circles) and Shibuya district defined by street address (yellow area) [Left]. The Plot of photos tagged, as 'Harajuku' [Right].

The left of Fig 1 shows the plot of photos tagged as "Shibuya" and Shibuya district defined by street address. (Shibuya-ward area is one of busy downtown area in Tokyo. Also this area has a lot of geotagged photos on Flickr.) As can be seen in this figure, we compared the area tagged 'Shibuya' in the geotagged photos with 'Shibuya' defined by the street address (yellow area located on the east side of Shibuya station). Outside the western boundaries of the Shibuya area, as defined by street addresses, many users tagged more of the area as "Shibuya" (blue circles in Figure 1). We can assume that many users recognize both the eastern and western areas of Shibuya station as Shibuya. The right of Fig 1 shows the points tagged as 'Harajuku.' Harajuku is not currently a street address, although 'Harajuku' was a street address located in the northeastern parts of the Jingumae intersection 50 years ago., close to where the points extend around Harajuku station. We can observe that the users recognize the place "Harajuku" by the station name and not by a street address. We can observe the difference between users' definition of the space and definitions of the street addresses.

2.1   Visualizing Spatial Definition Using Kernel Density Estimation

The public image often defines a space as an overlap, so it is difficult to describe a tree structure as merely street addresses. According to 'A City Is Not a Tree' by C. Alexander [3], a city is composed of many factors overlapping one another. Thus, the structure of the city is a semi-lattice form, not a tree. Alternately, a tree structure defines the structure of street addresses. Table 1 samples geotagged photos from Flickr that have the tag "Omotesando" in the map in Table 1. We can find other place names such as Tokyo, Harajuku, and Meiji-jingu (a Shinto shrine) in the photos (indicated red in a font). The users who took these photos tagged them with place names according to their recognition of the place. Social tagging allows users to collectively classify and find information from spatial, temporal, and social contextual metadata [4]. Using this metadata, we apply social tagging to the real space to visualize an image of the city that is easier for users to understand.

Table 1. The sample of photos tagged as "Omotesando"

Tags
,aoyama,...,omotesando,geo:lat=35.664...
Tokyo...omotesando,....aoyama ...
Tokyo,omotesando,....aoyama... tower,geotagged,earth@
...tokyo,....omotesando,harajuku,....,表参道,原宿,神宮前,jingumae,
Tokyo,jingumae,night,light,omotesando ...hills,geotagged,geo:...

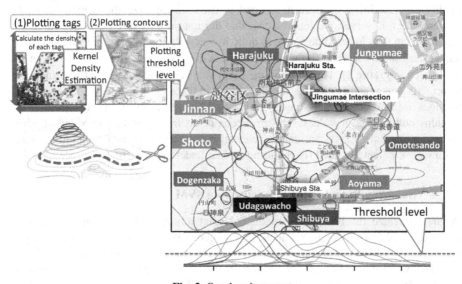

Fig. 2. Overlapping areas

Figure 2 shows the people-defined Shibuya map using kernel density estimation, plotted by using functions of the statistical programming language R. Kernel density estimation is an algorithm that makes it possible to extrapolate the data to the entire population. In this case, we use a library of R that is named "kde2d."[5] We extracted 7918 photos with tagged place names (street addresses, station, street name) from Flickr, and plotted contour lines of the place names. In this case, we calculated the density of these tags (Table 2) to indicate the areas of the geotagged objects, which we plotted with the following procedures:

Table 2. Frequency of place names occurring in tags

Name of place	Qty
shibuya (or "渋谷")	4250
harajuku (or "原宿")	2043
omotesando (or "表参道")	727
aoyama (or "青山")	301
dogenzaka (or "道玄坂")	150
jinnan (or "神南")	141
jingumae (or "神宮前")	140
udagawacho (or "宇田川町")	96
shoto (or "松濤")	14

1. Dividing each latitude and longitude axis of the area (Fig. 1) into 1000 parts, and plotting the geotagged photos in these areas, which are named according to the place names (Table 2: total of 7918 photos).
2. Estimating the density of the cluster of tags by the function "kde2d" (Fig. 2 (1))
3. Plotting the contour lines of these clusters of tags (Fig. 2(2)).
4. Extracting the contour line, thresholded 2% of the height of these clustered tags, and plotting it onto the map (Fig. 2).

2.1.1 Findings

As can be seen in this figure, the areas overlap each other, which is similar to what is shown in Figure 1. For example, three areas at Jingumae intersection surrounding the location. ("Omotesando" (green), "Harajuku" (red), and "Jingumae"(golden)). The result indicates that SGS users can utilize this map as a public image to aid cognition. In this case, defining the threshold level is used to optimize the density of each clustered tags; however, we found a case that did not produce a relevant definition of the area from the clustered tags, due to quite low density in the area. In the case of the tag cluster "shoto (or 松濤)", the defined area is divided into 2 areas (circled areas as light green in Figure 2). The photo in the north side is a shot of a post office, and was incorrectly geotagged photo (i.e, it did not exist in the area). Basically, social tagging provides information that is easily understood by using the user tags even if it contains outlier tags or values. The erroneous result indicates that we should find a minimum amount of tags that enable relevant definition of an area. In addition, this finding also indicates a need for requiring outlier detection by statistical procedures.

2.2 Visualizing Boundary of Districts Using SVM

People recognize the boundaries of districts that adjoin each other in their public images. Usually, we recognize a district by its geographical features or scenery (e.g., a government office quarter, a shopping zone, a park)[1]. Therefore, we recognize a boundary when the features of the scenery change. Some geotagged photos contain a tag that describes the geographical names using the users' spatial definition. The characteristics of the place also affect the tag. Thus, we classify geotagged photos to visualize the boundaries of districts using SVM (support-vector machines, which are methods used for classification and regression). SVM is a set of related supervised learning methods used for classification with an algorithm that is similar to a spam-filtering algorithm. In this study, we also borrowed the algorithm from functions "ksvm" of statistical programming language R [6].

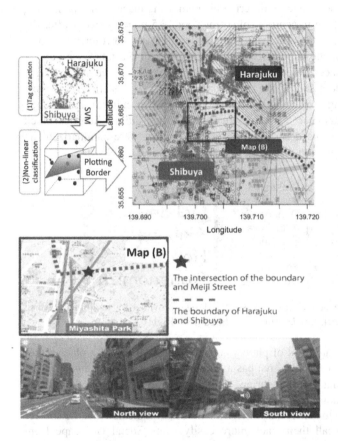

2.2.1 Findings

In Fig. 3, we classify the photos, which include a tag for "Shibuya" or "Harajuku," into two areas using SVM. The zoomed map in Fig.3 shows the point crossing the boundary line (red line) and Meiji-dori Street (the street lined by green lines). In the area around this point, the scenery changes from buildings lining the street to an area that is more open to the sky than the surroundings (Miyashita Park). In addition, Meiji-dori Street is curved. (The lower two photos in Fig.3 are from the Google street view.) According to 'The Image of the City', these visual features can be viewed as the boundaries of the district for residents. The north/south view of the crossing point indicates the suggested method can be used to find a boundary of districts.

Fig. 3. Plot of the boundary (Shibuya and Harajuku) by SVM using tags in geotagged photos from flickr (4250(Shibuya) and 2043(Harajuku) of 53522 photos in this area.)) In map (B), the boundary is plotted by SVM (the red line in the top figure). Around the intersection of the boundary and the street (blue star), the scenery changes from buildings lining the street to the park opened to the sky (the north and south views in the lower right photos), and the street is curved.

3   Preliminary Evaluations

3.1   Social Geoscape vs. Traditional Reverse Geocoding

We conducted an evaluation to compare normal reverse geocoding with Social Geoscape. In the experiment, the subject walked around with a GPS logger, but was not notified the aim of experiment. The GPS used in this experiment was a Holux M-241. After that we asked the subject to describe his path using place names he knows. We logged 3.2Km of his path in central Tokyo for about 5.5 hours. A week after the experiment, we interviewed the participant, to exclude affects of short-term memory. Fig.4 shows the results of the experiment. As can be seen in the table, the subject described his paths as places where he had walked. The subject did not describe "Sotokanda" (a street address near the Akihabara station. Akihabara is a largest electrical devices shopping area and a mecca of Japanese pop culture) and "Kanda surugadai" (a street address near "Ochanomizu station"), and did not describe block number (e.g. "1 chome"). The descriptions from the subject were summarized the same as SGS except "Yushima (a district of near the University of Tokyo)."

Fig. 4. Comparing with the activity logs by street address provided by traditional reverse geocoding (Left), SGS (Center), and description of the subject (Right)

In Yushima area, there are a lot of photos tagged with the name of a place rather than nearby other areas, because the area has a famous shrine named Yushima Tenjin (湯島天神) and places related to the shrine. According to the interview, the subject recognized the shrine is not close to his path of this experiment, as the subject has used a different path to go to the shrine. Otherwise the result indicated that the subject was able to review or recall their track more easily using Social Geoscape from Flickr's user tags than traditional reverse geocoding.

3.2   SGS vs. "The Image of the City" ~Drawing Cognitive Maps Using Geotagged Objects~

Comparing SGS with the cognition maps made for 'The Image of the City', in Lynch's research, he surveyed Boston, Los Angeles, and Jersey City in the 1960's. He plotted cognitive maps of these cities based on the result of interviewing to the residents and observing residents' behaviors. In this section, we compare Lynch's map with SGS's maps defined by social tagging in Los Angeles. In this case, we observe that both definitions have a connection to each other. In addition, we describe the interesting fact that the SGS map references the historical changes in Los Angeles.

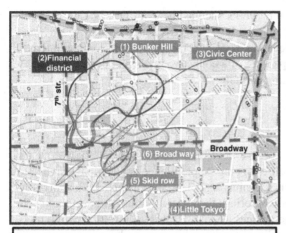

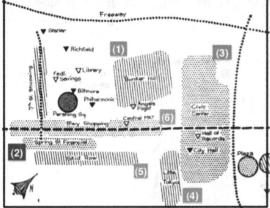

Fig. 5. Comparison of the significant elements of L.A. in the 1960's and the 2000's

Table 3. The number of tags from Downtown Los Angeles area on Flickr (Jun. 2010)

Place label	Qty
bunker hill	221
civic center	40
financial-district	178
little tokyo	3398
skid row	191
broadway	664
---	---
disney	3476
anime	6930

3.2.1   Comparison of the Significant Elements of L.A. in the 1960's and the 2000's

These two maps indicate the districts of the central part of Los Angeles (L.A.). The bottom map is from The Image of the City (Fig.5). This map shows the significant elements of L.A. in the 1960's. The top map indicates the same districts as the bottom one but uses SGS. In Table 3, the quoted photos were taken from 2003 to 2010 with "Bunker Hill" in the golden area (1), "Financial district" in the blue area (2), "Civic Center" in the purple area (3), "Little Tokyo" in the sky-blue area (4), "Skid Row" in the pink area (5), and "Broadway" in the green area. (6). As can be seen in the top map, it cannot find "Shopping districts." (There is no photo that was tagged as "shopping" in this map.) Actually, "Shopping district" are defined on the suburban area located outside of the map area. So we can guess the user did not choose to define the shopping district as "shopping area." "Little Tokyo" and "Broadway" are almost the same as the 1960's. These areas have had clear definitions by the people for nearly 50 years.

On the other hand, the definition of "Financial district" has completely changed. By the 1960's, the district was mainly located on Spring Street, however, between the 1970-1980's, the district began to decline and the main parts of the financial district have been moving to the western area of "Spring Street" until now [7]. "Bunker Hill", "Civic Center", and "Skid Row" have changed slightly. In addition, we found some quite vivid elements that emerged after the 1960's such as the Walt Disney Concert Hall. There are over 3000 tags related with this hall (tagged "disney", "disney hall", and "disney concert hall") around the location. Using geotagged objects from the Internet, these results indicate not only the plotting of a collective intelligent cognitive map by use but also reflecting on the changing of a city.

4   Applications

As an application of Social Geoscape, we developed 'Kioku Hacker' (kioku means memory in Japanese), a navigation/life-logging Apple iPhone application designed to apply our concept and to obtain user evaluations. The aim of this application is to assist the users in reviewing (or rediscovering) their activities and to grasp the image of their environs using their mobile devices. 'Kioku Hacker' allows the mobile users navigation and life logging functionalities, (1) providing people-defined geographical information (2) providing recommended tags from social tagging by user-generated geotagged objects using Flickr's API.

Fig. 6. This system enables overlaying the local maps and cognitive maps defined by geotagged social tagging. The user of the system is able to use zooming search the place by choosing the words from tags suggested by a use of this system.

4.1   Zoomable Socioscape Navigator

Fig. 6 shows a navigation user interface that enables overlaying the local maps and cognitive maps defined by SGS. The user can understand the scale of spatial keywords by simply tapping the tag (in Fig. 6) suggested through use of SGS. The interface is not always able to fit on the screen by using conventional geographical navigation systems, as can be seen in Fig. 6, the screen shots of this sample application. When the user selects the word "浅草 (asakusa)", the map zooms in (or out) to the area of the place quickly and to specify recommendation range of the tags define by SGS. Now we are developing a navigation tool that provides a better understanding of navigation supported by the folksonomic spatial definition using SGS as daily mobile navigation tool. (The spaces are defined by using kernel density estimation described in the previous section of this paper.) This system allows the user to access the 'navigate' function by jumping to a relevant area and adjusting the relevant scale of each area by selecting the recommended tags indicated on the screen, without using the keyboard on the mobile device.

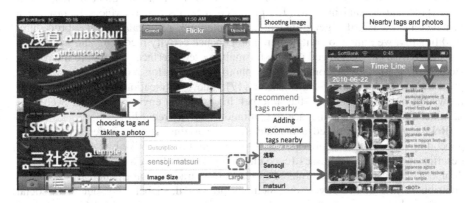

Fig. 7. Easy tagging Cam: Simultaneous photo capture and tagging conducted by tapping the overlaid tag recommendation. The taken photos are listed with nearby tags and photos as timeline style lifelog

4.2 Easy Tagging Cam: Tagging Recommendation System for Sustainable Life-Logging

'Kioku Hacker' is equipped with a digital image recording function equipped with multiple shutter buttons (Fig. 7). Tagging is a powerful method to retrieve (or find) user's records and to develop a re-usable life-log. At the same time, tagging is time consuming. This function lets users capture and tag photographs simultaneously. Hence allowing the user to be set free from tagging tasks. (According to Flickr, iPhone users tag 2% of their geotagged photos. Other non-smart mobile phone (Nokia N73) users tag 0.4% of their photos.) Watanabe et al., also developed 'WillCam', which enables users to capture various information, such as location, temperature, ambient noise, and photographer facial expression, aimed to avoid spending the time and effort to carry out annotation [8]. In our case, we utilized the system to provide recommended tags from social tagging, including geotagged photos on mobile devices. The user is able to develop a reusable life log and contribute to developing social tagging simultanously. This system also utilizes a life-log system, which facilitates the easy retrieval of information. Moreover, our application indicates both nearby photos and nearby tags on a unit of record to assist the user (Fig.7). According to the work of Kalnikaite et al., different types of memory promote the lifelog user's recollections [9]. In this figure is a case of a walk around Asakusa (An old town in Tokyo); nearby photos are laid out in order of the distance from a recorded point and nearby tags are indicated in order of the densities on the unit of the record. The user can view the image from the feature of both the sceneries (architectures) and the related words of its environs (e.g. temple, asakusa, matsuri (festival), sensoji (name of temple)). Through use of the function, the timeline augments the stream of the user's track by using geotagged objects.

5   Related Work

Kennedy et al. proposed a method of classifying photos using Flickr to automatically extract places and events from the assigned tags [10, 11, 12]. Persson et al [13], Masui et al. [14] and Nakanishi et al [15] proposed methods and interfaces to provide a visual/context based geographical information retrieval/sharing procedure. Additionally, we aimed to complement and enhance activity recording and navigation assistance by using geotagged objects for mobile user interfaces. There are interesting studies of spatial/social context-based photo browsing for mobile user interfaces, proposed as Mobiphos [16] and Zurfur [17]. These applications were designed for browsing/sharing photos via the Internet in a mobile environment but were not designed for navigation assistance or continuous activity recording.

Rekimoto et al. proposed a method of summarizing user activities with reverse geocoding [18]. They also provided lists that are more descriptive by labeling the user descriptions of street addresses (e.g., the street address for a user's home is labeled "home"). These methods are related in terms of extracting information from people-contributed media. Moreover, our methods provide the labels dug out from social tagging. Sellen et al. reported that the automatic way in which SenseCam captures these images results in cues which are as effective in triggering memory as images which people capture on their own initiative [19]. Kalnikaite et al. showed that there are multiple types of data that we might collect about our pasts, as well as multiple ways of presenting this data [9]. These previous works intended to enhance user's memory using the life logs that were recorded by the user itself. Additionally, our approach focused on the user's environmental understanding based on their public image, which we compared with social tagging on the Internet.

6   Discussion and Future work

6.1   Comments and Request Feedback from Users

Our proposed mobile applications aim to encourage users to assist navigation/activity recording by using geotagged photos/tags from Flickr as descriptions of the user's path. In order to confirm whether the system enhances the users' life logs, we conducted interviews about our application. Seven males and seven females (22–51 years old iPhone users) participated in the evaluation for 1–4 weeks. After the evaluation, we received comments and requests and we found possibilities that the system encourages users to recollect memories by using geo-tagged photos/tags from Flickr as descriptions of the user's path. According to comments such as "I was watching the timeline on the way to work in a train. That stimulated my recollections and helped me rediscover what I've missed in my daily life." by providing activity records enhanced by the life logs described by others' photos/tags, the participants experienced rediscovery of their environmental understanding. In addition, comments like "It (augmented life logging) is pretty close/ keeps the motivation of recording my life." imply that collective geotagged objects can be used for augmented life logging. At the same time, there were several requests. (More than two participants made requests.) According to requests "Viewing nearby photos by my friends through our group trip, will help talk up a storm." Participants in the system should be connected with multiple social network systems (SNSs) they use daily or with their buddies. This comment points out how this project would provide ordinary users with a sustainable life-log system.

6.2   Tag Clustering and Optimization

Social Geoscape is proposed for providing users with an easier way to grasp the public image of cities using Flickr's user tags (Fig.8). In our proposed application Kioku Hacker, we use the Flickr API (flickr.place.findByLatLon) that provides the searching functionality and sorting geotagged photos from their users. Kioku Hacker collects and processes these photos from Flickr APIs (maximum 200 photos within a 32km radius) to complement the periodic records in the user's life log. At the same time, the user tags included in these tags are created and ordered according their frequency. This system totals up the nearby tags to create a tag list, although this method sometimes produces the problem of outputting irrelevant tag clusters. For instance, many photos taken at (or nearby) the University of Tokyo (located in the Hongo district in Tokyo) are tagged "Hongo" and "University," but when the system indicates the tag clusters at the campus, the system outputs "Ueno" (next to Hongo district) because the number of photos taken at Ueno are more than that at Hongo. To solve the problem, this system optimizes tag clustering. Fig.8 shows the conceptual model of tag clustering optimization. As shown in the figure, this system multiplies a coefficient value (C) that is in inversely proportional to the distance (D) from the photo shooting point. As a result, "Hongo" tagged clusters are biased even if the number of tags is less than that for "Ueno." In addition, this system excludes tags that are unrelated to geographical or environmental factors (e.g., geotagged, Eye-Fi, Kodak) to indicate a more semantic tag description or recommendation.

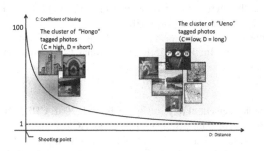

Fig. 8. Conceptual model of tag clustering optimization: "Hongo" tagged clusters are biased even if the number of tags is less than that for "Ueno"

Additionally, we observed several trends of image tagging between the each segment of the photos such as day/night, inhabitants/tourists, and recent/old days. For instance, in the case of Shinbashi area (A downtown area in Tokyo. Nearby this station, the area has a lot of bars and restaurants for businesspeople.), some sets of photos tagged "shinbashi" are also tagged "night", include the sceneries of nightspots such as nearby restaurants or bars. The cluster of night tagged photos spreads to the Ginza area (nearby district of Shinbashi also famous for night spot). We can guess that the users took these photos, and understood these areas as nightspot including bars and restaurants. On the other hand, we observe that the set of photos tagged "shinbashi" but not "night", include the sceneries of buildings, business persons, and billboards, in addition to many of these photos taken nearby Shinbashi station. The result indicates the area can be recognized through different perspectives, and there is a possibility of grasping the further aspects of the cities from user generated geotagged objects. We should consider this fact, however, our proposed method flattens out those different perspectives because the objects are not sufficient to cluster each other at present. To solve the problems, it is important to provide a user interface and user experience that encourages the motivation to contribute to developing social tagging.

References

[1] Lynch, K.: The Image of the City. MIT Press (1960)
[2] Lamere, P.: Social Tagging And Music Information Retrieval. Journal of New Music Research 37(2), 101–114 (2008)
[3] Alexander, C.: A city is not a tree (1965)
[4] Davis, M., et al.: From context to content: Leveraging context to infer media metadata. In: Proc. 12th Annual ACM International Conference on Multimedia (2004)
[5] 2dkde, http://stat.ethz.ch/R-manual/R-patched/library/MASS/html/kde2d.html
[6] R Documentation, http://rss.acs.unt.edu/Rdoc/library/kernlab/html/ksvm-class.html
[7] WikiPedia, http://en.wikipedia.org/wiki/Downtown_Los_Angeles
[8] Watanabe, et al.: WillCam: a digital camera visualizing users' interest. In: Proc. CHI 2007 Conference Proceedings and Extended Abstracts, pp. 2747–2752 (2007)
[9] Rattenbury, et al.: Towards automatic extraction of event and place semantics from flickr tags. In: Proceedings of the 30th Annual International ACM SIGIR Conference on Research and Development in Information Retrieval, July 23-27, Amsterdam, The Netherlands (2007)
[10] Kalnikaite, et al.: Now let me see where I was: understanding how lifelogs mediate memory. In: Proceedings of the 28th International Conference on Human Factors in Computing Systems CHI 2010, Atlanta, pp. 2045–2054 (2010)
[11] Kennedy, L., et al.: How flickr helps us make sense of the world: Context and content in community-contributed media collections. In: Proc. 15th International Conference on Multimedia, pp. 631–640 (2007)
[12] Tagmap, Yahoo! Research Berkeley, http://tagmaps.research.yahoo.com/worldexplorer.php
[13] Persson, P., et al.: GeoNotes: social enhancement of physical space. In: CHI 2001: CHI 2001 Extended Abstracts on Human Factors in Computing Systems, pp. 43–44. ACM Press (2001)
[14] Masui, T., Minakuchi, M., Borden IV, G.R., Kashiwagi, K.: Multiple-view approach for smooth information retrieval. In: Proceedings of the ACM Symposium on User Interface Software and Technology (UIST 1995), pp. 199–206. ACM Press (November 1995)
[15] Nakanishi, Y., Motoe, M., Matsukawa, S.: JIKUKAN-POEMER: Geographic Information System Using Camera Phone Equipped with GPS, and Its Exhibition on a Street. In: Brewster, S., Dunlop, M.D. (eds.) Mobile HCI 2004. LNCS, vol. 3160, pp. 486–490. Springer, Heidelberg (2004)
[16] Clawson, et al.: Mobiphos: a collocated-synchronous mobile photo sharing application. In: MobileHCI 2008 (2008)
[17] Hwang, A., et al.: Zurfer: Mobile Multimedia Access in Spatial, Social and Topical Context. In: Proc. Fifteenth ACM International Conference on Multimedia (2007)
[18] Rekimoto, J., Miyaki, T., Ishizawa, T.: LifeTag: WiFi-Based Continuous Location Logging for Life Pattern Analysis. In: Hightower, J., Schiele, B., Strang, T. (eds.) LoCA 2007. LNCS, vol. 4718, pp. 35–49. Springer, Heidelberg (2007)
[19] Sellen, K., et al.: Do life-logging, technologies support memory for the past? An experimental study using SenseCam. In: Conference on Human Factors in Computing Systems, Irvine, CA, pp. 81–90 (2007)

On the Spatio-temporal Information Content and Arithmetic Coding of Discrete Trajectories

Markus Koegel and Martin Mauve

Department of Computer Science, University of Düsseldorf, Germany
{koegel,mauve}@cs.uni-duesseldorf.de
http://www.cn.uni-duesseldorf.de/

Abstract. The trace of a moving object is commonly referred to as a trajectory. This paper considers the spatio-temporal information content of a discrete trajectory in relation to a movement prediction model for the object under consideration. The information content is the minimal amount of information necessary to reconstruct the trajectory, given the movement model. We show how the information content of arbitrary trajectories can be determined and use these findings to derive an approximative arithmetic coding scheme for trajectory information, reaching a level of compression that is close to the bound provided by its entropy. We then demonstrate the practical applicability of our ideas by using them to compress real-world vehicular trajectories, showing that this vastly improves upon the results provided by the best existing schemes.

1 Introduction

Gathering, storing and transmitting data on the movement of objects are common parts of many applications in the area of ubiquitous computing. These data, referred to as *trajectories*, basically comprise sequences of position and time measurements. Given that storage space and transmission capacity are valuable resources, in particular in the mobile domain, it is desirable to encode trajectories efficiently, e.g., by means of compression.

In general, compression methods seek to identify and remove redundancies from an input source; in this paper, we focus on redundancy within trajectories. This redundancy results from underlying principles of object mobility, such as kinematics or Newton's laws of motion. It is widely accepted that these principles cause mobility to be predictable to some degree; for example, several approaches have been proposed that use linear models for the compression of trajectories [1,2], though non-linear models have also been discussed recently [3,4].

However, no previous work has regarded the general upper bound for trajectory compression that is given by the *information content*, or *entropy*, of such a movement trace. In this paper, we therefore focus on the following question: given a prediction of how an object moves, how much information does a trajectory contain and what upper compression bound does this imply? Then, we use this knowledge to construct a compression scheme based on arithmetic coding that comes very close to reaching this bound.

A. Puiatti et al. (Eds.): MobiQuitous 2011, LNICST 104, pp. 13–24, 2012.

Throughout this work we use the vehicular domain as an example to illustrate our findings and to prove its applicability to real world data. However, the ideas presented here can be used to analyze and compress any form of trajectory, provided that a prediction model for the respective mobility can be constructed.

In the remainder of this paper, we present related work on trajectory compression and probabilistic positioning in Section 2. We introduce our idea of information content for trajectories and how to measure it in Section 3. In Section 4, we discuss how to apply this idea to vehicular trajectories and briefly describe details of an arithmetic coder implementing our model. The formal model and the arithmetic coder are finally evaluated in Section 5.

2   Related Work

The *compression of movement measurements* is frequently discussed in the context of *Mobile Object Databases (MODs)*. MODs receive trajectory updates from arbitrary mobile units and can handle spatio-temporal search requests. For MODs, compression techniques have been proposed that either require an already completed data collection (*offline* approaches, such as [5,6]) or that compress data on the fly (*online* approaches, such as [1,2]). For both approaches, line simplification or linear dead reckoning algorithms have been used. The compression performance of both are upper-bounded by the optimal line simplification proposed in [7]. The authors of [3] describe trajectories using so-called *minimax* polynomials, approximating a given function, so that the maximum approximation error is minimized for the employed parameter values. Further compression techniques that focus on vehicular trajectories use cubic splines [4] and clothoids [8] as described in [9]; in general, these non-linear approaches attempt to model the smoothness of vehicular movements or roadways.

In robot navigation, *Probabilistic Positioning* is employed for self positioning, e. g., within office buildings [10,11]: instead of precise positions, probabilities for the position on a discrete map are given. We work with a similar concept by defining a probability distribution over a limited region, but do not rely on previously known map material.

In [12], navigation decisions of pigeons are analyzed based on the stochastic complexity of trajectory sections by deriving the navigational confidence. The authors of [13] propose user movement estimation for cellular networks with Markov models. They determine state transition probabilities based on relative location frequencies and use these to derive compressed position update messages. Both approaches are special cases for information content measurements, but cannot directly be generalized to arbitrary movements. In this paper, we present a formal model that not only can be seen as a generalization of these approaches but can also be adapted to any other application area.

None of the existing approaches consider a general upper bound for trajectory compression that is given by the information content, or entropy, of such a movement trace. We will show in the following, that doing so will lead to significant improvements in the compression ratio of trajectories.

3   The Information Content of Trajectories

In this section, we will show what the information content of a trajectory is and how it can be measured. To this end, we will introduce a formal model for the entropy calculation of trajectories and discuss its components and parameters.

3.1   What Is the Information Content of Trajectories?

Any object movement, e. g., the migration patterns of flocks, the movement of astronomical objects or the trajectories of road vehicles can be described by a formal model. In general, such models can be used for movement predictions of particular objects based on previous position measurements, exploiting the redundancy and predictability of movements. Since typically not all factors influencing the mobility of an object can be modeled accurately, the *actual* position of the object might differ from the prediction. This deviation is commonly referred to as *innovation*, i. e., the uncertainty of the prediction process.

In this paper, we investigate the information content of the innovations. Let us start introducing the necessary information theoretical concepts from [14]: given an ensemble $X = (x, \mathcal{A}_X, \mathcal{P}_X)$, with the outcome x of a random variable over the finite set $\mathcal{A}_X = \{a_1, \ldots, a_I\}$ and according probabilities $\mathcal{P}_X = \{p_1, \ldots, p_I\}$: $p_i = P(x = a_i), \forall 1 \le i \le I : p_i \ge 0$ and $\sum_{i=1}^{I} p_i = 1$. We refer to $\mathcal{A}_X$ as the discrete *alphabet* and to $\mathcal{P}_X$ as the ensemble's *probability distribution*. The *Shannon information content* (in *bits*) of x is defined as $h(x) = \log_2(1/P(x))$, where $P(x)$ is the probability of its occurrence. Then, the *entropy* $H(X)$ refers to the *average information content* of an outcome of X and is defined as $H(X) = \sum_{x \in \mathcal{A}_x} P(x) h(x) = \sum_{x \in \mathcal{A}_x} P(x) \log_2(1/P(x))$. In other words, the entropy is the average number of bits that is needed to represent an outcome x.

If we apply this definition to our previous discussion, we can identify the estimation innovation as the outcome of each estimation step: it represents the estimation uncertainty and bears the information that was missing when the prediction was made. So, if the innovations of all position estimation steps are regarded, we can derive the information content of a whole movement trace. On the other hand, the ensemble's alphabet and the probability distribution yield the entropy of the outcome, being the average information content.

3.2   How to Determine the Information Content of Trajectories

Basically, each outcome x of an ensemble X is determined by the employed movement estimator. Therefore, we need to formalize all involved components: the *movement estimator* and the parts of X, namely the *alphabet* of possible values $\mathcal{A}_X$ and the set of corresponding probabilities $\mathcal{P}_X$.

The movement estimator is a function θ that determines a two-dimensional position based on an observation vector $m = (m_1, \ldots, m_{N-1})$ containing previously collected position measurements: $\theta : (\mathbb{R}^2)^{N-1} \to \mathbb{R}^2$, $\theta(m) = \hat{m}_N$. Then, the innovation i_N is the difference between the estimation and the actual measurement: $i_N = m_N - \hat{m}_N$, $i_N \in \mathbb{R}^2$. So, the innovation is a two-dimensional real vector itself and cannot directly be used for the outcome x, because $\mathbb{R}^2$ is uncountably infinite, i. e., neither countable nor bounded. To process the innovation into an outcome x, we need to overcome these two issues.

The innovation domain can be made countable by simple discretization: the real innovation vector is mapped onto a grid, with each grid node referring to a particular symbol in $\mathcal{A}_X$. The grid cell width and form are accuracy parameters, their choice is influenced by several aspects, e.g., the highest tolerable discretization error or the highest discretization error under which the movement model still produces reasonable results.

Once countable, the innovation domain can be bounded, while still keeping *all* reasonable innovations covered by $\mathcal{A}_X$. That is, all possible positions within reach in the time period since the last measurement need to be mappable to $\mathcal{A}_X$. Which positions can be reached depends, e. g., on the movement model, or measurement noise. The limitation of the innovation domain is important, because the resulting alphabet needs to be valid for the whole trajectory: if the limits are set too narrow, i. e., $\mathcal{A}_X$ misses reasonable innovations, such innovations could not be covered by the ensemble X. Contrariwise, too wide limits would include implausible innovations in $\mathcal{A}_X$ and thus would increase its entropy, which then could be significantly higher than the actual entropy of the trajectory.

Once the movement estimator and the alphabet are known, $\mathcal{P}_X$ is set up by assigning a probability to each symbol in $\mathcal{A}_X$. Like the alphabet, the probability distribution is crucial for the result of the entropy determination.

So, the entropy of an ensemble $X = (x, \mathcal{A}_X, \mathcal{P}_X)$ can be determined directly. To measure the information content of a trajectory, the deviations between the predicted positions and the actual position measurements are mapped to $\mathcal{A}_X$. Then, the information content of each measurement can be determined.

4 Exemplary Implementation of Information Measurement

We can now apply the necessary parts for the determination of a trajectory's information content to a specific use case and show how to implement these components for vehicular trajectories.

4.1 Movement Estimator

Consider position measurements $p = (p_x p_y) \in \mathbb{R}^2$; then, the velocity (v) and acceleration (a) vectors of a vehicle at the position p_i at the time t_i are given by: $v_i = (p_i - p_{i-1})/(t_i - t_{i-1})$, $a_i = (v_i - v_{i-1})/(t_i - t_{i-1})$. With these quantities, simple vehicular movement models can be set up as described in [15]: the first movement model only considers the last position and velocity vector:

$$\theta_{vel} = p_{i_{N-1}} + v_{i_{N-1}} \Delta t \ . \tag{1}$$

The second model extends the first one by using the approximated acceleration:

$$\theta_{acc} = p_{i_{N-1}} + v_{i_{N-1}} \Delta t + \frac{a_{i_{N-1}}}{2} \Delta t^2 \ . \tag{2}$$

Obviously, more complex movement models, e. g., using sensor data fusion, are conceivable. We will show that these simple models already perform very well and thus defer the investigation of other movement models to future work.

4.2   The Discrete Alphabet $\mathcal{A}_X$

As described above, the innovation domain can be made countable and bounded by projecting each innovation to a grid of limited size. It is clear that the specific design of the grid depends on the application context; for example, in the vehicular domain, a uniform approximation error for any region of the grid is desirable, making regularly tessellated grids an interesting option. Additionally, the grid cell dimensions and density can be easily adjusted by a maximal discretization error ϵ. We will thus use regular square grids for our examination.

While setting up the grid cells is a simple task, the limitation of the scope of the grid is more challenging, because the grid needs to cover all reasonable (and only those!) measurement innovations. For the use case of vehicular movements, the grid boundaries strongly depend on the possible movements of a vehicle. Therefore, we use kinematic model to determine them.

For the dimensioning of the grid, we will refer to a logical—not necessarily geometrical—grid center, at which the grid will be aligned along the movement direction. We set this grid center to the estimated next position according to the non-accelerated movement model (1), disregarding both acceleration and steering. This enables us to dimension the grid with a simple line of kinematic arguments: the longitudinal dimension—i. e., the dimension along the movement direction—directly results from the highest possible deceleration $\text{dec}_{\max}$ and acceleration $\text{acc}_{\max}$ that could cause a position deviation from the predictand. We calculate the lateral dimension—i. e., the dimension perpendicular to the movement direction—by the maximal possible change in steering since the last measurement: with Coulomb's friction law and common friction values [15], we can determine the highest velocity $v_{max}(r)$ that can be driven in curves with radius r. The lateral dimension is then calculated directly based on $v_{max}(r)$.

However, the grid dimensions depend, next to kinematic influences, on the positioning noise level. In extreme cases, increased noise levels may cause innovations to lie outside the analytically deduced boundaries. For such situations, we add a single extra symbol to $\mathcal{A}_X$, representing outliers; this minimally increases the alphabet size and the entropy of the ensemble, though. Additionally, expected or current noise statistics, e. g., *dilution of precision (DOP)* values, could be regarded for the grid dimensioning. This would result in some kind of *guard zone* around the analytically set up grid that could reduce, but not completely avoid the probability of outliers. The setup of such a zone is nontrivial and beyond the scope of this paper and thus remains future work.

These approaches can be implemented complementary, depending on the expected or experienced noise level. Furthermore, filters can be employed to odd out or smooth implausible position measurements. Some filters, such as the (extended) Kalman filter, even provide probabilities or covariances of the quality of the estimate that could be employed in dimensioning the grid.

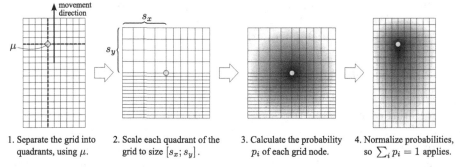

1. Separate the grid into quadrants, using μ.   2. Scale each quadrant of the grid to size $[s_x; s_y]$.   3. Calculate the probability p_i of each grid node.   4. Normalize probabilities, so $\sum_i p_i = 1$ applies.

Fig. 1. Skewing of the probability distribution and mapping it to the grid nodes

4.3   The Probability Distribution $\mathcal{P}_X$

The probability distribution of the ensemble X assigns a probability p_i to each symbol $a_i \in \mathcal{A}_X$, as described in Section 3. We expect $\mathcal{P}_X$ to be reasonably close to the normal distribution which is commonly used in the context of noisy position measurements [16]. While it is unlikely that the innovations during an estimation process will be perfectly normal distributed, we consider this to be a good approximation. This assumption will be further evaluated in Section 5.

As explained above, we derive the alphabet from a two-dimensional grid, so we need to employ a *bivariate* normal distribution $\mathcal{N}(\mu, \Sigma)$, $\mu = (\mu_x, \mu_y)$, $\Sigma = (\ (\sigma_x^2, \rho\sigma_x\sigma_y)^T, (\rho\sigma_x\sigma_y, \sigma_y^2)^T\ )$ with the standard deviations σ_x, σ_y and the correlation coefficient ρ [17]. The distribution's mean is set according to the estimated next position: while the grid is aligned using the non-accelerated movement model (1), the mean μ of the probability distribution can be determined using other models, e.g., the accelerated movement model (2). We do not expect the dimensions of the innovation domain to correlate, so $\rho = 0$. However, the normal distribution is symmetric, but the discretization grid may not necessarily be. For simplicity, we propose a projection of the grid to implement a skewed probability distribution, which is schematically depicted in Figure 1: the mean μ separates the grid into four quadrants, each of which is scaled to the dimensions $[s_x; s_y]$, where s_z is the number of standard deviations that are supposed to cover the z axis of each quadrant. Due to the scaling, the standard deviation of the distribution can be set to $\sigma = 1$ and so, the probabilities for the grid nodes can be determined using the simplified density function $f(x, y) = \frac{1}{2\pi} \exp(-\frac{1}{2}(x^2 + y^2))$. Afterwards, the assigned probabilities need to be normalized to eliminate scaling effects, so that $\sum_{i=1}^{I} p_i = 1$ applies again.

Alternatively, asymmetric probability distributions could be employed, e.g., the log-normal distribution.

4.4   Exemplary Alphabets and Their Entropies

We are now able to determine the entropy of particular ensembles, i.e., the expected information content per position measurement. Table 1 shows an overview

Table 1. Exemplary alphabet configurations and resulting entropies

Δt	ϵ	# symbols	entropy [bits] uniform	normal (3σ)	normal (4σ)
	0.1 m	199	7.64	6.32	5.55
0.5 s	0.5 m	16	4.00	2.38	1.77
	1.0 m	7	2.81	1.83	1.61
	0.1 m	2761	11.43	10.25	9.47
1.0 s	0.5 m	136	7.09	5.73	4.97
	1.0 m	41	5.36	3.86	3.20
	0.1 m	41580	15.34	14.20	13.42
2.0 s	0.5 m	1760	10.78	9.59	8.80
	1.0 m	476	8.89	7.65	6.86

of exemplary entropies for varying measurement intervals and accuracy bounds. For the regular square grid setup, we assumed an acceleration interval $[\text{dec}_{\max}; \text{acc}_{\max}] = [-11; 8]\frac{m}{s^2}$. Also, we calculated the entropies for probability distributions with two different standard deviations: We chose $s_x = s_y = 3\sigma$ and $s_x = s_y = 4\sigma$, thus assuming that approximately 99.7 % and 99.99 % of all measurement innovations will lie within the grid, respectively. Please note that the entropy, as an expected value, solely depends on the used movement model θ and ensemble X and not on actual measurements.

We can see from the table that even for very high accuracy demands, the expected average information content per symbol is very low: while position measurements are normally provided by off-the-shelf GPS receivers as fixed-point numbers with six digital places and thus can be encoded with 57 bits, the expected average information content at an accuracy bound of 0.1 m always lies below 16 bits. This would even be true if the probability distribution of the alphabet was normal distributed. According to our model, the entropy becomes smaller with the measurement interval. This is reasonable, because the more information is provided by measurements, the lower is the missing information for a perfect estimation.

4.5 Model Implementation: An Arithmetic Coder

The estimation results presented in Table 1 encouraged us to build an arithmetic coder based on our formal model, since we could expect compression rates of more than 90 % even at tight accuracy bounds. For the implementation, we used the arithmetic coding project of Bob Carpenter [18], version 1.1 as a basis.

The only modification to our formal model lies in the handling of outlier measurements: Instead of adding an extra outlier symbol, we stop the arithmetic encoding once an innovation cannot be mapped onto $\mathcal{A}_X$. This is inevitable, because the mapping of an discretized innovation to a code symbol needs to be bijective; this is not fulfilled in case of outliers. Once an innovation cannot be mapped to a grid node, it would not be possible to retrieve a valid grid node in the decoding process. Therefore, in this case the symbol stream is terminated

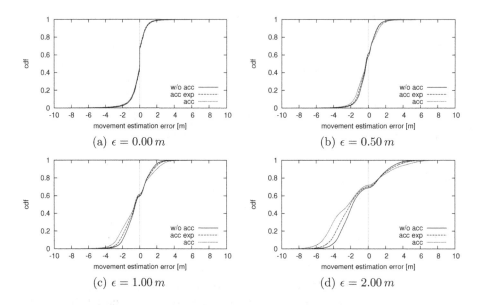

Fig. 2. Movement estimation error analysis (urban movement)

with the *End Of Stream* symbol, the probability distribution and the estimator are reset and a new encoding begins. This is an undesirable situation, because at least one position needs to be transmitted uncoded; so, even with the mentioned *guard zone*, using a robust estimator is crucial for the compression performance.

5   Evaluation

5.1   Movement Data

The results that we present here are based on real-world movement data from the *OpenStreetMap* project [19]. Those are available under the Creative Commons license BY-SA 2.0 [20]. We categorized each movement trace based on the highest object velocity v_{max} as *urban* ($8.3\,\frac{m}{s} < v_{max} < 17\,\frac{m}{s}$) or *highway* ($v_{max} \geq 17\,\frac{m}{s}$) movements. We then selected only those traces with 1 Hz measurement frequencies and more than 100 measurement points; in doing so, we retrieved 2263 and 4946 traces for the urban and highway pattern, respectively.

5.2   Movement Estimation

Since it is essential to use an accurate and robust movement model, we performed movement estimations with the non-accelerated and accelerated movement estimators. We were in particular interested in the influence of the discretization and therefore analyzed the movement estimation inaccuracies for varying discretization steps; the results are shown as cumulative distributions in Figure 2.

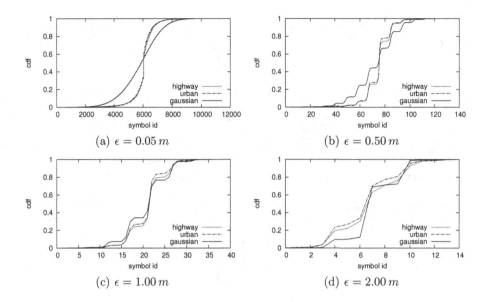

Fig. 3. Cumulative distribution analysis of the probability distribution $\mathcal{P}_X$

Without discretization (i. e., $\epsilon = 0$), the error was below 2 m in 90-95% of the cases, with slightly worse results for the highway topologies, which we left out for lack of space. For increasing ϵ, the error distributions widen, which indicates that coarser discretizations lower the quality of the estimator's observation vector. This in turn has a direct influence on the information content and the compression performance.

Unexpectedly, the non-accelerated estimator (w/o acc) outperforms the accelerated variant (acc). The latter is more impaired by the discretization, since it derives acceleration values from distorted velocities. To reduce this effect, we amended the accelerated estimator by smoothing the acceleration values exponentially (acc exp). Though this really improves the situation, it does not provide the same robustness as the non-accelerated estimator as shown in Figure 2.

5.3 Probability Distribution

To evaluate the probability distribution, we compare the assumed (gaussian) and actual cumulative distribution functions for both topologies over the respective $\mathcal{A}_X$ in Figure 3. To this end, we serialized the two-dimensional distributions over the grid to one-dimensional distributions over the ordered symbol set to gain a better overview: we concatenated the symbols from cross-sections along the lateral grid axis, causing stepped curves, where each "step" in the curves refers to one such cross-section. The cdf graphs for the normal distribution resemble the empirically determined ones, though the distributions for both the urban and highway topologies are denser, especially for lower values of ϵ. This basically

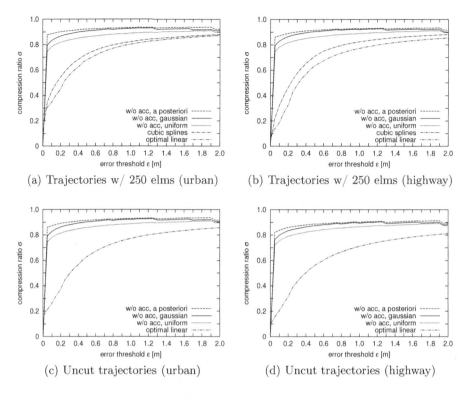

Fig. 4. Compression ratio comparison

confirms our assumption for $\mathcal{P}_X$, though it is also quite obvious that there is room for future research to improve the probability distribution and thereby the information content estimation and compression performance.

5.4 Compression

For the evaluation of the compression performance, we use the compression schemes based on optimal line simplification and cubic spline interpolation discussed in [9] as benchmarks for the work presented here.

The spline-based approach runs in $O(n^3)$ and was designed for relatively short trajectories of ∼250 elements; so, we selected typical trajectories of 1000-1300 positions and cut them to slices of 250 elements, each slice overlapping the previous one by 100 elements, and thus gained 318 and 327 shorter traces for the urban and highway topologies, respectively. In doing so, we avoid side effects and spread both advantageous and disadvantageous effects on multiple slices.

Both the line simplification and the arithmetic coding are capable of handling trajectories of several thousand measurements, so we additionally apply these to uncut traces in order to gain a broader basis for the analysis and to examine the ability of these approaches to handle data streams of variable length.

As an optimal benchmark for the arithmetic coder, we have performed compressions using *a posteriori* knowledge: we measured the empirical distributions of the code symbols for each trajectory and used these as stochastic models for the arithmetic coder. This is only a theoretical optimum, because for a productive operation, this distribution would have to be transmitted along with the code bit stream and would cause a serious overhead.

Figures 4(a) – 4(d) depict the average compression ratios against the discretization threshold ϵ. For all configurations, the same ranking of compression techniques is visible: the optimal line simplification algorithm performs worst, being outperformed by the approach driven by cubic splines (only for the trajectories with 250 elements in Figures 4(a) and 4(b)). The arithmetic coding approach performs best, especially for very tight accuracy bounds of $\epsilon < 1.0\,\mathrm{m}$ and even if a uniform probability distribution is used for $\mathcal{P}_X$ as reference. When a normal distribution is used, the compression ratios improve by another 20-30%. The results for using a posteriori knowledge are significantly better for $\epsilon < 0.5\,\mathrm{m}$, but thereafter are almost reached by the compression ratios with the normal distribution assumption. This underlines our findings from the probability distribution analysis that for growing ϵ, the impact of the probability distribution decreases. We only plot the compression results achieved with the non-accelerated movement estimator for a better overview. According to Section 5.2, it yielded slightly better compression ratios than the accelerated models.

An interesting effect are the visible drops of the compression ratios for very high ϵ that occur for all distributions and topologies alike. These originate from the discretization grid that is getting coarser for growing ϵ.

6 Conclusions

In this paper we determined the information content and entropy of trajectories with respect to a prediction model. Further, by using these findings we were able to specify a compression scheme based on arithmetic coding. We demonstrated the practical applicability of our ideas by using them to compress vehicular trajectories and applied this to a large number of heterogeneous real-world vehicular movement traces. The results from this evaluation show that our approach is far superior to the best existing compression scheme for vehicular trajectories.

There are two aspects of the work presented here that could be improved further. First, the prediction model we use is rather simple. It might make sense to investigate other models. After all, the more accurate the prediction is, the lower will be the information content of the trajectory in relation to that model. Second, we have used a normal distribution to assign probabilities to the alphabet. While this is an acceptable approximation it might pay off to investigate other ways to assign those probabilities.

Acknowledgments. The authors wish to thank Dennis Dobler for his work on the prototype of the arithmetic coder and the formal model. Also, the authors thank Bob Carpenter for the source code of his arithmetic coder and his support.

References

1. Lange, R., Farrell, T., Dürr, F., Rothermel, K.: Remote real-time trajectory simplification. In: PerCom 2009: Proceedings of the 7th IEEE International Conference on Pervasive Computing and Communications, pp. 184–193 (March 2009)
2. Hönle, N., Großmann, M., Reimann, S., Mitschang, B.: Usability analysis of compression algorithms for position data streams. In: GIS 2010: Proceedings of the 18th ACM SIGSPATIAL International Conference on Advances in Geographic Information Systems (November 2010)
3. Ni, J., Ravishankar, C.V.: Indexing Spatio-Temporal Trajectories with Efficient Polynomial Approximations. IEEE Transactions on Knowledge and Data Engineering 19, 663–678 (2007)
4. Koegel, M., Kiess, W., Kerper, M., Mauve, M.: Compact Vehicular Trajectory Encoding. In: VTC 2011-Spring: Proceedings of the 73rd IEEE Vehicular Technology Conference (May 2011)
5. Civilis, A., Jensen, C.S., Pakalnis, S.: Techniques for efficient road-network-based tracking of moving objects. IEEE Transactions on Knowledge and Data Engineering 17(5), 698–712 (2005)
6. Cao, H., Wolfson, O., Trajcevski, G.: Spatio-temporal data reduction with deterministic error bounds. VLDB Journal 15(3), 211–228 (2006)
7. Imai, H., Iri, M.: Computational-geometric methods for polygonal approximations of a curve. Computer Vision, Graphics, and Image Processing 36(1), 31–41 (1986)
8. Baran, I., Lehtinen, J., Popovic, J.: Sketching Clothoid Splines Using Shortest Paths. In: Computer Graphics Forum, pp. 655–664 (2010)
9. Koegel, M., Baselt, D., Mauve, M., Scheuermann, B.: A Comparison of Vehicular Trajectory Encoding Techniques. In: MedHocNet 2011: Proceedings of the 10th Annual Mediterranean Ad Hoc Networking Workshop (June 2011)
10. Fox, D.: Markov localization: A probabilistic framework for mobile robot localization and navigation. Ph.D. dissertation, University of Bonn, Germany (1998)
11. Roy, N., Burgard, W., Fox, D., Thrun, S.: Coastal navigation – mobile robot navigation with uncertainty in dynamic environments. In: ICRA 1999: Proceedings of the IEEE Int'l Conference on Robotics and Automation, pp. 35–40 (August 1999)
12. Roberts, S., Guilford, T., Rezek, I., Biro, D.: Positional entropy during pigeon homing i: application of bayesian latent state modelling. Journal of Theoretical Biology 227(1), 39–50 (2004)
13. Bhattacharya, A., Das, S.K.: LeZi-update: an information-theoretic approach to track mobile users in PCS networks. In: MobiCom 1999: Proceedings of the 5th Annual ACM/IEEE Int'l Conf. on Mobile Computing and Networking (July 1999)
14. MacKay, D.J.C.: Information Theory, Inference & Learning Algorithms. Cambridge University Press, New York (2002)
15. Kuchling, H.: Taschenbuch der Physik, 17th edn. Fachbuchverlag Leipzig im Carl Hanser Verlag (August 2007) (in German language)
16. van Diggelen, F.: GPS Accuracy: Lies, Damn Lies and Statistics. GPS World 9(1), 41–45 (1998)
17. Timm, N.: Applied multivariate analysis. Texts in statistics. Springer (2002)
18. Capenter, B.: Arithcode project: Compression via arithmetic coding in java. version 1.1, online resource (2002),
http://www.colloquial.com/ArithmeticCoding/
19. The OpenStreetMap Project, online resource,
http://www.openstreetmap.org/
20. Creative Commons BY-SA 2.0,
http://creativecommons.org/licenses/by-sa/2.0/

A Proposal on Direction Estimation between Devices Using Acoustic Waves

Yasutaka Nishimura, Naoki Imai, and Kiyohito Yoshihara

KDDI R&D Laboratories Inc.
Ohara, 2-1-15 Fujimino, Saitama, Japan
{yu-nishimura,naoki,yosshy}@kddilabs.jp

Abstract. How can you easily find a partner in rendezvous whom you have not met before (e.g., a new friend on social network service, a customer in delivery service)? One answer is to display the distance and direction to the partner on your smartphone. Although conventional work has provided keys to perform distance estimation with only commodities like smartphones, direction estimation requires pre-planned infrastructure or special hardware. In this paper, we newly propose a direction estimation method, which monitors Doppler Effect of acoustic waves generated by user's simple motion. Moreover, we implemented the proposed method, and measured its performance under real-world conditions. The experimental results show that the estimation error ranges within 18.0 degrees, which is practical for the above use cases.

Keywords: Direction Estimation, Acoustic Wave, Smartphone, Doppler Effect.

1 Introduction

The increasing popularity of Internet services, e.g., SNS (Social Network Service) and BBS (Bulletin Board System), has allowed communication with many people, and created a need for new forms of rendezvous. One example is meeting an SNS friend whom you have not met before. Other examples are rendezvous between a customer and a deliveryman in delivery service and between a worker registering a part-time job via Internet and the supervisor. Even in cases of rendezvous with a person without real world acquaintance like these examples, partner searching must be facilitated.

One of the ways of achieving such rendezvous is to provide the accurate distance and direction to the partner. A well-known solution is to share locations obtained from GPS (Global Positioning System). However, the accuracy of location, which includes error of several meters, is insufficient to find a partner in such rendezvous. Alternatively, by the transmission and reception of acoustic waves between user devices, like smartphones and mobile phones, the correct distance can be estimated [1]. In terms of direction, multiple methods to estimate the direction have been proposed [2]-[8]. However, these methods require not only the user devices, but also pre-planned infrastructures, like Wi-Fi AP (Access Point), or special hardware,

A. Puiatti et al. (Eds.): MobiQuitous 2011, LNICST 104, pp. 25–36, 2012.

like a directional radio antenna and microphone. So, too much initial cost causes bottleneck to deploy.

One of the ways to estimate direction without initial cost is the transmission and reception of radio signals or acoustic waves between devices via Wi-Fi and Bluetooth antennas and microphone/speaker, which are equipped with commercially available devices. However, it is difficult to estimate direction only by simple transmission and reception alone, because of omni-directional nature intrinsic to radio signals and acoustic waves transmitted from commercially available devices. Meanwhile, the known problem with distance and direction estimations using radio signals and acoustic waves is the increase in estimation error due to reflection from objects, such as walls and ceilings [1]. The estimation error may also increase, when a device misrecognizes noise as acoustic wave. To facilitate rendezvous not only outdoors, like in shopping malls and parks, but also indoors, e.g. in cafés or station yards, the increase in estimation error at the reflection wave and noise sites must be prevented.

This paper newly proposes a direction estimation method between devices using acoustic waves, to realize a precision required for the rendezvous without any pre-planned infrastructures and special hardware. In order to do this, the proposed method exploits Doppler Effect on transmission and reception of acoustic waves. Meanwhile, to prevent the estimation error from increasing due to reflection waves and noise, the devices tries to remove them using acoustic wave information, including the transmission count and the transmission interval of acoustic waves. Moreover, we implement the proposed method as a smartphone application and measure its performance. Through the experiment, we evaluate from the viewpoint of the impact of the distance between devices, reflection wave, noise and crowdedness on the estimation error, since these should be taken into account for the real world use.

This paper is organized as follows. Chapter 2 shows related work, while Chapter 3 newly proposes a direction estimation method between devices using acoustic waves. Chapter 4 describes the implementation of the application of the proposed method, and Chapter 5 evaluates it using the implemented application. Chapter 6 concludes this paper.

2   Related Work

Some methods to estimate the direction between devices have been proposed. These methods are classified into two approaches. The first one uses pre-planned infrastructures, and the second one transmits and receives signals directly between devices.

In the first approach using infrastructures, each device initially obtains its location from infrastructure, and then the devices exchange respective locations. A well-known solution to obtain location is GPS (Global Positioning System). The application to share locations obtained from GPS [2] has been available. Since the sufficient GPS satellites have been introduced and most user devices have GPS receivers, the application needs hardly initial cost. However, the accuracy of location, which includes error of several meters, is insufficient to find a partner without real world acquaintance in the rendezvous. In addition, the location may include more error in urban areas and indoors.

The other methods to obtain location from infrastructure use Wi-Fi AP (Access Point) [3], UWB (Ultra Wide Band) AP [4] or ultrasound transmitters and receivers [5] [6]. These methods require the introduction of multiple infrastructures and location of the infrastructures beforehand. In these methods, the location of the device is obtained through measuring distances to more than three infrastructures. The distance is measured by ToA (Time of Arrival) during the transmission and reception of radio signals or ultrasounds between a device and each infrastructure. These methods can obtain more precise location than GPS. In particular, the precision of location in methods [5] [6] is about 10 cm, because the speed of sound is relatively slower than that of radio signal. Also, the location even in urban and indoor areas can be obtained. However, excessive initial cost of infrastructures is required.

In terms of the second approach to transmit and receive signals directly between devices, the direction is estimated using a directional radio antenna or microphone [7] [8]. In concrete terms, a device calculates the DoA (Direction of Arrival) of a signal transmitted by the other device, and then the device estimates the direction to be that of DoA. However, it is difficult to apply these methods to commercially available devices, since those devices are not equipped with directional radio antennas and microphones.

As abovementioned, though several methods to estimate direction have been proposed, some lack sufficient direction precision, or others require excessive initial cost of infrastructures and a special hardware. Therefore, in the next chapter, we propose a new direction estimation method, which realizes a precision required for the rendezvous without initial cost.

3   Direction Estimation between Devices Using Acoustic Waves

We newly propose a direction estimation method between devices using acoustic waves. Acoustic waves are usually chosen to elevate the accuracy, because of their relatively slower speed than radio signals. The proposed method is based on the following approaches:

Approach 1: We use Doppler Effect for the direction estimation (See Section 3.2 for more details). For producing the Doppler Effect, a user motion is used (See Section 3.1 for more details).

Approach 2: For recognition of the Doppler Effect, the pulse-pair method [9] or FFT (Fast Fourier Transform) method is generally used. We use the former, since its processing load is lower. In concrete terms, the devices transmit and receive multiple pulse-type acoustic waves and detect the change between transmission and reception intervals of acoustic waves (See Section 3.2 for more details).

Approach 3: To reduce the estimation error due to reflection waves and noise, the device tries to remove them, using acoustic wave information including the

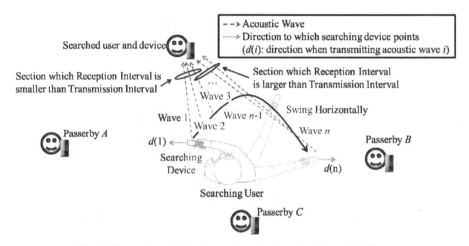

Fig. 1. The outline of direction estimation based on Doppler Effect

transmission count and the transmission interval of acoustic waves (See Section 3.3 for more details). This information is exchanged beforehand via Bluetooth, Wi-Fi and so on.

In the rest of this paper, we refer to a user requiring direction to a partner and his/her partner as searching and searched users, respectively. Similarly, we refer to the devices of the searching and searched users as searching and searched devices, respectively. The basic procedure of the proposed method is as follows:

Basic Procedure 1: The searching and searched devices exchange the acoustic wave information.

Basic Procedure 2: While the searching device is transmitting acoustic waves, a Doppler Effect is produced by the searching user motion. Also, the searching device detects its direction to which it points, when transmitting each acoustic wave. The detection is performed with magnetic sensor or gyrocompass.

Basic Procedure 3: After receiving acoustic waves, the searched device calculates the reception interval of the acoustic waves, whereupon it notifies the calculated reception interval back to the searching device.

Basic Procedure 4: The searching device estimates the direction by the change of transmission and reception intervals based on the Doppler Effect.

The rest of this Chapter is organized as follows. Section 3.1 explains the user motion to generate the Doppler Effect, while Section 3.2 describes the direction estimation based on the Doppler Effect. Section 3.3 states the procedure used to calculate the reception interval of acoustic waves, and Section 3.4 shows the whole procedure for the direction estimation of the searching and searched devices.

3.1   Searching User Motion for Generation of Doppler Effect

When the searching user requires direction to the searched user, he/she is naturally unaware of the location of the searched user. So, generating a Doppler Effect to all directions is required. One example of the user motions is to swing the searching device horizontally as if drawing a half circle, as illustrated in Fig. 1. In specific term, the searching user stretches the arm while holding the searching device, and then swings it horizontally through 180 degrees.

3.2 Direction Estimation Using Acoustic Waves Based on Doppler Effect

The outline of direction estimation based on the Doppler Effect is depicted in Fig. 1. The searching device transmits multiple pulse-type acoustic waves at a transmission interval, during swing. Also, the searching device detects its direction pointing to, when transmitting each acoustic wave. As a result, the searched device receives the acoustic waves at an interval different from the transmission interval. Based on the Doppler Effect, in the section in which the searching device is approaching the searched device, the reception interval is smaller than the transmission interval (hereafter, referred to as the approaching section). Conversely, in the section that the searching device is withdrawing from the searched device, the reception interval is larger than the transmission interval (hereafter, referred to as the withdrawing section). By detecting these sections from the change between the transmission and reception intervals (hereafter, referred to as change of interval), the direction can be estimated, when the searched user is located not only in front of the searching user like Fig. 1, but also to the right, left and back sides of the searching user like passers-by A, B and C in Fig. 1.

The concrete procedures are as follows. First, the searching device calculates the change between the transmission and reception intervals. Second, it estimates the direction by the change of interval. Now, the acquisition of transmission interval is possible by generation of a music file, which plays acoustic waves at a specified interval. According to the reception interval, the searched device calculates it and notifies it to the searching device. Calculation of the reception interval is described in Section 3.3. In the rest of this section, let the transmission count of acoustic waves be n and the direction to which the searching device points in transmission of acoustic wave i ($i=1, 2, \ldots , n$) be $d(i)$. Also, let the transmission and reception intervals between the acoustic waves i and j be $SI(i, j)$ and $RI(i, j)$ ($i=1, 2, \ldots , n$-1, $j=i+1, i+2, \ldots , n$), respectively. We assume that the searching device is swung clockwise, as shown in Fig. 1. In the last part of this section, we show how the proposed method can estimate direction during swing in counter clockwise manner.

Calculation of the Change of Interval: The searching device calculates the change of interval $CI(i)$ with the transmission and reception intervals as follow: $CI(i) = SI(i, i+1) - RI(i, i+1)$.

Direction Estimation: The procedure of direction estimation with the change of interval $CI(i)$ is illustrated in Fig. 2. In the procedure, there are 4 patterns of the direction: front, right, left and back.

If the change of interval $CI(i)$ is initially negative, and then becomes positive, this means that the approaching and withdrawing sections occur in turn. Thus, the searched device is located in front of the searching device (Line 4 in Fig. 2). In this

```
 1.    if (CI(1) < 0)
 2.        for(i = 1: i < n: i = i − 1)
 3.            if (CI(i) > 0)
 4.                D = d(i). break;         Front
 5.            end
 6.            if (i == n − 1)
 7.                D = d(n);               Right (Clockwise)
 8.            end                         (Left (Counter Clock wise))
 9.        end
10.    else
11.        for(i = 1: i < n: i = i − 1)
12.            if (CI(i) < 0)
13.                D = d(i) − 180: break;   Back
14.            end
15.            if (i == n − 1)             Left (Clockwise)
16.                D = d(1);               (Right (Counter Clock wise))
17.            end
18.        end
19.    else
```

Fig. 2. The procedure of direction estimation with change of interval of acoustic waves

case, the searching device detects the acoustic wave of boundary between both sections, and then estimates the direction at that of the searching device in transmitting the detected acoustic wave.

Conversely, when the change of interval $CI(i)$ is initially positive (including zero) and becomes negative, it means that the withdrawing and approaching sections occur alternately, and the searched device is located at the back side of the searching device (Line 13 in Fig. 2). In this case, the searching device detects the acoustic wave of the boundary and estimates the direction at the right back of the direction of the searching device in transmitting the detected acoustic wave.

Where all the values of the change of interval $CI(i)$ are negative (positive), this indicates that only the approaching (withdrawing) section occurs, whereupon the searched device is judged to be on the right (left) side of the searching device (Line 7 (Line 16) in Fig. 2). Here, the searching device estimates the direction as one of the searching device in transmitting the last acoustic wave n (first acoustic wave 1).

Now, we assume that the searching user swings the searching device clockwise. The difference between clockwise and counter clockwise is judgment whether the searched device is located to the right or left side at Lines 7 and 16 in Fig. 2. However, the estimated direction is same in both cases, so the direction can be estimated if swung counter clockwise.

3.3   Calculation of Reception Interval of Acoustic Waves

We describe how the searched device calculates the reception interval of acoustic waves. Now, the calculation is realized by recording acoustic waves as the file once, and then analysing the file, as shown in [1]. This enables us to prevent errors between the actual time of reception and the time of recognition of reception of the acoustic wave.

```
1.    A = {1,2, ... , n} : i = 1: B₁ = φ
2.    while( A ≠ φ)
3.        A' = A
4.        if( B = φ )
5.            x = min( A' ): B = B ∪ {x}: A' = A'-{x}:
6.        else
7.            while( A' ≠ φ )
8.                y = max( B ): z = min( A' ): A' = A'-{z}:
9.                if( SI(y, z) - RI(y, z) < Threshold )
10.                   B = B ∪ {z}:
11.               end
12.           end
13.           A = A - B: i = i - 1: B = φ:
14.       end
15.   end
16.
17.   temp = 0:
18.   for( j = 1: j < i: j = j - 1)
19.       if( temp < B )
20.           temp = B: index = j:
21.       end
22.   end
```

(Division of Set of Acoustic Wave)
Abstracting sets of acoustic waves of which transmission and reception intervals of acoustic waves differ less than threshold

(Removal of Reflection Wave)
Acoustic waves except the member of the maximum set are removed

Fig. 3. The procedure of removal of reflection wave

The concrete procedures are as follows. Both devices initially exchange the acoustic wave information. Next, the searched device detects the reception time of the acoustic waves, and then calculates the reception interval of them. After that, it tries to remove the reflection waves and noise with the acoustic wave information.

Exchange of Acoustic Wave Information: The Acoustic wave information, including the transmission count n, transmission interval $SI(i, j)$ and the frequency of acoustic waves f, is exchanged between both devices beforehand.

Detection of the Reception Time of Acoustic Wave: The reception time is detected by correlation between the recorded file and a reference signal in the time domain. The reference signal can be generated with the acoustic wave information. The time of the maximum peak of correlation is concluded as the reception time $R(i)$ ($i=1, 2, \ldots , n$).

Calculation of Reception Interval of Acoustic Wave: The reception intervals between the arbitrary two acoustic waves i and j ($i=1, 2, \ldots , n-1, j=i+1, i+2, \ldots , n$) are calculated as follows: $RI(i, j) = R(j) - R(i)$.

Removal of Reflection Waves and Noise: The searched device tries to remove reflection waves and noise based on the following approach. If the transmission and reception intervals of two acoustic waves differ by more than a threshold, at least one of the two acoustic waves is a reflection wave. If the arm length is 70cm, the change of distance between both devices by the swing depicted in Fig. 1 is indicated as a maximum 140cm. Thus, the change of transmission and reception intervals peaks at 4.3ms ($\fallingdotseq$140cm / the speed of sound), so the threshold is set as 4.3ms.

The searched device tries to remove reflection waves and noise, based on the procedure shown in Fig. 3. Initially, set A composed of n acoustic waves is divided

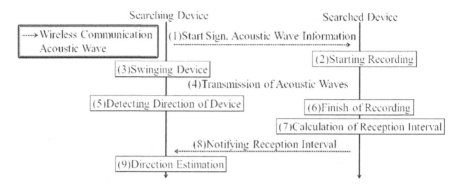

Fig. 4. The whole procedure of searching and searched devices

into sets composed of acoustic waves, which the transmission and reception intervals of the two waves have differences less than the threshold (from Lines 1 to 15 in Fig. 3). Then, if the number of abstracted sets exceeds 1, the acoustic waves, except the member of the maximum set B_{index}, are removed (from Lines 17 to 22 in Fig. 3).

Finally, the searched device notifies the reception interval and the set B_{index} to the searching device. Now, the set B_{index} is used by the searching device, only if some acoustic waves are removed. In that case, the number of transmission interval exceeds that of the reception interval, whereupon the searching device recalculates the transmission interval adaptive to the reception interval with the set B_{index}.

3.4   Whole Procedure for Direction Estimation of Searching and Searched Devices

We explain the whole procedure of the searching and searched devices using Fig. 4. First, the searching device notifies a start sign and the acoustic wave information to the searched device (Fig. 4 (1)). After receiving this, the searched device starts to record (Fig. 4 (2)). After that, when the searching device is swung (Fig. 4 (3)), it transmits acoustic waves (Fig. 4 (4)). At the same time, it detects its direction in transmission of each acoustic wave (Fig. 4 (5)). After finishing recording (Fig. 4 (6)), the searched devices calculates the reception interval (Section 3.3) (Fig. 4 (7)), and then notifies the reception interval (Fig. 4 (8)). On receiving the reception interval, the searching device estimates the direction (Section 3.2) (Fig. 4 (9)).

4   Implementation

We implement the proposed method as an application on smartphones (Android 2.1), in order to evaluate it. We show the implementation outline.

● Bluetooth is used as the form of radio communication to notify the acoustic wave information and the reception interval.

- A chirp signal is selected as an acoustic wave, with sampling frequency and signal length of 44.1 kHz and 50ms, respectively.
- Some parameters, such as the frequency range of the chirp signal, the transmission count and the transmission interval, can be selected via the application setting menu.
- A magnetic sensor is used to detect the direction in which the searching device points.
- To adjust the detection timing of the direction in which the searching device points and transmission of each acoustic wave, the timer is set in line with the transmission interval.
- To adjust the start timing of swing and transmission of acoustic waves, the application shows the countdown on the display.
- The estimated direction is shown via an arrow on the display of smartphone. After the estimation, the arrow is dynamically adjusted to point to the estimated direction by detecting the direction to which the searching device points continuously.

5   Experiment and Evaluation

To evaluate the proposed method, we measure its performance, through the implemented application. First, we evaluate the distance between devices within which the proposed method works enough for practical use, since an acoustic wave attenuates according to propagation distance. Now, if we supposed rendezvous outdoors and indoors, such as in shopping malls, parks, cafés and station yards, factors, such as reflection waves, noise and crowdedness would impact on the results. Thus, we also evaluate from the viewpoint of impact of reflection waves, noise and crowdedness.

5.1   Experimental Method

We use estimation error as an evaluation metric, which is calculated as the absolute difference between the estimated and actual directions.

We set the parameters as follows: frequency range of the chirp signal of 14-16kHz, the transmission count of 15 and the transmission interval of 200ms. In the experiment, the directions in which the searching user turns is six patterns: the front, right and left 45 degrees, right and left 90 degrees and back, based to the direction relative to the searched user, as illustrated in Fig. 5. Also, the searching user swing clockwise.

The experimental conditions are shown in Table. 1. In the first experiment, the distances between devices are set as 10m, 20m and 30m outdoors. The second experiment is performed in a room that is approximately 8m x 8m to generate reflection waves. The third experiment is performed, while playing a music file on a PC. The loudness level near the searched device shows 80dB, which is compatible to a noisy urban city in daytime [10]. The frequency of the music file ranges under 5kHz. The fourth experiment is performed near a station. Many people pass through between devices. The loudness level near the searched device shows 80dB. The estimation error is measured 30 times under each condition.

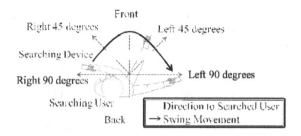

Fig. 5. Directions of searching user based on direction to searched user

Table 1. Experimental Condition

Experimental Content	Distance between Devices	Place	Remarks
1. Distance between Devices	10m, 20m, 30m	Outdoors	Quiet
2. Reflection Wave	10m	Indoors (Room by 8m x 8m)	Quiet
3. Noise	10m	Indoors (Room by 8m x 8m)	Loudness level 80dB (Playing music file)
4. Crowdedness	10m	Outdoors	Passers-by (Loudness level 80dB)

5.2   Experimental Results

We illustrate the experimental results of distance between devices in Fig. 6 (a), and also depict those of the impact of reflection waves, noise and crowdedness in Fig. 6 (b). The vertical and horizontal axes imply estimation error and the direction in which the searching user turns, respectively. Each plot includes averaged values of 30 trials under each condition. Also, the plot averaged for the direction in which the searching user turns is shown at the far left in the Fig. 6 (a) and (b). Now, for comparison, the result of 10m outdoors is also plotted in Fig. 6 (b).

Distance between Devices: From the experimental results, we can see little difference in estimation error among distances. For instance, the averaged values range from 9.6 (P1 in Fig. 6 (a)) to 12.6 degrees (P2 in Fig. 6 (a)). Meanwhile, it is confirmed that the estimation error increases due to attenuation of acoustic waves, when we measured it in case of distance of 40m. Thus, the proposed method works enough for practical use, where the distance between devices is within 30m.

Impact of Reflection Wave, Noise and Crowdedness: The experimental results of Fig. 6 (b) show that all estimation errors are kept within 18.0 degrees.

In terms of reflection waves, the averaged value is 12.2 degrees (P4 in Fig. 6 (b)), while that of the first experiment with 10m is 9.6 degrees (P3 in Fig. 6 (b)), meaning the impact of reflection wave is small. Hence, it is indicated that reflection waves are sufficiently removed by the procedure in Section 3.3.

In the case of noise, the averaged value is 11.8 degrees (P5 in Fig. 6 (b)), so that we can say that the impact of noise is also small. This is because the frequency of acoustic waves (14-16kHz) is different from that of the music file (under 5kHz).

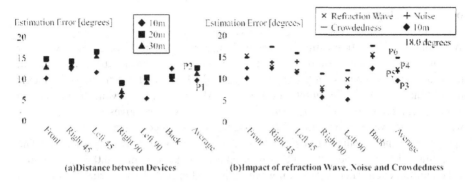

(a)Distance between Devices   (b)Impact of refraction Wave. Noise and Crowdedness

Fig. 6. Experimental results of Estimation Error

Similarly, since the frequency of noise made by humans and cars is different, the impact of noise in shopping malls and parks is also considered small. Just in case if there is noise with high frequency, by scanning frequency of present noise, it is possible to select the frequency different from present noise.

Regarding crowdedness, the experimental results show that the averaged value is 14.9 degrees (P6 in Fig. 6 (b)), meaning the impact is slightly larger than that in other cases. This is due to interception of some acoustic waves by passers-by. As a result, the number of acoustic waves used for the estimation is reduced. However, the estimation error is still kept within 18.0 degrees.

Direction of Searching User: The estimation errors in the cases of right and left 90 degrees are smaller than that in other cases. For example, all plots of the former case in Fig. 6 (a) range under 10.3 degrees, while those in the latter case range over 10.0 degrees. This is because only approaching or withdrawing section occurs in the former case. Conversely, the both sections occur in the latter case, so the detection of boundary between both sections is required. In this detection, there is few change of distance near the boundary, as shown in acoustic waves 2 and 3 in Fig. 1. Hence, the estimation error is a little increased.

5.3   Evaluation

The experimental results show that the direction estimation is possible where the distance between devices is within 30m. In the rendezvous, it is likely to approach the partner within 30m by sharing the rendezvous place. Otherwise, by combining the proposed method with existing location services like GPS, it would be possible to lead a user to near the partner. Meanwhile, the estimation error is kept within 18.0 degrees under conditions where reflection wave, noise and crowdedness are factors. By obtaining the direction of an error of within 18.0 degrees, the direction in which the partner would be located is limited to 1/10 (=18.0*2/360). In case that there is only one person in the estimated direction, this person must be specified as the partner. Otherwise, if there are multiple persons in the estimated direction, we can make a short list of the candidate persons by 1/10. This enables the user to easily find his/her partner. Therefore, the proposed method is practical for the rendezvous with the person who is not acquaintance in the actual world.

6   Conclusion

We proposed a direction estimation method enabling users to have a rendezvous for the first time which requires neither any additional infrastructures nor special hardware on user devices. In the proposed method, Doppler Effect produced by a user movement is used for the direction estimation. Meanwhile, to prevent the estimation error from increasing due to reflection waves, the device removes reflection waves with acoustic wave information. We implemented the mechanism as a smartphone application and evaluated its performance under real-world conditions. The experimental results show that the estimation error is kept within 18.0 degrees under the condition even where reflection wave, noise and crowdedness occur. This implies that the direction in which the partner would be located is limited to $1/10$ (=18.0*2/360) in the rendezvous. As this enables the user to find a partner easily, the proposed method is practical for the rendezvous.

References

1. Chunyi, P., Guobin, S., Yongguang, Z., Yanlin, L., Kun, T.: Beepbeep: a high accuracy acoustic ranging system using cots mobile devices. In: Proceedings of the 5th International Conference on Embedded Networked Sensor Systems (2007)
2. GPS Share,
   https://market.android.com/
   details?id=com.kkinder.sharelocation
3. Hui, L., Houshang, D., Pat, B., Jing, L.: Survey of wireless indoor positioning techniques and systems. IEEE Transactions on Systems, Man, and Cybernetics Part C 37(6), 1067–1080 (2007)
4. Muthukrishnan, K., Hazas, M.: Position Estimation from UWB Pseudorange and Angle-of-Arrival: A Comparison of Non-linear Regression and Kalman Filtering. In: Choudhury, T., Quigley, A., Strang, T., Suginuma, K. (eds.) LoCA 2009. LNCS, vol. 5561, pp. 222–239. Springer, Heidelberg (2009)
5. Andy, W., Alan, J., Andy, H.: A new location technique for the active office. IEEE Personal Communications 4(5), 43–47 (1997)
6. Adam, S., Hari, B., Michel, G.: Tracking moving devices with the cricket location system. In: Proceedings of the 2nd International Conference on Mobile Systems, Applications, and Services (Mobisys 2004), pp. 190–202 (2004)
7. Myungsik, K., Nak, Y.C., Wonpil, Y.: Robust DOA estimation and target docking for mobile robots. Intelligent Service Robotics 2(1), 41–51 (2009)
8. Yoshifumi, N., Toyota, F., Masato, A.: Two-dimensional DOA estimation of sound sources based on weighted wiener gain exploiting two-directional microphones. IEEE Transaction Audio, Speech and Language Processing 15(2), 416–429 (2007)
9. Seman, S.A.: Performance of Pulse-Pair Method of Doppler Estimation. IEEE Transactions on Aerospace and Electronic Systems 34, 520–531 (1998)
10. USA PRO Shoreline Technology LLC, SOUND LEVELS,
    http://www.usaproshoreline.com/pdf/Decibel_Levels.pdf

Using SIFT and WiFi Signals to Provide Location-Based Services for Smartphones

Antonio J. Ruiz-Ruiz, Oscar Canovas, Ruben A. Rubio Muñoz,
and Pedro E. Lopez-de-Teruel Alcolea

Department of Computer Engineering, University of Murcia, Spain
{antonioruiz,ocanovas,rrm15947,pedroe}@um.es

Abstract. This paper introduces how to fuse the data acquired from different sensors available in commodity smartphones to build accurate location-based services, pursuing a good balance between accuracy and performance. Using scale invariant features from the images captured using the smartphone camera, we perform a matching process against previously obtained images to determine the current location of the device. Several refinements are introduced to improve the performance and the scalability of our proposal. Location fingerprinting, based on IEEE 802.11, will be used to determine a cluster of physical points, or zone, where the device seems to be according to the received signal strength. In this way, we will reduce the number of images to analyze to those contained in the tentative zone. Additionally, accelerometers will be also considered in order to improve the system performance, by means of a motion estimator. This set of techniques enables a wide range of new location-based applications.

Keywords: SIFT, image processing, 802.11, probabilistic techniques.

1 Introduction

Location technologies provide a way of associating information to a user position. For a diverse set of areas including tracking, geographic routing or entertainment, location-sensing systems have been an active research field. We will focus on indoor environments, where the Global Positioning System (GPS) suffers from several obstacles blocking the radio signals.

In recent years, the wide adoption of smartphones equipped with several sensors has simplified the process of obtaining the required context information and provides an exceptional starting point to develop location-based services, like augmented-reality applications [10]. Localization systems might benefit from the images that users obtain from the camera in order to display the augmented reality. Indeed, those images can be used to provide a better estimation of the users' position, offering a seamless integration of the sensor and the display. There are several augmented-reality applications which do not require a real time response, such as those designed to display location-aware reminders or notes [19], or to obtain information about who is behind the door of a particular room or laboratory. We find our approach a valuable contribution for this kind of

A. Puiatti et al. (Eds.): MobiQuitous 2011, LNICST 104, pp. 37–48, 2012.

location-based services, since we have obtained the required tradeoff between a fine-grained accuracy and an acceptable response time using data from multiple sensors.

In our proposal, we make use of the scale invariant feature transform (SIFT) [14], an image processing technique suitable for object recognition, to deal with the images captured by the smartphone camera. Our system looks for matching features between the current image and a geo-tagged database of features that were extracted using representative images of the application environment.

Despite we use the images obtained from the camera as the main piece of data to infer the position of a particular device, we can benefit from other sensors in order to limit the amount of information to be examined. Most of the well-known proposals for indoor positioning are based on the received signal strength intensity (RSSI) of transmitted 802.11 packets. In fact, several works have demonstrated that significant accuracy can be obtained in indoor scenarios by means of fingerprinting techniques [7]. As we will show, using fingerprinting methods, we can obtain a cluster of physical points where there is a high probability of locating the device. This cluster is then used to reduce the amount of images in the database to check against, since only those images contained in the selected cluster are analyzed. Additionally, the use of a RSSI-based fingerprinting technique is an added-value service for our purposes, since we will be able to calculate a coarse-grained location estimation which can be useful in those situations when the images obtained by the camera are useless.

Our system achieves acceptable performance distributing the required functionality between the mobile devices and dedicated servers. Additionally, in-built accelerometers will be used to infer coarse-grained user-motion, so reducing the required amount of operations to perform in some circumstances. The system can currently complete an entire cycle, from obtaining data from sensors to providing a location estimation, in less than 3 seconds.

2   Related Work

Indoor positioning is a research field that has been addressed by several authors and disciplines. Several types of signals (radio, images, sound) and methods have been used to infer location. Each method has specific requirements as to what types of measurements are needed. Most of the pattern recognition methods, like fingerprinting [7], estimate locations by recognizing position-related patterns. The analysis of RSSI patterns is a technique that has been examined by several authors [4,8], obtaining an accuracy ranging from 0.5 to 3 meters.

Better results can be obtained by integrating the information captured by multiple sensors. SurroundSense [3] is an interesting mobile phone-based location system for indoor environments via ambience fingerprinting of optical, acoustic and motion attributes. However, the optical recognition techniques proposed in SurroundSense are too limited, since the authors are only considering pictures of the floor in order to extract information about light and color. With SIFT, our work avoids typical variations related to light, color or scale, and provides robustness and better accuracy.

In [1,22], the authors performed a preliminary analysis of how techniques like SIFT can be used to improve the accuracy in location based systems. However, both works fail to show an exhaustive analysis of the enhanced possibilities of such techniques when combined with the additional sensors commonly available on smartphones.

Miyaki et al. [15] described an object tracking system for outdoor environments fusing information from CCTV cameras and WiFi signals using a particle filter. While this proposal is based on object tracking (especially people), our work is focused on object recognition in the scene captured by the smartphone camera carried by the user.

Other works also use WiFi signals and image recognition to estimate positions, such as [9] and [17]. However, they are based on two-dimensional landmarks that must be placed in the scenario of interest, which involves the inclusion of obtrusive elements. As we will show, we can obtain good accuracy without imposing such requirements.

3   Experimental Environment

The testbed where our experiments were conducted is located on the third floor of our Faculty where several students, researchers and professors move around constantly. The dimension of the testbed is 35 meters by 30 meters, and includes 26 rooms. We have defined a discrete space model of 94 cells where we can link location-based information.

To deploy the fingerprinting system based on RSSI, we distributed six 802.11 access points throughout our dependencies (red dots in Figure 1). Access points already deployed in the scenario might also be used since there are no specific requirements imposed. During the corresponding training phase we collected 250 RSSI observations at each cell. For our database of images, we have obtained a set of seed images, where the number of images captured at each cell depends on the cell type (zoom on Figure 1). Thus, a cell in a corridor is associated to as many images as possible directions of movement, whereas inside the rooms we build panoramic images covering the whole dependency. For larger scenarios we plan to develop some technique like the one presented by Park et al. in [18] in

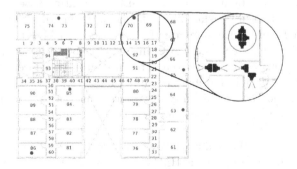

Fig. 1. Experimental environment

order to populate larger databases of images and RSSIs using the data provided by the users as they make use of the available location services.

Our experiments were carried out using several hardware devices. The training observations were captured with an Asus Eee 1201 laptop with a Realtek TRL8191SE Wireless LAN 802.11n card. In addition, during the online phase we have also used HTC Desire and HTC Legend smartphones with Android. We developed the appropriate software client for each device in order to collect RSSIs and images and to send them to a repository. Applications were programmed in C++ and Java, depending on the requirements imposed by each device. We have used Linksys WRT54G access points with 802.11abg support. Their locations were chosen so as to provide consistent coverage throughout the entire scenario, guaranteeing that every cell is covered by, at least, 3 access points.

For image processing we use the SIFTGPU library, a GPU Implementation of Scale Invariant Feature Transform (SIFT), implemented by Changchang Wu. SiftGPU requires a high-end GPU, that makes it impossible to be managed by smartphones, so we use a nVidia GeForce 9800GT supporting both GLSL (OpenGL Shading Language) and CUDA (Compute Unified Device Architecture). This GPU has been installed in a Intel(R) Pentium(R) Dual-Core CPU E2160 server. This computer is responsible for estimating the location of the different devices. The resolution of the training images is 640x480 pixels for corridors and 2900x360 pixels for panoramic images of offices and laboratories, and they were captured using a HTC Desire smartphone.

The system has been tested by five different users. They held the phone out in front of them, facing ahead in order to obtain location-aware information related to their current cell or to a zone containing the cell. We are aware that the use of these augmented-reality applications based on images would be sporadic, since we do not envision realistic scenarios where users are comfortable holding their phones facing ahead all the time. Therefore, when the smartphone is inside the pocket, facing the floor, or obtaining useless images (unfocused, uniform), the location estimation will be based mainly on the RSSI measurements.

4   Clustering Based on RSSI

As mentioned, several research works have demonstrated that a significant accuracy can be obtained by means of location fingerprinting based on RSSI. We have performed several tests using different techniques in order to compare their results [4,8]. In Figure 2 we compare the accuracy provided by the different techniques that we analyzed. These experiments have been carried out using the training observations as inputs for our estimator and, therefore, we are aware that these results can only be obtained under ideal conditions. We decided to represent the position as a probability distribution using Bayesian inference. As we can see, a histogram-based representation of the sensor model performs better in our scenario.

Accuracy is considerably enhanced by introducing a Hidden Markov Model (HMM) [11]. We have designed the HMM chain as a matrix of NxN size, where N is the number of cells within our scenario. Our matrix has been initialized

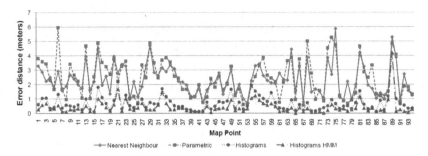

Fig. 2. Estimation error using RSSI

using the adjacency relationship between cells and considering that users do not usually move faster than 2 meters per second.

One of the most interesting conclusions that can be obtained from the fingerprinting methods is their suitability to define geographical areas where signals show a similar behavior. Lemelson et al. [12] proposed the Fingerprint Clustering algorithm, which makes use of the training RSSIs to find clusters. It is based on the idea that the signals collected in nearby cells tends to cover only a limited range of the possible values. In order to show how this proposal can be applied in our interests, we have calculated the clusters, shown in Figure 3 (cells pertaining to the same cluster are displayed using the same color), and then we performed several tests where most of the already-analyzed techniques obtain a high cluster hit percentage, up to 93%. According to these experiments, we have defined four overlapping zones joining adjacent clusters in order to reduce the search space when other sensors are also analyzed.

As we will see, the main drawback of using images is the elevated computational cost, especially in huge scenarios, where the number of images to analyze is excessive, involving serious scalability problems. The use of the mentioned clustering technique and the defined zones reduces the number of processed images to those contained in a specific zone of the entire scenario, so performing a fine-grained localization and improving the system scalability.

5 SIFT Analysis

The Scale Invariant Feature Transform [13,14] is a widely adopted technique in computer vision research. It provides a method for extracting a collection of features from images, and these features are invariant to image translation, scaling and rotation, and partially invariant to illumination changes and affine distortion or change in 3D camera viewpoint. These features are well localized in both the spatial and frequency domains, reducing the probability of disruption by occlusion, clutter, or noise. One of the most important characteristics of SIFT is that each feature vector is highly distinctive, which allows a single feature to be correctly matched with a high probability against a large database of features, providing a basis for object and scene recognition.

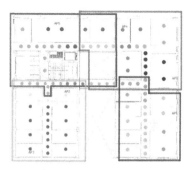

Fig. 3. Clusters distribution

There are several efficient algorithms to extract distinctiveness feature vectors from images, proposed by Lowe [14] or by Vedaldi [21]. Turcot and Lowe have taken an additional step in [20], improving performance by selecting only a small subset of the training features.

Since the SIFT extractor algorithm is based on a Gaussian pyramid of the input image, there are several parameters that influence its performance. We have empirically analyzed the SIFT extractor algorithm in order to find the input parameters that best fit our images and scenario characteristics. We tested different values for the number of octaves, for the index of the first octave, and finally for the number of levels per octave of the pyramid. Selected values are: 5 octaves, first octave equal to 0 and 5 levels per octave. Thus, we obtain 250 stable keypoints per image on average.

Since each keypoint descriptor is defined as a 128-dimensional feature vector, there is no algorithm able to identify the exact nearest neighbors in such high dimensional spaces that is any more efficient than exhaustive search. There are some algorithms, such as the Best-Bin-First proposed by Beis and Lowe [5], that return the closest neighbor with high probability. Another useful algorithm is proposed by Arya and Mount [2], based on the use of kd-trees and bd-trees, that support both exact and approximate nearest neighbor searching in spaces of various dimensions. We have used the kd-tree version implemented within the ANN (Approximate Nearest Neighbor) library by Mount and Arya [16] to carry out our experiments.

Our image database contains a set of 45374 data points in real 128-dimensional space. However, with a tree structure, the nearest neighbor can be found efficiently. ANN allows us to select the number of returned k-nearest neighbors, where $k \geq 1$. For $k = 2$, we compute the distance between these two nearest neighbors in order to check whether it is a real match. As Figure 4 shows, we evaluated three different values for the distance ratio R (between the closest and the next closest neighbor), and we reject those matchings with a ratio greater than the specified value. In our scenario, the best results for performance and accuracy are obtained with $R = 0.75$ (close to the $R = 0.8$ suggested by Lowe in [13]).

Another important parameter of our matching algorithm is the number of individual matches required to consider that there is strong evidence of a global image matching. Since the number of features for each image may be high, we

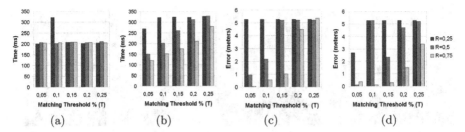

Fig. 4. Matching parameter analysis. a) Global tree performance; b)Clustering-based trees performance; c) Global tree accuracy; d) Clustering-based trees accuracy

can specify a matching threshold T (a percentage of matches against the number of features per image) to define a match as valid. We have experimented with different T values (x axis of Figure 4), finding that 0.1 is a good value to maximize performance and accuracy. That is, given a query image, we consider that there is match when at least 10% of its features are found in a particular image of the database. It proves that SIFT features are very descriptive.

Once we have chosen the right parameters for an optimal image search, we can show the appropriateness of using a multisensor system to improve the accuracy and the performance of the location estimation process. As we mentioned above, using the clustering technique based on the RSSIs analysis, we divided our scenario into four zones. Figure 4 (a,c), shows the performance and accuracy results, respectively, obtained from a experiment using a tree of images that contains all the images of the database. However, Figure 4 (b,d) shows the performance and accuracy results, but with five different trees. Four of them contain the images of each zone, and the fifth one is a global tree containing all the images in the scenario. Analyzing these results, we can conclude that when using smaller trees we get better performance results, around 25% reduction in the search time, even improving accuracy. We are aware that our scenario is not so large, meaning that in larger scenarios this difference of using a global tree against clustering-based trees will suppose a higher performance improvement and, therefore, a better scalability.

Finally, it is worth noting that SIFT features provide a good distinctiveness even in environments with many similarities between different physical emplacements. Figure 5 shows different images, and their related features, extracted from the experimental environment. Each feature is represented by a circle indicating the corresponding scale and by a vector showing the orientation. Red circles are light blobs on dark background, green ones are dark blobs on light background, and a specific feature is drawn as a blue histogram, for illustration purposes. As Figure 5 shows, despite corridors A and B are similar, there is a significant difference regarding the number of features matching the captured image.

6   Motion Analysis

In several situations there is no need to perform continuous estimations about the user location. Once the right position has been determined with a high confidence,

(a) Features   (b) Matching with corridor A   (c) Matching with corridor B

Fig. 5. SIFT features and matching of images

the information obtained by the built-in inertial sensors of a smartphone might be used to determine whether the user moves or remains still. In this latter case, there is no need to acquire additional data from other sensors, or to calculate a new location estimation. The integration of this type of sensors improves the performance of our system, supporting a higher number of users. Additionally, regarding to power consumption, we will be able to save energy and avoid unnecessary operations and transmissions.

We infer the physical state of the mobile phone from a built-in 3-axis accelerometer, so we are able to characterize user movements. Since it is too difficult to get a better motion recognition with mobile phone accelerometers, we decided to identify just two states: still and motion.

To identify these states we use a simple perceptron [6], because we are dealing with two linearly separable sets, and that technique performs reasonably well. In order to train the perceptron, we first got 150 readings from a phone held by a user in a static position. Then we recorded another 150 samples from a user walking with the phone. Once this phase was finished, we trained our perceptron with these 300 samples. We performed this entire process several times using different patterns of movement to obtain different perceptrons. Once we finished this learning stage, we tested the perceptrons in the real scenario and we selected the one providing better results, which was trained with slow movements.

7   Sensor Fusion

The sensor fusion of our location system is designed to reduce the computational cost, to minimize the amount of information transmitted and, therefore, to preserve the smartphone battery life. The smartphone uses two different threads running in parallel in order to capture images and to obtain information about RSSI. Access points are analyzed in order to determine whether we are in a location supported by our system. Additionally, we have to check whether the image is useful, that is, it is focused enough to allow the extraction of SIFT features (a gradient model is used to discard blurry and uniform images). In that case we send to a database the image along with the RSSI information and a motion estimation performed locally, otherwise the image is not sent. Finally, once motion is detected or a timer expires, the process is repeated.

Once the information has been stored, the location service is able to estimate the position. RSSIs are processed to get a probability distribution vector indicating the likelihood of being located at each cell of the scenario. SIFT features are computed, and using the ANN kd-tree matching algorithm, a probability distribution is obtained according to the number of matches found.

The matching process proceeds as follows. We select the subtree linked to the cluster containing the cell with higher probability after the RSSI analysis. We compare our input image features with those stored in the selected subtree. If the result does not exceed the matching threshold T (mentioned in Section 5), we select another subtree containing that cell, if available, and the process is repeated. Finally, if we do not exceed T we select the global tree to perform a new search. According to the results shown in Figure 4, the performance of using subtrees in our testbed is up to 25% better than a global tree search.

The fusion process uses Bayes' Rule to obtain a probability distribution indicating the likelihood of being located at each cell of the scenario. Being π a probability distribution vector over each cell, $C = \{c_1, .., c_m\}$ the set of cells that make up the finite space state, n the amount of RSSI measurements in the current observation O_j, and $Pr(\lambda_\beta | a_\beta, c_i)$ the probability of taking a measurement from the access point a_β at reference cell c_i with a signal strength λ_β, there is a first estimation based only on RSSI:

$$\pi_i' = \frac{\pi_i Pr(O_j | c_i)}{\sum_{\alpha=1}^{m} (\pi_\alpha Pr(O_j | c_\alpha))} \quad \text{where } Pr(O_j | c_i) = \prod_{\beta=1}^{n} Pr(\lambda_\beta | a_\beta, c_i) \quad (1)$$

Considering π_h' as the highest value in π', we can constrain the analysis of the image in Oj to the cluster of cells where c_h is included. $Pr(f|c_c)$ is the probability of seeing an image f at cell c_c contained in the selected cluster, and it is defined as follows:

$$Pr(f|c_c) = \frac{matches_{f,c_c}}{\sum_{k=1}^{l} (matches_{f,c_k})} \quad (2)$$

All the images related to that cluster are analyzed to determine the image with a higher number of matching features. If $Pr(f|c_c) > T$ (T was defined in Section 5), we consider that there is strong evidence of being at cell c_c. Those cells not related with the selected cluster are assigned a negligible probability value (to avoid zero probability distribution). Finally we recalculate the probability distribution π' by fusing the already estimated π_i' with the corresponding $Pr(f|c_i)$ probability.

8 Experimental Analysis

In order to validate the accuracy and performance of our multisensor system we carried out several realtime tests where users were still and moving. Five different users pertaining to our research group participated in these tests daily during four weeks, making use of a augmented-reality prototype able to display location-aware notes. Every cell in the scenario was linked to a virtual note. Users were able to provide feedback through the application in order to confirm

Table 1. Cell hit (including adjacent) using different sensors

Cell hit / Fused Sensors	Still	Motion
RSSI	68.75% (93.75%)	5.5% (38.9%)
RSSI + Acc	56.25% (90.65%)	5.5% (38.9%)
Images + RSSI + Acc	82.85% (97.14%)	55% (94.44%)

their estimated positions, or to provide the right cell when the estimation was not correct, and this was our way to establish the ground truth.

During all these tests we obtained information from all the available sensors (images, RSSI and accelerometer). We have divided the tests into two different categories: still tests where users remain still at the same place, and motion tests where users move along the dependencies. The still tests took place at several cells, in corridors, offices and laboratories. During the motion tests, we covered several paths mainly along the corridors. Location was estimated with three different combinations of sensors: using RSSI only, using RSSI and accelerometer and using all the sensors, in order to check the accuracy of each combination. Table 1 shows that, for motion tests, we are able to estimate the right cell 55% of cases using images (94.44% of the estimations are exact or directly adjacent to the right cell). It is worth noting that the results improve the accuracy obtained using only WiFi, both for still and motion cases.

Regarding to the system performance, Figure 6 shows the distribution of time among the different tasks to be performed during the whole cycle needed to estimate locations. The required mean time is around three seconds using a HTC Desire smartphone and, as mentioned, our main intention was to find a good tradeoff between accuracy and performance. We consider that the extra time required to deal with images is acceptable for some of the envisioned applications requiring better accuracy. Furthermore, most of the time required for some tasks included in Figure 6 will be reduced significantly using future smartphones. For example, RSSI acquisition requires 35% (one second) since we perform a passive scanning. However, devices supporting active scanning might reduce this time drastically. In relation to images, we have considered the required time for auto focus, but this is not necessary once the focus is completed and we want to obtain more pictures. Additionally, communications have an important overload (25%), and most of this time is consumed by the transmission of images. It is worth reminding that we employ accelerometers in order to save energy and calculations in those situations where the handset remains still, and images are discarded when the device is in the pocket or in similar cases. Transmission of images is a requirement due to the limitations of current smartphones to perform the extraction of SIFT features. However, some manufacturers are announcing new smartphones with built-in GPUs, like NVIDIA TEGRA 2, that will be able to perform that extraction locally. This is especially interesting in order to reduce the required time to estimate the position by the location server, which is 13% (around 400ms) but including the calculation of SIFT features.

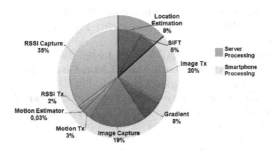

Fig. 6. Time latency of the localization process

9 Conclusions

The multisensor localization system presented in this paper provides an accurate method for estimating the user location. We have concentrated our efforts on integrating the context information obtained by using the available sensors in current smartphones.

As mentioned during the paper, the main drawback of using images is the elevated computational cost of the matching process in huge scenarios. Though our experimental scenario is relatively small, we have demonstrated that by using RSSI information we can reduce the search time up to 25%. In larger scenarios this performance improvement will be meaningfully higher since the complete tree of features will contain a higher amount of descriptors. Realtime experiments provide good results for still and motion scenarios, respectively, while the system can currently complete an entire cycle, from obtaining data from sensors to providing a location estimation, in approximately three seconds. Additional optimizations have been added by considering the information from the accelerometer and discarding useless images.

There are several augmented-reality applications which do not require a real time response. Therefore, we find our approach a valuable contribution for this kind of location-based services, since we have obtained the required tradeoff between a fine-grained accuracy and an acceptable response time using data from multiple sensors.

Acknowledgments. This work was supported by the Spanish MICINN, Plan E funds, under Grant TIN2009-14475-C04-02/01. It was also partly supported by the Funding Program for Research Groups of Excellence (04552/GERM/06) established by Fundación Séneca.

References

1. Arai, I., Horimi, S., Nishio, N.: Wi-Foto 2: Heterogeneous device controller using Wi-Fi positioning and template matching. In: Proc. Pervasive 2010 (2010)
2. Arya, S., Mount, D.M., Netanyahu, N.S., Silverman, R., Wu, A.Y.: An optimal algorithm for approximate nearest neighbor searching in fixed dimensions. In: ACM-SIAM Symposium on Discrete Algorithms, pp. 573–582 (1994)

3. Azizyan, M., Constandache, I., Roy Choudhury, R.: SurroundSense: Mobile Phone Localization via Ambience Fingerprinting. In: Proc. of the 15th MOBICOM, pp. 261–272 (2009)
4. Bahl, P., Padmanabhan, V.N.: RADAR: An In-Building RF-based User Location and Tracking System. In: Nineteenth Annual Joint Conference of the IEEE Computer and Communications Societies, vol. 2, pp. 775–784 (2000)
5. Beis, J., Lowe, D.G.: Shape indexing using approximate nearest-neighbour search in high-dimensional spaces. In: Proc. CVPR 1997, pp. 1000–1006 (1997)
6. Block, H.D.: The perceptron: a model for brain functioning. I, pp. 135–150. MIT Press, Cambridge (1988)
7. Chandrasekaran, G., Ergin, M.A., Yang, J., Liu, S., Chen, Y., Gruteser, M., Martin, R.P.: Empirical Evaluation of the Limits on Localization Using Signal Strength. In: Proc. SECON 2009, pp. 333–341 (2009)
8. Haeberlen, A., Flannery, E., Ladd, A.M., Rudys, A., Wallach, D.S., Kavraki, L.E.: Practical Robust Localization over Large Scale 802.11 Wireless Networks. In: Proc. MOBICOM 2004, pp. 70–84 (2004)
9. Hattori, K., Kimura, R., Nakajima, N., Fujii, T., Kado, Y., Zhang, B., Hazugawa, T., Takadama, K.: Hybrid indoor location estimation system using image processing and WiFi strength. In: Proc. WNIS 2009, pp. 406–411 (2009)
10. Hile, H., Borriello, G.: Positioning and orientation in indoor environments using camera phones. IEEE Computer Graphics Applications 28, 32–39 (2008)
11. Konolige, K., Chou, K.: Markov Localization using Correlation. In: Proc. IJCAI 1999, pp. 1154–1159 (1999)
12. Lemelson, H., Kjærgaard, M.B., Hansen, R., King, T.: Error Estimation for Indoor 802.11 Location Fingerprinting. In: Choudhury, T., Quigley, A., Strang, T., Suginuma, K. (eds.) LoCA 2009. LNCS, vol. 5561, pp. 138–155. Springer, Heidelberg (2009)
13. Lowe, D.G.: Object Recognition from Local Scale-Invariant Features. In: Proc. ICCV 1999, pp. 1150–1157 (1999)
14. Lowe, D.G.: Distinctive Image Features from Scale-Invariant Keypoints. International Journal of Computer Vision 60, 91–110 (2004)
15. Miyaki, T., Yamasaki, T., Aizawa, K.: Tracking persons using particle filter fusing visual and WiFi localizations for widely distributed camera. In: Proc. ICIP 2007, pp. 225–228 (2007)
16. Mount, D.M., Arya, S.: Ann a library for approximate nearest neighbor searching. In: 2nd CGC Workshop on Computational Geometry (1997)
17. Mulloni, A., Wagner, D., Barakonyi, I., Schmalstieg, D.: Indoor Positioning and Navigation with Camera Phones. IEEE Pervasive Computing 8, 22–31 (2009)
18. Park, J.G., Charrow, B., Curtis, D., Battat, J., Minkov, E., Hicks, J., Teller, S., Ledlie, J.: Growing an organic indoor location system. In: Proc. MobiSys 2010, pp. 271–284 (2010)
19. Sohn, T., Li, K.A., Lee, G., Smith, I., Scott, J., Griswold, W.G.: Place-Its: A Study of Location-Based Reminders on Mobile Phones. In: Beigl, M., Intille, S.S., Rekimoto, J., Tokuda, H. (eds.) UbiComp 2005. LNCS, vol. 3660, pp. 232–250. Springer, Heidelberg (2005)
20. Turcot, P., Lowe, D.: Better matching with fewer features: The selection of useful features in large database recognition problems. In: Proc. ICCV 2009 (2009)
21. Vedaldi, A., Soatto, S.: Features for recognition: viewpoint invariance for nonplanar scenes. In: Proc. ICCV 2005, pp. 1474–1481 (2005)
22. Werner, M., Kessel, M., Marouane, C.: Indoor Positioning Using Smartphone Camera. In: Indoor Positioning Indoor Navigation (IPIN) (September 2011)

What's around Me? Spatialized Audio Augmented Reality for Blind Users with a Smartphone

Jeffrey R. Blum, Mathieu Bouchard, and Jeremy R. Cooperstock

McGill University, Montréal, Québec, Canada
{jeffbl,matju,jer}@cim.mcgill.ca

Abstract. Numerous projects have investigated assistive navigation technologies for the blind community, tackling challenges ranging from interface design to sensory substitution. However, none of these have successfully integrated what we consider to be the three factors necessary for a widely deployable system that delivers a rich experience of one's environment: implementation on a commodity device, use of a pre-existing worldwide point of interest (POI) database, and a means of rendering the environment that is superior to a naive playback of spoken text. Our "In Situ Audio Services" (ISAS) application responds to these needs, allowing users to explore an urban area without necessarily having a particular destination in mind. We describe the technical aspects of its implementation, user requirements, interface design, safety concerns, POI data source issues, and further requirements to make the system practical on a wider basis. Initial qualitative feedback from blind users is also discussed.

Keywords: spatialized audio, blind navigation, GPS, smartphone, audio augmented reality.

1   Introduction

Guide dogs and canes have long been the staple assistive devices used by the blind community when navigating city streets. More recently, GPS has broadened the possibilities for autonomous exploration. Efforts to date have largely been focused on guiding a user from one location to another, usually via turn-by-turn spoken directions, much as a car GPS system operates for drivers. A blind user can use such a system, although since the device and the database of geographic information are designed for automotive applications, they have significant limitations when used for pedestrian navigation by the visually impaired [19]. Devices designed specifically for the blind often run on custom hardware, and are for the most part single-purpose and relatively expensive, or else run on commodity hardware, but with significant limitations on functionality. Existing commercial audio-based tools typically rely exclusively on speech to

A. Puiatti et al. (Eds.): MobiQuitous 2011, LNICST 104, pp. 49–62, 2012.
© Institute for Computer Sciences, Social Informatics and Telecommunications Engineering 2012

indicate the distance, direction, and type of locations around a user. Unfortunately, this form of content delivery is intrusive or distracting, thus discouraging continuous use. Considerable research has been invested in using spatialized audio to navigate or render waypoints and points of interest (POI) information, but the resulting systems require the use of bulky, expensive, or custom hardware and are thus not well-suited for wide deployment. Many research systems also depend on proprietary POI databases that cover only a small area, and are not easy to generalize to multiple cities or countries.

The confluence of advanced smartphone technology and widely available geospatial databases offers the opportunity for a fundamentally different approach. The current generation of smartphones is sufficiently powerful to render multiple voices of spatialized audio, and also integrates GPS, compass, accelerometer and other sensors that allow for a complete audio augmented reality system that is useful and enriching to the blind community. Our objective is to create a solution usable by simply installing a piece of software on a widely available device, without additional hardware beyond the phone and a pair of headphones, and without depending on customized databases. Although this significantly limits the achievable accuracy, reliability and functionality of the resulting system, it allows for potentially much more widespread use.

In this context, we describe our smartphone application, In Situ Audio Services (ISAS). Rather than navigation assistance, ISAS exploits the resources noted above to provide the blind community with a greater sense of environmental awareness. Specifically, ISAS enables blind users to sense locations in their vicinity such as restaurants and shops. Our key criterion for success is not enabling users to navigate themselves through the door of a new restaurant without assistance, but rather walk down the street and serendipitously *notice* a restaurant of which they were previously unaware.

Although ISAS is specifically designed for the blind and vision-impaired community, the implications of this system extend beyond. Anyone whose eyes are occupied with other tasks, driving being an obvious example, could make use of many of the ideas and implementations described in this paper. We expect that in the future, much of the functionality we describe here will be adopted in various forms by the general population.

The contributions described by this paper center on our effort to combine three key items to form a practical audio augmented reality system for blind users: a readily available and unmodified smartphone platform, a commercial location database, and an audio spatialization implementation for orientation awareness. These are coupled with a novel user interface that addresses the needs of someone walking in an urban environment while simultaneously holding a cane or guide dog harness. Our implementation thus represents a "snapshot in time" that tests whether current platforms and POI services are indeed sufficiently capable to fulfil the longstanding vision of a small, mobile platform for such exploration, and if not, what specific issues remain before such a system can be practically deployed.

2   Previous Work

Numerous commercial systems exist for blind navigation, e.g., the HumanWare Trekker Breeze[1] and Mobile Geo,[2] the latter powered by Sendero GPS software,[3] which provide not only navigation assistance, but also POI information along the route. The free Loadstone GPS software for Nokia phones[4] allows users to import POI information and be informed when they approach the locations they have chosen to load into memory. Intersection Explorer[5] for Android smartphones lets users explore nearby streets and intersections by dragging their finger on the phone's touchscreen. Further systems are listed in a recent literature review [14]. However, none of these tools utilize spatialized audio, despite demonstrations that for wayfinding, the cognitive load of spatialized content is lower than when using language, e.g., spoken "left" or "right" instructions [7]. For recent systems, this is generally not due to hardware limitations, since some spatialized rendering capability is often included on the device for gaming applications, e.g., a limited OpenAL library on the iPhone. Although the iPhone implementation appears to be quite limited, a full head-related transfer function (HRTF) implementation for rendering 3D sound is built in to Nokia N95 phones, and has been shown to be effective [18].

Spatialized audio has, however, been employed in previous research systems. An early example is the Personal Guidance System (PGS), which used a GPS, compass and spatialized speech to guide blind users by rendering nearby waypoints and POI information, either organized by proximity or presented in a clockwise fashion around the user [5,4]. Experiments using this system were conducted on the University of California Santa Barbara campus, where the research team had access to highly detailed map information and a nearby differential GPS base station 20 km from their site [4]. Similar systems followed, albeit lacking spatialized audio, including Drishti [13,6] and MoBIC [11,12].

The SWAN project continues in the vein of PGS, enabling experimentation with rendering an audio scene while a user moves in the real world. To provide full functionality, SWAN requires add-on external devices such as a head-mounted inertial sensor or digital compass for orientation sensing. Using a portable Windows PC as its platform, SWAN can render spatialized sound using a full HRTF via OpenAL, while still fitting into a relatively small shoulder bag [23]. The user interface relies on a combination of speech recognition and audio menus, and is primarily targeted at waypoint finding and navigation, although it also supports user annotation of locations. POI support is mentioned, but it is unclear what sort of database is used and how many locations are covered. Similar multi-component hardware platforms have been used to render spatialized audio for environmental awareness [17]. The trend has been toward smaller and lighter systems as technology improves [9].

---

[1] http://www.humanware.com
[2] http://www.codefactory.es/en/products.asp?id=336
[3] http://www.senderogroup.com/products/GPS/allgps.htm
[4] http://www.loadstone-gps.com
[5] http://www.googlelabs.com/
show_details?app_key=agtnbGFiczIwLXd3d3IVCxIMTGFicOFwcE1vZGVssGIHDtwIM

Other efforts modify the environment itself by distributing IR transmitters, radio receivers[6] or RFID tags [15] over an area of interest.

More generally, researchers have attempted to sonify information usually represented via visual maps, tables and charts, or images. The most direct way to do this is simply to speak a description, but this approach quickly becomes tedious. Thus, efforts have focused on using techniques such as abstract musical tones (earcons [1]), sped up spoken text (spearcons [21]), and recorded sounds (auditory icons [3]), to represent a thing or idea. These techniques can reduce the time spent representing information to a blind user, as well as provide additional features such as an overview of large data sets or *gist* [25]. Of recent note, the Timbremap project uses an iPhone and stereo sonification to allow users to learn an indoor map by providing audio cues that convey different shapes [16]. Although focused on exploration rather than navigation, users are always expected to stop and focus entirely on the application, rather than passively experiencing ambient information about their surroundings while walking.

3   The ISAS Application

Noting the lack of an attempt to merge the best features of existing research platforms, such as spatialized audio and auditory icons, with the low cost and ubiquity of commodity smartphone devices, as well as with commercial POI databases, we developed the ISAS application. This involved four main challenges addressed in this section: rendering a spatialized audio scene; designing a practical user interface; compensating for, or at least degrading gracefully in the face of, unreliable GPS and orientation sensors; and relying on existing large-scale, but imperfect, location data sources.

We recognized immediately that a commodity smartphone would restrict the accuracy of the sensors and data, as well as the processing power available for rendering the audio scene. The question we wanted to answer was whether a useful system could still be implemented despite these constraints, or else identify the specific issues still blocking such a system from practical deployment.

3.1   Hardware

Due to its audio capabilities, position and location sensors, powerful CPU and blind accessibility features (VoiceOver), our initial implementation runs on the Apple iPhone 4. The only external hardware required by the system is a pair of headphones. Given the importance to blind users of unobstructed audio of their environment, e.g., traffic sounds, we recommend either open ear headphones,[7] whose speakers are placed in front of each ear, or bone conduction headphones,[8] which rest on the bone in front of the ear. Admittedly, the sound quality of these technologies is inferior to over-the-ear solutions, and positioning the AirDrive

---

[6] Two examples are http://talkingsigns.com and http://eo-guidage.com.

[7] http://www.airdrives.com

[8] http://www.audioboneheadphones.com

headphones correctly is initially quite difficult, thus impacting the quality of spatialization. Despite these drawbacks, the trade-off for safety reasons is clearly worthwhile. We note with interest that others are not only successfully using bone conduction headphones for similar purposes [20], but are also discussing solutions for overcoming their limitations when used for spatialization [22].

3.2   Audio Scene Rendering and Spatialization

The iPhone's SDK includes an OpenAL implementation, but it appears that its 3D sound spatialization falls back to simple stereo panning, lacking the robustness of a full HRTF implementation, which attempts to model how the human anatomy, in particular, the head and external ears (pinna), filter sound before it reaches the eardrums. One recent attempt to improve the iPhone's built-in OpenAL 3D sound support was inconclusive in its benefits [8]. We briefly attempted to use the open-source earplug~ HRTF implementation,[9] but found that even a single voice consumed prohibitive amounts of CPU. Thus, we decided to improve on the built-in spatialization, but not attempt a full HRTF implementation. To do this, we use the libpd[10] implementation of PureData (Pd) that runs on many platforms including smartphones. This allowed us to create a Pd patch that uses not only simple panning techniques, but also interaural time difference and filtering effects to spatialize the sound. A low-pass filter helps to distinguish locations in back of the user, which results in the sounds being more "muffled" and somewhat quieter as they move further behind the user's head. Volume falls off depending on the distance of the item from the user's current position. The application can render up to four simultaneous spatialized items; when an additional one is requested, the first is stopped. Note that we expect built-in 3D sound rendering to improve rapidly on mobile devices in the near future, primarily driven by increases in processing power and the demands of gaming applications. As noted previously, technical feasibility of HRTF implementations has already been demonstrated on the Nokia N95.

The user interface, described in the next section, renders up to three audio representations of a location depending on user preference and current mode:

- Spatialized *category name:* A spoken pre-recorded category name rendered by a text-to-speech (TTS) system, e.g., "restaurant," "shop," or "cafe."
- Spatialized *category audio icon:* A short sound, e.g., ice clinking in a glass representing a bar, or a drum beat for entertainment.
- Non-spatialized *details:* The full name of the location, usually with spoken confirmation of bearing and distance.

Audio icons have several advantages over spoken words. In particular, we expected that walking mode, described below, would benefit from shorter, clearer indications of locations surrounding the user. There is a trade off, however, against the greater specificity possible when using words. For example, a verbal

---

[9] http://puredata.info/community/projects/software/earplug
[10] http://http://gitorious.org/pdlib

category name for a restaurant can easily differentiate between fast food, a food court, and a normal restaurant. Designing icons to represent location categories turned out to be surprisingly difficult, as they must satisfy multiple criteria:

1. They must be easily distinguishable from real environmental sounds. For example, a siren sound for a fire station risks confusion with a real siren, thus connoting danger rather than safety.
2. A strong onset (attack) helps disambiguate one long sound from overlapping repetitions, and avoids masking from other nearly simultaneous icons.
3. Since the icons may be filtered, e.g., when they are behind the user, they must contain a sufficient distribution of frequencies so that the effect of filtering is perceptible, differentiated from other filtering effects, and leaves the sound in a recognizable state.

3.3   Application Design

As noted earlier, our system is not intended for navigation assistance but for exploration and discovery within one's environment. This functionality is provided by two primary modes. *Walking mode* is designed to be used while users are walking down the street, and not actively interacting with the device until they notice something of interest. This can be viewed as a background voice, designed to be turned on continuously as a user walks down the street. *Stop & listen mode* is designed for actively searching the immediate vicinity.

Walking Mode. This mode is engaged when the device is kept in a vertical position (i.e., as if in a front shirt pocket). We implemented two different sound triggering mechanisms for walking mode, similar to those described in the earlier PGS system [4]. The *radar* mechanism plays sound nodes out to as far as 150 m from the user, sequentially in a clockwise sweep around the user's head. The *shockwave* mechanism instead plays the sounds in order from near to far. Unlike the PGS implementation, we repeat the playback continuously as long as the user remains in walking mode. In an earlier experiment [2], we tested variants of these two mechanisms, with subjects sitting in a chair, and concluded that there were few meaningful performance differences between them. However, in a mobile context, with the user walking down the street, we found that a simple version of the radar mechanism seemed less intrusive and easier to comprehend.

One revolution of the radar sweep takes 12 seconds. However, in dense areas with many locations, the sweep is dynamically slowed to avoid an overwhelming number of simultaneous sounds. A short spatialized tick is played every 15° to indicate where in the sweep the radar is currently playing, and a more intense sound is played at the cardinal points to assist in registration. These cues indicate that walking mode is still active and operating, they reinforce the spatialization by creating a circular "sweep" around the user's head, and they allow the user to anticipate where spatialized locations will next play. To avoid cluttering the audio scene with objects the user has already passed, we only play locations to the front and sides. While each location is always spatialized relative to the device's (and we assume, the user's) current orientation, the radar sweep itself progresses independently. This ensures that user movement or swaying does not lead to repetitions or variations in playback rate.

To hear details in walking mode, the user touches a finger on the screen, which pauses the radar sweep and begins playing additional information for the last location heard. Sliding the finger to the left allows the user to hear details for locations further back (counter-clockwise) in the sweep. Lifting the finger restarts the radar sweep from where it was paused.

Stop and Listen Mode. When the user tips the device so it is parallel to the ground, it enters *stop & listen mode*. In this mode, the user can more actively explore the area around them by running their thumb up and down the screen. The bottom of the screen represents nearby locations, and the top represents locations 150 meters away. As the user drags their finger, they cross sound nodes, which are played as they are crossed. Thus, the user can "look" out ahead of their current location in a more controlled way than in radar mode, since they actively control the triggering of the sound nodes. The device can then be tipped to the side while the finger or thumb remains on the screen to hear the same unspatialized details that can be heard in walking mode. If the user keeps the device tipped to the side, the details for the next closest four locations to the initial one will also be read. This is particularly helpful in very dense areas, when it can be difficult to isolate a single location while dragging a finger. To "look" further, the left edge of the screen can be used in a similar fashion to "see" out to 750 m. Note that when the user switches from stop & listen mode to walking mode, walking mode starts its sweep with the last location played in stop & listen mode in order to provide some continuity between the two modes.

Sensor Reliability. Accurate location and orientation information is key to implementing a working spatialized audio system. For the compass, magnetic interference is a significant issue. In ad-hoc testing, for example, we observed a repeatable difference of $30°$ in the compass reading when bringing the device near a parked sport utility vehicle. In addition to the magnetic compass, the iPhone also includes a gyro-based sensor which provides device rotation readings, although they are not relative to the cardinal directions. Since the compass provides an accuracy estimate with each reading, we implemented a sensor fusion between the gyro and the compass in order to improve the reliability of the heading information. When ISAS starts, it needs one good compass reading before it can function, since the compass is the only hardware sensor capable of finding north, which we require for calculating the bearing to surrounding POIs. Once this reading is obtained, we calibrate the gyro with this value. From then on, we use the calibrated gyro reading for all heading values. Every time a valid compass reading is received, the gyro is recalibrated to north, both to correct for gyro drift as well as to benefit from potentially more accurate compass information. When the compass loses its heading entirely or the reported accuracy is worse than $±30°$, the readings are ignored. Thus, once we have a single good compass heading, we can rely on the gyro to carry the system though periods where the compass is known to be unreliable. Although we cannot overcome the sensor limitations entirely, we are designing the system to be as robust as possible to sensor errors, as suggested in previous work attempting to use unreliable GPS on handheld devices [10]. In our current implementation:

- If the GPS or the compass reports an error that exceeds a predetermined threshhold, synthesized speech explicitly informs the user regularly.
- Even when the GPS and compass readings are valid, we provide a low-level white noise in the background that varies in intensity based on their reported accuracy. This provides a continuous indicator analogous to the shaded GPS error circle visible in the iPhone's map application.
- Locations within the current GPS error are rendered without spatialization (and thus currently sound like they are in front of the user), and the details report they are nearby, rather than providing a specific direction or distance.
- When describing the direction to a location, we use either clock directions (e.g., "1 o'clock" or "9 o'clock") or descriptions based on 45° segments (e.g., "front" or "back left"), to avoid conveying more precision than warranted.

Thus, we depend on the sensors providing valid error estimates. Unfortunately, we see the same issue of poor error estimates from both the iPhone compass and GPS as documented for other mobile phone GPS implementations [24], with indications of "good accuracy" when it is in fact off by 180° or two city blocks. When this occurs, we do not even know that the results are inaccurate, and thus that nearby locations are rendered in the wrong directions. In the end, we must reinforce that ISAS does not replace a guide dog or cane, and there will be times when the information is simply inaccurate, without any warning or other indication. We expect this problem to fade as sensors improve, but it is a significant concern for any deployment on currently available smartphone hardware, and reinforces the decision to provide a system for exploration rather than navigation.

3.4 Location Data

In addition to relying on the sensors in the device, ISAS also depends on good location information. Other systems have used data sets generated specifically for the project, or databases for small areas such as a University campus, which limits the area in which the tool is practically useful, and also imposes an ongoing maintenance burden. Due to increasing interest in location based service (LBS) products such as Foursquare, providers including OpenStreetMap, Google Places, the Yellow Pages Group and SimpleGeo are offering application developers access to constantly updated databases of geographic content including businesses and other points of interest.

Initially, we were attracted to the OpenStreetMap service due to its openness and the ability to add our own data into the system. However, although the data was generally accurate, the quantity was insufficient. We now use the Google Places API to furnish data to the ISAS application, which provides an almost

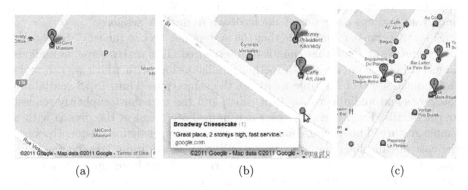

Fig. 1. Examples demonstrating Google Places data issues for pedestrian use

overwhelming amount of information on dense urban streets. Unfortunately, the way the data is generated causes some issues for ISAS.

A substantial portion of the latitude/longitude data appears to be generated by interpolating the location along the street using nothing more than the address to determine where along the street it lies. For example, the McCord Museum in Figure 1a is located on the opposite side of the sidewalk from the actual building, and past the building along the street. For car navigation, this is not a significant issue, as it is accurate to the city block, but for a blind pedestrian, this means that while walking on the sidewalk in a northeast direction, she would pass the actual museum on the right side, while hearing it spatialized off to the left. Then, immediately after passing the building, she would hear it directly to her left, despite it being to her back right. Further, the data is inconsistent, as in Figure 1b, which shows three restaurants all in the same building. One of them (the Subway restaurant) is placed exactly at the entrance door, which is the best possible case. Art Java is near enough to the entrance door that the error is not likely to be significant compared to GPS and compass errors on the device. However, the Broadway Cheesecake restaurant is placed on the street corner, far from the building, resulting in the same issue seen in Figure 1a. Fortunately, these issues subside somewhat in areas of the city where there are more discrete buildings with individual addresses, as in Figure 1c, although a significant portion of the data is still placed directly on the street.

In addition, location names are usually not tagged by language, so we cannot easily indicate the correct text-to-speech voice to use. In bilingual Montréal, it is difficult to understand the French voice speaking "Ye Olde Orchard Tavern."

4   User Feedback

Quantitatively evaluating a system like ISAS, which seeks to improve the quality of life for blind users, is difficult. Although we are in the process of designing more formal tests, we have carried out informal usability evaluations with sighted team members and two blind participants walking in downtown Montréal. Several important findings came out of the feedback from these sessions.

First, there was an insistence that the system not "get in the way" by playing long segments of audio that cannot be interrupted. This makes sense, as audio is largely a linear communication method, unlike vision, with which we can more easily make sense of multiple inputs at the same time. Thus, ISAS spatialized categories and audio icons are kept short, and the user must explicitly request longer details. Even then, the user can immediately cancel the details with a simple gesture. This decision encourages the user to get details frequently, since the cost of cancelling the operation is minimal. In addition, keeping the communication terse is crucial to a good experience. Aside from carefully wording messages to be as short as possible, we also round distance values as they are further from the user, since "one hundred forty seven meters" is longer than a rounded "one hundred fifty meters," and in French, "quatre-vingt-dix-neuf" (99) is significantly longer than "cent" (100).

Not surprisingly, our experience confirmed that feedback obtained in a laboratory environment is often of limited value, or worse, occasionally misleading. Sitting in a quiet environment listening to test versions of the software, we would frequently overrate the amount of information a user could handle. These naive estimates were quickly dispelled after trying the system on a real (noisy) street. This pitfall not only applied to the sighted members of the ISAS team. For example, a blind user tried the system in a quiet indoor environment, and indicated it would be good if the details for a location would be spatialized along with the category indicator. However, at a later date, while using the system outdoors and walking down a busy street with a guide dog harness in one hand and ISAS in the other, the same user explicitly indicated it was good that the details were not spatialized since it was more important that the details cut through all of the distractions and surrounding noise.

Accompanying blind users while they use ISAS has illustrated several other interesting effects. For example, one user heard the actual sounds of people eating on a restaurant terrace. He commented that he would like to know the restaurant's name, so he entered *stop & listen* mode, pointed the device in the direction of the (real) sound, and attempted to find the restaurant. Unfortunately, it was not in the database at that time, but we note that the combination of real-world sounds with the augmented reality provided by ISAS can form a powerful combination. This same blind user, while in walking mode, paused to get details on a restaurant, then while gesturing in the correct direction, mentioned he did not know there was a cheesecake restaurant over there. These are the types of serendipitous discovery we hope ISAS will enable for more users.

5   Future Work

We are currently conducting more formal user tests and revising the ISAS application based on the feedback being received. An initial round of usability testing involved six blind participants, using ISAS to accomplish specific tasks on a street in Montreal, with the sessions observed by a sighted experimenter. For this experiment, we also prototyped the ability to play the name of the location in walking (radar) mode, albeit unspatialized, in addition to the spatialized audio icon or category name. Users generally found this to be more useful than hearing only the audio icon or category name. For example, participant 6 indicated, "I find this one [with the location name read after the spatialized category] better, I find it more at ease... it gives you more information, it is less frustrating... you do not have to concentrate as much... and is less physical (you do not have to tap constantly)... I find this one gives you more information." However, the additional information spoken by the system results makes this method significantly more intrusive.

In addition, we questioned the ecological validity of a short-term experiment outside of the user's usual context, compounded by the presence of an accompanying experimenter. To address these concerns, we are now in the midst of longer-term trials in which the participants are loaned a device to use in their daily routine for a week or more, allowing them to provide more informative feedback regarding their experiences with the system within their daily environment. Feedback received to date points to user excitement for ISAS, albeit with two important problems that we are currently addressing. First, users frequently felt overwhelmed by the quantity of information when using walking mode. Second, participants strongly prefer to avoid having to hold the device continuously while walking. This motivates our investigation of a suitable harness that supports the smartphone in a stable position while allowing easy manual interaction with the device.

Our ongoing work also includes refinement of the accuracy and reliability of the system and porting to other platforms such as Android. We are also adding features such as user tagging, where users can record new POIs based on their current location, which are uploaded to our server and provided to future visitors to the same location. We expect this to be most useful for identifying hazards or other information most useful to blind users, as a supplement to the generic location information provided by existing online POI databases. We have also not yet explored filtering of content by category or other criteria to reduce the overwhelming nature of areas with many POIs nearby. This is crucial, since initial usability testing and longer-term trials indicate that our current simple model of rendering points is too intrusive; making the walking mode "smarter" about what information it plays is our current priority. Although not the focus of this work, we have also considered adding support for optional hardware such as a head-mounted compass, which may not only be more reliable than the built-in smartphone sensor, but also allow the user to orient their head independently of the smartphone to better localize sounds.

Last, there are several practical issues that need to be resolved. For example, we are currently using the built-in iPhone text-to-speech engine, which makes ISAS ineligible for the Apple App Store, and thus limits its potential distribution. Switching to another TTS engine would resolve this issue. We are also integrating additional (and commonly requested) data sets into ISAS which are specific to Montreal, such as bus stop and subway data, which is currently only licensed for research use, and thus cannot be widely deployed. We have not found a global source for this type of information, so this may need to be accomplished on a city-by-city basis for the near future.

6   Conclusion

We created a smartphone application that uses spatialized audio to render nearby locations to blind users as they walk down the street. We accomplished this using only built-in sensors to obtain location and orientation information, allowing it to be installed on any iPhone 4. Initial feedback indicates the system is promising as a practical tool. However, limitations in the iPhone hardware sensors and currently available location databases mean the system not only fails in some cases, but cannot always know, and therefore indicate, significant errors in the presented information. We conclude that given current smartphone capabilities, a practical system is possible only for non-critical exploration of an environment, and not for high-accuracy navigation tasks. We have thus focused ISAS on exactly these use cases. Further user testing, especially over longer periods of time, will reveal whether blind users find the system useful on an ongoing basis, or whether the issues we have discussed are too great to overcome in practice. More work is also required to refine the ISAS user interface, as existing user feedback has pointed out several areas that need improvement. Although only a snapshot in time, ISAS illustrates how close a practical system is, especially for a system targeted at exploration and ambient location information rather than navigation. Given the rapid rate of improvement in phone technology and geographic data sets, we have high hopes for such a system in the coming years. We expect that in the not-too-distant future, an application similar to ISAS will provide the blind community with an experience that matches the capabilities of research platforms such as SWAN, but implemented on a commodity smartphone, and deployed on a truly global scale.

Acknowledgments. This work was made possible thanks to the financial support of the Québec Secrétariat du Conseil du trésor through the *Appui au passage à la société de l'information* program, as well as additional funding from a Google Faculty Research Award. The authors would like to give special thanks to Florian Grond, who implemented the original spatialization patches and consulted on numerous audio issues throughout the project, as well as Adriana Olmos, Dalia El-Shimy, Sabrina Panëels, Zack Settel, and Mike Wozniewski. Stephane Doyon and Lucio D'Intino graciously provided feedback on the system as it was in development.

References

1. Blattner, M., Sumikawa, D., Greenberg, R.: Earcons and icons: Their structure and common design principles. Human-Computer Interaction 4(1), 11–44 (1989)
2. El-Shimy, D., Grond, F., Olmos, A., Cooperstock, J.R.: Eyes-free environmental awareness for navigation. Springer Journal on Multimodal User Interfaces, Special Issue on Interactive Sonification (2011) (in press)

3. Gaver, W.: Auditory Icons: Using Sound in Computer Interfaces. Human-Computer Interaction 2(2), 167–177 (1986)
4. Golledge, R.G., Klatzky, R.L., Loomis, J.M., Speigle, J., Tietz, J.: A geographical information system for a GPS based personal guidance system. International Journal of Geographical Information Science 12(7), 727–749 (1998)
5. Golledge, R.G., Loomis, J.M., Klatzky, R.L., Flury, A., Yang, X.L.: Designing a personal guidance system to aid navigation without sight: Progress on the GIS component. Int. J. of Geographical Information Science 5(4), 373–395 (1991)
6. Helal, A.S., Moore, S.E., Ramachandran, B.: Drishti: An integrated navigation system for visually impaired and disabled. In: ISWC 2001 Proceedings of the 5th IEEE International Symposium on Wearable Computers (4514203), p. 149. IEEE Computer Society (2001)
7. Klatzky, R., Marston, J., Giudice, N., Golledge, R., Loomis, J.: Cognitive load of navigating without vision when guided by virtual sound versus spatial language. Journal of Experimental Psychology. Applied 12(4), 223–232 (2006)
8. Linell, M.: Comparison between two 3d-sound engines of the accuracy in determining the position of a source. Master's thesis, Luleå U. of Technology (2011)
9. Mariette, N.: From Backpack to Handheld: The Recent Trajectory of Personal Location Aware Spatial Audio. Media-Space Journal 1(1) (2008)
10. McGookin, D., Gibbs, M., Nivala, A.-M., Brewster, S.: Initial Development of a PDA Mobility Aid for Visually Impaired People. In: Baranauskas, C., Abascal, J., Barbosa, S.D.J. (eds.) INTERACT 2007. LNCS, vol. 4663, pp. 665–668. Springer, Heidelberg (2007)
11. Petrie, H., Johnson, V., Strothotte, T., Raab, A., Fritz, S., Michel, R.: MOBIC: Designing a Travel Aid for Blind and Elderly People. Journal of Navigation 49(01), 45–52 (1996)
12. Petrie, H., Johnson, V., Strothotte, T., Raab, A., Michel, R., Reichert, L., Schalt, A.: MoBIC: An Aid to Increase the Independent Mobility of Blind Travellers. British Journal of Visual Impairment 15(2), 63–66 (1997)
13. Ran, L., Helal, S., Moore, S.: Drishti: an integrated indoor/outdoor blind navigation system and service. In: Proceedings of the Second IEEE Annual Conference on Pervasive Computing and Communications, pp. 23–30 (2004)
14. Roentgen, U.R., Gelderblom, G.J., Soede, M., de Witte, L.P.: Inventory of electronic mobility aids for persons with visual impairments: A literature review. Journal of Visual Impairment & Blindness 102(11), 23 (2008)
15. Stewart, J., Bauman, S., Escobar, M., Hilden, J., Bihani, K., Newman, M.W.: Accessible contextual information for urban orientation. In: Proceedings of the 10th International Conference on Ubiquitous Computing, pp. 332–335. ACM (2008)
16. Su, J., Rosenzweig, A., Goel, A., de Lara, E., Truong, K.N.: Timbremap: enabling the visually-impaired to use maps on touch-enabled devices. In: Proceedings of the 12th International Conference on Human Computer Interaction with Mobile Devices and Services, pp. 17–26. ACM (2010)
17. Sundareswaran, V., Wang, K., Chen, S., Behringer, R., McGee, J., Tam, C., Zahorik, P.: 3D audio augmented reality: implementation and experiments. In: Proceedings of the Second IEEE and ACM International Symposium on Mixed and Augmented Reality, pp. 296–297 (2003)
18. Vazquez-Alvarez, Y., Brewster, S.: Investigating background & foreground interactions using spatial audio cues. In: Extended Abstracts CHI 2009, p. 3823 (2009)

19. Völkel, T., Kühn, R., Weber, G.: Mobility Impaired Pedestrians Are Not Cars: Requirements for the Annotation of Geographical Data. In: Miesenberger, K., Klaus, J., Zagler, W.L., Karshmer, A.I. (eds.) ICCHP 2008. LNCS, vol. 5105, pp. 1085–1092. Springer, Heidelberg (2008)
20. Walker, B.N., Lindsay, J.: Navigation performance in a virtual environment with bonephones. In: Proceedings of the International Conference on Auditory Display (ICAD 2005), vol. 3(3), pp. 1–26 (2005)
21. Walker, B.N., Nance, A., Lindsay, J.: Spearcons: Speech-based earcons improve navigation performance in auditory menus. In: Proceedings of the International Conference on Auditory Display, London, UK, pp. 63–68 (2006)
22. Walker, B.N., Stanley, R.: Thresholds of audibility for bone-conduction headsets. In: International Conference on Auditory Display, Limerick, Ireland, pp. 218–222 (2005)
23. Wilson, J., Walker, B., Lindsay, J., Cambias, C., Dellaert, F.: SWAN: System for Wearable Audio Navigation. In: 2007 11th IEEE International Symposium on Wearable Computers, pp. 1–8 (October 2007)
24. Zandbergen, P., Barbeau, S.: Positional Accuracy of Assisted GPS Data from High-Sensitivity GPS-enabled Mobile Phones. J. of Navigation 64(03), 381 (2011)
25. Zhao, H., Plaisant, C., Shneiderman, B., Duraiswami, R.: Sonification of geo-referenced data for auditory information seeking: Design principle and pilot study. In: Proceedings of ICAD 2004-Tenth Meeting of the International Conference on Auditory Display (2004)

Real-Time Detection of Anomalous Taxi Trajectories from GPS Traces

Chao Chen[1], Daqing Zhang[1], Pablo Samuel Castro[1],
Nan Li[2,3], Lin Sun[1], and Shijian Li[4]

[1] Institut TELECOM/TELECOM SudParis, CNRS SAMOVAR, France
{chao.chen, daqing.zhang, pablo.castro, lin.sun}@it-sudparis.eu
[2] National Key Laboratory for Novel Software Technology, Nanjing University, China
lin@lamda.nju.edu.cn
[3] School of Mathematical Sciences, Soochow University, China
[4] Department of Computer Science, Zhejiang University, China
shijianli@zju.edu.cn

Abstract. Trajectories obtained from GPS-enabled taxis grant us an opportunity to not only extract meaningful statistics, dynamics and behaviors about certain urban road users, but also to monitor adverse and/or malicious events. In this paper we focus on the problem of detecting anomalous routes by comparing against historically "normal" routes. We propose a real-time method, *iBOAT*, that is able to detect anomalous trajectories "on-the-fly", as well as identify which parts of the trajectory are responsible for its anomalousness. We evaluate our method on a large dataset of taxi GPS logs and verify that it has excellent accuracy (AUC ≥ 0.99) and overcomes many of the shortcomings of other state-of-the-art methods.

1 Introduction

With the increasing pervasiveness of GPS devices, there is an enormous amount of information available to researchers [24]. The traces left behind by GPS-enabled vehicles provide us with an unprecedented window into the dynamics of a city's road network. This information has been analyzed to uncover traffic patterns [17], city dynamics [27], driving directions [23], and a city's "hot-spots" [5,28]. Much of this work has made use of the data from GPS-equipped taxis, often using it to provide useful information for the taxi drivers themselves [5,19,20].

Mining large GPS traces has been investigated for a number of different problems, and one interesting amongst these is using GPS traces to develop new ways to detect taxi drivers' anomalous activities. One kind of anomaly could be caused by greedy taxi drivers, who aim to overcharge passengers by deliberately taking unnecessary detours. It would be useful if we could detect the anomalous behavior while it is occurring as well as which parts of the trajectory (sub-trajectories) are abnormal, thereby reducing the number of passengers that fall prey to taxi fraud. Another anomalous situation could occur when there are abnormal traffic conditions such as traffic accidents, resulting in certain road segments being

A. Puiatti et al. (Eds.): MobiQuitous 2011, LNICST 104, pp. 63–74, 2012.

blocked, forcing taxi drivers to find alternate routes. Real-time traffic monitoring of blocked road segments can be achieved through the real-time detection of anomalous sub-trajectories.

The aforementioned problem is the focus of this paper, where we aim to detect driving routes that are considered *anomalous* in the sense that they differ significantly from the norm. Given that one of the main motivations for this work is the detection of fraudulent taxi drivers, the anomaly detection will be with respect to fixed source and destination *areas*. Accurate detection of these anomalous driving patterns can be useful for detecting adverse traffic events, road network changes and taxi fraud, amongst others. We believe successful methods should be able to identify which parts of a trajectory are anomalous, as well as assign an *ongoing anomaly score* which can be used to rank the different trajectories. Our main contributions are a real-time method which accurately identifies anomalous sub-trajectories with very little processing overhead, as well as computes an evolving anomaly score which can indicate how severely the anomalous route deviates from normal routes. We begin by reviewing related work in Section 2. The algorithm is defined in Section 3, and an empirical evaluation along with an analysis of its differences with a closely related method are presented in Section 4. Finally, we present concluding remarks and point to future research directions in Section 5.

2   Related Work

There have been many recent works on mining large GPS traces. Liao, et al. [15] devise methods to predict a user's mode of transportation and daily routine to provide reminders when needed, while [19,12] uncover taxi drivers' operating patterns. Other works show how to predict the route and destination based on historical GPS traces [10,6,29], in addition to providing driving directions by exploiting taxi drivers' knowledge [23]. GPS traces have also been used for uncovering interesting "hot-spots" for tourists [28,26], for passengers searching for vacant taxis [20], or for classifying the social functions of different regions in a city [21].

Anomaly detection has its roots in the more general problem of outlier detection. In most cases the data is static, rather than evolving over time. There are a number of different methods available for outlier detection, including supervised approaches [1], distance-based [2,9], density-based [3], model-based [8] and isolation-based methods [18].

Recent work on detecting anomalous moving vehicles include the following. In [11], a trajectory is split into various partitions (at equal intervals) and a hybrid of distance and density based approaches is used to classify each partition as anomalous or not. In [7], the authors compute a score based on the evolving moving direction and density of trajectories, and make use of a decay function to include previous scores. In [4], Bu et al. present a method for monitoring anomalies over continuous trajectory streams by using the local continuity characteristics of trajectories to cluster trajectories on a local level; anomalies are then identified by a pruning mechanism. Somewhat related, but addressing a different problem, Li et al. [14] identify outlier road segments by detecting drastic changes between current data and historical trends. Finally, some recent work has used learning methods to identify anomalous trajectories [13,16,22]. However, these last methods require training data which is expensive to label.

Most of these methods identify anomalous trajectories based on their physical distance to "normal" clusters or their orientations. Based on the idea of isolating anomalies [18], Zhang et al. [25] devise a method which identifies trajectories as anomalous when they follow paths that are rare with respect to historical trajectories. Our paper adopts this characterization of anomalous trajectories but goes a step further: in addition to identifying anomalous trajectories online, our method is able to specify which *parts* of the trajectory are anomalous. In comparison with some of the more sophisticated methods mentioned above, whose running time may disqualify them from real-time situations, our method is fast and can be used in a real-time manner.

3   iBOAT: Isolation Based Online Anomaly Trajectory Detection

Definition 1. *A **trajectory** t consists of a sequence of points $\langle p_1, p_2 \ldots, p_n \rangle$, where $p_i \in \mathbb{R}^2$ is the physical location (i.e. latitude/longitude). We will use t_i to reference position i in t, and for any $1 \leq i < j \leq n$, $t_{i \to j}$ denotes the **sub-trajectory** $\langle p_i, \ldots, p_j \rangle$.*

The points p_i occur in a continuous domain, so dealing with them directly is difficult. In order to mitigate this problem, we assume we have access to a finite decomposition of the area of interest. Specifically, let G be a finite set of elements, and $\rho : \mathbb{R}^2 \to G$ a function that maps locations to elements in G.

Definition 2. *A **mapped trajectory** $\bar{t}$, obtained from a trajectory t, consists of a sequence of elements $\langle g_1, g_2 \ldots, g_n \rangle$, where for all $1 \leq i \leq n$, $g_i \in G$ and $\bar{t}_i = \rho(t_i)$. We will write $g \in \bar{t}$ when $\bar{t}_i = g$ for some $1 \leq i \leq n$.*

Henceforth we will only deal with mapped trajectories, so we will drop the *mapped* qualifier. Let $\mathbb{T}$ denote the set of all mapped trajectories. Define the function $pos : \mathbb{T} \times G \to \mathbb{N}^+$, where given a trajectory t and element g returns the first index in t that is equal to g (or ∞ if $g \notin t$).

$$pos(t, g) = \begin{cases} \arg\min_{i \in \mathbb{N}^+} \{t_i = g\} & \text{if } g \in t \\ \infty & \text{otherwise} \end{cases}$$

For example, if $t = \langle g_3, g_4, g_5, g_4, g_3, g_6 \rangle$, then $pos(t, g_4) = 2$, and $pos(t, g_7) = \infty$.

Given a fixed source-destination pair with a set of trajectories T and a sub-trajectory $t = \langle g_1, g_2, \ldots, g_n \rangle$, we would like to verify whether t is **anomalous** with respect to T. We say a sub-trajectory t is anomalous with respect to T (and the fixed source-destination pair) if the path it follows rarely occurs in T. We define a function $hasPath : \mathcal{P}(\mathbb{T}) \times \mathbb{T} \to \mathcal{P}(\mathbb{T})$ that returns the set of trajectories

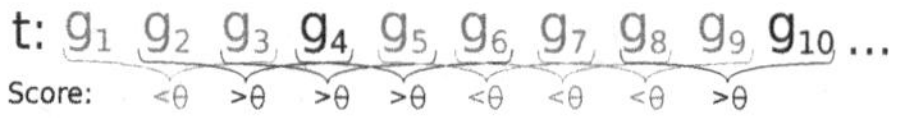

$$\text{t: } g_1 \; g_2 \; g_3 \; \mathbf{g_4} \; g_5 \; g_6 \; g_7 \; g_8 \; g_9 \; \mathbf{g_{10}} \ldots$$

Score: $<\theta$ $>\theta$ $>\theta$ $>\theta$ $<\theta$ $<\theta$ $<\theta$ $>\theta$

Fig. 1. Example of fixed-window approach with $k = 3$. There are two anomalous sub-trajectories detected: $\{g_1, g_2, g_3\}$ and $\{g_5, g_6, g_7, g_8, g_9\}$.

from T that contain all of the points in t in the correct order.[1] Note, however, that the points need not be *sequential*, it suffices that they appear in the same order.

$$hasPath(T,t) = \left\{ t' \in T \left| \begin{array}{l} \text{(i) } \forall 1 \leq i \leq n. \; g_i \in t' \\ \text{(ii) } \forall 1 \leq i < j \leq n. \; pos(t', g_i) < pos(t', g_j) \end{array} \right. \right\} \quad (1)$$

For instance, if $T = \{t1, t2, t3\}$, where $t1 = \langle g_1, g_2, g_3, g_4, g_5, g_8, g_9, g_{10} \rangle$, $t2 = \langle g_1, g_2, g_4, g_5, g_6, g_8, g_{10} \rangle$, and $t3 = \langle g_1, g_3, g_4, g_3, g_6, g_8, g_{10} \rangle$, and an ongoing trajectory $t = \langle g_1, g_2, g_5, g_8 \rangle$, then $hasPath(T,t) = \{t1, t2\}$.

We now formalize what it means for a sub-trajectory t to be anomalous with respect to a set T by observing the proportion of trajectories agreeing with t.

Definition 3. *Given a threshold $0 \leq \theta \leq 1$, a sub-trajectory t is θ-***anomalous*** with respect to a set of trajectories T if*

$$support(T,t) = \frac{|hasPath(T,t)|}{|T|} < \theta \quad (2)$$

We will use this definition of θ-anomalousness to describe two variants of our proposed algorithm.

Fixed-Window: We fix a window size k, indicating the number of grid cells in the trajectory to check for anomalousness. Given a set of trajectories T and an ongoing trajectory $t = \langle g_1, g_2, \ldots \rangle$, we verify whether the last k-sized sub-trajectory from t occur with enough frequency in T to determine if it is anomalous. An example of this approach is illustrated in Figure 1, where $k = 3$. Note that when $k = 1$, we have the density method used for comparison in [25].

Adaptive: In this approach we maintain a *working set* of trajectories (initially equal to T). After i entries received, our partial trajectory t consists of $\langle g_1, g_2, \ldots, g_i \rangle$ and we have a working set T_i. Upon arrival of entry g_{i+1}, we compute $support(T_i, t)$. If its value is less than θ, then point g_{i+1} is anomalous so it is added to the set of anomalous points, and we set $T_{i+1} = T$; otherwise, we set $T_{i+1} = hasPath(T_i, t)$. This procedure is repeated as long as new entries are arriving. Note that $T_0 = T$, and that every time an anomalous point is encountered, the working set is reset to the original trajectory set T. See Figure 2 for an illustration of this process. This resetting is what enables our adaptive algorithm to accurately detect anomalous sub-trajectories in real-time with a finer granularity than the fixed-window approach (with $k > 1$). Additionally, by reducing the working set with each incoming point, the adaptive approach has a computational advantage over the fixed-window approach.

---

[1] $\mathcal{P}(X)$ is the power set of X.

t:	g_1	g_2	g_3	g_4	g_5	g_6	g_7	g_8	g_9	g_{10} ...
Working set:	T_0	T_0	T_0	T_1	T_2	T_3	T_0	T_0	T_1'	T_2'
Working set size:	$>\theta$	$<\theta$	$<\theta$	$>\theta$	$>\theta$	$>\theta$	$<\theta$	$<\theta$	$>\theta$	$>\theta$

Fig. 2. Example of adaptive window approach. Two anomalous sub-trajectories are detected: $\{g_2, g_3\}$ and $\{g_7, g_8\}$. Note that $T_1 = hasPath(T_0, \langle g_3, g_4 \rangle)$ and $T_1' = hasPath(T_0, \langle g_8, g_9 \rangle)$.

Anomaly Score: We assign an ongoing score based on the length of the anomalous sections so far. Let $dist : G \times G \to \mathbb{R}$ be a distance function on the elements of G (this will usually be the standard Euclidean distance). Given a trajectory t along with a set of anomalous points, we define the *score* as the sum of the distance between all anomalous points g_i and the previous point g_{i-1} from t. The detected anomalous points in Figure 2 are $\{g_2, g_3, g_7, g_8\}$, then the score will be the sum of $dist(g_1, g_2)$, $dist(g_2, g_3)$, $dist(g_6, g_7)$ and $dist(g_7, g_8)$.

4   Empirical Evaluation

For our experiments, we make use of a large database of GPS logs from over 7600 taxis in Hangzhou, China. Each log contains the latitude, longitude and taxi status (free/occupied), amongst other things. The logs were collected over a period of twelve months at a sample rate of around one entry per minute. In this work we will only make use of trajectories where the taxi is occupied, as one of the applications of this method is in aiding passengers to avoid fraud. We restrict our attention to the Hangzhou metropolitan area, with longitude and latitude ranges of $[120.0°E, 120.5°E]$ and $[30.15°N, 30.40°N]$, respectively. We decompose the area just mentioned into a matrix of 100×200 grid cells (*i.e.* $|G| = 20000$), where the area of each grid cell is roughly $250m^2$. Thus, the function ρ simply maps a latitude/longitude pair into the grid cell g enclosing it.

Because of the rate at which GPS entries are received and the small size of our grid cells, there may be gaps between consecutive mapped points (black squares in Figure 3). We augment all the trajectories to ensure that there are no gaps in the trajectories by (roughly) following the line segment (green line in left panel) between the two cells in question (gray cells). When we are testing whether a trajectory t is anomalous, even though it may be following the same

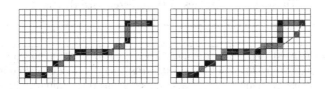

Fig. 3. Left: An example of a trajectory with augmented cells. Right: Comparing existing trajectory with a new trajectory.

path as most of the trajectories in T, the GPS points may fall in different cells. In the right panel of Figure 3 we display the augmented trajectory from the left panel, along with a new testing trajectory (colored squares and green line). Some of the grid cells fall on the augmented path (blue squares), while others fall in "empty" grid cells (orange and red cells). There is the possibility that the augmented path was not completely accurate, so we must account for this type of error when testing with a new trajectory: If a grid cell of the new trajectory is adjacent to one of the augmented cells, we consider it as if it were along the same path (orange cells), while if it is not adjacent to any augmented cells, we consider it as following a different path (red cell).

We picked nine source-destination pairs (T-1 through T-9) that had sufficient trajectories between them (at least 450, but on average over 1000), and asked three volunteers to manually label whether trajectories are anomalous or not (averaged at around 5.1% over the nine datasets). We then only labeled trajectories as anomalous if it received a majority of "votes" from the volunteers.

4.1 Results

To test *iBOAT*, we selected a trajectory t as an ongoing trajectory from a dataset T and used our two approaches with $\theta = 0.05$. This was done for all trajectories and all datasets. In the left panel of Figure 4 we display the output of our method for two test trajectories from T-1, where we plot the normal trajectories in light blue; for the test trajectories, the anomalous points are drawn in red and the rest (normal points) in dark blue. As can be seen, our method can accurately detect which parts of a trajectory are anomalous and which are normal. In the right panels of Figure 4 we plot $support(T - \{t\}, t)$ (see equation (2)) for the ongoing trajectory t. We can see that the value of *support* is a clear indication of when trajectories become anomalous, and that there is little difference between the different variants of *iBOAT*. Note, however, that there is a trailing *lag* for the fixed-window approach, equal to k. This is because the last anomalous point in an anomalous sub-trajectory will be included in the following k sub-trajectories. Although setting $k = 1$ will solve the lag problem, this minimal window size contains no contextual information of the trajectory, and will therefore have poor prediction quality. This was observed in [25] (therein referred to as the density method), and will be evident in the figures below. A classified trajectory will fall into one of four scenarios: True Positive (TP), when an anomalous trajectory is

Table 1. AUC values of the different algorithms

	T-1	T-2	T-3	T-4	T-5	T-6	T-7	T-8	T-9
iBAT	0.9868	0.9970	0.9970	0.9909	0.9944	0.9997	0.9983	0.9972	0.9998
$k = 1$	0.9629	0.9364	0.8023	0.8518	0.9108	0.9227	0.8806	0.9380	0.9788
$k = 2$	0.9904	0.9900	0.9735	0.9582	0.9887	0.9914	0.9846	0.9735	0.9989
$k = 3$	0.9805	0.9890	0.9386	0.9571	0.9879	0.9899	0.9841	0.9728	0.9986
Adaptive	0.9982	0.9952	0.9962	0.9890	0.9967	0.9953	0.9935	0.9936	0.9995

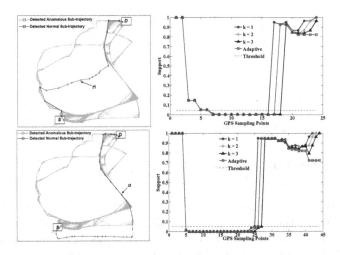

Fig. 4. Left: Detected anomalous sub-trajectories from T-1 using *iBOAT*. Right: Plot of ongoing *support*.

correctly classified as anomalous; False Positive (FP), when a normal trajectory is incorrectly classified as anomalous; False Negative (FN), when an anomalous trajectory is incorrectly classified as normal; True Negative (TN), when a normal trajectory is correctly classified as normal. The True Positive Rate (TPR), defined as $TPR = \frac{TP}{TP+FN}$, measures the proportion of correctly labeled anomalous trajectories; the False Positive Rate (FPR), defined as $FPR = \frac{FP}{FP+TN}$, measures the proportion of *false alarms* (*i.e.* normal trajectories that are labeled as anomalous). A perfect classifier will have $TPR = 1$ and $FPR = 0$. In a ROC curve, we plot FPR on the x-axis and TPR on the y-axis, which indicates the tradeoff between false alarms and accurate classifications. By measuring the Area Under Curve (AUC), we can quantify the tradeoff between correct positive classification and false alarms. In Figure 5 we plot the ROC-curve for T-1 and T-8, and in Table 1 we display the AUC values for all datasets and the different algorithms. To generate this plot we ranked all the instances according to the scores from each algorithm and used the *perfcurve* function in MATLAB, which generates the ROC curve. Using *iBAT*, $k = 2$ and the adaptive variants of *iBOAT* have the best overall performance with little significant difference between them. In Section 4.3 we will discuss some important differences between adaptive *iBOAT* and the fixed-window and *iBAT* approaches.

4.2   *iBOAT* versus *iBAT*

iBAT is a recent anomaly detection method introduced in [25] that is similar to our approach. In order to determine whether a trajectory is anomalous, *iBAT* picks cells from the testing trajectory at random to split the collection of trajectories into those that contain the cell and those that do not. This process is

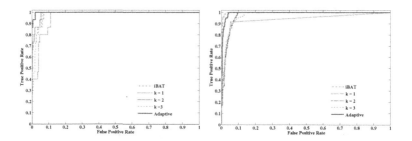

Fig. 5. The ROC curves for T-1 (left) and T-8 (right)

repeated until the trajectory is isolated, or until there are no more cells in the trajectory. Usually the number of cells required to isolate anomalous trajectories will be much less than the number of cells in the trajectory. This isolation procedure is repeated a number of times and $\mathbb{E}(n(t))$, the average number of cells required to isolate a trajectory, is used to compute the score, which is proportional to $2^{-\mathbb{E}(n(t))}$.

Our proposed method is a clear improvement over *iBAT* on two levels. First of all, we are able to determine which *parts* of a trajectory are anomalous, in contrast to *iBAT* which only classifies *full* trajectories as anomalous. Second of all, our method works in *real-time*: we can detect anomalous sections immediately, and do not require a full trajectory as an input.

In Figure 6 we show an example where a road block has forced a taxi to retrace its path and search for another route to its destination. We focus on the first part of the trajectory where the taxi retraces its steps. In the right panel of Figure 6 we can see the *support* is accurately identifying the anomalous section of the trajectory. We determined what anomalous ranking (based on the scores) both methods assign this partial trajectory in comparison with all other trajectories[2]. Out of 1418 trajectories, *iBOAT* ranked this trajectory in 48th place, while *iBAT* ranked it in 831th place. Furthermore, *iBAT* assigned this trajectory a score of 0.4342, which is below the usual 0.5 threshold. Thus, while *iBAT* is unable to detect that this trajectory is anomalous, *iBOAT* has ranked it amongst the top 3% of anomalous trajectories, as well as identifying which part is anomalous. The reason *iBAT* fails in this example is that their method does not take the *order* the points appear in into consideration; despite the fact that the taxi is retracing its steps and actually going *away* from the destination, it is only visiting "normal" grid cells.

Now consider the hypothetical example in Figure 7. In this simple situation, the value $\mathbb{E}(n(t))$ for *iBAT* is just the expected number of times their algorithm must pick cells before an anomalous cell (in red) is picked. This is essentially a Bernoulli trial with "success" probability p equal to the proportion of anomalous cells to total number of cells in the trajectory. It is well known that the expected number of trials before reaching success in a Bernoulli trial is given by $1/p$. Let

---

[2] A higher ranking means higher degree of anomalousness.

Fig. 6. A trajectory where the taxi had to retrace its path due to a blocked route. Left: illustration of situation; Middle: Real trajectory; Right: Ongoing *support* from *iBOAT*.

n be the number of cells in the straight line between S and D, then trajectories of the form on the left will have $2n - 2$ anomalous cells and $5n - 4$ total cells, while trajectories of the form on the right will have $2n - 2$ anomalous cells and $2n + 2$ total cells. It follows that for trajectories of the form on the left $\mathbb{E}(n(t)) = \frac{5n-4}{2n-2} \to \frac{5}{2} \Rightarrow score \approx 0.1768$; for trajectories of the form on the right $\mathbb{E}(n(t)) = \frac{2n+2}{2n-2} \to 1 \Rightarrow score = 0.5$. Thus, *iBAT* will qualify trajectories of the form on the right as more anomalous than those on the left. This runs contrary to intuition, which would perceive trajectories like the one on the left at least as anomalous as the one on the right, given that the path taken is much longer and they are clearly taking longer routes than necessary. Our scoring method, which uses the distance of the anomalous sub-trajectories, would assign the left trajectory an anomalous score around 33% higher than the one on the right. Finally, we compared the running time of both algorithms on all the datasets, and we display the results in Figure 8. We computed the running time for checking each trajectory in each dataset, and averaged over the size of the dataset. Although *iBAT* will usually check fewer grid cells than *iBOAT* (since one anomalous cell is enough to classify the trajectory as anomalous), *iBAT* is based on random cell selections, so they must average over m runs; as in [25], we set $m = 50$. We can see that *iBOAT* is consistently faster than *iBAT* on all datasets.

4.3   Adaptive versus Fixed-Window Approach

As was evident in the previous figures, the performance of the fixed-window approach with $k = 2$ and the adaptive approach are nearly identical. The advantage

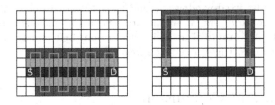

Fig. 7. Two anomalous trajectories of different types. The normal trajectory between S and D is in blue, cells adjacent to normal cells are in orange, and anomalous cells in red.

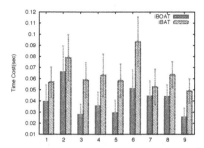

Fig. 8. Running times of *iBOAT* and *iBAT* on all the datasets

of the fixed-window approach is that it requires a very small amount of memory for real-time anomalous detection, while the adaptive method requires memory proportional to the size of the longest "normal" sub-trajectory. In practice, this difference is negligible. On the other hand, we will demonstrate that the adaptive approach has an advantage over the fixed-window approach due to its use of longer historical "contexts". In Figure 9 we display an anomalous trajectory that "switches" from one normal route to another. The fixed-window method with $k = 2$ will not detect this anomalous switch. The transition from point 19 to point 20 will seem normal since this sequence occurs in route A, and the transition from point 20 to point 21 will also seem normal since it occurs in route B. On the other hand, *iBOAT* would maintain the entire route up to the point when the driver switches routes and would immediately detect it as an anomalous point. Although this example is specific to window sizes equal to 2, similar situations (with longer overlaps between routes) will produce a similar effect for larger window sizes.

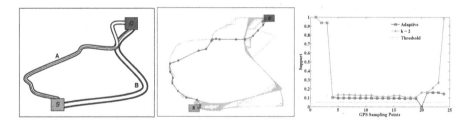

Fig. 9. A situation the fixed-window method ($k = 2$) fails to classify as anomalous: two normal routes (route A and B) are in dark blue; an anomalous trajectory (in red) switches from route A to route B at their intersection. Left: illustration of situation; Middle: Real trajectories; Right: ongoing *support* from *iBOAT*.

5   Discussion and Conclusion

In this paper we have proposed a new algorithm for fast *real-time* detection of anomalous trajectories obtained from GPS devices that can use fixed and variable window sizes. In addition to classifying full trajectories as anomalous, *iBOAT* can work with ongoing trajectories and can determine which parts of a trajectory are responsible for its anomalousness.

We validated *iBOAT* on a large dataset of taxi GPS trajectories recorded over a month and found our method achieved excellent performance (AUC$\geq$ 0.99 for all datasets) which is comparable to *iBAT*'s performance; however, we demonstrated a number of examples that highlight *iBOAT*'s advantage over *iBAT* and the sliding window method.

Given that one of the main applications of this work is taxi fraud detection, information such as speed can be crucial for more accurate detection. We plan on extending our work to use additional attributes such as speed, distance, orientation, taxi fare, etc., as this information can help distinguish fraudulent detours from other types of anomalous trajectories (such as road closures). The work presented in this paper was not meant to distinguish the different types of anomalous trajectories, but is an important first step in this direction. We have recently constructed a digital map of Hangzhou along with a mechanism for mapping GPS points onto the digital map; we are currently investigating *iBOAT*'s performance on this map and preliminary results are promising. This would give us access to detailed information about possible accidents, road closures, etc., which would be of great benefit to drivers, passengers, and traffic monitoring organizations.

Acknowledgements. The authors would like to thank the three anonymous reviewers for their valuable comments as well as Prof. Zhi-hua Zhou for the precious inputs. Chao Chen would like to thank the Chinese Government for his PhD funding. This research was supported by the Institut TELECOM "Futur et ruptures" Program, NSF of China (No.60975043, No.60803109), and the High-Tech Program of China (863) (No.2011AA010104).

References

1. Abe, N., Zadrozny, B., Langford, J.: Outlier detection by active learning. In: Proc. KDD (2006)
2. Angiulli, F., Fassetti, F.: Dolphin: An efficient algorithm for mining distance-based outliers in very large datasets. ACM-TKDD 3(1) (2009)
3. Breunig, M.M., Kriegel, H.P., Ng, R.T., Sander, J.: LOF: Identifying density-based local outliers. In: Proc. SIGMOD (2000)
4. Bu, Y., Chen, L., Fu, A.W.C., Liu, D.: Efficient anomaly monitoring over moving object trajectory streams. In: Proc. KDD (2009)
5. Chang, H., Tai, Y., Chen, H., Hsu, J.Y.: iTaxi: Context-aware taxi demand hotspots prediction using ontology and data mining approaches. In: Proc. of TAAI (2008)
6. Froehlich, J., Krumm, J.: Route prediction from trip observations. In: Proc. SAE (2008)
7. Ge, Y., Xiong, H., Zhou, Z.H., Ozdemir, H., Yu, J., Lee, K.C.: Top-Eye: Top-k evolving trajectory outlier detection. In: Proc. CIKM (2010)
8. He, Z., Xu, X., Deng, S.: Discovering cluster-based local outliers. Pattern Recognition Letters 24(9-10), 1641–1650 (2003)

9. Knorr, E.M., Ng, R.T., Tucakov, V.: Distance-based outliers: Algorithms and applications. VLDB Journal 8(3-4), 237–253 (2000)
10. Krumm, J., Horvitz, E.: Predestination: Inferring Destinations from Partial Trajectories. In: Dourish, P., Friday, A. (eds.) UbiComp 2006. LNCS, vol. 4206, pp. 243–260. Springer, Heidelberg (2006)
11. Lee, J., Han, J., Li, X.: Trajectory Outlier Detection: A Partition-and-Detect Framework. In: Proc. ICDE (2008)
12. Li, B., Zhang, D., Sun, L., Chen, C., Li, S., Qi, G., Yang, Q.: Hunting or waiting? Discovering passenger-finding strategies from a large-scale real-world taxi dataset. In: PerCom Workshops (2011)
13. Li, X., Han, J., Kim, S., Gonzalez, H.: ROAM: Rule- and motif-based anomaly detection in massive moving object data sets. In: Proc. SDM (2007)
14. Li, X., Li, Z., Han, J., Lee, J.G.: Temporal outlier detection in vehicle traffic data. In: Proc. ICDE (2009)
15. Liao, L., Patterson, D.J., Fox, D., Kautz, H.: Learning and inferring transportation routines. Artificial Intelligence 171(5–6), 311–331 (2007)
16. Liao, Z., Yu, Y., Chen, B.: Anomaly detection in GPS data based on visual analytics. In: Proc. VAST (2010)
17. Lippi, M., Bertini, M., Frasconi, P.: Collective Traffic Forecasting. In: Balcázar, J.L., Bonchi, F., Gionis, A., Sebag, M. (eds.) ECML PKDD 2010, Part II. LNCS, vol. 6322, pp. 259–273. Springer, Heidelberg (2010)
18. Liu, F.T., Ting, K.M., Zhou, Z.: Isolation Forest. In: Proc. ICDM (2008)
19. Liu, L., Andris, C., Ratti, C.: Uncovering cabdrivers' behavior patterns from their digital traces. Computers, Environment and Urban Systems 34, 541–548 (2010)
20. Phithakkitnukoon, S., Veloso, M., Bento, C., Biderman, A., Ratti, C.: Taxi-Aware Map: Identifying and Predicting Vacant Taxis in the City. In: de Ruyter, B., Wichert, R., Keyson, D.V., Markopoulos, P., Streitz, N., Divitini, M., Georgantas, N., Mana Gomez, A. (eds.) AmI 2010. LNCS, vol. 6439, pp. 86–95. Springer, Heidelberg (2010)
21. Qi, G., Li, X., Li, S., Pan, G., Wang, Z.: Measuring Social Functions of City Regions from Large-scale Taxi Behaviors. In: PerCom Workshop (2011)
22. Sillito, R., Fisher, R.B.: Semi-supervised learning for anomalous trajectory detection. In: Proc. BMVC (2008)
23. Yuan, J., Zheng, Y.: T-Drive: Driving Directions Based on Taxi Trajectories. In: ACM SIGSPATIAL GIS (2010)
24. Zhang, D., Guo, B., Yu, Z.: The Emergence of Social and Community Intelligence. IEEE Computer 44(7), 21–28 (2011)
25. Zhang, D., Li, N., Zhou, Z., Chen, C., Sun, L., Li, S.: iBAT: Detecting Anomalous Taxi Trajectories from GPS Traces. In: Proc. of UbiComp (2011)
26. Zheng, V.W., Cao, B., Zheng, Y., Xie, X., Yang, Q.: Collaborative filtering meets mobile recommendation: A user-centered approach. In: Proc. AAAI (2010)
27. Zheng, Y., Liu, Y., Yuan, J., Xie, X.: Urban Computing with Taxicabs. In: Proc. of Ubicomp (2011)
28. Zheng, Y., Zhang, L., Xie, X., Ma, W.: Mining interesting locations and travel sequences from gps trajectories. In: Proc. WWW (2009)
29. Ziebart, B.D., Maas, A.L., Dey, A.K., Bagnell, J.A.: Navigate Like a Cabbie: Probabilistic Reasoning from Observed Context-Aware Behavior. In: Proc. of Ubicomp (2008)

Scalable Data Processing for Community Sensing Applications[*]

Heitor Ferreira, Sérgio Duarte, Nuno Preguiça, and David Navalho

CITI-DI-FCT-UNL, Caparica, Portugal

Abstract. Participatory Sensing is a new computing paradigm that aims to turn personal mobile devices into advanced mobile sensing networks. For popular applications, we can expect a huge number of users to both contribute with sensor data and request information from the system. In such scenario, scalability of data processing becomes a major issue. In this paper, we present a system for supporting participatory sensing applications that leverages cluster or cloud infrastructures to provide a scalable data processing infrastructure. We propose and evaluate three strategies for data processing in this architecture.

Keywords: participatory sensing, distributed processing, mobile computing.

1 Introduction

Participatory Sensing [2,5] aims to leverage the growing ubiquity of sensor capable mobile phones as the basis for performing wide-area sensing tasks. Taking advantage of people's movements in their daily routines, Participatory Sensing promises an enormous potential for gathering valuable data at a fraction of the cost associated with the deployment of dedicated sensor infrastructures. Examples of this potential are well illustrated in [8,11,16], which concern road conservation and traffic monitoring, based on accelerometer and GPS readings collected by mobile devices.

Realizing the potential of Participatory Sensing poses several challenges, in particular, that of large-scale support, since the appeal of the paradigm can make its applications popular, with a very large number of users contributing with sensor data and obtaining information from the system. Many of the application examples found in the literature [8,11,16] use centralized architectures with a single server to process sensor data received from mobile users. These approaches are appropriate only for small-scale, proof-of-concept experiments.

For supporting large communities, a single server will be insufficient to process all data and reply to all queries. Thus, there is a need for partitioning data processing among multiple node. One possible approach is to use a decentralized solution composed by nodes scattered across the Internet. For example, in [9], we

---

[*] This work was supported partially by project #PTDC/EIA/76114/2006 and PEst-OE/EEI/UI0527/2011 - CITI/FCT/UNL/2011-12.

A. Puiatti et al. (Eds.): MobiQuitous 2011, LNICST 104, pp. 75–87, 2012.

have proposed such a system, with data processing being performed in a peer-to-peer network with nodes contributed by participants in the system. Such completely decentralized solutions involve a lot of complexity for achieving good performance and fault tolerance.

An alternative approach is to leverage current cluster and cloud computing infrastructures and perform data processing in such infrastructures. Several solutions for data processing in these environments have been proposed recently [6,13,4], but few are appropriate for processing streams of continuous data, as required by real-time participatory sensing applications. The solutions fit for processing continuous data (e.g. [4]) only focus on server execution, while a Participatory Sensing system can start data processing in the mobile nodes.

In this paper we present the Cloud 4 Sensing (C4S) system for supporting participatory sensing applications, allowing application developers to define the computation performed in the system. This includes the computations performed in the mobile nodes and in the system servers executing either in a cluster or in a cloud computing infrastructure. Computation is partitioned across server nodes according to a distribution strategy that defines how data is acquired by the system, where it is processed, and how it is aggregated. We propose three distribution strategies for processing data and evaluate these strategies in the context of a traffic monitoring application.

If the way programmers express computations is mostly inherited from our previous work [9], C4S runs in a completely different computation infrastructure (cluster/cloud vs. peer-to-peer). This leads to differences in the way information is propagated by mobile nodes and processed in the servers. Additionally, unlike our previous work, we propose several different distribution strategies.

The rest of the paper is structured as follows. Section 2 provides an overview of the C4S system. Section 3 details the three processing strategies proposed in this paper, followed by the results of their experimental evaluation in Section 4. The paper concludes with an overview of related work and some conclusions, respectively, in Sections 5 and 6.

2   System Overview

2.1   System Architecture

The C4S system architecture (Figure 1) comprises two kinds of nodes. A large number of mobile nodes, equipped with sensors, is the main source of data for the system, whereas a much smaller set of data center nodes forms a fixed infrastructure that provides computing, storage and networking resources.

Mobile nodes, typically smartphones, are expected to have limited computational power, battery life and communications capabilities. As such, they will mainly support user interaction and run data acquisition and simple processing services on behalf of the applications hosted at the fixed infrastructure. Mobile nodes do not interact directly, and connect to the fixed infrastructure to upload sensory data and obtain processed information via a frontend service.

Fixed nodes are deemed to be server-grade machines, well connected by a high-throughput and low-latency data center network. They form a loose overlay network, where the key characteristic is that they all know and can interact with each other. Moreover, each fixed node is assigned with a set of virtual geographic positions, chosen randomly from each of the target sensing areas. These locations are the basis for supporting decentralized processing strategies based on geographic partitioning. And, they also determine how mobile nodes bind to the fixed infrastructure.

2.2 Data Model

Applications access participatory sensing data by issuing queries over *virtual tables* - the main high-level data abstraction provided by C4S for naming a collection of data with a particular schema and semantics. Virtual tables have a global scope within a particular instance of the C4S platform. Issuing a query over a virtual table serves two purposes, it allows applications to request data and, at the same time, restrict its scope to a subset of the whole, in the form of spatial and temporal constraints.

While flexible regarding the actual schema, virtual tables handle geo-referenced and time-stamped data. As such, virtual table data is represented as a set of named attributes and, as a common denominator, each data tuple must include a temporal attribute, i.e., a timestamp, and a spatial component, in the form of physical coordinates or a geographic extent. A query over a virtual table will then result in a sequence of data tuples to be forwarded to the requesting application, confined to the requested geographic area and time period.

Virtual tables are purely logical entities, in the sense they do not necessarily need to refer to data already present in some physical storage medium. Interfacing applications with persisted (stored) data is just one of the facets of this construct. Virtual tables can also target data that does not yet exist and that may never be stored, including data intended to be produced and consumed with (near) realtime requirements. Moreover, another central concept to virtual tables is that they refer to data produced as a result of applying a set of transformations to raw sensor inputs and other virtual tables. As such, virtual tables embody a generic inference mechanism that creates high-order data from simpler constituents. This design is intended to facilitate and promote data sharing and cooperation among otherwise unrelated applications.

2.3 Data Transformation

Data transformation is achieved by specifying the execution of a *pipeline* of successive operations. Starting with raw sensor samples, or data from other virtual tables, a derived class of data can be produced, based on the output of a combination of pipeline operators. Data transformations typically involve *mapping*, *aggregation* and *condition detection* operations. Mapping adds new attributes to individual data elements, such as tagging a GPS reading with a street segment

Definition 1. TrafficHotspots virtual table specification

```
sensorInput( GPSReading )
dataSource {
    process{ GPSReading r ->
        r.derive( MappedSpeed, [boundingBox: model.getSegmentExtent(r.segmentId) ])
    }
    timeWindow(mode: periodic, size:10, slide:10)
    groupBy(['segmentId']){
        aggregate( AggregateSpeed ) { MappedSpeed m ->
            sum(m, 'speed', 'sumSpeed')
            count(m, 'count')
} } }
globalAggregation {
    timeWindow(mode: periodic, size:10, slide:10)
    groupBy(['segmentId']){
        aggregate( AggregateSpeed ) { AggregateSpeed a ->
            avg(a, 'sumSpeed', 'count', 'avgSpeed')
    } }
    classify( AggregateSpeed ) { AggregateSpeed a ->
        if(a.count > COUNT_THRESHOLD &&
                a.avgSpeed <= SPEED_THRESHOLD * model.maxSpeed(a.segmentId))
            a.derive( Hotspot, [confidence: Math.min(1, a.count/COUNT_THRESHOLD*0.5) ])
} }
```

identifier. Aggregation combines several samples into one and often involves statistical operators, such as *count*, *average*, etc., over temporal data snapshots. Finally, condition detection generates new data indicative of a particular noteworthy event, such as a congested street.

The *TrafficHotspots* virtual table, c.f. Definition 1, exemplifies the inference logic for an application devoted to realtime traffic monitoring, which is later detailed. In this example, starting with discrete GPS readings collected by mobile nodes, a stream of *Hotspot* tuples is generated, representing real-time detections of congested road segments, when certain thresholds are exceeded. In between, data is progressively transformed into intermediate forms, such as *MappedSpeed* and *AggregateSpeed* representing for each road segment, respectively, an individual speed measurement and the average car speed for the last 10 seconds. In section 4 we detail this application. The domain-specific language for specifying virtual tables and data transformations is detailed elsewhere [9].

A key aspect about data processing in virtual tables is that it is split between two transformation pipeline stages. One, *dataSource*, processes data locally available to the node, i.e., data already stored locally, or data that is being acquired or uploaded by mobile nodes. The *globalAggregation* merges the contributions of several nodes. Simple pipelines, with no *globalAggregation* stage can run entirely in mobile devices, and produce transformed data to feed another pipeline.

The two pipeline stages abstract the C4S distributed data processing facet. Consequently, their operation is very closely tied to the distribution strategy employed, which among other things determines the shape and properties of the data aggregation infrastructure used, as discussed further on.

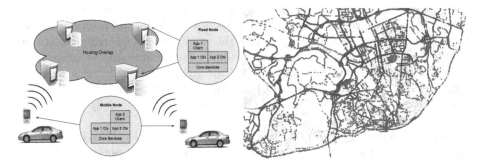

Fig. 1. C4S Architecture

Fig. 2. Snapshot of the traffic hotspots application for the Lisbon metropolitan area, showing congested spots in dark/red

2.4 Data Dissemination

When a node issues a query, the system instantiates data processing pipelines in the necessary fixed infrastructure and mobile nodes, depending on the geographic coverage of the standing queries, and according to the distribution strategy in use, as discussed in the next section. For returning query results to clients, C4S adopts a push-based model that leverages a publish/subscribe, content-based routing substrate. So, issuing a query translates to the client subscribing data conforming to a particular pattern/type, confined to a certain geographic area of interest and time period.

C4S is primarily designed for handling queries covering a large fraction of the target sensing areas. Supporting many "narrow" queries is made possible and efficient by merging them whenever they overlap geographically. For simplicity, the extent of the resulting compound query is used. The goal is to minimize the number of pipeline instantiations and avoid redundant data processing. To that end, the publish/subscribe substrate is used to filter out the query results that are outside of a client's request.

3 Distribution Strategies

Distribution strategies specify how the pipeline specification is materialized in the C4S infrastructure. Each strategy determines how data is acquired by the system, where it is processed, and how it is aggregated. Different strategies strive for different strengths. We next describe the three strategies we have implemented in the C4S platform.

3.1 RTree

The main rational behind RTree (Random Tree) is to leverage a simple partitioning of the acquired sensor data, backed by a random tree to aggregate and process data towards a root node of the fixed infrastructure.

In RTree, each mobile node maintains a long lasting association to a particular fixed node, established by selecting the fixed node with virtual position closest to a static reference location that defines the usual, general whereabouts of the mobile node. As a result, acquired data is immediately available for processing at each fixed node, but it is also partitioned among the fixed nodes without taking into account the actual spatial attributes of each sample. Therefore, the determining aspect of RTree is that every fixed node potentially hosts data relevant to any particular query.

In a given RTree instance (associated with a particular query), fixed nodes are organized into a random tree of a chosen degree, where they perform the same role and will instantiate both the data source and global aggregation pipeline stages. Since a node cannot determine if it has complete information for a particular spatial extent, data aggregation and processing may have to proceed along the tree until the root is reached, leading, potentially, to increased processing latency and raising issues of load imbalance. In particular, this can be an issue for virtual tables whose inference logic requires detecting the absence of certain data patterns. Early detections can, however, be published as soon as they are produced in any point of the aggregation tree. A straightforward way to address load balancing issues in RTree is to build a new random aggregation tree periodically to average the load of the nodes over time.

3.2 QTree

In QTree (Quad Tree), the idea is to do an *a priori* geographic partition of the data by performing a regular recursive subdivision of the sensing space into quadrants. Under this scheme, acquired sensor data is committed and bound to any of the fixed nodes that lie in the smallest quadrant that fully encloses the data's coordinates or geographic extent. Therefore, in QTree, dataSource pipeline stages will process data samples acquired by any mobile node. As for the global aggregation pipeline stages, QTree organizes them into a random quad tree, which is built, recursively, by picking a random node located in each subquadrant.

The key characteristic of QTree lies in that all the data processed in the deepest levels of the aggregation tree pertains to the immediate neighborhood of the processing node. This enables QTree to potentially detect highly localized phenomena early in the aggregation tree. As in RTree, load balancing issues may be mitigated by rebuilding the aggregation tree periodically.

3.3 NMap

NMap (Node Map) partitions data based on a geographic hashing approach. Each incoming data tuple is hashed to a geographic position and assigned to the fixed node closest to that point - its *nearest neighbour*. The hashing function can be tailored to the type and attributes of the sensor data, provided it preserves data locality. For instance, data that refers to a geographic extent can use the extent's centroid as the input for the hashing function. Besides spatial proximity, other attributes can be used to cluster data and enhance the notion of proximity. The idea is to process geographically related data tuples on the same node to reduce the overall computation latency and, consequently, maximize the chances for earlier pattern detection.

NMap uses a bottom up approach to build the aggregation structure. Initially, in each node, the dataSource pipeline will process data samples acquired by any mobile node. The resulting data tuples are then hashed and forwarded to the corresponding nearest neighbour nodes, where they are processed by their respective global aggregation pipelines. Since data can be re-maped at the global aggregation stage with new coordinates, the process can be repeated to create a multi-level aggregation path that converges at some virtual rendezvous point. Provided the nodes share a consistent membership view of the fixed node infrastructure, closely related data tuples (according to the hashing functions used) will flow towards the same final processing node. As such, NMap provides a distributed processing model that has similarities to the Map/Reduce model [6].

In NMap, load-balancing issues may arise if too much data is allowed to flow towards a small subset of the available processing nodes. This could happen, for instance, as a consequence of particular patterns in the sensory data or the hashing functions used. To address this issue, besides using different hashing functions to different virtual tables, one possible solution is to change periodically the virtual geographical positions assigned to the nodes.

4 Case-Study and Experimental Evaluation

Performance metrics of the three distribution strategies were evaluated using a case-study application that concerns realtime road traffic monitoring. The application, *Traffic hotspots*, provides information about the congested areas based on GPS data, sampled at periodic intervals by in-transit vehicles. It relies on the TrafficHotspots virtual table, presented earlier as Definition 1, which supports querying for congestion detections computed from average speeds.

In the TrafficHotspots's *dataSource* pipeline stage, GPS samples are augmented to include the identifier of the road segment the vehicle is in. In this case, as this step requires accessing a database of road segments, it runs in the fixed nodes. For each road segment, an *AggregateSpeed* sample is generated with aggregate information of the cars in the segment. These *AggregateSpeed* samples are propagated every 10 seconds for processing by the *globalAggregation* stage. In that stage, a sliding window of the *AggregateSpeed* samples received in the last 10 seconds is maintained. For each road segment, the total number of cars and the average car speed is computed. With this information, an hotspot is signaled for some segment if the number of cars in the segment and their average speed crosses some thresholds (that depend on the type of road). A client application can use these detections, for instance, to render maps of the current state of the target sensing area, as shown in Figure 2.

4.1 Evaluation

For the system evaluation, we use the Open Street Map [18] vectorial representation of the road network of Lisbon city. This data is used to map geographic coordinates to road segments, to determine the spatial extent of segments and their associated road type. The model used in the evaluation divides roads, as needed, into segments with a maximum of 1 Km and uses separate segments for each driving direction. Each road is assigned an expected (uncongested) driving speed according to its type: highway, primary to tertiary and residential.

In the simulation experiments, 50000 mobile nodes populate the sensing area. They simulate in-transit vehicles, according to a traffic model, and report GPS readings every 5 seconds, as they follow the assigned paths. They interact with the infrastructure frontend, resulting in the delivery of raw GPS data with no latency. For the fixed insfrastructure, besides a single server solution, we evaluated performance using 50 and 500 fixed nodes. In this case, fixed nodes are assigned virtual positions distributed randomly across the sensing area.

A common clock is used to timestamp readings; any effects of clock desynchronization are not considered.

Traffic is modeled by emulating a fleet of vehicles driving through random routes. The maximum speed for a given segment is the same value used for congestion detection and depends on the road type. An average speed, for each road segment at a given time, is determined by its current car density and used to generate the random speed individually for each vehicle, according to a normal distribution. In the experiments performed, congestion occurs in segments with a density of at least 50 vehicles. Vehicle paths are determined by choosing a random start position and sequence of road intersections; a new path is assigned whenever a vehicle reaches its destination. Figure 2 shows a rendering of the traffic simulation.

In the following results, we scrutinize the effects of a single query covering 25% of the overall simulation area in an area with high density of mobile nodes. Note that having a query over a large area is what happens when multiple queries over nearby small areas (e.g., several points in the city downtown) are merged in our algorithms. The set of metrics captured was averaged over 5 runs, corresponding to different fixed node placements.

4.2 Workload Distribution

We have started by analyzing how the effort to evaluate a query is spread among the fixed nodes in the different distribution strategies. For comparison, we have computed the effort that a solution with a single central node would experience.

The workload is measured as the number of data tuples processed in both *dataSource* and *globalAggregation* stages at each node. Figure 3 shows the workload distribution using the different distribution strategies, when considering 50 and 500 fixed nodes, for the top 25 most loaded nodes. The workload is presented as a percentage of the workload experienced by a single, centralized node.

The results show that when using the proposed strategies, both QTree's and NMap's most loaded node processes only a fraction of the tuples of a single

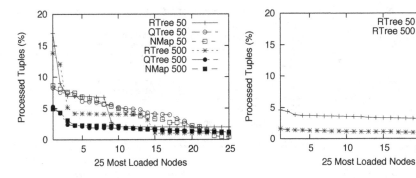

Fig. 3. Workload distribution   **Fig. 4.** Workload - RTree Rebalance

node solution (below 9% when considering 50 fixed nodes, and below 5% when considering 500). These values show the scalability of our solution - for example, C4S could still work properly even if the workload of the system exceeds by 10× the workload that a single node can process.

RTree presents a clearly skewed load distribution, with some nodes (those at the top of the aggregation) doing significantly more work. To address this load-balancing issue, RTree can rebuild the aggregation tree from time to time. Figure 4 summarizes the results when the tree is rebuilt every 10 minutes (for a total of 2 hours). It shows clearly that just a few tree updates are very effective at better spreading the load among the infrastructure nodes.

4.3   Detection Latency

Detection latency measures the lag between the occurrence of a segment congestion and its detection by the system. Transient congestions (lasting less than 20 seconds) were not considered for the evaluation. As the traffic patterns produced by the traffic model are highly dynamic compared to real world conditions, with frequent short lived congestions, these experiments represent a challenging scenario to the system.

Figure 5 plots the detection latency for the accumulated level of successful detections. Results show clearly that QTree and NMap detect congestions faster than RTree, regardless of the number of considered fixed nodes. Their performance is comparable to the centralized solution. In RTree aggregation progress is slower because it is maily driven by the degree of the tree, rather than by strong spatial coherence, as in QTree or NMap.

Failures. We implemented a simple failure recovery mechanism consisting in rebuilding the aggregation tree periodically or when failures exceed a certain threshold in RTree and QTree. For NMap, sensory data is distributed disregarding the failed nodes upon their detection.

Our experiments allowed us to conclude that different distribution strategies present different behaviors that are hard to reflect in average results. Figure 6

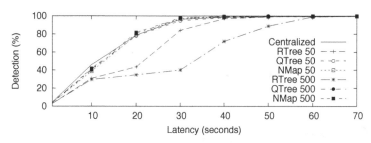

Fig. 5. Detection latency

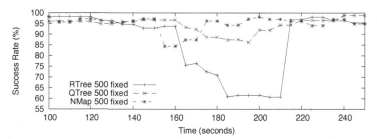

Fig. 6. Success rate in the presence of node failures

shows a selected run for each distribution strategy that exemplifies the impact of failures, when observed.

In RTree, the influence in the success rate observed depends hugely on the position of nodes failed in the aggregation tree. When nodes are mostly leaf nodes, little to no influence is observed, as data redundancy still allows detections to be observed. On the other hand, when nodes higher in the tree hierarchy are affected, the impact in the success rate is high.

QTree exhibits a similar behavior with stronger consequences for failures at lower levels and weaker consequences for failures at higher levels. The former can be explained by the fact that sensory data for a given region is processed by fewer nodes - the failure of a few of these nodes has an important impact in the final result. The latter can be explained by the fact that by aggregating the sensory data closer to the leaves, detections are often performed in lower levels of the tree, which makes inconsequent a failure in an higher level node.

NMap is the extreme case of impact in the failure of nodes - the failure of a node will always lead to a drop in the success rate, as results computed by that node are lost. However, as the recovery solution implemented is simpler, the success rate returns to the initial values quickly.

5   Related Work

Our work has been influenced by works in different areas.

Participatory sensing has become popular recently [2,5], and a large number of supporting systems have been designed. Some systems (e.g., BikeNet [7], PEIR [17], CarTel [11,8]) rely on a centralized approach, where mobile nodes propagate sensing data to a central node responsible for processing information. Our system is also based on a centralized approach, but unlike previous works focus on the scalability of data processing in the servers.

In other systems, computation is performed by a combination of fixed nodes scattered across the Internet (e.g., COSMOS [15], SenseWeb [10], 4Sensing [9]). Some of these solutions address the scalability issue by spreading the load across multiple nodes in a peer-to-peer fashion. Although these solutions are interesting, the churn usually observed in nodes of a peer-to-peer network make solution complex for providing adequate quality of service and fault tolerance, and incur in a large communication overhead. Our solutions are inspired in some of the ideas proposed in these works, adapted to the target environment.

Sensor networks [1], while operating under a different context and communication assumptions, provided us with inspiration on how to gather and share data among nodes. TinyDB [14] extends the standard SQL syntax with a continuous query semantics, providing highly flexible queries as well as summarization and event detection. Directed Diffusion [12] presents a data-centric solution, where a node requests data by sending *interests* for named data. Data matching this query is then gathered towards the node. In our system, the sensor definition, virtual table and pipeline models separate querying from acquisition and data operations, embodying characteristics of topic-based publish-subscribe systems and SQL based queries.

In wireless sensor networks, a large number of algorithms have been proposed for processing information [21]. However, these algorithms tend to focus on minimizing energy usage and nodes can only communicate with nearby nodes. Thus, the topologies that are formed to aggregate results have very different constraints when compared to our approach.

A large number of solutions have been proposed for stream and data processing - e.g. [3,13,6,4]. While these systems usually only focus on the processing in the servers, our solution spans both the servers and mobile nodes, which feed geo-referenced data into the servers periodically. Nevertheless, our work is inspired by some of these works. In NMap, data of a given region is processed by a single node in a way similar to a map-reduce computation [4], where the reduce step processes all data that has been mapped to the same key.

Quad trees have been previously used for a large number of goals, including for addressing geographical-related problems concerning the monitoring and tracking of moving objects [20] and for querying data in peer-to-peer networks [19]. QTree is inspired by these works, building a query specific tree during query dissemination.

6   Conclusions

This paper presents a system for supporting Participatory Sensing applications, focusing on data processing. In our system, data processing spans both mobile nodes and a set of server nodes, deployed in a cluster or cloud infrastructure. We present three algorithms for performing data processing in the servers. RTree is the simplest solution, leveraging random aggregation trees. QTree combines random trees with regular, *a priori*, subdivision of geographic space for improved performance. In NMap, all closely related sensory data is aggregated and processed in a single node.

The experimental evaluation using simulation and a case-study application, allows us to draw the following conclusions. The three distribution strategies distribute the load across multiple nodes, with the most loaded node processing only a fraction of the tuples of a single node solution. NMap and QTree exhibit overall better load balancing when compared with RTree. The results also show that NMap and QTree can compute results faster than RTree, and with a latency similar to a single node solution. Thus, C4S with either NMap or QTree presents a scalable solution for processing data in participatory sensing applications. Compared to QTree, NMap offers the additional flexibility afforded by the use of hashing functions to distribute (and cluster) processing, as they can be tailored to match the application scenario closely.

As for future work, we intend to continue studying solutions for improving load balancing, processing overhead and query success and latency in all strategies. Additionally, we intend to extend the support for processing information in mobile nodes, thus further reducing the load experienced by server nodes and helping to improve the overall scalability of the system.

References

1. Akyildiz, I.F., Su, W., Sankarasubramaniam, Y., Cayirci, E.: A survey on sensor networks. IEEE Communications Magazine 40(8), 102–114 (2002)
2. Campbell, A.T., Eisenman, S.B., Lane, N.D., Miluzzo, E., Peterson, R.A., Lu, H., Zheng, X., Musolesi, M., Fodor, K., Ahn, G.-S.: The rise of people-centric sensing. IEEE Internet Computing 12(4), 12–21 (2008)
3. Cherniack, M., Balakrishnan, H., Balazinska, M., Carney, D., Çetintemel, U., Xing, Y., Zdonik, S.B.: Scalable distributed stream processing. In: CIDR (2003)
4. Condie, T., Conway, N., Alvaro, P., Hellerstein, J.M., Elmeleegy, K., Sears, R.: Mapreduce online. In: NSDI 2010: Proceedings of the 6th USENIX Symposium on Networked Systems Design and Implementation (2010)
5. Cuff, D., Hansen, M., Kang, J.: Urban sensing: out of the woods. Commun. ACM 51(3), 24–33 (2008)
6. Dean, J., Ghemawat, S.: Mapreduce: simplified data processing on large clusters. In: Proc. 6th Symp. on Operating Systems Design & Implementation (2004)
7. Eisenman, S.B., Miluzzo, E., Lane, N.D., Peterson, R.A., Ahn, G.-S., Campbell, A.T.: The bikenet mobile sensing system for cyclist experience mapping. In: SenSys 2007: Proc. 5th Int. Conf. on Embedded Networked Sensor Systems (2007)
8. Eriksson, J., Girod, L., Hull, B., Newton, R., Madden, S., Balakrishnan, H.: The Pothole Patrol: Using a Mobile Sensor Network for Road Surface Monitoring. In: Proc. 6th Int. Conf. on Mobile Systems, Applications, and Services (June 2008)
9. Ferreira, H., Duarte, S., Preguiça, N.: 4Sensing - Decentralized Processing for Participatory Sensing Data. In: 16th International Conference on Parallel and Distributed Systems (ICPADS 2010). IEEE (2010)
10. Grosky, W., Kansal, A., Nath, S., Liu, J., Zhao, F.: Senseweb: An infrastructure for shared sensing. IEEE Multimedia 14(4), 8–13 (2007)

11. Hull, B., Bychkovsky, V., Zhang, Y., Chen, K., Goraczko, M., Miu, A.K., Shih, E., Balakrishnan, H., Madden, S.: CarTel: A Distributed Mobile Sensor Computing System. In: 4th ACM SenSys (November 2006)
12. Intanagonwiwat, C., Govindan, R., Estrin, D.: Directed diffusion: a scalable and robust communication paradigm for sensor networks. In: MobiCom 2000: Proc. 6th Int. Conf. on Mobile Computing and Networking, pp. 56–67 (2000)
13. Isard, M., Budiu, M., Yu, Y., Birrell, A., Fetterly, D.: Dryad: distributed data-parallel programs from sequential building blocks. In: Proc. 2nd EuroSys European Conference on Computer Systems, EuroSys 2007, pp. 59–72 (2007)
14. Madden, S.R., Franklin, M.J., Hellerstein, J.M., Hong, W.: Tinydb: an acquisitional query processing system for sensor networks. ACM Trans. Database Syst. 30, 122–173 (2005)
15. Marie Kim, Y.J.L., Lee, J.W., Ryou, J.-C.: Cosmos: A middleware for integrated data processing over heterogeneous sensor networks. ETRI Journal 30(5) (October 2008)
16. Mohan, P., Padmanabhan, V., Ramjee, R.: Nericell: Rich Monitoring of Road and Traffic Conditions using Mobile Smartphones. In: Proceedings of ACM SenSys 2008 (November 2008)
17. Mun, M., Reddy, S., Shilton, K., Yau, N., Burke, J., Estrin, D., Hansen, M., Howard, E., West, R., Boda, P.: Peir, the personal environmental impact report, as a platform for participatory sensing systems research. In: MobiSys 2009: Proc. of the 7th Int. Conf. on Mobile Systems, Applications, and Services, pp. 55–68. ACM (2009)
18. OpenStreeMap (April 2010), http://www.openstreetmap.org
19. Tanin, E., Harwood, A., Samet, H.: Using a distributed quadtree index in peer-to-peer networks. VLDB Journal 16, 165–178 (2007)
20. Tayeb, J., Ulusoy, Ö., Wolfson, O.: A quadtree-based dynamic attribute indexing method. Comput. J. 41(3), 185–200 (1998)
21. Yick, J., Mukherjee, B., Ghosal, D.: Wireless sensor network survey. Comput. Netw. 52(12), 2292–2330 (2008)

Gander: Personalizing Search of the Here and Now

Jonas Michel[1], Christine Julien[1], Jamie Payton[2], and Gruia-Catalin Roman[3]

[1] The University of Texas, Austin, TX, USA
{jonasrmichel,c.julien}@mail.utexas.edu
[2] The University of North Carolina, Charlotte, NC, USA
payton@uncc.edu
[3] The University of New Mexico, Albuquerque, NM, USA
gcroman@unm.edu

Abstract. In Personalized Networked Spaces (PNets), people and devices are integrated with the environment and demand fluid interactions to enable connectivity to information, services, and people. PNet applications exhibit significant *spatiotemporal* demands in which connectivity to resources and information is personalized and focused on the *here* and *now*. We introduce *Gander*, a personalized search engine for the here and now. We examine how search expectations are affected when users and applications interact directly with the physical environment. We define a formal conceptual model of search in PNets that provides a clear definition of the framework and ultimately enables reasoning about relationships between search processing and the relevance of results. We assess our model by evaluating sophisticated Gander queries in a simulated PNet.

1 Introduction

In Personalized Networked Spaces (PNets), people and machines interact to make the physical environment more digitally accessible. PNets are made possible by wireless and sensor technology, cyber-physical systems, and a deeper understanding of the importance of social networks. Key PNet features are spatiotemporal locality and a rapidly changing world; knowing what is happening to me and around me now is of the essence. PNets are likely to become ubiquitous and critical to our economy and social life.

PNets will serve different purposes and entail different interactions than the Internet, but the same fundamental need to access information exists. PNets, however, require tight spatiotemporal integration of user behavior and the immediate environment; information needs are immediate, personalized, and localized. Internet search engines treat the Internet as a large (relatively static) library for rapid access to relevant information; enormous technological, intellectual, and organizational resources support such a massive undertaking. In contrast, a PNet search engine needs to facilitate immediate interactions with one's surroundings without infrastructure and advance indexing.

Fluidity and extreme dynamics are defining features of PNets that motivate the kinds of search users need. In the Internet, one may ask for webcams in Geneva; in a home one may want to find where the dog is hiding using motion detectors and webcams. Using an Internet search engine one may find available trains from Rome to Florence; while hurrying to board a crowded train at the station one may need to find an available seat in a second class car. In the Internet, one might ask for an aerial photo of a forest fire, which may be acceptable even if a few hours old; when running away from the fire one needs to know the relation between fire and wind in the immediate neighborhood.

A. Puiatti et al. (Eds.): MobiQuitous 2011, LNICST 104, pp. 88–100, 2012.
© Institute for Computer Sciences, Social Informatics and Telecommunications Engineering 2012

An Internet-centric perspective might frame the question as how to extend an existing search engine to PNets. However, PNets' dynamic and heterogeneous nature give rise to novel challenges. We pose a fundamental research question: *Given a PNet, what mechanisms are required to provide search capabilities without reliance on Internet connectivity?* The latter requirement is justified by practical considerations. There are indeed situations in which Internet access is costly, inconvenient, nonexistent, or simply unnecessary; a home is managed better by exploiting local wireless connectivity, an exploration team may be far from any connectivity other than a satellite, in underdeveloped countries connectivity to the Internet may be sparse or financially unattainable.

This paper's contribution is to introduce *Gander*—a personalized search engine for PNets—and to investigate how existing query protocols can be used to support personalized search of the here and now. Gander queries about "me, here, and now" have a strong spatiotemporal component; the location of the user is a key point of reference. Our conceptual model is based on a worldview in which reachable nodes have locations, are semantically related, and have attributes of interest to the user. An important departure from traditional query processing is the tight integration of *personalized relevance* (the PNet analog to page ranking) into query processing. This personalized relevance is dynamic and reflects the user's personalized priorities here and now; it affects the perception of the search process in a fundamental and novel way and it holds the promise to reduce the cost of processing by leveraging relevance in the query protocol.

2   Background and Motivating Example

We first consider a concrete motivating scenario; we then look at the state of the art in related areas to demonstrate the important gap that the Gander approach fills.

2.1   Application Example

While planning a trip to an amusement park, visitors may use the Internet to find directions, opening hours, etc. Most of this information is static or updated sporadically. In the park, visitors' information needs change. A visitor may want to know which rides have the shortest wait right now, where the nearest exit is, or how others like a ride. Providing this information via the Internet is problematic: the volume of information is too great to be shipped and stored centrally, the lifespan of information is short, and the ratio of data used to data available is minute. A visitor's requests for information "here and now" must be served by local, dynamically formed networks of devices in the park.

Consider a visitor, Maya, who wants to discover if she has time to go on a ride before meeting her friends for lunch. She submits a query over a dynamically formed network of infrastructure and personal mobile devices that are reachable (possibly across multiple hops) from her mobile device. Visitors' devices may provide information about density of visitors in regions of the park and information collected about attractions or restaurants they have recently encountered. Constraints on the query can restrict the logical search space; to meet her friends for lunch, Maya needs to find a ride close to a food vendor, so her query uses a proximity constraint to restrict the search space.

Although the constraints limit the search scope, several rides may satisfy Maya's query. Since Maya needs to make it to lunch in time, her query emphasizes a combination of the ride wait time and the distance from the ride to the food vendor. Such relevance metrics may be evaluated over devices and their associated data that are not part of the result set for the query and its constraints. For example, wait time information may be acquired from the mobile devices of other visitors in line for the ride. Many other queries are possible with different search parameters, constraints, and ranking metrics. The concepts are clearly not limited to this particular domain. The notions of using semantic relationships among data items to evaluate queries and providing a description of relevance with each query to provide personalized search of the here and now can be generalized and applied to many other applications and spaces.

2.2   Related Work

Mobile devices, location-based services, and the embedding of computation sets the stage for search capabilities that are inherently intertwined with our personalized spaces. This section examines the state of the art and identifies the gap Gander fills.

Mobile Information Retrieval. Recent work has assessed requirements for information retrieval and identified relationships between users' information needs and their *context*, including location, time, and even activity [17,23]. Such studies have exposed influences on people's willingness to share information about themselves; for example, people may be willing to share with other co-located users (even unknown ones) what they would not be willing to share publicly (i.e., on the Internet).

Systems have extended spatiotemporal search techniques to mobile applications. WebPark [23] provides geographically relevant information using geographic filters to capture spatial relevance. Ahlers and Boll enrich spatial context with temporal aspects [1]. GeoRel [26] develops metaphors for assessing relevance of geospatial features. These systems allow users to search relatively *static* information (e.g., landmarks) and focus on how to use geographic context to determine which information is most relevant. In a PNet, the data searched is *ephemeral*; such transient data cannot be easily indexed and associated with a relevant spatial context outside of the here and now.

Moving object databases [9,10] and spatiotemporal databases [15] have driven spatiotemporal data representation. Erwig et al. use abstract data types that map time onto points, lines, and spatial regions, enabling spatiotemporal predicates, relationships between spatial entities changing over time [13,14]. This and similar approaches enable effective spatiotemporal search; however, they require access to a centralized library of continuously cataloged information. PNets, in contrast, demand the ability to access instantaneously available local information with transient spatial relationships.

The Internet of Things. The Internet of Things [3] envisions a world in which ordinary objects are imbued with computation, sensing, and networking capabilities. Such a vision makes possible and necessary the ability to perform real-time local searches. A fundamental building block of this vision are *smart objects* [7,18]; the wide availability of such smart objects drastically increases the amount of dynamic and transient information in our spaces. Successful applications in the Internet of Things must be able to search this large volume of data here and now efficiently.

Dyser [24] is a search engine that supports real-time search for sensors with a user-specified current state. Searches are optimized using a technique called sensor ranking [12] by assuming that searchable entities are persistently accessible via the Internet. In a PNet, however, reachability is volatile and must be assessed instantaneously.

Relevance and Recommender Systems. Relevance in traditional web search is well-understood [22], even along multiple dimensions [2]. Geographic digital libraries [1,5,19] use geospatial metadata (e.g., coordinate representations of geographic objects) to support storage and retrieval of geographic information. A document's relevance may be computed in terms of its geospatial metadata's topological relation to a query (e.g., size, shape, location, distance) in addition to its content's relation to a search query [11].

Gander demands a richer awareness of *context* in determining relevance, yet contextually influenced information retrieval is challenging due to an inability to appropriately index information when it is generated [20]. Collaborative filtering combines results from multiple users to make recommendations, using a variety of techniques to acquire a user's context [27]; the approaches falter in PNets because explicit computation and comparison of rich contexts is complex even for simple queries [8]. Our approach does not *index* data relative to its context but instead performs the query *in* the context. Future extensions to Gander could dovetail more explicitly with collaborative filtering, learning how other users interact with the information in this space at this time.

3   The Gander Conceptual Model

Personalized search of the here and now entails two components: (1) *query processing*: i.e., how to distribute a query (and its responses) using local interactions; and (2) *relevance determination*: i.e., how to rate results' relevance to the query. We next describe the Gander conceptual model, which is essential for providing a rigorous understanding of the *quality* of a Gander query and its ability to represent the here and now.

3.1   Gander Conceptual Model Components

A *PNet* is a collection of nodes connected via a dynamic topology. Nodes issue queries that are evaluated across information stored at other nodes. A *data item* is an atom (ν, d), where ν is a data value (e.g., a measure of some condition in the environment), and d is meta-data associated with that piece of data (e.g., the device(s) that generated the data, the data's location, a timestamp, etc.). This representation reflects existing work in capturing and representing context in ubiquitous computing [6].

For every valid result for a query, the result's ν must "match" the search string. A query can include one or more additional *query constraints*. For each constraint c, valid results are those whose ν values match the search string and $c((\nu, d))$ returns true. A *query relevance metric* compares valid results against each other. For each relevance metric m, $m((\nu, d))$ returns a value; these values can be ordered. A query can use multiple metrics evaluated independently or using weighted statistics. A *query processing protocol* executes in a distributed multihop fashion to select a subset of the PNet to distribute a query to; this subset includes only "reachable" nodes in the PNet. Gander query processing can use the search string, constraints, and relevance metrics.

3.2   Gander Query Processing

A Gander query is a function $G_h : D \to \Phi$, where D contains all data items in the world, Φ is the domain of the relevance metric, and h is the node issuing the query. A query processing protocol is a *partial function* $QP_h : D \to D$; QP_h is not required to be defined for every element of its domain, D. Informally, $QP_h((\nu, d)) = (\nu, d)$ if $(\nu, d) \in D$ is a "valid" result; otherwise $QP_h((\nu, d))$ is undefined. One can view QP_h as a *filter* on D. The three components of are the following.

Reachability. The partial function $\mathcal{R}_h : D \to D$ expresses whether the data item (ν, d) is *reachable* from h; if not, $\mathcal{R}_h((\nu, d))$ is not defined. This is a specialization of a general reachability function; $\mathcal{R} : H \times H \to \{0, 1\}$, written as $\mathcal{R}(h_1, h_2)$, which expresses whether h_2 is *reachable* from h_1. We focus on *query* reachability, the ability to send a query from h_1 to h_2 *and* receive a response [25]. $\mathcal{R}$ is related to $\mathcal{R}_h$ as: $\mathcal{R}_h((\nu, d)) = (\nu, d) \Leftrightarrow \langle \exists h_2 : (\nu, d) \in h_2 :: \mathcal{R}(h, h_2) \rangle$, where $(\nu, d) \in h_2$ indicates that (ν, d) is "owned" by h_2. Clearly $\mathcal{R}$ depends on both physical communication capabilities and communication protocols used in the PNet.

Query Resolution. The partial function $\mathcal{S} : D \to D$ is defined for each $(\nu, d) \in D$ that matches the search string. In our application scenario, $\mathcal{S}$ indicates whether or not the data item (ν, d) is a reachable data item describing a ride.

Query Constraint. The partial function $\mathcal{C} : D \to D$ is defined for each $(\nu, d) \in D$ that satisfies the query constraints. $\mathcal{C}$'s resolution may rely on the *meta-data* (d), which may provide the context of that data item in the PNet. In our scenario, an example constraint is whether (ν, d) refers to a ride near a food vendor.

These three functions filter D to the subset of reachable data items that match the search string and satisfy the constraints. Given a snapshot of all data items in the PNet, Fig. 1 shows the composition of reachability, query resolution, and query constraints; $QP_h = \mathcal{C} \circ \mathcal{S} \circ \mathcal{R}_h$. This model assumes complete knowledge of the PNet. Practically, this is not reasonable, but this formulation of query processing as a composition of partially defined functions allows us to incrementally compute a query's result.

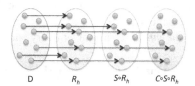

Fig. 1. Query processing functions

3.3 Gander Relevance Model

A Gander query defines regions of the PNet from which to draw data to satisfy a personalized search of the here and now. Gander query constraints and relevance definitions provide criteria by which data in these regions is selected for delivery to the query issuer. Our goal is not to collect all of the data but only the data that is most relevant.

A Gander *relevance metric*, $\mathcal{M}_i : D \to \phi_i$, is a partial function; ϕ_i is the domain of the relevance metric $\mathcal{M}_i$. Elements of ϕ_i should be scalar; $\mathcal{M}_i((\nu, d))$ gives the distance of a data item (ν, d) from an ideal (with respect to the relevance metric $\mathcal{M}_i$). A Gander query may entail more than one relevance metric; given a query's n relevance metrics, the complete relevance metric is the partial function $\mathcal{K}_{\{\mathcal{M}_1, \mathcal{M}_2, ..., \mathcal{M}_n\}} : D \to \phi_1 \times \phi_2 \times \cdots \times \phi_n$, or simply $\mathcal{K}_{\{\mathcal{M}_1, \mathcal{M}_2, ..., \mathcal{M}_n\}} : D \to \Phi$. A Gander query, G_h, composes the complete relevance metric with a query processing protocol: $G_h = \mathcal{K}_{\{\mathcal{M}_1, \mathcal{M}_2, ..., \mathcal{M}_n\}} \circ \mathcal{C} \circ \mathcal{S} \circ \mathcal{R}_h$. This combination of query processing with relevance maps valid results to a multidimensional space whose dimensions are given by $\Phi = \phi_1 \times \phi_2 \times \cdots \times \phi_n$.

$G_h((\nu, d))$ is not defined if (ν, d), is not reachable or does not satisfy the search string or query constraints; otherwise $G_h((\nu, d))$ is an n-tuple, where field i has the value $\mathcal{M}_i((\nu, d))$. We can plot each valid result in a multidimensional space, where each axis represents one of the n metrics; results closer to the origin are more relevant[1].

We give two examples of computing the distance from a point in this multidimensional space to the origin: *lexicographical ordering* and *weighted combination*. The former is less expressive but more flexible since any metrics can be combined. A weighted combination requires the metrics to be expressed in domains that are comparable (or could be made comparable by applying scaling factors) but is more expressive.

Lexicographically Ordered Relevance Metrics. In lexicographical ordering, the order of the metrics matters; data items are ranked first based on the first metric, and later relevance metric values break ties. Given two n-tuples k and k' representing relevance values for (ν, d) and $(\nu, d)'$, (ν, d) is more relevant if and only if:

$$\langle \exists i : 1 \leq i \leq n : k[i] < k'[i] \land \langle \forall j : 1 \leq j < i :: k[j] = k'[j] \rangle \rangle$$

Maya wants to maximize the thrill for the rides she experiences. Her query looks for rides she has not yet ridden, favoring first rides with the highest thrill and breaking ties by favoring those that are closer. Her friend Alex also likes thrill rides, but he wants to go on as many rides as possible. His query also looks only at rides he has not yet ridden, but first uses a relevance metric of distance and then one for thrill.

Weighted Combination of Relevance Metrics. This approach requires as input a vector $\mathcal{W}$ that associates a weight with each metric. We map each n-tuple to a single value: $m : \Phi \to \mathbb{R}^2$. Given $\mathcal{W} = \langle w_1, w_2, \ldots w_n \rangle$, we can map a result's n-tuple to a weighted sum of the tuple's constituents: $m_{\mathcal{W}}^+((\nu, d)) = \sum_{i=1}^{n}(w_i \times \mathcal{M}_i((\nu, d})))$. $\mathcal{W}$ normalizes Φ's dimensions so metrics can be numerically combined. As an example, Maya's relevance metrics can express the travel time to a ride from her location, the travel time from that ride to a food vendor, and the ride's wait time; by weighting these component metrics equally and summing their values, we can order the rides according to the total time it would take Maya to ride the ride and meet her friends.

The multiplicative combination, $m_{\mathcal{W}}^{\times}$, can be defined similarly. This combination can support a user who wants to ride the most thrilling rides but only has two hours. The wait time relevance metric maps to a value between 0 and 1. When this wait time metric is part of a multiplicative combination with a thrill metric, rides that the user does not have time to enjoy will have a total relevance ranking of 0.

These approaches to combining multidimensional relevance linearly order the results; future work will consider more complex yet expressive relevance combinators. In the remainder of this paper, we examine how well existing query protocols for mobile networks support this conceptual model. This paper's novelty is in defining the conceptual model and using existing query protocols to distribute personalized queries

---

[1] We assume the origin is absolute and relevance metrics are defined relative to an ideal. The origin could itself be relative to the results; this causes a translation of the axes of the multidimensional space to move the origin. The same distance functions can be applied.

[2] We use $\mathbb{R}$ as the function's range; for other combinations, the range could be any set over which a partial order can be defined.

of the here and now. We do not define novel protocols; instead we use our evaluation of the Gander conceptual model to posit how existing protocols could be modified (or replaced) to better support personalized search of the here and now.

4   Evaluation

In this section, we evaluate the Gander conceptual model to ascertain how well existing protocols for mobile networks can support personalized searches of the here and now.

We developed a simulation-based imple-mentation that executes each query over a model of PNet data and dynamics and returns a list of ranked results. We use our amuse-ment park scenario and data we collected about Disney World's Magic Kingdom in Or-lando, Florida. Our simulation includes static nodes that represent 30 attractions, 12 restau-rants, and 8 restrooms. We populated the park with 20,000 visitors and simulate visitors' movements along paths at an average speed of 0.5 mph. Fig. 2 shows an example of the input; yellow discs are rides, green discs are restaurants, orange discs are restrooms, and

Fig. 2. The data input to our query simulator

pink spots indicate visitors. In this figure we only placed 100 visitors so that other ele-ments are visible. We use ride wait times published by Lines [21]; we collected wait time data every 60 seconds on a single day. Simulated visitors carry timestamped data about amenities they have visited recently. Static nodes provide data about fixed entities and metadata (e.g., ride name, its thrill factor and location).

In our prototype, a Gander query can choose from one of four protocols: *flooding*, *probabilistic propagation*, *location-based*, and *probabilistic sampling*, which are repre-sentative of commonly used paradigms in mobile querying. Fig. 3 depicts each protocol. Our evaluation focuses on the utility of Gander's relevance metrics to personalize search and the impact of different query protocol behaviors on the quality of search results.

We issued six queries, all with the same string ("thrill ride") and constraint ("within 75 ft of a restaurant") but different relevance metrics: **Q1:** wait time; **Q2:** distance from me; **Q3:** thrill; **Q4:** wait time then distance from me; **Q5:** wait time then thrill; **Q6:** thrill then wait time. We report results using three of Gander's protocols: flooding with a range of three hops, probabilistic with a range of three hops and propagation probability of 0.5, and probabilistic sampling with a probability of responding of 0.5; we limit propagation to within 10 hops for tractability. A node is considered reachable from another if the two are within 7.5 feet of each other; we model dropped packets using a loss probability associated with a link and experiment with different link qualities.

Fig. 4 shows a sample result. Here, the Gander result is a subset of the ideal with small differences. One result is missing (Tom Sawyer Island), and some data is old (as mea-sured by timestamps). This results in stale data (e.g., the wait time for Pirate Tutorial). Such differences are likely to be small in PNets (since the data collected is relatively

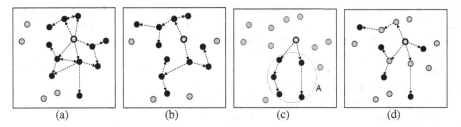

Fig. 3. Query routing protocols. (a) Flooding. Every node in a given range (2 hops) retransmits the query. (b) Probabilistic Propagation. Every node in a given range (3 hops) that receives the packet retransmits it to 2 random neighbors. (c) Location. The query reaches nodes in region A. (d) Probabilistic Sampling. The query reaches any 5 nodes.

fresh), but they can impact relevance rankings. The alternative, i.e., searching via the Internet, would be more severely impacted by even moderately out of date data. This highlights a fundamental differences between PNets and the Internet: data volatility.

```
2011-04-09 15:00:00.0 Tom Sawyer Island {waittime=5.0, thrill=2}
2011-04-09 15:00:00.0 Regal Carrousel {waittime=5.0, thrill=3}
2011-04-09 15:00:00.0 Mickey's PhilharMagic {waittime=10.0, thrill=4}
2011-04-09 08:37:00.0 Pirate Tutorial {waittime=26.0, thrill=5}
2011-04-09 15:00:00.0 Dumbo {waittime=19.0, thrill=5}
2011-04-09 15:00:00.0 Snow White {waittime=17.0, thrill=6}
2011-04-09 15:00:00.0 Pirates of the Caribbean {waittime=12.0, thrill=6}
2011-04-09 15:00:00.0 Tomorrowland Speedway {waittime=29.0, thrill=8}
2011-04-09 15:00:00.0 Splash Mountain {waittime=29.0, thrill=10}
```
(a)

```
2011-04-09 15:00:00.0 Regal Carrousel {waittime=5.0, thrill=3}
2011-04-09 15:00:00.0 Mickey's PhilharMagic {waittime=10.0, thrill=4}
2011-04-09 15:00:00.0 Dumbo {waittime=19.0, thrill=5}
2011-04-09 08:32:00.0 Pirate Tutorial {waittime=21.0, thrill=5}
2011-04-09 15:00:00.0 Snow White {waittime=17.0, thrill=6}
2011-04-09 14:55:00.0 Pirates of the Caribbean {waittime=12.0, thrill=6}
2011-04-09 15:00:00.0 Tomorrowland Speedway {waittime=29.0, thrill=8}
2011-04-09 14:20:00.0 Splash Mountain {waittime=29.0, thrill=10}
```
(b)

Fig. 4. Results for Query 3. (a) ideal query results. (b) Gander query results with flooding.

Gander Queries Reflect the Ground Truth. We evaluate Gander using the discounted cumulative gain (DCG) [16] of a ranked list of results, which compares how useful a result is to the user and its ranked position in the set. The intuition is simple: since a result with a lower ranking is less likely to be used, a result's gain is discounted as the position decreases. We compare the result of executing a Gander query with the *ground truth*, i.e., we compute the DCG for a list of search results as: $DCG_p = \sum_{i=1}^{p} \frac{rel_{d_i}}{\log_2(i+1)}$, where p is the size of the result set, and rel_{d_i} is an integer that reflects the result's position in the ideal query's rankings. A query result d returned with ranking i is graded on a scale from 1 (least relevant) to n, where n is the number of items returned by the ideal query. The value of rel_{d_i} is determined by the ranked position j of the item in the ideal result: $rel_{d_i} = n/j$. We normalize computed DCG values based on the ideal result by calculating the DCG for the ideal result ($IDCG$) and dividing each DCG by $IDCG$, generating a set of normalized values, $nDCG$.

We use DCG values to evaluate how well queries reflect the PNet, and we plot this for varying connection qualities for Query 1 (Fig. 5). Different query protocols perform differently. All of the protocols do a good job of reflecting the ground truth, especially under reasonable connection qualities ($> 50\%$ success of delivery). Probabilistic Sampling performs poorly when the connection quality is poor; this is because the queries propagate over longer paths, sampling a wider space of

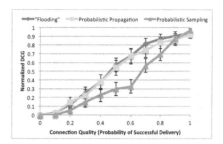

Fig. 5. Query Quality vs. Link Quality

the PNet. These longer paths are more susceptible to low link quality, as the probability of a dropped packet is multiplicative. However, when the quality of the links is high, Probabilistic Sampling's performance surpasses the other protocols, motivating that certain queries need to broaden their search space and query protocols that enable such capabilities are necessary. Flooding and Probabilistic Sampling, on the other hand, sampling sometimes suffer from localization around the query issuer.

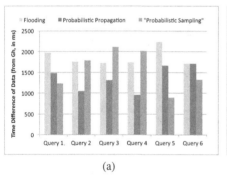

(a)

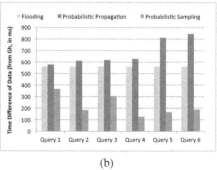

(b)

Fig. 6. Age of responses (a) 50% of packets dropped (b) perfect connectivity

Another way to highlight the difference between the Gander query and the ideal one is to look at the difference in results' time stamps. Fig. 6 shows the measured time stamp differences for the three protocols across all six queries. Fig. 6(a) shows that, given faulty communication links, the time stamp differences between an ideal query and a Gander query result vary widely. However, as the quality of the links increases, we see a drastic difference between the freshness of the data returned by Probabilistic Sampling in comparison to the other protocols. This is especially evident when the loss probability decreases to 0, shown in Fig. 6(b). The density of connections in a PNet (our nodes had an average of 18 network neighbors) makes it possible to select nodes at random to sample, and this Probabilistic Sampling achieves better coverage than flooding or probabilistic sampling since the latter end up restricting their searches to nearby devices. This latter result specifically motivates that some situations may demand reliable communication protocols that better enable search to reflect the ground truth efficiently. More generally, these results demonstrate that having a formal understanding of the structure of the results of queries given different query processing protocols could be informative in selecting the appropriate query protocol for a given query, user, and environment. Future work will build on our existing conceptual model to create an understanding of incremental Gander query processing that relates the results of a query processing protocol (including relevance rankings) to the ideal result. This will allow formal mathematical reasoning about the quality of a Gander query result.

Relevance Matters. It is common to compare rankings by counting *inversions* [4]. Given two rankings, we fix one set of rankings and compute how much out of order results in the other ranking are. To demonstrate that using different relevance metrics has a significant impact on results, we com-

Query	1	2	3	4	5	6
1	0	3.74	2.29	0.85	0.91	1.08
2		0	3.40	3.65	3.93	3.53
3			0	2.35	2.12	0.78
4				0	0.96	2.12
5					0	1.91
6						0

Fig. 7. Average inversion counts

pute the number of inversions returned by queries that are identical other than their use of relevance. Fig. 7 compares our six queries, given everything else (the network, the location of the query issuer, and the state of the data) is held constant. This identifies two equivalence classes of queries: {Query 1, Query 4, Query 5} and {Query 3, Query 6}. The average number of inversions of rankings from Query 3 and Query 6 was 0.78. Within the class {Query 1, Query 4, Query 5}, the average number of inversions was always less than 1. For all other combinations, there was a significant number of inversions ($>\sim$ 2) when comparing two result sets' rankings. Given our relevance metrics, this is reasonable. For example, Query 1 uses only the single relevance metric wait time, while Query 4 uses a relevance metric of wait time breaking ties using the distance from the query issuer. Inversions in rankings returned by these two queries result exactly from resolving ties.

Clearly, personalized relevance metrics have a dramatic effect on which results are presented and in what order. This could drive future work in assistive Gander interfaces that help users identify similar queries or queries that will help them more effectively distinguish physical aspects of the PNet environment.

It is apparent that existing query processing protocols for dynamic networks are a feasible starting point for supporting personalized search of the here and now. Our evaluation and conceptual model have exposed two key aspects necessary for Gander queries in these dynamic environments: (*i*) search processing must be tailored to PNets and search of the here and now and (*ii*) the semantics of search execution must be formalized (i.e., Q, the Gander query, must be formally related to G_h, the ideal result).

5   Conclusions

PNet Search Requires Tailored Reflective Protocols. Different styles of search processing provide different qualities of results in terms of their timely reflection of the ground truth. Gander queries inherently carry information that can benefit the protocols' execution, for example by directing queries towards areas of the PNet more likely to have relevant results or by taking advantage of reliable connectivity when possible to achieve a wider coverage of the space sampled by the query. Thus the results above motivate *reflective* protocols that can adapt their behavior to the nature of the PNet, its capabilities, the data it contains, and the results of previous similar searches.

We omitted a performance evaluation in this paper. As we develop protocols tailored for Gander queries, it will be essential to perform a thorough performance evaluation that measures the network aspects of Gander query processing from all directions, including measuring the overhead (in terms of communication, storage, and energy consumed on users' devices) and delay in receiving query results, coupling evaluation in simulation with evaluation in live PNets.

Search Execution Demands Formal Semantics. More interestingly, the use of partial functions in our conceptual model maps intuitively to *incremental evaluation* in which a search execution starts with a completely undefined function and gradually increases the size of the subset of the domain for which the function is defined.

One may expect that query execution should yield G_h, but achieving this exact reflection of the environment is unreasonable in practical PNets. Instead, we want to provide guarantees with which a query protocol realizes G_h in computing Q. If the protocol maintains a relationship between Q and G_h that has certain structural properties, we can reason about the results in the context of the posed query. An example of a query protocol that exhibits good structure is one that ensures that $Q \subseteq G_h$, i.e., Q will never contain a result that is not in G_h, but there may exist valid results we have not (yet) discovered. Results' relevance values are correct in G_h, i.e., the relative ordering of elements a and b in Q is the same as their relative ordering in G_h. We could envision a weaker relationship in which Q is always less defined than G_h, but in addition the values returned in Q may be somewhat different (within some τ) of the actual values. We could also envision the opposite: that $Q \supseteq G_h$, i.e., we start by assuming that the set of valid results is *larger* than the ideal query and gradually trim results out of Q. Explicitly relating the structure of Q to G_h allows us to reason about the *fidelity* of a query (and its query protocol). Our goal is to create query protocols that (provably) maintain structural relationships between G_h and Q, though practically we can never know G_h.

As the digital world becomes increasingly accessible, we need to access the vast amount of information available in our Personalized Networked Spaces. We introduced Gander, a search engine for personalized search of the here and now. A key contribution of Gander is use of a multi-dimensional specification of relevance, which provides a personalized search of a PNet from the perspective of a query issuer. We derived a conceptual model that mathematically defines Gander query processing and relevance in terms of partial functions. This model gives a formal foundation that maps to the formulation of protocols that incrementally evaluate a Gander query and allows us to reason about the semantics of results returned by a distributed implementation of a Gander query. We have provided a simulation-based evaluation in a large-scale PNet; our results illustrate the expressiveness of this approach and highlight the fact that using personalized relevance metrics can give increased value to the user of ranked search results.

References

1. Ahlers, D., Boll, S.: Beyond position–spatial context for mobile information retrieval systems. In: Proc. of WPNC, pp. 129–134 (2009)
2. Assa, J., Cohen-Or, D., Milo, T.: Displaying data in multidimensional relevance space with 2d visualization maps. In: Proc. of Visualization, pp. 127–134 (1997)
3. Atzori, L., Iera, A., Morabito, G.: The internet of things: A survey. Computer Networks 54(15), 2787–2805 (2010)
4. Bansal, M., Fernandez-Baca, D.: Computing distances between partial rnakings. Information Processing Letters 109(4), 238–241 (2008)
5. Beard, K., Sharma, V.: Multidimensional ranking for data in digital spatial libraries. Int'l. J. on Digital Libraries, 153–160 (1997)
6. Bettini, C., Brdiczka, O., Henricksen, K., Indulska, J., Nicklas, D., Ranganathan, A., Riboni, D.: A survey of context modelling and reasoning techniques. Pervasive and Mobile Computing 6(2), 161–180 (2010)
7. Bolliger, P., Ostermaier, B.: Koubachi: A mobile phone widget to enable affective communication with indoor plants. In: Proc. of MIRW, pp. 63–66 (2007)
8. Chen, A.: Context-Aware Collaborative Filtering System: Predicting the User's Preference in the Ubiquitous Computing Environment. In: Strang, T., Linnhoff-Popien, C. (eds.) LoCA 2005. LNCS, vol. 3479, pp. 244–253. Springer, Heidelberg (2005)
9. de Almeida, V., Guting, R., Behr, T.: Querying moving objects in secondo. In: Proc. of MDM, p. 47 (May 2006)
10. Djafri, N., Fernandes, A.A., Paton, N.W., Griffiths, T.: Spatio-temporal evolution: querying patterns of change in databases. In: Proc. of ACMGIS, pp. 35–41 (2002)
11. Egenhofer, M., Franzosa, R.: Point-set topological relations. Int'l. J. of Geographical Info. Sys. 5(2), 161–174 (1991)
12. Elahi, B.M., Römer, K., Ostermaier, B., Fahrmair, M., Kellerer, W.: Sensor ranking: A primitive for efficient content-based sensor search. In: Proc. of IPSN, pp. 217–228 (2009)
13. Erwig, M., Schneider, M.: Developments in spatio-temporal query languages. In: Proc. of DEXA, pp. 441–449 (1999)
14. Erwig, M., Schneider, M.: Spatio-temporal predicates. IEEE Trans. on Knowledge and Data Eng. 14, 881–901 (2002)
15. Güting, R.H., Böhlen, M.H., Erwig, M., Jensen, C.S., Lorentzos, N., Nardelli, E., Schneider, M., Viqueira, J.R.R.: Chapter 4: Spatio-temporal Models and Languages: An Approach Based on Data Types. In: Sellis, T.K., Koubarakis, M., Frank, A., Grumbach, S., Güting, R.H., Jensen, C., Lorentzos, N.A., Manolopoulos, Y., Nardelli, E., Pernici, B., Theodoulidis, B., Tryfona, N., Schek, H.-J., Scholl, M.O. (eds.) Spatio-Temporal Databases. LNCS, vol. 2520, pp. 117–176. Springer, Heidelberg (2003)
16. Järvelin, K., Kekäläinen, J.: Cumulated gain-based evaluation of IR techniques. ACM Trans. on Info. Sys. 20, 422–446 (2002)
17. Jones, Q., Grandhi, S., Karam, S., Whittaker, S., Zhou, C., Terveen, L.: Geographic place and community information preferences. CSCW 17(2-3), 137–167 (2008)
18. Kortuem, G., Kawsar, F., Fitton, D., Sundramoorthy, V.: Smart objects as building blocks for the internet of things. IEEE Internet Computing 14(1), 44–51 (2010)
19. Kreveld, M., Reinbacher, I., Arampatzis, A., Zwol, R.: Multi-dimensional scattered ranking methods for geographic information retrieval. GeoInform 9, 61–84 (2005)
20. Lamming, M., Newman, W.: Activity-based information retrieval: Technology in support of personal memory. In: Proc. of IFIP World Computer Congress on Personal Computers and Intelligent Systems – Information Processing (1992)

21. Disney World Lines App (Touring Plans),
    `http://www.touringplans.com/walt-disney-world-lines`
22. Manning, C.D., Raghavan, P., Schutze, H.: Intro. to Information Retrieval (2009)
23. Mountain, D., MacFarlane, A.: Geographic information retrieval in a mobile environment: evaluating the needs of mobile individuals. J. of Info. Science 33, 515–530 (2007)
24. Ostermaier, B., Römer, K., Mattern, F., Fahrmair, M., Kellerer, W.: A real-time search engine for the web of things. In: Proc. of IOT, pp. 1–8 (2010)
25. Rajamani, V., Julien, C., Payton, J., Roman, G.-C.: Inquiry and Introspection for Non-deterministic Queries in Mobile Networks. In: Chechik, M., Wirsing, M. (eds.) FASE 2009. LNCS, vol. 5503, pp. 401–416. Springer, Heidelberg (2009)
26. Reichenbacher, T.: Geographic relevance in mobile services. In: Proc. of LocWeb (2009)
27. Si, H., Kawahara, Y., Kurasawa, H., Morikawa, H., Aoyama, T.: A context-aware collaborative filtering algorithm for real world oriented content delivery service. In: Proc. of Metapolis and Urban Life Workshop (2005)

A Mean-Variance Based Index for Dynamic Context Data Lookup

Shubhabrata Sen and Hung Keng Pung

School of Computing, National University of Singapore
{shubhabrata.sen,dcsphk}@nus.edu.sg

Abstract. primary functionality of context aware applications is the retrieval of different types of context data from various context sources and adapting their behavior accordingly. In order to facilitate context aware application development, a context aware middleware must provide an effective context data management and lookup strategy. The use of a traditional index for indexing dynamic context data is not feasible due to the high update overhead. In this paper, we propose a context data indexing mechanism that utilizes the statistical properties of data viz. the mean and variance to cluster similar data values together and minimizes the need for frequent index updates. Experimental results indicate that the performance of the proposed index structure is satisfactory with respect to the query response time and query accuracy together with a low maintenance overhead.

Keywords: Context-awareness, Dynamic data, Context data management, Context Lookup.

1 Introduction

The recent advances in the fields of pervasive and ubiquitous computing have led to an increased focus towards the development of sophisticated context-aware applications. Context-aware applications need to efficiently retrieve and manage context data from different context sources. A context source here refers to an entity (physical or virtual) that is responsible for the generation of context data. In order to facilitate the development of context-aware applications, there has been an increased research interest towards the development of context-aware middleware [1][2]. An integral component of a context-aware middleware is a data management component that can effectively manage multiple different types of context data from a variety of context sources as well as support the context lookup operation over multiple context sources. The context lookup process can be defined as the process of identifying the context sources that an application should acquire data from and the retrieval of the data from these sources.

The notion of 'context' [3] can be defined as any data that can be used to characterize the situation of an entity involved in the user-application interaction. Context data can be either static or dynamic. Dynamic context data changes asynchronously and frequently such as the location of a person and the temperature in an office. As context-aware applications primarily operate by adapting to context

A. Puiatti et al. (Eds.): MobiQuitous 2011, LNICST 104, pp. 101–112, 2012.

changes, the context data involved in these applications is primarily dynamic. The involvement of dynamic attributes makes the context lookup process more challenging as the applications need to deal with continuously changing data values. An index structure designed to work with dynamic data needs to handle the update overheads caused due to frequently changing data.

Context-aware applications often need to identify a subset of context sources from a collection that satisfy some particular conditions. Such context lookup queries are similar to the range queries observed in databases. As part of our current research project Coalition [4] aimed towards developing a prototype of a context-aware middleware, semantic peer-to-peer overlays are used to aid context data lookup. Context sources are grouped according to the semantics of the data provided by them. However, even within a single semantic group, there can be a large number of context sources that can hamper the processing of range queries as the query needs to be sent to every context source.

In this paper, we propose an indexing mechanism that attempts to provide an index structure similar to that of databases for dynamic context data. The index functions by partitioning context data into multiple range clusters and reduces the search space for a query. In order to minimize the index update overhead for dynamic data, we utilize the observation presented in [5] that states that the statistical properties of data viz. the mean and variance are more resistant to change than the actual data values and can be used to construct indexes for dynamic data. Our proposed index utilizes this observation to develop an index for dynamic context data that can be utilized by applications to resolve range and point queries over context data.

The rest of the paper is organized as follows. We give an overview of our Coalition system in Section 2. Section 3 gives the description of the mean-variance calculation process over dynamic data. We discuss the index construction and context lookup operations in Section 4. The current experimental results are described in Section 5. The related work is discussed in Section 6. Section 7 concludes the paper with future research directions.

2   System Overview

The Coalition middleware uses two concepts to provide an abstract representation of context data – *operating spaces* and *context spaces*. The context data representation techniques used in Coalition is illustrated in Fig. 1. An operating space is defined as a person, object or place that provides a common interface for managing the context data retrieved from the context sources affiliated to it. This interface is maintained as a software module defined as the *operating space gateway (OSG)*. Coalition categorizes the operating spaces into multiple domain classes termed as *context spaces* such as shops and person where each context space has a set of attributes. OSGs sharing an attribute within a particular context domain are grouped into a P2P network with the OSGs as the peers. This P2P network is defined as a *semantic cluster*. Context-aware applications can use Coalition to acquire context data through a SQL-based query interface [6]. The query processor of Coalition receives and parses queries to identify the relevant context space and semantic cluster.

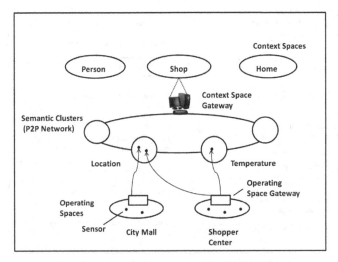

Fig. 1. Context Data representation in Coalition

The query is then distributed within the semantic cluster and each OSG processes the query against its local data store as no data is stored within the middleware. In the absence of any ordering within a semantic cluster, the only option for resolving the query is by flooding the entire p2p network which can prove to be expensive if the number of OSGs within a semantic cluster is large. In this paper, we attempt to address this issue by providing an index that creates an ordering amongst the OSGs in a semantic cluster.

3 Using Mean and Variance to Index Dynamic Data

As mentioned previously, the mean-variance based indexing scheme proposed in this paper is partly based on the idea described in [5].The motivation behind using the mean and variance properties of data to build an index is that even though a data item may be dynamic, the associated mean and variance values are relatively stable. For example, sensory data like temperature changes continuously but the changes are confined within a range for a significant period of time. Hence, indexes constructed using the statistical properties of data are expected to have a lower index updating cost. If a data attribute A is dynamic and continuously changing and has a set of historical values A_1, A_2, A_3, ..., A_n, the mean value of A is denoted by μ_A and is calculated as the sum of the values divided by the sample size. The variance for attribute A is denoted by δ_A and the formula for calculating the bias-corrected sample variance is given by

$$\delta_A = 1/(n-1) \sum_{k=1}^{n} (A_k - \mu_A)^2 \tag{1}$$

The mean and variance values calculated for a given context attribute are used to generate the range clusters that constitute our proposed index. We utilize the basic structure of the mean and variance calculation process as discussed in [5]. The calculations are carried out within the OSG of an operating space. An overview of the mean-variance calculation process is given in Fig. 2.

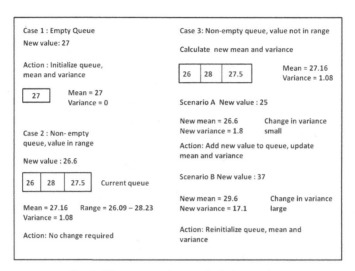

Fig. 2. The mean-variance calculation process

A dynamic data attribute results in a continuous influx of data values and attempting to use the entire set of data values for calculation will be expensive in terms of memory as well as processing. We use a dynamic queue to hold the values over which the mean and variance is calculated as compared to the sliding window approach adopted in [5]. As observed, no changes are required as long as the data value stays within the mean-variance interval. Since the data changes according to the expected pattern, the mean-variance parameters are left unchanged. If the data value exceeds the interval, the mean-variance values are updated and the change in the variance is used to assert whether the data pattern is changing. The change in variance is compared against a pre-defined threshold. A large change in the variance causes the queue to be reinitialized and the process is restarted whereas in the other case, the mean-variance values are updated and the new data value is added to the queue.

4   Mean-Variance Based Index for Context Data Lookup

4.1   Index Structure for Context Lookup

The proposed index structure utilizes the mean and variance values calculated within each OSG to partition the OSGs into multiple range clusters that can reduce the search space for a query. As the index is required to operate within a context aware middleware where OSGs can leave and join the system in a dynamically, a clustering algorithm that can generate clusters incrementally as new data values are received needs to be used. The sequential leader clustering algorithm [7] generates clusters incrementally according to the sequence of input values and can produce a large number of small sized clusters. We propose a clustering algorithm as part of our index structure that is a variant of the leader clustering algorithm that strives to avoid this problem.

The proposed index structure operates within the scope of a single semantic cluster. As of now, only single valued numerical context data attributes are supported. As every OSG in a semantic cluster contains the data value for the corresponding attribute, each OSG represents a data sample. All the OSGs are assigned to a single cluster during the initial phase of index construction when no clusters are present. This process is continued till the size of the cluster exceeds a system-defined threshold for the maximum cluster size.

The first step in the clustering process consists of the server retrieving the current value from every OSG within the cluster for the following parameters: the mean-variance range bounds ($[\mu\text{-}\delta, \mu\text{+}\delta]$), the data value for the context attribute and a unique identifier assigned by the server to the OSG during registration. These values are stored in separate tables and are indexed using the unique identifier. The process of identifying the initial clusters is highlighted in Fig. 3.

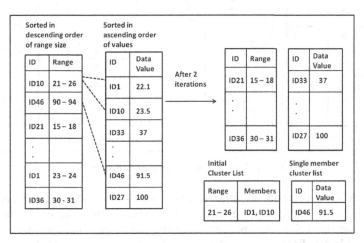

Fig. 3. The identification of the initial clusters

The clustering process aims to group OSGs with similar data change patterns. In order to achieve this, the mean-variance ranges are taken to be the cluster bounds and the data values falling within a particular mean-variance range are assigned to the same cluster. In order to facilitate this operation, the mean-variance range table is sorted in descending order of range size as the larger sized ranges will have a better chance of accommodating more data values and the data value table is sorted in ascending order. Once a data value is assigned to a cluster, the corresponding identifier is used to delete the corresponding entries from both the tables so that these entries are not considered further. If the only data value falling within a particular mean-variance range is found to be the one corresponding to the same OSG, the OSG is added to the single member cluster list. The cluster identification process is carried out until the range table is empty. The main operation of the algorithm involves the assigning of data values to the clusters. Since the data values are stored in a sorted table, an approach similar to binary search can be used to identify the subset of values to be considered for every cluster bound. With this assumption, the running time of the algorithm can be taken to be as O(nlogn) where n is the number of data values. However, since the size of both the tables is expected to decrease gradually due to the removal of the matching values, the running time of the algorithm in practice is expected to be faster.

The next step is the generation of the clusters that constitute the index. Since there can be a large number of small sized clusters generated during the initial phase, these clusters are merged to keep the total number of clusters low. After the initial clusters have been identified, they are arranged in order of their cluster bounds in preparation for merging. The final cluster generation process is described in Fig. 4.

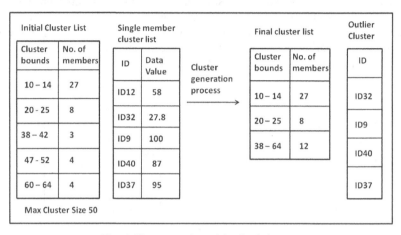

Fig. 4. The generation of the final clusters

A cluster is merged with its adjacent cluster only if the following two conditions are satisfied – both the size of the cluster being merged as well the size of the cluster after merging stay below 50% of the maximum cluster size. This heuristic is utilized to keep the clusters lightly loaded. After the final clusters are generated, the extent of some of the cluster bounds will increase due to merging. Consequently, some of the OSGs in the single member cluster list can now be allotted to one of the clusters. If the single member cluster list still contains some members after this operation, these indicate data values that are not part of any of the present clusters. In a typical clustering scenario, these values would be considered as outliers. However, they still represent valid values in our case and we cannot discard them. In order to handle these values, we designate a special cluster known as an *outlier cluster*. The outlier cluster is used to store the values that cannot be currently assigned to any of the existing clusters. After all the clusters have been finalized, the corresponding OSGs register with their allotted clusters. The semantic cluster now consists of a number of range clusters each of which forms a separate P2P network.

4.2   Maintenance of the Index Structure

After the initial clusters have been identified, subsequent OSGs are assigned to one of the clusters depending on their attribute values. The outlier cluster is used to accommodate the OSGs that cannot be currently assigned to any cluster. Whenever a cluster or an outlier cluster exceeds the maximum cluster size threshold, the clustering process discussed above is invoked within that cluster. Hence, even though the initial cluster bounds may not be very fine-grained, the clustering performance improves as more data values are received. The index structure keeps evolving continuously as OSGs join and leave the system. After an OSG has been assigned to a cluster, it is possible for the OSG to move to a different cluster if its data pattern changes. A large shift in the variance value during the mean-variance calculation process can be taken as the indication to check if a cluster update operation is required. Alternatively, the OSG can periodically check its value against the cluster bounds and decide if it needs to move to a different cluster. This policy cannot be dictated by the server and it needs to be enforced within an OSG. The server periodically checks the cluster sizes in order to ensure that smaller size clusters are merged with adjacent clusters to keep the number of clusters low. Also, clusters with no members are removed from the system.

4.3   Context Lookup Using the Index

The context lookup in Coalition is carried out by issuing SQL style queries that specify the data acquisition conditions using range-search conditions. Since the query issuer is not expected to know the number of OSGs satisfying the query conditions, each application submits the number of answers expected for the query. The Coalition query processor redirects the query to the appropriate semantic cluster. The query parameters are compared against the range clusters to generate a set of candidate clusters that are expected to have the answer. The query processing operation is depicted in Fig. 5. In case the query parameters are not confined in a single cluster, the outlier cluster is included as part of the candidate cluster set. The processing of a query within a single cluster is controlled using the number of query answers received and a system-defined timeout that controls the duration for which a query is processed within the cluster.

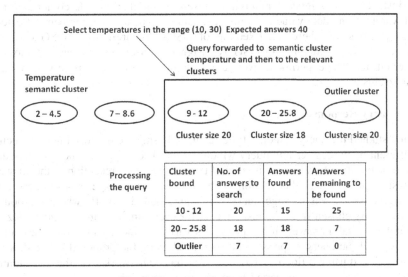

Fig. 5. The context lookup operation

The query is processed by flooding it in every cluster in the candidate set. For each cluster, the number of expected answers is compared with the cluster size and the number of answers received is compared with the lesser of the two values. This ensures that the number of answers to be searched within a cluster takes the current cluster size into account. This operation is then repeated in the next cluster in the candidate cluster list with all the parameters suitably updated as observed in Fig. 5. This process ensures that the response time for a query is minimized by customizing the search operation in each range cluster. The context lookup operation terminates either when all the requested number of answers have been received or when the timeout value expires for the last cluster in the candidate cluster list.

5   Experimental Results

The proposed index structure was implemented and integrated with a prototype of the Coalition middleware. A Dell PowerEdge T300 server with four 2.83 Ghz quad-core Intel Xeon CPU was used as the server. Multiple operating spaces were simulated by running multiple instances of the OSG module on 6 desktop PCs where each PC had an Intel Core 2 Duo 2.83 GHz CPU and runs the Windows XP OS. The data set used for testing comprised of a combination of real world and simulated values to ensure randomness. Half of the values were drawn from the Intel lab data set [8]. This set has multiple sensor readings of different physical properties like temperature, humidity etc over a period of time. The test data was generated by taking samples of different lengths from the data stream associated with a sensor for different sensors. The mean and variance values were then calculated over these samples. The simulated data was obtained using a random number generator. A set of values randomly chosen from the set (0, 1000) were designated to be the mean values as well as the data values whereas the variance values were chosen randomly from the set (0, 1.5). Each OSG instance was assigned a randomly chosen unique data sample comprising of a mean, variance and data value from this test data set. The test environment reflected a stable system state wherein a fixed no of OSGs are present, no OSG enters or leaves the system and after an OSG is assigned to a cluster it does not move to another cluster. The experiments were conducted using a context space with a single semantic cluster.

5.1   Query Response Time

We first studied the query response times achieved using the proposed index structure for different network sizes and query window sizes. The response time was measured as the time duration between the issuing of the query and the reception of the answers. The results presented in this section were taken as the average of 400 query runs. Each query issued was a range query with range bounds (A, B) where the bounds were randomly chosen from the test data set for each run. The query window size or the number of valid answers for a query was varied by modifying the range bounds. We compared the query response times achieved using the proposed index structure to that achieved using a flooding based approach. The network size (the total number of OSGs in the system) was varied from 250 to 1500 and the query window size was varied from 10 to 150. The maximum cluster size was set to 50. We highlight the results achieved for the query response time comparison for the case with query window size as 150. The results are illustrated in Fig. 6.

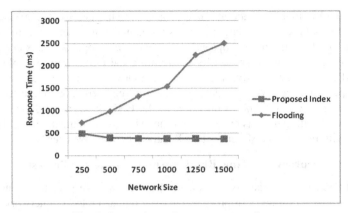

Fig. 6. Comparison of query response times

The results indicate that the proposed index performs quite better than the flooding based approach in terms of variations in query response times with an increase in network size. The increase curve for our proposed index is quite flat as compared to the steep increase for the flooding based approach. This indicates that the proposed approach is scalable with increase in network size. The minimal variation of response time in our approach can be attributed to the fact that the range clusters constituting the index efficiently reduce the search space for a query as compared to flooding.

We further examined the variation in the query response times by varying the network sizes for a particular query window size. The results are illustrated in Fig. 7.

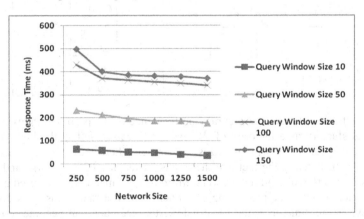

Fig. 7. Query response times with different query window sizes

The results achieved show that the response time increases with an increase in the query window sizes which is expected. It is also observed that for a given query window size, the response time decreases as the network size is increased. The ratio of query window size to network size gives the % of OSGs that contain the valid answers for a query. In Fig. 7, the query window size is kept fixed and the network size is varied. In this case, the ratio gradually decreases which indicates that the subset of the network containing the valid answers becomes smaller as the network size increases. Intuitively, in the absence of any ordering among the OSGs, a larger network size should result in a larger response time which is observed from the results in Fig. 6 for the flooding based approach. However, the proposed index compensates for the increase in the network size by partitioning the OSGs into multiple clusters. Also, as discussed previously, the proposed index is expected to improve its clustering performance as more data values are received. As the range clusters become more fine-grained, the localization of the OSGs with a valid answer occurs faster thereby resulting in a faster response time. The results indicate the scalability of the system with respect to different network and query window sizes.

5.2   Query Accuracy and Time Breakdown for Clustering Process

We first studied the accuracy of the index structure with respect to the number of answers received for a query. In order to measure the accuracy, the network size was kept constant and the query window size was varied. For each query window size, the accuracy measurements were taken as the average of 200 query runs and the query range bounds were varied for each run. The results for a network size of 1500 are highlighted in Table 1.

Table 1.   Accuracy results and timeout values

Accuracy ranges	% of answers received for an accuracy range for different query window sizes				Timeout values for different cluster sizes	
	10	50	100	150	Size	Timeout (ms)
90% - 100%	94	98.5	97.5	97	0 - 10	25
					10 - 20	35
80% - 90%	4	1.5	2.5	1.5	20 - 30	45
70% - 80%	2			1.5	30 - 40	55
					40 - 50	60

The results indicate that the accuracy performance of the proposed index structure is quite satisfactory as a majority of the answers received fall in the high accuracy range for different query window sizes. The cases where the accuracy falls below 90% can be attributed to the fact that the range clusters are P2P networks and are not always expected to return all the answers. Moreover, a timeout value is used as one of the parameters control the processing of a query within a range cluster as discussed previously. If this timeout value is very low, the accuracy can become low and a higher timeout can result in a larger response time. The timeout values used are expected to have a bearing on the query accuracy as well as the response time. We vary the timeout values according to the cluster size and timeouts used in the experiments are highlighted in Table 1.

We next analyzed the time breakdown for the operations involved in the clustering process when a single cluster is split into multiple range clusters. Table 2 shows the time required for the different steps in the clustering process. It is observed that the time required for the clustering process is dominated by the re-registration process that assigns all the OSGs to their respective range clusters. The re-registration overhead will also be present when two clusters are merged. This indicates that unless the dynamism of context data and the membership of OSGs are very high, the frequency of the re-registration process will be low and the latency will not affect the overall system performance.

Table 2. Time breakdown for clustering process

Operation	Time Taken (ms)
Retrieval of data values from OSGs	167
Generating clusters	25
Re-registering OSGs to assigned clusters	560

6   Related Work

Dynamic data indexes need to focus on minimizing the index update overhead. We discuss some of these index structures in this section.

Research efforts in the area of data management for moving objects have led to the development of R-tree based index structures [9][10] that try to reduce the number of index updates. This is achieved by representing the motion of an object as a function and updating the index according to the variation in function parameters. Alternatively, the physical properties of moving objects like the motion trajectories are used to make indexing decisions. These indexing techniques are not generic as they are designed for a particular category of applications and use the special properties of the application class as part of their index design. Hence, these indexes lack applicability outside their target application domain. Sensor networks are also an important area where support for dynamic data management is required. Indexes for sensor networks [11][12] are usually query-driven and operate proactively or reactively according to the query frequency. In order to store frequently changing sensor data in databases, database systems are augmented with uncertainty management components [13]. These databases associate a data value with an interval and probability distributions functions and handle queries using probabilistic operators that define the answer quality. These indexes operate at the sensor level and directly interact with sensor data as compared to our scenario where we consider large scale context sources over wide areas where each context source encompasses multiple sensors.

There have been efforts to support range queries in p2p systems by extending the DHT based data lookup techniques [14][15]. Since DHT systems utilize hash functions to store and lookup data, the usage of these algorithms with dynamic context data will prove to be difficult as the hash value will need to be continuously updated. Also, the DHT model involving a set of nodes which store data according to the key-node mapping is structurally different from our Coalition middleware architecture as we consider multiple autonomous context sources. Since the context sources are autonomous, it will be difficult to impose a DHT based overlay structure in our system. These problems prevent the adoption of DHT based range query techniques as part of our context aware middleware.

7   Conclusion and Future Work

We have presented a mean-variance based index structure to support dynamic context lookup in a context-aware environment and provide support for range and point queries over context data. This index structure uses an incremental clustering approach to partition the OSGs within a semantic cluster into multiple range clusters based on their mean and variance values. The mean and variance values are used as they are relatively more stable than the actual data which changes frequently. The initial experimental results demonstrate that the proposed index structure achieves good response times and is scalable with respect to the increase in network size. The results also indicate that the performance of the index with respect to accuracy is good and the time required for the clustering process is reasonably small. As part of our future work, we plan to carry out more extensive testing of the index and study the impact of the frequent leave/join operations of OSGs on the index performance, provide support for join operations involving multiple attributes and extend the index structure to support string and composite attributes.

References

1. Baldauf, M., Dustdar, S., Rosenberg, F.: A survey on context-aware systems. IJAHUC, 263–277 (2007)
2. Kjær, K.E.: A survey of context-aware middleware. In: 25th Conference on IASTED International Multi-Conference (2007)
3. Dey, A.K.: Understanding and Using Context. Personal and Ubiquitous Computing, 4–7 (2001)
4. Context-Aware Middleware Services and Programming Support for Sentient Computing, http://lucan.ddns.comp.nus.edu.sg:8080/PublicNSS/researchContextAware.aspx
5. Xia, Y., Cheng, R., Prabhakar, S., Lei, S., Shah, R.: Indexing continuously changing data with mean-variance tree. IJHPCN, 263–272 (2008)
6. Xue, W., Pung, H.K., Ng, W.L., Gu, T.: Data Management for Context-Aware Computing. In: EUC (1), pp. 492–498 (2008)
7. Hartigan, J.A.: Clustering Algorithms. Wiley. New York (1975)
8. Intel Lab Data, http://db.csail.mit.edu/labdata/labdata.html
9. Silva, Y.N., Xiong, X., Aref, W.G.: The RUM-tree: supporting frequent updates in R-trees using memos. VLDB J, 719–738 (2009)
10. Saltenis, S., Jensen, C.S., Leutenegger, S.T., Lopez, M.A.: Indexing the Positions of Continuously Moving Objects. In: SIGMOD Conference, pp. 331–342 (2000)
11. Dyo, V., Mascolo, C.: Adaptive Distributed Indexing for Spatial Queries in Sensor Networks. In: DEXA Workshops, pp. 1103–1107 (2005)
12. Diao, Y., Ganesan, D., Mathur, G., Shenoy, P.J.: Rethinking Data Management for Storage-centric Sensor Networks. In: CIDR, pp. 22–31 (2007)
13. Cheng, R., Singh, S., Prabhakar, S.: U-DBMS: A Database System for Managing Constantly-Evolving Data. In: VLDB 1271–1274 (2005)
14. Gao, J., Steenkiste, P.: An Adaptive Protocol for Efficient Support of Range Queries in DHT-Based Systems. In: ICNP, pp. 239–250 (2004)
15. Li, D., Cao, J., Lu, X., Chen, K.: Efficient Range Query Processing in Peer-to-Peer Systems. IEEE Trans. Knowl. Data Eng, 78–91 (2009)

HiCHO: Attributes Based Classification of Ubiquitous Devices

Shachi Sharma[1], Shalini Kapoor[1], Bharat R. Srinivasan[2], and Mayank S. Narula[3]

[1] IBM Research Laboratory, New Delhi, India
[2] Georgia Institute of Technology, Atlanta, United States
[3] Indian Institute of Technology, Kharagpur, India

Abstract. An online and incremental clustering method to classify heterogeneous devices in dynamic ubiquitous computing environment is presented. The proposed classification technique, HiCHO, is based on attributes characterizing devices. These can be logical and physical attributes. Such classification allows to derive class level similarity or dissimilarity between devices and further use it to extract semantic information about relationship among devices. The HiCHO technique is protocol neutral and can be integrated with any device discovery protocol. Detailed simulation analysis and real-world data validates the efficacy of the HiCHO technique and its algorithms.

1 Introduction

Ubiquitous Computing as envisioned by Mark Weiser [14], is a computing paradigm where interconnected computational devices are part of day to day human life and are used invisibly to accomplish a task. Users work with a wide range of heterogeneous devices. These devices can be desktop devices, mobile communicators, digital assistants, wrist watches, game consoles, consumer electronics (e.g., TVs, radios, and refrigerators), cars, sensors, smart meters, video surveillance equipments etc. In many cases, users interact with multiple heterogeneous devices simultaneously. For example, a morning alarm clock instructs coffee machine to start preparing coffee automatically, road sensors inform arrival of vehicles to traffic signal so that it turns on. The alarm clock, coffee machine, road sensors and traffic signal are altogether different types of devices communicating with each other. Hence, design and development of smart applications and systems in ubiquitous computing environment require these heterogeneous devices to discover, identify and communicate with each other.

Today, discovery and identification of the devices is limited by the fact that devices following same protocol standard can find and interconnect with each other. There are instances when (i) devices are to be searched based on criterion like location, functionality, owners, services, etc i.e. the attributes characterizing devices and not by any protocol standard (ii) not only the singleton device but a group of devices sharing some characteristics are to be discovered. For example, consider a smart building with thousands of devices installed by several vendors.

A. Puiatti et al. (Eds.): MobiQuitous 2011, LNICST 104, pp. 113–125, 2012.

This may include air-conditioners, light sensors, access controls, web cams, video surveillance equipments, elevator sensors, telephones, utility meters etc. Each vendor provides its own monitoring capability. Moreover, generic monitoring tools use ip addresses based identification method to act on the remote devices. There is a need to monitor all devices in the building and apply some operations on a set of devices based on their attributes. Suppose if power consumption goes high on a particular day then all the devices (irrespective of the make) in the smart building with high energy consumption are to be switched off; similarly in case of outside temperature falling low, all the air-conditioners in the building are to be instructed to increase temperature. Another example can be of smart grid comprising of sub-stations, voltage regulators, capacitors, meters, reclosers, transmission lines etc. In case of some emergency situation such as fire in some part of the grid, a set of devices in the grid are to be discovered based on attributes such as location so that all the affected devices can be turned off instantly. Hence, one of the requirement for smart applications in ubiquitous computing environment is to *design and develop methods for classifying devices into groups based on criterion like logical attributes.* Based on such classification, it is easy to apply rules and policies, provide secure access control to a group of devices and perform finer grained device management.

Several protocols like Bluetooth, Jini, UpnP enable devices to locate each other [2] [12]. Bluetooth allows finding a set of devices in immediate vicinity based on device type [2]. However, these protocols do not have capability to group devices based on logical attributes as they do for physical attributes. The standard Zigbee defines notion of clusters [15]. In Zigbee, a cluster is a message or collection of messages pertaining to a given application domain. The idea behind clusters is to provide reusability by abstracting clusters across several application domains and placing them in a library organized according to pre-defined functional domains (e.g., lighting, closures, HVAC). *A generic technique to classify devices into groups based on their characteristics is not present today.* There are expected to be 50 billion devices worldwide by 2020, this mechanism, brings in a new paradigm where devices are identified and discovered based on the attributes they support.

In this paper, we propose a technique HiCHO to classify the ubiquitous devices using their logical attributes. This technique is independent of any protocol standard and can be implemented for all protocols. Another important point of discussion is that the set of logical attributes might change with time. For example, for a video camera at traffic signal, measurement of number of vehicles passing through is an important attribute whereas the model of video camera or the RAM it possesses to store images is not important for certain set of policies. Also over a period of time as devices within the vehicle itself become advanced, the measurement of number of cars, vis a vis truck would become increasingly important. Hence there is need to keep the classification mechanism open to add newer attributes.

We believe HiCHO can be used by several enterprises as they create their own intranets of things. With an increase in volume of ubiquitous devices in coming years, a need will arise to control such devices beyond their physical attributes alone. The paper is organized into four sections. Section 2 discusses in detail the HiCHO method. This method is evaluated through simulated devices and also for real-world devices in section 3. The last section 4 contains concluding remarks.

2 HiCHO: Classification Technique for Ubiquitous Devices

Devices in real world have many characteristics such as color, manufacturer, type, owner, number of components, memory etc often known as their attributes. Following [3] [1] attribute and value can be defined as follows,

Definition 1. An Attribute *is a category in which a device can be classified such as 'color'.*

Attributes can be physical such as 'model', 'make' or logical such as 'owner', 'location'.

Definition 2. A Value *is the device's classification within that category, for example, 'red.'*

Attributes and values are free-form strings. Together, an attribute and its associated value form an attribute-value pair or av-pair. A set of av-pairs describes a device. We define,

Definition 3. Characteristics Set (CS) *as the set of all the possible av-pairs possessed by a device.*

For example, a mobile phone may have its *CS* as {(manufacturer, 'Nokia'); (model, 'N72'); (color, 'black'); (wifi, 'no'); (camera, 'yes'); (owner,'john')}. In ubiquitous computing domain, we can assume that the universal attributes set *A* is finite and is known in advance. Such an assumption is not too stringent to make as one can think of a scenario where the vendors and manufacturers of devices provide the information about attributes to standardizing agency whenever they launch a new device or upgrade an existing one. The other option to exempt this assumption is by learning the universal attributes set. It means whenever a device specifies a new attribute, the same is added to the universal attributes set automatically by the system implementing HiCHO technique. However, determining the value domain of an attribute may be difficult in many cases, for example, IP address. Hence, we do not make any assumption on the value set.

There are multiple ways to classify devices. One possibility is on the basis of physical attributes like device type, manufacturer ID, serial number, memory, hardware configuration. Such classification has limitations because - (i) physical attributes fail to provide a high level picture of importance of devices. The administrators instead have to find and feed this information. (ii) Many times, physical attributes are not known to the outside world, especially, human users. Some network tools and probes can retrieve this information but these tools themselves may give inaccurate and incomplete information. (iii) If there is some

```
<?xml version="1.0" ?>
  <!-- Sample XML Document -->
  <ns:deviceData xmlns:ns="urn:foo">
    <ns:attribute id="1">
      <ns:name>deviceType</ns:name>
      <ns:value>MobilePhone</ns:value>
    </ns:attribute>
    <ns:attribute id="2">
      <ns:name>manufacturer</ns:name>
      <ns:value>Nokia</ns:value>
    </ns:attribute>
  <ns:attribute id="3">
      <ns:name>model</ns:name>
      <ns:value>N72</ns:value>
    </ns:attribute>
  ...
  ...
  ...
  </ns:deviceData>
```

Fig. 1. XML document for specifying CS : mobile phone example

change or enhancement in physical attributes, for example, memory increase, CPU change, then devices class may change necessitating re-classification.

Another option could be of grouping the devices manually based on logical attributes. Obviously, manual method is not scalable for huge number of devices. Also, such a classification becomes incomplete and outdated as new devices are added, new attributes are added or existing attributes undergo change. Hence, it is essential to automate the classification process based on logical attributes.

There is an immediate questions how devices specify their CS. The next subsection discusses this.

2.1   Specification of Characteristics Set

There are numerous ways by which a device can specify its CS. We opt to choose XML (Extensible Markup Language) because of its wide usage and applicability. XML is a mature standard and is already in practice for mobile and embedded devices. Menten etal [9] have used XML in designing network device management tools. XML-based messaging system for enabling communication between mobile devices is implemented by Kangasharju etal [7]. XML security specification has been extended and implemented for mobile devices [8]. The usage of XML has increased to the extent that now there are specialized devices in the network that control and manage XML traffic. The World Wide Web Consortium (W3C) has introduced a compression standard (Efficient XML Interchange i.e. EXI Format 1.0 [4]) for XML to bring the web data exchange standard to smart-phones and other power constrained mobile and embedded devices. Figure 1 shows the sample XML document of a mobile phone CS. Note that each attribute is a tuple - (name, value).

2.2   Clustering Devices

Many devices are almost identical to each other and share many similar av-pairs. There can be applications which may be interested in class level information or which are developed for a particular class. Hence, there is a need to classify devices. We resort to clustering methods to partition devices into classes (called clusters) such that (i) devices that belongs to same cluster are similar in some ways (ii) devices that belongs to different clusters are dissimilar in some ways. Clustering is an extensively studied field and is widely used in domains like machine learning, data mining, bio-informatics, databases and statistics. *However, to the best of our knowledge, clustering is neither studied nor employed in the ubiquitous computing domain for classifying devices.* The ubiquitous computing devices have some specific requirements that a clustering method based on logical attributes must adhere to - (i) **on-line:** Since clustering method is to be based on logical attributes possessed by devices, values of these logical attributes may change over time. In some cases, even the attributes may undergo change. Also, clustering should allow devices to register and get classified in a cluster and de-register for de-allocating its class. This is important as in ubiquitous computing domain complete shutdown of devices is unacceptable if some hardware dependent softwares or application softwares are upgraded. (ii) **incremental:** The complete universe of the devices is not known in advance. Hence, clusters are built incrementally over time. This is in contrast to typical data mining problems where complete data set is available beforehand. (iii) **attributes and their values based:** The classification of devices in different groups must be such that while retrieving devices from a large population, it should not consume time. Devices can be searched by specifying complete or partial CS. The search of devices based on input criterion is time critical. If devices are first classified based on attributes then the search domain gets squeezed instantly. Then within those classes, av-pairs are used to find the final answers. Hence, the proposed method is *hierarchical in nature with two levels.* (iv) **capable of working with numeric as well as categorical data:** Attributes are free-form strings but values can be strings or numeric. The clustering method must be able to handle both types of values. The existing literature on clustering addresses the requirements mentioned above individually and not as a complete family. Work by Friedman [5] on attribute based clustering requires complete data set to be available. The clusters are created by calculating the distance between two data points and hence this method works only for numeric data. Real-time clustering algorithm (real-time OPTICS), by Shao etal [10] and stream data clustering by Shuyun etal [13] requires some training data to be available before deploying the algorithm in the environment. Real-time OPTICS is density based clustering method where clusters are constructed around core objects. This method is based on core-distances and hence applies only to numeric data set. Stream data clustering by Shuyun etal [13] first identifies micro-clusters using entropy measures, the online process of updating the micro-clusters is initiated afterwards where these micro-clusters represent the current snapshot of clusters which change over the course of the stream as new points arrive. There are specialized clustering algorithm for categorical data [11] but suffers from short comings like been non real-time and not incremental.

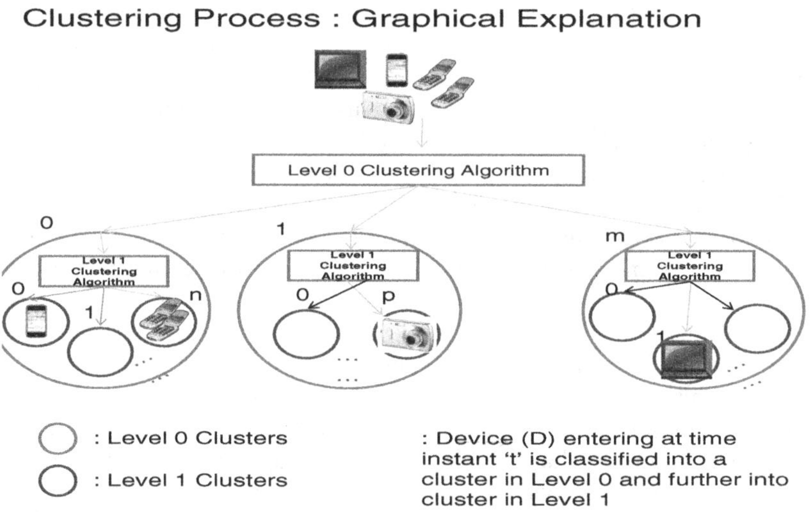

Clustering Process : Graphical Explanation

Fig. 2. Overview of HiCHO Technique

We propose a hierarchical (with two levels) clustering method - Level0 clustering based on attributes and Level1 clustering based attribute-values. As mentioned above, the reason behind designing a two step hierarchical method lies in reducing the search time. The overview of the HiCHO method is shown in Figure 2. We next present the methodology of these two steps in detail.

2.3   Level0 Clustering

The main idea of level0 clustering is to group together the devices whose attribute set is as close to each other as possible. The devices in different clusters have attribute sets as different from each other as possible. Consider two devices D_i and D_j with their attribute sets as A_i and A_j respectively where $A_i \subseteq A$ and $A_j \subseteq A$ where A is the universal attribute set and is known in advance. One possible measure to compute similarity between two attribute sets is by using Jaccard Index [6]. Let C_{ij} be the count of common attributes and U_{ij} be the count of uncommon attributes between devices D_i and D_j, then we define an index, termed as Commonality Index (CI) (Jaccard Index [6]) between D_i and D_j as,

$$CI(D_i||D_j) = \frac{C_{ij}}{C_{ij} + U_{ij}} \qquad (1)$$

We also define cluster representative or CR as,

Definition 4. A Cluster Representative or CR *is a virtual device whose attribute set is the union of attribute sets of all the devices belonging to that cluster.*

Algorithm 1. Level0 Clustering Algorithm

    Input: $C, Re, \varepsilon_0, D_{new}, A_{new}, m$
    Output: probably a new C and Re
1 $max = 0;$
2 $cluster_{num} = 0;$
3 $tempCI[m];$ //a dummy array of size equal to number of clusters to store CI temporary
4 $i = 0;$
5 **if** $(C = \phi)$ **then**
6 | create a new cluster $C_{new};$
7 | assign D_{new} to $C_{new};$
8 | $C = C \cup C_{new};$
9 | create a new cluster representative $R_{new} = A_{new};$
10 | $R = R \cup R_{new};$
11 | return;
12   └

13 **while** $(i < m)$ **do**
14 | Calculate C_{newi} and $U_{newi};$
15 | $CI(D_{new}||Re_i) = C_{newi}/(C_{newi} + U_{newi});$
16 | $tempCI[i] = CI(D_{new}||Re_i);$
17   └ $18\,i++;$

19 //compute maximum of the array values and returns maximum value and cluster index
20 $cluster_{num} = MAXIMUM(tempCI, max);$
21 **if** $(max \geq \varepsilon_0)$ **then**
22 | assign D_{new} to cluster $C_{cluster_{num}};$
23 | $Re_{cluster_{num}} = Re_{cluster_{num}} \cup A_{new};$
24   └

25 **else**
26 | create a new cluster $C_{new};$
27 | assign D_{new} to $C_{new};$
28 | $C = C \cup C_{new};$
29 | create a new cluster representative $R_{new} = A_{new};$
30 | $R = R \cup R_{new};$
31   └

The basis of level0 clustering algorithm are CI and CR. Let there are m clusters and $C = \{C_1, C_2, ..., C_m\}$ be collection of all the clusters and $Re = \{Re_1, Re_2, ..., Re_m\}$ be corresponding collection of cluster representatives at any time t at level 0 when a new device D_{new} enters. Let A_{new} be the attribute set of device D_{new}. Then CI is calculated between D_{new} and cluster representatives of all the m clusters. D_{new} is allocated to the cluster with maximum commonality i.e. the one with maximum value of CI. The cluster representative of selected cluster is then expanded to include new attributes. The complete algorithm is presented in Algorithm 1. A new cluster is created if $CI(D_{new}||Re_k) < \varepsilon_0, \forall k = 1, 2, ..., m$ i.e. D_{new} does not have any significant commonality with any of the existing cluster. When the very first device enters, there is no cluster and a new cluster with first device is created. Here, ε_0 is the level0 clustering parameter and controls the size and number of clusters. We discuss the sensitivity of level0 clustering algorithm with ε_0 in section 3.

2.4 Level1 Clustering

Level1 Clustering is applied on each of the clusters of level0. This clustering is based on av-pairs. Here, we assume that attributes have some weights attached to them. The weights of an attribute may be its importance, its dispersion in the devices population or entropy. Let $W = \{w_1, w_2, ..., w_N\}$ be set of weights

---

Algorithm 2. Level1 Clustering Algorithm

Input: $C_{x1}, \varepsilon_1, D_{new}, A_{new}, nx$
Output: probably a new C_{x1}

```
1   max = 0;
2   cluster_num = 0;
3   tempAvgSI[nx]; //a dummy array of size equal to number of clusters to store SI temporary
4   tempSI[]; // another dummy array to store intermediate values of SI
5   i = 0;
6   j = 0;
7   if (C_{x1} = φ) then
8   |   create a new cluster C_{new};
9   |   assign D_{new} to C_{new};
10  |   C_{x1} = C_{x1} ∪ C_{new};
11  |   return;
12  └
13  while (i < nx) do
14  |   while (j < |C_{x1_i}|) do
15  |   |   tempSI[j] = SI(D_{new}||(D_j ∈ C_{x1_i}));
16  |   └
17  |   tempAvgSI[i] = SUM (values of tempSI)/|C_{x1_i}|;
18  └
19  //compute maximum of the array values and returns maximum value and cluster index
20  cluster_num = MAXIMUM(tempAvgSI, max);
21  if (max ≥ ε_1) then
22  |   assign D_{new} to cluster C_{cluster_num};
23  └
24  else
25  |   create a new cluster C_{new};
26  |   assign D_{new} to C_{new};
27  |   C_{x1} = C_{x1} ∪ C_{new};
28
```

---

of attributes where w_i is weight of attribute a_i. These weights are normalized weights,

$$\sum_{i=1}^{N} w_i = 1 \qquad (2)$$

Between two devices D_i and D_j, we compute following quantities:

1. Find the set of same av-pairs i.e. between characteristic set of CS_i of device D_i and CS_j of device D_j calculate

$$Z_{ij} = CS_i \bigcap CS_j \qquad (3)$$

2. Between D_i and D_j, find the set of those attributes a_k such that
$a_k \in \left\{ Z'_{ij} = A_i \cap A_j \right\}$ and
$\forall a_k \in Z'_{ij}, \quad v_{a_k}(i) \neq v_{a_k}(j)$
where $v_{a_k}(i)$ is the value of attribute a_k for device D_i.

We then define a Similarity Index (SI) between D_i and D_j as,

$$SI(D_i||D_j) = (\alpha + \beta) \sum_{av_k \in Z_{ij}} w_{a_k} + \alpha \sum_{a_k \in Z'_{ij}} w_{a_k} \qquad (4)$$

Here, $\alpha > 0$ and $\beta > 0$ are two parameters that controls the importance given to attributes and av-pairs respectively. One obvious thing is to chose $\alpha < \beta$, assign more importance when av-pair is same. In order to keep SI normalized, a required condition is $\alpha + \beta = 1$.

Let a new device D_{new} finds $C_{x1} = \{C_{x1_1}, C_{x1_2}, ..., C_{x1_{nx}}\}$ nx level 1 clusters within level 0 cluster $C_x \in C$ upon its arrival. For a level0 cluster C_{x1_i}, SI is calculated between D_{new} and all the members of C_{x1_i}. The mean value of SI_{mean} for that cluster is then computed. The process is repeated for all the nx clusters. The device D_{new} is then allocated to that cluster from C_{x1} which has maximum value of SI_{mean} and is greater than the clustering parameter ε_1. The level1 clustering algorithm is presented in Algorithm 2.

3   Performance Evaluation of HiCHO

In this section, we discuss the performance results of our proposed HiCHO technique. Our principal objective here is (i) to demonstrate the scalability of the HiCHO algorithms through simulation (ii) to study the sensitivity of clustering algorithms with respect to clustering parameters ε_0 of level0 and ε_1 of level1 (iii) to show the applicability of the HiCHO for real-world devices. We focus on two performance metrics : (i) average number of clusters created at each level and (ii) the average size of clusters i.e. the average number of devices in a cluster at each level.

We have implemented a simulator that generates characteristics set of devices in XML (as depicted in Figure 1). The attributes from the universal attributes set are chosen following Uniform and Pareto distribution. Uniform distribution is an obvious choice as it corresponds to an extreme case where all attributes have equal probability to be possessed by the devices. In practice, some attributes tend to occur in a large number of devices (e.g. color) than others (e.g. service). This behavior can be modeled by choosing a skewed distribution for selecting attributes. We opt for Pareto distribution because of its wider usage in modeling skewed behavior. The performance of level0 algorithm of HiCHO is shown Figures 3. As depicted in Figure 3 (a), Uniformly distributed CS devices result in more number of clusters compared to Pareto distributed CS devices. This is because of the way CS's are generated by the simulator. For Pareto distributed CS devices, the fewer number of attributes are selected repeatedly whereas for Uniformly distributed CS devices all the attributes are chosen. For a fixed value of ε_0 and maximum size of CS, the number of clusters increase sharply initially as devices enter and then almost becomes constant. The average size of the cluster representatives also remains constant with number of devices as illustrated in Figure 3 (b). The average size of clusters increases gradually with increase in number of the devices as presented in Figure 3 (c). These facts shows scalability of the level0 clustering algorithm. Figures 3 (d)-(f) present sensitivity of level0 clustering algorithm with clustering parameter ε_0 for fixed number of devices and maximum CS size of 10. Lower values of ε_0 results in small number of large clusters whereas high value of ε_0 gives rise to large number of small clusters.

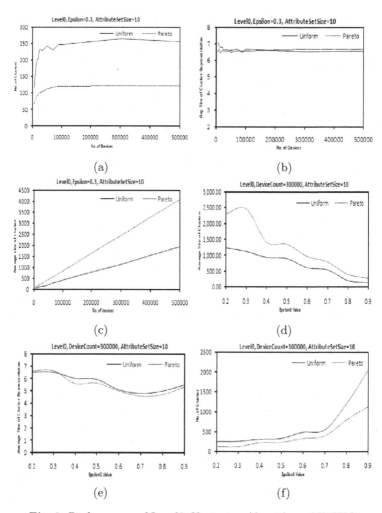

Fig. 3. Performance of Level0 Clustering Algorithm of HiCHO

Hence, fixing ε_0 to middle range is expected to give a balance between number of clusters and cluster sizes. Level1 Clustering is carried out within each cluster created at Level0. The performance results of level1 clustering algorithm is shown in Figures 4. Figure 4 (a) and (b) show that high value of the parameter β compared to α results in large number of small clusters for Uniformly distributed CS devices. Whereas for Pareto distributed CS devices, the choice of parameters α and β have very little impact on number of clusters and cluster sizes as is clear from Figure 4 (c) and (d). For Uniformly distributed CS devices, both the number of clusters and cluster size becomes constant as the clustering parameter ε_1 tends to one. This phenomenon is not observed for Pareto distributed CS devices. In order to validate the feasibility of the HiCHO to real-world devices, we have gathered the attribute-value data of 20 devices owned by

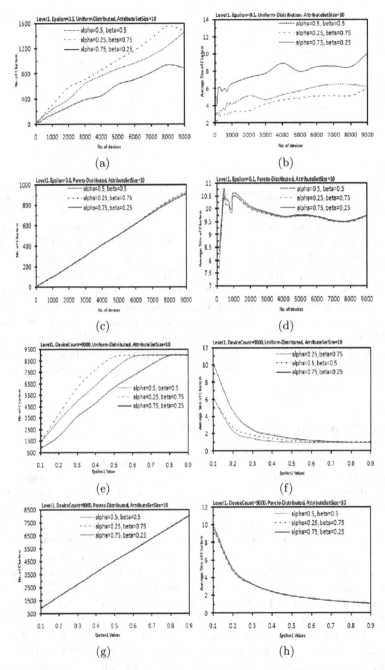

Fig. 4. Performance Results of Level1 Clustering Algorithm of HiCHO

our colleagues at the IBM. These devices are laptops, mobile phones and digital cameras. These 20 devices have maximum of 18 attributes including pixels,

Table 1. Level0 Results of Real world Devices

Cluster id	Cluster Size
0	4
1	7
2	8
3	1

Table 2. Level1 Results of Real world Devices

Cluster id	Cluster Size
01	3
02	1
11	2
12	3
13	2
21	2
22	3
23	3
31	1

owners, model, functional capabilities etc. We fix the level0 clustering parameter ε_0 to 0.6 and level1 clustering parameters α and β to 0.5; ε_1 to 0.45. We then run the HiCHO methods on characteristics set of these 20 devices and results are presented in Table 1 and 2. In spite of the fact that the HiCHO method is applied to a small-scale real world data set, it allows us to understand the clustering pattern in practice. Level0 of HiCHO classifies the 20 devices into 4 classes. The formation of clusters is not based on single attribute such as device type or color rather the combination and presence of attributes govern the creation of clusters at level0. The second step of level1 clustering fine grains clusters within level0 clusters based on both attributes and values. We observe that all the devices of same color and make are combined, or devices belonging to same owner are clubbed together into one cluster, or devices with same protocol like bluetooth are grouped together at level1.

4   Conclusion and Future Work

A classification technique, HiCHO, based on attribute-value pairs of devices is proposed. These attributes are logical including capabilities, functionalities, customized data etc. Devices specify the attribute-value pairs, called Characteristics Set (CS), in XML. In practice, we either expect CS to be available with devices through some configuration or network probes to obtain and transfer CS to back-end server running HiCHO algorithms. The method itself is not tied to any protocol and hence can be integrated with any device discovery protocol. This type of classification is useful in generating class-level logical identifiers and in creating repository of devices for future networks like Internet of Things (IoT). Though we have explained HiCHO in relation to logical attributes, but it can be very well applied to a combination of physical and logical attributes. This will become important for IoT where objects needs to be classified by a combination of physical and logical attributes. So far, we have tested HiCHO for a small set of real-world devices to show the feasibility of the technique. As a future work, we would like to establish the scalability of HiCHO method to a large set of real-world devices.

References

1. Adjie, W.: The design and implementation of an intentional naming system. In: 17th ACM Symposium on Operating Systems Principles, pp. 186–201 (1999)
2. Blueetooth website, http://www.bluetooth.com/
3. CCITT. The Directory Overview of Concepts, Models and Services, X.500 series recommendations (1988)
4. Efficient XML Interchange, http://www.w3.org/TR/exi
5. Friedman, J.H.: Clustering objects on subsets of attributes. Journal of Royal Statistical Society 66(4), 815–849 (2004)
6. Jaccard, P.: Étude comparative de la distribution florale dans une portion des Alpes et des Jura. Bulletin de la Société Vaudoise des Sciences Naturelles 37, 547–579 (1901)
7. Kangasharju, J., Lindholm, T., Tarkoma, S.: Xml messaging for mobile devices: From requirements to implementation. Computer Networks: The International Journal of Computer and Telecommunications Networking 51(16) (2007)
8. Kangasharju, J.: Efficient Implementation of XML Security for Mobile Devices. In: IEEE International Conference on Web Services, pp. 134–141 (2007)
9. Menten, L.E., Murray, H.: Experiences in the application of xml for device management. IEEE Communications Magazine 72(7), 92–100 (2004)
10. Shao, F., et al.: A new real-time clustering algorithm. Journal of Information and Computational Science 7(10), 2110–2121 (2010)
11. Li, T., Ma, S., Ogihara, M.: Entropy-based criterion in categorical clustering. In: Proceedings of the 12th International Conference on Machine Learning (2004)
12. UpnP, http://www.upnp.org/
13. Wang, S., et al.: Entropy based clustering of data streams with mixed numeric and categorical values. In: IEEE/ACIS International Conference on Computer and Information Science, pp. 140–145 (2008)
14. Weiser, M.: The Computer for the Twenty-First Century. Scientific American, 94–104 (1991)
15. Zigbee website, http://www.zigbee.org/

On the Effects of Input Unreliability on Classification Algorithms

Ardjan Zwartjes, Majid Bahrepour, Paul J.M. Havinga,
Johann L. Hurink, and Gerard J.M. Smit

University of Twente
Drienerlolaan 5
7522NB Enschede
The Netherlands
{g.j.zwartjes,m.bahrepour,p.j.m.havinga,j.l.hurink,g.j.m.smit}@utwente.nl

Summary. The abundance of data available on Wireless Sensor Networks makes online processing necessary. In industrial applications, for example, the correct operation of equipment can be the point of interest. The raw sampled data is of minor importance. Classification algorithms can be used to make state classifications based on the available data for devices such as industrial refrigerators.

The reliability through redundancy approach used in Wireless Sensor Networks complicates practical realizations of classification algorithms. Individual inputs are susceptible to multiple disturbances like hardware failure, communication failure and battery depletion. In order to demonstrate the effects of input failure on classification algorithms, we have compared three widely used algorithms in multiple error scenarios. The compared algorithms are Feed Forward Neural Networks, naive Bayes classifiers and decision trees.

Using a new experimental data-set, we show that the performance under error scenarios degrades less for the naive Bayes classifier than for the two other algorithms.

1 Introduction

Online data processing is an important, but complex, task on Wireless Sensor Networks (WSNs) [3]. Even on small WSNs the amount of data that can be sampled by the sensor nodes is considerable. Simple micro-controllers can acquire samples of rates above 10kHz; far more than what can practically be transmitted using current WSN radios. For most applications, however, the raw data itself is not of interest. For example, in domestic fire detection [6] carbon-dioxide readings never need to reach a human operator. The presence of a fire however, is important information. In logistics the state of the monitored products is of importance, while 10-bit temperature readings are of limited value.

Online data processing comes in many forms, ranging from simple schemes to compress the data, to complex event recognition algorithms that draw intelligent conclusions. This last group of algorithms can result in considerable reductions

A. Puiatti et al. (Eds.): MobiQuitous 2011, LNICST 104, pp. 126–137, 2012.

in communication by removing the need to transmit raw sensor readings. Considering that the energy needed to transmit a few bytes of data is significant[10], it is clear that online intelligent processing is a promising area of research.

1.1 Problem Description

Implementing complex intelligent algorithms for WSNs, is a complicated matter. Unreliability of inputs is not taken into account in traditional research in this area [26]. For WSNs however, correctly handling input failure is a key requirement.

In this paper, we investigate the problems related to unreliable inputs for three widely used classification algorithms: Feed Forward Neural Networks (FFNN), decision trees and naive Bayes. The analysis of these problems identifies the algorithm that handles the unreliability of individual inputs on WSNs best.

The target application for this study is logistics. This application leads to some assumptions: First of all, we assume that the network consists of relatively small clusters of sensor nodes collaborating in the detection of local conditions; second, we assume that all nodes within such a cluster have a bidirectional communication path to all other nodes in the cluster.

Scenarios in which such a cluster can occur include sensors attached to machinery, for example a cooling cell for food storage, or sensors inside a container with products that need to be monitored.

The scope of this research is limited to algorithms that do periodic classifications, without considering the evolution of data over time. This aspect is left for further research.

1.2 Related Work

Online classification on WSNs has been an area of research for considerable time now. Event detection [27,28,30], context recognition [20], outlier detection [8] and classification [19] are different techniques to automatically draw conclusions from sensor data.

Given the limited hardware capabilities of wireless sensor nodes, classification based on fixed threshold values is often applied [27,28,29,6]. More sophisticated events, however, cannot be detected in this manner. Pattern matching and machine learning techniques are better suited for these complicated tasks.

Based on the scale of the network and the application requirements and constraints, classification algorithms can be executed on the base-station [19,30], locally on the sensor nodes [7], or distributed over the network [8,16,18,21,23]. Distributed execution uses the potential of WSN technology, by providing robustness for sensor failures, reduced communication and distribution of energy consumption. On the other hand, distributed execution provides the most challenges when considering implementation.

Naive Bayes [7], FFNNs [7] and decision trees [9] all have been used to detect events locally on individual sensor nodes. Distributed approaches, using collaboration between nodes, range from techniques based on distributed fuzzy engines [22], map based pattern matching [17], FFNNs, and naive Bayes classifiers [5].

1.3 Contributions

In this paper, we give the results of a comparison between three algorithms: FFNNs, naive Bayes classifiers and decision trees. By analyzing the way the algorithms handle failing inputs, we demonstrate that, compared to the other two algorithms, naive Bayes classifiers shows a superior performance.

A key difference of this comparison, compared to other research, is that we look into the effect of failing inputs on the classifiers without retraining. Retraining a distributed classifier every time an input fails, for example due to a drained battery or a lost connection, would put considerable demands on the available resources of a WSN.

A part of this research was the gathering of a new experimental data-set [32]. This data-set consists of 11 streams of data from heterogeneous sensors. Three different states have been labeled for this data-set. These states differ on frequency and randomness of occurrence and can occur simultaneously, thereby causing interference in the sensor readings. This data-set can be a valuable resource for studies into various applications of WSNs and will be made publicly available.

1.4 Structure of the Paper

The remainder of this paper is organized as follows: The approach used to create the results of this study is described in Section 2. Section 3 describes the actual results. Directions of future research are handled in Section 4. This paper is concluded by Section 5.

2 Method

This section describes the method used to create the results of this research. This section is divided in the method used to gather the experimental data-set (in Section 2.1), the selection of the algorithms (in Section 2.2) and the method used to compare the algorithms (in Section 2.3).

2.1 Data-Set

The scope of this research is the application of WSNs in the field of logistics. Cold-chain management is an important branch of logistics where WSN technology can be applied [11,12,13]. Situations to be monitored in a cold chain include the correct functioning of machinery like cooling cells and the human interaction with this machinery. Pieces of machinery in cold-chains are usually not perfectly isolated, which means that sensor readings can be influenced by other machines, humans, etc.

An application where similar conditions occur is the refrigerator in the social room of our research group. Suitable sensor interference is provided by the coffee machine positioned on top of this refrigerator. Because of these similarities, we have chosen this refrigerator as the environment from which we have created a new sensor data-set.

2.1.1   Conditions of Interest

In this research, we focus on the classification of three different binary conditions for the refrigerator and coffee machine:

1. Is the cooling system of the refrigerator running? This is a frequent and predictably occurring condition, without human interaction.
2. Is the coffee machine running? This is a less frequent condition, triggered by human interaction.
3. Is the refrigerator open? This is the rarest situation we look at, also triggered by human interaction.

We chose these conditions because of the variation in event types they provide. The frequency in which these conditions occur differs in orders of magnitude. Furthermore, there are human-triggered, and automatically initiated conditions.

The fact that the two machines are situated in the social corner of our research group, resulted in frequent and uncontrolled human interaction. Another aspect of these conditions, is the expected correlation between sensor readings. Opening the fridge door, for example, results in vibrations on the fridge door. These vibrations can also be seen on the coffee machine, but to a lesser extent. These factors together provide a realistic and challenging environment in which to do classification.

2.1.2   Set Up of the Experiment

To detect the state of the fridge door, coffee machine and fridge we used Sun SPOT [1] sensor nodes. Sun SPOTs come equipped with a number of sensors [2]. We used the 3D accelerometer, the light sensor and the thermometer. Furthermore, we equipped one of the Sun SPOTs with additional sensors to measure the current through and voltage over the refrigerator and coffee machine. The current and voltage for the coffee machine and refrigerator were combined on one power outlet.

Table 1 show the placement of the sensor nodes and the sample rates used in our experiment. We chose this placement to give relevant and redundant information for the three conditions of interest.

The sample rates were chosen based on the type of sampled data. For example, light and temperature are mostly influenced by relatively low frequency phenomena, increasing the sampling rate above 10Hz does not add extra data about those phenomena. Furthermore, the sample rates are limited by hardware capabilities. For example, current and voltage samples could only be stored reliably at a rate of 160Hz.

To get a complete data-set, without the risk of losing samples due to interrupted wireless communication, we connected all the Sun SPOTs to a central

Table 1. Sample rates for various sensors

Node location	Temperature	Light	3D Acceleration	Current	Voltage
Power outlet	-	-	-	160Hz	160Hz
Inside fridge door	10Hz	10Hz	100Hz	-	-
Outside fridge door	10Hz	10Hz	100Hz	-	-
Back coffee machine	10Hz	10Hz	100Hz	-	-

computer using USB cables. This data was stored on the computer using a MySQL database. Although this means that our experimental setup was no WSN in a strict sense, data collection was more reliable and resulted in a better data-set as base for our research. When needed in future work, the effects of wireless communication can be introduced in simulations.

2.1.3 Labeling of the Data
All human interactions with the coffee machine and refrigerator were recorded using two webcams and the open-source motion detection application "Motion" [25]. Using the captured videos and the data streams from the sensors, we manually labeled the three conditions of interest for a period of roughly two weeks.

2.1.4 Data Features
Since we are targeting WSN architectures, there is a limit to the number of classifications that can be made per unit of time. Therefore we preprocessed the data to reduce the sample rates. For this research, we chose a 1Hz frequency.

The risk of reducing the sample frequency is the loss of information. In order to keep valuable information in our data-set, we split the sensor streams into multiple feature streams. An example of a feature is the RMS value of a signal over the last second. For voltage and current, this provides a meaningful indication of the power consumed. A good selection of features can make classification more straightforward.

In this research, we have used the following features for the various sensor streams.

3D Acceleration: Peak magnitude without gravity of the last second and magnitude of the resampled signals.

Light: The first derivative of the low pass filtered signal (at a cut-off frequency of 1Hz) and the resampled value of the low pass filtered signal (at a cut-off frequency of 1Hz)

Temperature: The first derivative of the low pass filtered signal (at a cut-off frequency of 1Hz) and the resampled value of the low pass filtered signal (at a cut-off frequency of 1Hz)

Voltage: RMS value of the last second.
Current: Peak value of the last second and the RMS value of the last second.

Using these features for the streams shown in Table 1, resulted in 21 new streams. These 21 streams were used as input for the classification algorithms.

2.2 Selection of Algorithms

A comparison of all available classification algorithms is outside the scope of this research. Therefore, we opted to make a selection of three different algorithms. For successful WSN implementation the used algorithms need to be computationally cheap, but able to perform efficient classifications. Based on related work on WSNs [6,9,18,5] we selected the FFNN algorithm, the naive Bayes algorithm and the decision tree algorithm. These three algorithms are commonly used and have been implemented on WSNs before.

2.2.1 Feed Forward Neural Networks

An algorithm that is frequently used for recognition tasks is the FFNNs algorithm[15]. FFNNs can be seen as directed acyclic graphs where the nodes without predecessors are used to feed information into the network (the input layer). Nodes without successors give the resulting output of the FFNN (the output layer). Each node in the graph is a processing element (neuron) that combines its inputs and generates an output.

Parameters that change the neuron's output include the weights assigned to the inputs, the transfer function and the bias. Learning algorithms are used to automatically adapt these parameters to generate a desired output for a given input.

The simple structure of FFNNs makes them easy to implement and leaves some options to see how the model works after the learning phase.

2.2.2 Naive Bayes Classifiers

Naive Bayes classifiers use Bayesian statistics and Bayes' theorem to find the probability $P(C|E)$ that a given input $E = (x(s_1,t), x(s_2,t), ..., x(s_n,t))$ belongs to a class C. This probability $P(C|E)$ is estimated using Equation (1) [31]. In order to make a binary classification, the naive Bayes algorithm calculates both $P(c = 1|E)$ and $P(c = 0|E)$. The class with the highest probability is the final classification.

$$P(C|E) = \frac{P(E|C)P(C)}{P(E)} \tag{1}$$

In this case, class C can, for example, be the class of samples where the fridge is open, $x(s_i,t)$ is the output of sensor s_i on time t. The algorithm is called naive because of the assumption that all the inputs $x(s_i,t)$ have an independent contribution to $P(C|E)$.

The most time and resource consuming part of the naive Bayes classifier is the computation of $P(E|C)$. Accurately estimating this probability is important for the classification result. In current literature of pattern recognition and machine learning, it is proposed that this probability can be estimated using standard data distributions, such as the Gaussian or Poisson distribution [4].

Another approach is the use of histograms. In this approach, the input space is partitioned into several intervals. The number of occurrences of each condition is counted for each interval. This number is used to determine the probability that an input will fall in a certain interval given classification C.

2.2.3 Decision Trees

Decision trees are classification algorithms that use tree like graphs to model and evaluate discrete functions [28,27]. The input of a decision tree can contain either continuous or discrete values. The output, however, contains only discrete values.

Construction of a decision tree for classification can be done using a training algorithms like ID3 and C4.5[24]. Training algorithms use a data-set to find a decision tree of minimal depth that performs the classification. The number of nodes or depth of the decision tree should be minimized to reduce time and memory complexities. The training algorithms are usually local search greedy algorithms that result in a locally optimal decision tree.

2.3   Metrics

Rating the performance of classification algorithms is not always a straightforward task. Calculating the classification accuracy alone does not necessarily give a good indication for how well a classifier discriminates between classes. When classifying rare states, for example, a high accuracy can be reached by never detecting the state. A more complete insight in classification performance can be given by calculating the sensitivity, specificity, positive predictive value and negative predictive value for a classifier. With this approach however, it is difficult to say which metric is the most important.

In order to make a direct comparison between classifiers, we have used a technique coming from Receiver Operator Characteristics (ROC) analysis [14]. In ROC analysis, a plot is made of the sensitivity on the Y-axis versus the False Positive Rate (FPR) on the X-axis. The FPR is defined as $FPR = 1 - Specificity$. In this plot (Figure 1), the line $y = x$ is called the no discrimination line, classifiers on this line are not able to discriminate between the classifications in any way. Each classifier can be assigned a point in this graph based on the FPR and the sensitivity. The distance from this point to the no discrimination line is an indication of how well the classifier can discriminate between the classes.

In this research we compare the impact of failing inputs on various classification algorithms. To make this comparison the absolute value of this distance is of limited importance. In order to demonstrate the impact of failing inputs we have normalized over the performance using all inputs. This allows us to directly compare the relative performance penalty for failing inputs for all the algorithms.

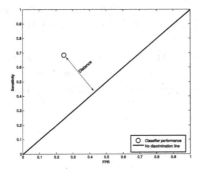

Fig. 1. The distance to the no discrimination line is an indicator for classifier performance

2.4   Classifier Training

In this research, we have trained classifiers using each of the three algorithms, for each of the three conditions, resulting in a set of nine trained classifiers. The classifiers were trained over a training set and their performance was assessed using a verification set.

The training sets were selected at random from the complete data-set. The only non random aspect of the training set selection is the bias between samples with positive and negative labels. For FFNNs and naive Bayes, this bias was changed to ensure a sufficient representation of both classification options.

The size of the training-set was 10000 samples for all the training runs, except for classification of rare conditions. In our case, we had to reduce the number of training samples for the "fridge open" classifications, because of the limited number of positive samples. The size of the verification set was roughly one million samples and was formed by all data, except for the training-set.

For each algorithm, the training was repeated 20 times and the classifier performing the best on the verification set was selected. The nine resulting classifiers, one of each type for each condition, are used for the rest of this paper.

2.5   Robustness

In order to be suitable for WSNs, the used algorithms should keep working without intervention when one or multiple sensors fail. In case of sensor failure, some loss of performance is unavoidable, but the impact should be minimal for suitable algorithms.

We have investigated the impact of sensor failure on the three algorithms. To compare the three algorithms, we analyzed the selected trained classifiers for each algorithm and created a ranking of the features in order of influence on the classification result. The analysis of the feature importance for the FFNN algorithms was done by calculating the weight of each input throughout the FFNN starting from the output. For naive Bayes, we looked at how much the one vs. zero ratios of the intervals deviated from the global one vs. zero ratio. The

feature ranking for the decision tree algorithm was made based on the purity of
the split made by each decision node, weighted over the probability of the node
being used in a classification.

Using this ranking, we ran the classifiers in scenarios with an increasing number of failing inputs. We started by running the algorithms with all features as
input and continued by dropping the most important feature until just the least
useful feature was left.

3   Results

This section describes the results gathered during the course of this study.

3.1   Data-Set

Data was gathered using the experimental setup over a period of two weeks.
Using the video results and Matlab scripts, the three conditions of interest were
labeled and the feature streams were produced. Figure 2 shows an example where
the fridge is opened, as observed by multiple sensors.

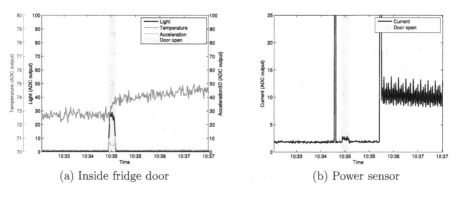

(a) Inside fridge door   (b) Power sensor

Fig. 2. Door open event seen by 2 different nodes

As expected, the frequency of occurrence of the three different conditions are
in different orders of magnitude. The "fridge running" condition occurs 23.7% of
the time, the coffee machine is on 0.65% of the time and the fridge door is open
0.05% of the time.

3.2   Robustness

Figure 3 shows the performance of the algorithms in various scenarios. When
using a FFNN classifier, it can be seen that more then one failing feature has a
severe impact on the performance.

The performance of the decision tree algorithm already shows a large drop when a single feature is dropped. This effect can be explained by the way this algorithm works. Decision trees, unlike FFNNs and naive Bayes classifiers, do not combine multiple results into an answer where all the inputs have a small influence. Only a subset of the inputs are used for sequential binary decisions. If one of those inputs is left out, entire parts of the decision tree become unreachable.

The naive Bayes classifier performs quite well, up to a certain point, when features are dropped. Depending on the condition that is being classified, multiple important features can be dropped without large effects on the classification performance.

Altogether, the naive Bayes classifier handles the error scenarios best.

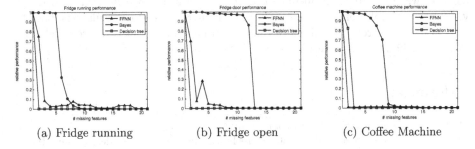

(a) Fridge running   (b) Fridge open   (c) Coffee Machine

Fig. 3. Performance for various classifications

4 Future Work

Although this paper highlights some important aspects of the various algorithms with respect to WSNs, there are many obstacles before a viable implementation is ready. This section describes some areas with room for further research.

A key aspect of WSNs is their distributed nature. Since radio communication costs a significant amount of memory, radio usage should be kept to a minimum. Therefore, the amount of communication involved in the distribution of classification algorithms is an important consideration. Over the years numerous distributed classifiers have been developed, but a fundamental investigation of the properties that allow or limit the distribution of algorithms remains of interest.

Another direction of research is the maintenance required to keep a classifier working. With respect to classification algorithms, maintenance costs provide some interesting areas of research. The complexity of adding new nodes to a network running a classifier, for example, could increase the Total Cost of Ownership (TCO) for dynamic applications. Another example is the reprogramming of the network to do an additional classification. If this is a very time consuming process, the involved man-hours could cost a significant amount of money. Investigating the effects of these two aspects on the TCO, for various algorithms is a promising direction for further research.

5 Conclusion

When looking into the effects of unreliable inputs, FFNN and decision tree classifiers show clear drawbacks. The high dependence on individual inputs and the inherently discrete nature of decision trees make this algorithm sensitive to input failure. Although naive Bayes is also influenced by sensor failure, we firmly believe that this algorithm overall shows the best compatibility with WSN architectures.

With respect to the problem of classification on WSNs in general, we believe that careful consideration of the compatibility of algorithms with WSN architectures can prevent complications during implementation.

A final note is on the data-set created for this research. The fact that this data-set was created in an uncontrolled environment and was labeled for events visible on multiple sensors makes it an excellent resource for simulations based on real data. Therefore, we believe that it can be valuable for other researchers. We will make it publicly available [32].

References

1. Sun spot world, http://www.sunspotworld.com/
2. Sun spot edemo technical datasheet. Technical datasheet, Sun Microsystems Inc., 16 Network Circle, Santa Clara, CA, USA (2010)
3. Akyildiz, I.F., Su, W., Sankarasubramamiam, Y., Cayirci, E.: A survey on sensor networks. IEEE Communications Magazine 40(8), 102–114 (2002)
4. Alpaydin, E.: Introduction to machine learning. MIT Press (2004)
5. Bahrepour, M., Meratnia, N., Havinga, P.: Sensor fusion-based event detection in wireless sensor networks. Sensor Fusion, pp. 1–8 (2009)
6. Bahrepour, M., Meratnia, N., Havinga, P.J.: Automatic fire detection: A survey from wireless sensor network perspective. Technical report, Centre for Telematics and Information Technology (2007)
7. Bahrepour, M., Meratnia, N., Havinga, P.J.: Use of ai techniques for residential fire detection in wireless sensor networks. In: AIAI 2009 Workshop Proceedings (2009)
8. Bahrepour, M., Zhang, Y., Meratnia, N., Havinga, P.J.: Use of event detection approaches for outlier detection in wireless sensor networks. In: ISSNIP 2009 (2009)
9. Cayirci, E., Tezcan, H., Dogan, Y., Vedat, C.: Wireless sensor networks for underwater survelliance systems. Ad Hoc Networks 4, 431–446 (2006)
10. Chohan, N.: Hardware assisted compression in wireless sensor networks (2007)
11. Evers, L., Bijl, M., Marin-Perianu, M., Marin-Perianu, R., Havinga, P.: Wireless sensor networks and beyond: A case study on transport and logistics (2005)
12. Evers, L., Havinga, P., Kuper, J.: Flexible sensor network reprogramming for logistics. In: IEEE International Conference on Mobile Adhoc and Sensor Systems, pp. 1–4 (2007)
13. Evers, L., Havinga, P.J., Kuper, J., Lijding, M.E., Meratnia, N.: Sensorscheme: Supply chain management automation using wireless sensor networks. In: IEEE Conference on Emerging Technologies and Factory Automation, pp. 448–455 (2007)
14. Fawcett, T.: An introduction to roc analysis. Pattern Recognition Letters 27, 861–874 (2006)

15. Haykin, S.: Neural Networks: a comprehensive foundation, 2nd edn. Prentice Hall (1999)
16. Jin, G., Nittel, S.: Ned: An efficient noise-tolerant event and event boundary detection algorithm in wireless sensor networks. In: 7th International Conference on Mobile Data Management (2006)
17. Khelil, A., Shaikh, F.K., Ayari, B., Suri, N.: Mwm: A map-based world model for wireless sensor networks. Autonomics (2008)
18. Krishnamachari, B., Iyengar, S.: Distributed bayesian algorithms for fault-tolerant event region detection in wireless sensor networks. IEEE Transactions on Computers 53(3) (2004)
19. Li, D., Wong, K.D., Hu, Y.H., Sayeed, A.M.: Detection, classification and tracking of targets. IEEE Signal Processing Magazine 19, 17–29 (2002)
20. Lombriser, C., Roggen, D., Stäger, M., Tröster, G.: Titam: A tiny task network for dynamically reconfigurable heterogeneous sensor networks. Kommunikation in Verteilten Systemen 3, 127–138 (2006)
21. Luo, X., Dong, M., Huang, Y.: On distributed fault-tolerant detection in wireless sensor networks. IEEE Transactions on Computers 55(1), 58–70 (2006)
22. Marin-Perianu, M., Havinga, P.: D-FLER – A Distributed Fuzzy Logic Engine for Rule-Based Wireless Sensor Networks. In: Ichikawa, H., Cho, W.-D., Satoh, I., Youn, H.Y. (eds.) UCS 2007. LNCS, vol. 4836, pp. 86–101. Springer, Heidelberg (2007)
23. Martincic, F., Schwiebert, L.: Distributed event detection in sensor networks. In: Proceedings of the International Conference on Systems and Networks Communications, p. 43 (2006)
24. Murthy, S.K.: Automatic construction of decision trees from data: A multidisiplinary survey. Data Mining and Knnowledge Discovery 2, 345–389 (1998)
25. Pack, R.D.: Motion - web home, http://www.lavrsen.dk/foswiki/bin/view/Motion/WebHome
26. Russel, S., Norvig, P.: Artificial Intelligence A Modern Approach. Prentice Hall Series in Artificial Intelligence. Prentice Hall (1995)
27. Segal, M.L., Antonio, F.P., Elam, S., Erlenbach, J., de Paolo, K.R., Beach, S.: Method and apparatus for automatic event detection in a wireless communication system. US. Patent (2000)
28. Vu, C.T., Beyah, R.A., Li, Y.: Composite event detection in wireless sensor networks. In: Performance, Computing and Communications, pp. 264–271 (2007)
29. Werner-Allen, G., Lorincz, K., Welsh, M., Marcillo, O., Johnson, J., Ruiz, M., Lees, J.: Deploying a wireless sensor network on an active volcano. IEEE Internet Computing, 18–25 (2006)
30. Xue, W., Luo, Q., Chen, L., Liu, Y.: Contour map matching for event detection in sensor networks. In: Proceedings of the 2006 ACM SIGMOD International Conference on Management of Data (2006)
31. Zhang, H.: The optimality of naive bayes. In: 17th Florida Artificial Intelligence Research Society Conference (2004)
32. Zwartjes, A.: Fridge dataset, http://ps.ewi.utwente.nl/Datasets.php

Unsupervised Power Profiling for Mobile Devices

Mikkel Baun Kjærgaard and Henrik Blunck

Aarhus University, Denmark
{mikkelbk,blunck}@cs.au.dk

Abstract. Today, power consumption is a main limitation for mobile phones. To minimize the power consumption of popular and tradition-ally power-hungry location-based services requires knowledge of how in-dividual phone features consume power, so that those features can be utilized intelligently for optimal power savings while at the same time maintaining good quality of service. This paper proposes an unsuper-vised API-level method for power profiling mobile phones based on ge-netic algorithms. The method enables accurate profiling of the power consumption of devices and thereby provides the information needed by methods that aim to minimize the power consumption of location-based and other services.

Keywords: power profiling, mobile devices, power consumption.

1 Introduction

Today, mobile phones include more and more positioning and sensor technologies such as GPS, cellular positioning, accelerometers and compasses. This develop-ment enables location-based services that aim to provide high-end user experi-ences, such as location-based search, games, sports trackers, social networking and activity recognition [12]. However, the power consumption of such location-based services is in many cases above 1 watt, which is twenty times higher than a mobile phone's standby consumption and thus significantly shortens the battery lifetime [9]. The high consumption requires frequent battery recharges which is often inconvinient, or, for instance in deserted areas, not possible. Therefore, power consumption inhibits the use of many promising always-on location-based services. The problem can only to a small extend be addressed by lowering hard-ware consumption because it is the total use of the hardware by software that is the problem in the same manner as faster CPUs alone do not lead to fastest answers if an inefficient algorithm invokes the instructions on the CPU. Our previous studies [8,10,11] have shown that power savings are possible if posi-tioning and sensor technologies are managed in a smarter way: up to 73% for a continuous moving device and up to 95% for a periodically moving device.

To successfully minimize power consumption requires knowledge of how much power a specific phone feature consumes and how fast it powers on and off. To understand the power consumption of mobile phones one could as a first step consult their specifications (e.g. [13]). However, these will often not give the

A. Puiatti et al. (Eds.): MobiQuitous 2011, LNICST 104, pp. 138–149, 2012.

full picture, because values are missing (e.g. the power consumption for CPU operations) and dynamic aspects are not considered. The dynamic aspects are due to that features do not instantly power on or off, e.g., a 3G radio needs several seconds to power on before it is able to send or receive data. Similarly, also the radio powering off does not happen instantly, due to a prior initiation of a proper disconnection, maybe preceded by a short period of waiting for a potential next radio request. Therefore, the power consumed for sending or receiving data cannot be simply modeled as a static value, which is applied just for the span of the actual sending period. Similar holds for other phone features, e.g. for the in-phone GPS during the acquisition of a positioning fix. A solution for accurately modeling dynamic aspects of power consumption is via power profiling a device to learn the dynamic behavior of its features. However, a manual approach to power profiling has the drawback that it does not scale, considering that many of the different mobile platforms and models currently existing may soon be outdated and replaced by newer models. Even worse, a power model may even sooner be invalidated just by a software upgrade that alters the phone model's power profile. E.g., we observed for Symbian phones, that power consumption for location based services changes by more than a factor of two with the OS version, which is amongst others related to how often GPS assistance data is requested over the cellular network in the different OS versions.

Efforts to manually power profile recent smart phones can be found in Carroll et al. [5], Rice et al. [15] and Zhang et al. [16], all of which employed external hardware, and our earlier work [11], which utilized software APIs. To use a power model proactively it must be able to predict future power consumption; this is enabled by our model based on conditional functions presented in [11], whereas the linear model proposed by Dong and Zhong [6] and Zhang et al. [16] depends directly on system level metrics inhibiting prediction, since the model can not over time prescribe changes of the metrics and thereby of the modeled power consumption. Zhong et al. [6] recognize the need for unsupervised power profiling but also do not provide a model that enables prediction.

This paper proposes PowerProf, an unsupervised method for power profiling mobile phones based on genetic algorithms. Genetic algorithms, operating on profile measurements collected on the phone, are utilized to estimate a power model consisting of a set of conditional functions. This method enables accurate profiling of the power consumption on a wide selection of devices and thereby provides the information needed by methods that reduce the power consumption of location-based services. The proposed method has been evaluated on several generations of phones (N97, N8, C7) and has generated models that can predict the power consumption for the mentioned devices with a high accuracy.

2   Related Work

The power consumption of smart phones has been studied from several angles to provide measurement tools, analysis results and models of power consumption. Rice et al. [15] propopes a mobile measurement tool for decomposition of the power consumption of smart phones by designing an artificial measurement battery. Carroll et al. [5] provide an analysis based on external measurement equipment and Kjærgaard et al. [11] provides an analysis of the power consumption of Nokia phones using measurements from the internal battery interface.

Related work on modeling power consumption can be classified according to several dimensions. Firstly, according to how the measurements are collected for building the model: Measurements can either be collected using *external* equipment or using an *internal* smart battery interface, if existent, and the respective choice has a direct impact on the requirements for building new models. Secondly, according to what type of information the model is built from. A model for power consumption can be deduced from i) measurements of system *utilization*, e.g., disk and processor statistics available from the operating system, from ii) power consumption measurements per *system call* made to the operating system, or from iii) power consumption measurements per *API call* made in a specific programming language. Thirdly, according to what type of information the model can provide. The model can enable either solely the *estimation* of the current power consumption, or it can allow additionally for the *prediction* of the power consumption ahead of time. Fourthly, according to how the model is constructed: is it a human supervised process or an unsupervised process performed entirely by a software component. Table 2 provides a summary of related work according to these four dimensions.

	Kjærgaard [11]	PowerTutor [16]	Sesame [6]	Pathak [14]	PowerProf
External		x		x	
Internal	x	x	x		x
Utilization		x	x		
System-call				x	
API-call	x				x
Estimation	x	x	x	x	x
Prediction	x				x
Supervised	x				
Unsupervised		x	x	x	x

In this paper we propose PowerProf that utilizes measurements from the internal battery of a phone enabling models to be built on user demand, whenever a new model is needed, e.g. for a new phone type or after a software upgrade that might alter the power management and thus the power profile of the phone. Dong and Zhong [6] compared the accuracy of power models constructed based on measurements from internal battery interfaces versus external equipment and found that models constructed utilizing internal battery interfaces where only marginally less accurate than models built from external equipment. PowerProf builds models that captures the phone's power consumption per API call issued in the utilized programming language. This is enabled by utilizing a program language API to the battery interface. This API solution enables in-code placement of power consumption measurements with explicitly defined start and end times, which enables optimal synchronization between code timing and measurements. This in turn allows all code to be placed at the application layer, thus avoiding i) changes to the operating system such as those needed for detecting system calls [14], as well as avoiding ii) a strong dependence on the operating system to read out runtime statistics [6,16]. This also ensures that the resulting PowerProf-built models capture the logic of a program language interpreter or virtual machine that can have a large impact on the power consumption as they, e.g., define how resources are allocated and deallocated. Furthermore, the models built by PowerProf enable prediction which allows, e.g., sensor scheduling algorithms to make decisions comparing the predicted power consumption of different possible actions. The method of PowerProf aims –in agreement with related work– for unsupervised building of models, but does not require any predefined thresholds as earlier work uses to separate different power states [14]; e.g., PowerProf's modelling is able to identify new states without requiring from them, that they change the power consumption by more than a given threshold.

3   Automatic Power Profiling

In this section we will present the proposed method PowerProf, which is enabled by the increasing availability of smart battery interfaces on mobile devices. These interfaces include software APIs that provide access to measurements of voltage, current and other battery statistics [6]. The PowerProf method requires that a set of training measurements is collected to build models from. During collection, relevant phone features are exercised sequentially and independently of each other. Note, that the collection of these measurements does not require any user interaction and can thus be carried out when the device is not needed by the user for other tasks. Alternatively, the training can be performed as an installation step, thus making the process invisible to device users.[1] The training might then be reapplied if an application detects that an interpreter or operating systems has been updated to a new version or has been reconfigured, e.g., if the GPS is reconfigured to use (a different scope of) GPS assistance data.

Overall System Structure. The structure of and the individual steps when applying the PowerProf system are illustrated in Figure 1. First, a request is sent to a software API that interfaces with the smart battery to start providing time-stamped power measurements (1). Relevant phone features are independently exercised and time-stamps for the starts of features and for the return of results are logged (2). Measurements are processed and prepared, and additionally directly observable characteristics are determined, e.g., background power

---

[1] Also, accuracy in power modeling may be further increased through training in several environment types, e.g. indoors and outdoors, which differ in reception properties, and thus also in time and energy required for obtaining, e.g. GPS fixes or GSM communication. Detecting the type of environment, a phone is currently in, can be done in real-time on-device, e.g. via analysis of GPS reception quality data [4].

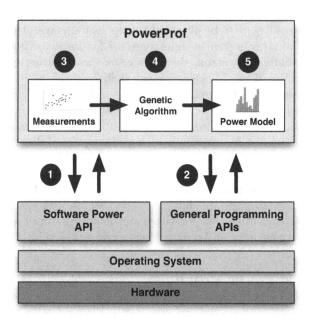

Fig. 1. Steps of the PowerProf system from measuring to generating power models

consumption (3). A genetic algorithm [7] is used to search for optimal parameter values for the power model (4). This step is delegated to a server as an extensive amount of processing is involved in running the genetic algorithm. The fitness function of the algorithm calculates the difference between the power consumption as predicted by the current model and as actually measured on the device. Finally, the parameter values resulting from minimizing the fitness function are used as input to the final power model (5).

Power Model Design. A power model, as built by PowerProf, is given by one conditional function per phone feature. Such a function models the feature's power consumption in dependence of the input parameter t, which resembles the time span, since the feature was last requested via a programming API call. Each conditional function is restricted to four power states, defined by four time parameters t_1, t_2, t_{result} and t_{end} where the first two parameters are free variables and the second two are the time that it takes the function to return, and the time when the power consumption finally drops to background consumption, respectively. The two free variables t_1 and t_2 defines the transition times between state one and two, and state three and four, respectively. The power consumption for each of the four states is defined by a parameter p_1, p_2, p_3 and p_4, respectively. The form of the resulting conditional function is given in Equation 1, and Figure 2 illustrates an example of the resulting power profile for such a conditional function. The restriction to four parameters is applied to decrease the search space when fitting the functions to actual measurements.

Furthermore, this restriction has been chosen based on the number of power states identified in our earlier work [11]. If the same function is exercised several times in the training phase, average values are used for t_{result} and t_{end}. The drop to background consumption is detected, when the average power consumption over three consecutive measurements is below $\mu_{background} + \sigma_{background}$, the sum of the mean and the standard deviation of the background consumption, respectively. Note, that the this sum is well separated from the power consumption when using a phone feature, since the latter use considerably more power than experienced by fluctations in background consumption.

$$\mathcal{P}(t) = \begin{cases} p_1 & \text{if } t <= t_1 \\ p_2 & \text{if } t > t_1 \text{ and } t <= t_{result} \\ p_3 & \text{if } t > t_{result} \text{ and } t <= t_2 \\ p_4 & \text{if } t > t_2 \text{ and } t <= t_{end} \end{cases} \tag{1}$$

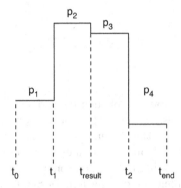

Fig. 2. Power Model for a single phone feature

Power Model Construction. The reason for choosing a genetic algorithm for finding model parameters, i.e. an algorithm which searches for an optimal solution based on the principles of natural evolution, is that it is a well known technique for finding approximate solutions to intractable parameter optimization problems [7] and especially to real world optimization problems on the basis of noisy data, e.g. noisy power consumption measurements.

To apply genetic algorithms, one needs, firstly, to define the format of the *chromosome* that has to be evolved towards a solution using the principles of natural evolution. Secondly, a fitness function is applied iteratively to evaluate the last generation's chromosomes, which are developed by the genetic algorithm, to only let the fittest survive. Our chromosomes consist, as shown in Figure 3, of the parameters of the power model that need to be found. Thus, a chromosome consists of six entries for each phone feature to represent the six unknowns in Equation 1: t_1, t_2, p_1, p_2, p_3 and p_4. Note, that t_{result} is recorded by in-code measurement as the time span from API call till the return of the call, and t_{end} is found as the time till the power drops down to background consumption.

Fig. 3. Chromosome consisting of parameters for $1...n$ features

To evaluate the fitness of a developed chromosome $\mathcal{C}$, we use the n training measurements, which consist of the time-stamps $t_i, i = 1, \ldots n$ during which phone features were exercised and the corrsesponding measurements of power consumptions m_i on the phone. From a chromosome $\mathcal{C}$ we parametrise a power model $\mathcal{P}_{\mathcal{C}}$ and use it together with the training time-stamps to predict the power consumption during each measurement phase i for $i = 0 \ldots n$, so that each predicted power value is aligned in time with its actual measurement. The fitness of the chromosome is then found as the inverse sum of absolute differences as defined in Equation 2. Therefore, as the differences decrease, the fitness value will increase.[2]

$$fitness = \frac{1}{\sum_i^n |\mathcal{P}_{\mathcal{C}}(i) - m_i|} \tag{2}$$

4   Evaluation

To evaluate PowerProf we have implemented and tested the system on three different mobile device types. In our evaluation we consider the accuracy of the respective power models and the dependence of the accuracy on the number of the training iterations and on the number of generations that the genetic algorithm is allowed for evolving the chromosomes.

PowerProf has been implemented in python for S60 [2] to run on different mobile devices supporting the Symbian operating system. The implemented PowerProf system consists of the components shown in Figure 1. To interface with the smart battery interface of the devices we use a python software API that interfaces with the Nokia energy profiler [1]. The Nokia energy profiler provides power measurements at the same sample rate of 4 Hz as provided by the python software API. To implement the genetic algorithm component we utilize the Pyevolve software library for genetic algorithms [3], using the library's standard parameters, which specify a population size of 80 individuals, a mutation rate of 2%, a crossover rate of 80% and that a ranking selector is used. To enable our evaluation of the dependency between the accuracy and the number of training measurements and evolved generations, the genetic algorithm part has for the evaluation been implemented and run on a server.

To evaluate the PowerProf method, we have collected three datasets for each of the three Nokia Phones N97, N8 and C7. In each dataset we iterate three

---

[2] We decided against the alternative of using squared differences, since the latter strategy would result in power models that attempt to fit (potentially irregular and random) spikes in the power consumption, rather than more regular, and thus more likely reoccuring, patterns.

times over the functions for different phone features, where each iteration takes around five minutes. Table 1 lists the exercised phone features. Note, that for various applications, further phone features may be of interest. In such cases, the respective application developer should extend PowerProf's feature set and its set of training measurements accordingly. Besides the PowerProf program no other programs were running on the phone during data collection. The measurements were collected outdoors, and prior to the measurements a single GPS fix was obtained, and with it the current A-GPS data, so that we subsequently power profile only the GPS device, provided that the phone is configured not to obtain A-GPS data via the radio for every invocation. Note, that the latter A-GPS data, once obtained, is valid for several hours. The reason for choosing a measurement duration as long as five minutes is that we need to separate the usage of individual features by at least thirty seconds to be able to analyse the time it takes the individual features to power off. The thirty seconds as lower limit was selected based on prior work [11].

Table 1. Functions for features exercised

Feature	Scenario
WiFi	WiFi Scanning at 1 Hz during ten seconds to provide measurements for WiFi positioning
Accelerometer	Acceleration measurements for ten seconds at the hardware-provided frequency
Compass	Compass measurements for ten seconds at the hardware-provided frequency
GSM	GSM scanning at 1 Hz during ten seconds to provide measurements for GSM positioning
CPU	Calculate π with 1500 decimals
HTTP	Read 'www.google.com' using an HTTP connection
GPS	Receive one GPS position

Before presenting our evaluation we provide with Figure 4 an exemplary comparison of the predictions of a model, generated by PowerProf, and real power measurements for a C7 phone. Generally, as indicated by the overlap of the two graphs, the predictions match the real measurements with a few exceptions. One such exception is, that the HTTP feature is predicted to power off too early, which is due to that both power on and off time spans vary for this feature to some extent between calls, due to changes in the network characteristics.

To analyse the performance of PowerProf we evaluate it based on the prediction error defined as the difference between the predicted power consumption and the measured one. We use the three datasets for each phone type, and to devide this data into training and test data we perform three-fold cross validation where each fold only contains data from one dataset. To evaluate specific aspects of our approach, we also vary i) the number of iterations included in the datasets used for training and ii) the number of generations that the chromosomes had to evolve. Furthermore, we have repeated each genetic evolution three times, so

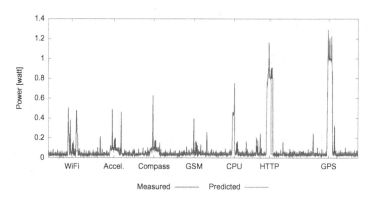

Fig. 4. Comparison for a C7 phone of model predictions and real measurements

that the results presented here are less dependent on the random elements of the evolution process.

Figure 5 shows a cumulative distribution over the prediction errors in each of the three datasets for each device type. The best performance is achieved for the C7 and N8 devices. For the N97 datasets the performance is a bit worse with a higher degree of large errors, the two reasons having been identified as the background consumption being less stable for the N97 phones, and the power consumption being often more spiky than for C7 and N8 devices.

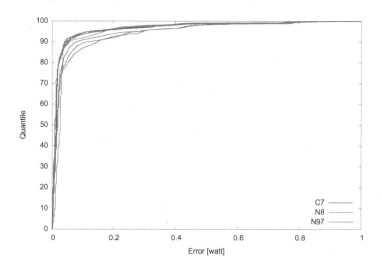

Fig. 5. Cummulative distributions for model accuracy after 200 generations

To evaluate how many generations are necessary for our genetic algorithm to evolve stable chromosomes, we list in Table 2 results in terms of prediction error of the modeled power consumption for chromosomes evolved for a varying

Table 2. Results with different number of generations

| | 25 gen. [watt] | | 100 gen. [watt] | | 200 gen. [watt] | | 400 gen. [watt] | |
	Median	95-quantile	Median	95-quantile	Median	95-quantile	Median	95-quantile
C7	0.013	0.159	0.013	0.148	0.013	0.145	0.013	0.145
N8	0.012	0.182	0.012	0.171	0.012	0.172	0.012	0.171
N97	0.015	0.298	0.015	0.290	0.015	0.290	0.015	0.290

Table 3. Results with different number of iterations for 200 generations

| | 1 iteration [watt] | | 2 iterations [watt] | | 3 iterations [watt] | |
	Median	95-quantile	Median	95-quantile	Median	95-quantile
C7	0.013	0.155	0.013	0.154	0.013	0.145
N8	0.012	0.177	0.012	0.166	0.012	0.172
N97	0.015	0.318	0.015	0.294	0.015	0.290

number of generations.[3] Generally, the improvement of the models with additional generations is more significant for the 95-quantile than for the median prediction errors: To obtain an accurate model for the power consumption for the respective phone model, which can only be insignificantly improved in further generations, 25 (resp. 200) generations seem sufficient, when considering (the granularity of) the median (resp. the 95-quantile) error measurements.

We also considered the number of training iterations used. Each iteration contains one set of training measurements for each of the features, listed in Table 1. The results with one, two and three iterations, as listed in Table 3, indicate a significant gain in model accuracy by collecting more than one iteration for the 95-quantile, though not for the median error. The gain is caused by the extra training measurements increasing the model's generality and therefore increasing its ability to predict the test measurements.

Finally, we have also evaluated the model's performance in a real location-based-service use-case scenario, featuring more frequent and overlapping feature usage. For this test, we considered a deployment dataset of our system $EnTracked_T$ [10], that has been designed to provide energy-efficient user position and trajectory tracking. The deployment was conducted with a N97 phone configured to use A-GPS seldom, and during the experiment the phone logged both time-stamped function calls within $EnTracked_T$ as well as power consumption. In the following, we compare the power consumption predicted by a PowerProf-built model for the N97 phone with the measured power consumption. Figure 6 shows both the predicted and measured power consumption during an experiment where a person was walking in a city area while being position tracked by $EnTracked_T$. As we can observe from the figure, the model produced by PowerProf is able to capture the overall power consumption, whereas occasional spikes are not accurately captured. This is expected as the model will

---

[3] Note, that within PowerProf and given settings, computing one generation took on average 1.2 seconds on a PC, featuring a Intel X3430 processor and 8GB RAM.

be unable to capture non-repetitve phenomena. The overall prediction accuracy for both the previously described experiment and another one, where the target person was driving in a car, exhibited a median error of 0.143 watt and a 95th quantile error of 0.313 watt. This indicates that PowerProf models power consumption accurately and that the 95-quantile and worst-case error can be properly predicted from the PowerProf training measurements, whereas the average error increased with the more frequent and overlapping feature usage as it is to be expected when using location based services 'in the wild'.

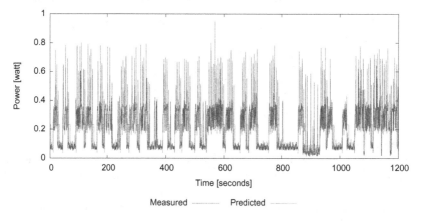

Fig. 6. Comparison of predicted and measured power consumption during a try out of the $EnTracked_T$ system

5   Conclusions

In this paper we presented PowerProf, an unsupervised API-level method for power profiling mobile phones based on genetic algorithms. The method has been evaluated for building models of common phone features utilized by location-based services. Evaluation results provide evidence that the system for the three tested phone types achieves predictions with high accuracy, with average errors of 0.012 watt for the median and 0.145 watt for the 95th quantile. Evaluation results for a real use-case scenario with the energy-efficient position tracking system $EnTracked_T$ showed an increase in the median error to on average 0.143 watt, but only a slight increase of the 95th quantile error.

Future work items are to evaluate whether the profiling accuracy of PowerProf can be further increased by extending the search space by adding more states to each conditional feature function and by experimenting with different strategies and parameters for the genetic algorithms PowerProf employs. Additionally, we would like to consider the impact on model accuracy of applying averaging filters to remove non-periodic power spikes.

Acknowledgements. The authors acknowledge the financial support granted by Nokia and the Danish National Advanced Technology Foundation for the project Galileo: A Platform for Pervasive Positioning under J.nr. 009-2007-2. We thank Niels Aleksander Mårup Christensen for helping with the implementation and Morten Videbæk Pedersen for providing access to a Python API for the Nokia Energy Profiler.

References

1. Nokia - Energy Profiler (2008), http://www.nokia.com
2. Python for S60 (2008), http://sourceforge.net/projects/pys60
3. Pyevolve (2011), http://pyevolve.sourceforge.net
4. Blunck, H., Kjærgaard, M.B., Toftegaard, T.S.: Sensing and Classifying Impairments of GPS Reception on Mobile Devices. In: Lyons, K., Hightower, J., Huang, E.M. (eds.) Pervasive 2011. LNCS, vol. 6696, pp. 350–367. Springer, Heidelberg (2011)
5. Carroll, A., Heiser, G.: An analysis of power consumption in a smartphone. In: Proc. 2010 USENIX Annual Technical Conference, pp. 1–12 (2010)
6. Dong, M., Zhong, L.: Self-constructive high-rate system energy modeling for battery-powered mobile systems. In: Proc. 2011 Intl. Conf. Mobile Systems, Applications, and Services, pp. 335–348 (2011)
7. Kantardzic, M.: Chapter 10 - Genetic Algorithms. Data Mining: Concepts, Models, Methods, and Algorithms. John Wiley & Sons (2003)
8. Kjærgaard, M.B.: On Improving the Energy Efficiency and Robustness of Position Tracking for Mobile Devices. In: Sénac, P., Ott, M., Seneviratne, A. (eds.) MobiQuitous 2010. LNICST, vol. 73, pp. 162–173. Springer, Heidelberg (2012)
9. Kjærgaard, M.B.: Minimizing the Power Consumption of Location-Based Services on Mobile Phones. IEEE Pervasive Computing 11(1), 67–73 (2012)
10. Kjærgaard, M.B., Bhattacharya, S., Blunck, H., Nurmi, P.: Energy-efficient trajectory tracking for mobile devices. In: Proc. 9th Intl. Conf. Mobile Systems, Applications, and Services, pp. 307–320. ACM (2011)
11. Kjærgaard, M.B., Langdal, J., Godsk, T., Toftkjær, T.: Entracked: energy-efficient robust position tracking for mobile devices. In: Proc. 7th Intl. Conf. Mobile Systems, Applications, and Services, pp. 221–234 (2009)
12. Küpper, A.: Location-Based Services: Fundamentals and Operation. Wiley (2005)
13. Nokia. S60 Platform: Effective Power and Resource Management. Nokia (2007)
14. Pathak, A., Hu, Y.C., Zhang, M., Bahl, P., Wang, Y.-M.: Fine-grained power modeling for smartphones using system call tracing. In: Proc. of the Sixth European Conference on Computer Systems, pp. 153–168 (2011)
15. Rice, A.C., Hay, S.: Decomposing power measurements for mobile devices. In: Proc. 8th Annual IEEE Intl. Conf. Pervasive Computing and Communications, pp. 70–78 (2010)
16. Zhang, L., Tiwana, B., Qian, Z., Wang, Z., Dick, R.P., Mao, Z.M., Yang, L.: Accurate online power estimation and automatic battery behavior based power model generation for smartphones. In: Proc. 8th Intl. Conf. Hardware/Software Codesign and System Synthesis, pp. 105–114 (2010)

Towards a New Classification of Location Privacy Methods in Pervasive Computing

Mads Schaarup Andersen and Mikkel Baun Kjærgaard

Department of Computer Science
Aarhus University
{masa,mikkelbk}@cs.au.dk

Abstract. Over the last decade many methods for location privacy have been proposed, but the mapping between classes of location based services and location privacy methods is not obvious. This entails confusion for developers, lack of usage of privacy methods, and an unclear roadmap ahead for research within location privacy. This paper presents a two-dimensional classification of existing methods for location privacy grouping them by the type of location based service to which they apply and location privacy method category. The types of location based services identified are *Point-of-Interest, Social Networking, Collaborative Sensing*, and *Route Tracing*, and the high level location privacy method categories are *Anonymization, Classical Security, Spatial Obfuscation, Temporal Obfuscation*, and *Protocol*. It is found that little work exists on location privacy in the areas of Social Networking and Collaborative Sensing, and that insufficient work has been done in Route Tracing. It is concluded that none of the existing methods cover all applications of Route Tracing. It is, therefore, suggested that a new overall method should be proposed to solve the problem of location privacy in Route Tracing. Furthermore, future challenges are identified.

Keywords: Location Privacy, Pervasive Computing, Ubiquitous Computing.

1 Introduction

With the number of smart phones based on Android and iOS soon exceeding the number of stationary and laptop computers on the Internet, applications for these devices, usually referred to as Apps, are penetrating the everyday life of people. One of the interesting aspects of Apps is that they are able to incorporate sensor data from the device and use it to provide services based on this. Currently, many apps are available for these devices and a subset of these use the location of the device (computed in some way using one or more sensors) as an integrated and essential part. These are called location based services (LBSs). In February 2010, there were 6,400 LBSs in Apples AppStore and more than 1,000 LBSs in Androids Marketplace[1]. Using location as an integrated part of

---

[1] http://skyhookwireless.com/locationapps/

A. Puiatti et al. (Eds.): MobiQuitous 2011, LNICST 104, pp. 150–161, 2012.
© Institute for Computer Sciences, Social Informatics and Telecommunications Engineering 2012

an application has enabled a number of new application domains such as navigation, friend finder, route tracking, etc. However, these services require the user to disclose his location. This introduces the concern of preserving the privacy of the user. In 1993, Bellotti and Sellen recognized that ubiquitous computing is particularly prone to attack on privacy [5] and in 2001, Langheinrich proposed six guidelines to system design to include privacy concerns [26]. Since then a lot of different methods for location privacy have been introduced, but each of them for a specific application domain and usually to solve a very specific problem. This makes it difficult for a developer to choose how location privacy should be obtained, and hence location privacy methods are often not added. Furthermore, there seems to be a lack of work in location privacy for other than Point-of-Interest (POI) services, e.g., GPS navigation, where a user can query a service for route to an address. However, during recent years new types of LBSs have emerged where the usage of location has become increasingly complex. Position is no longer shared only with a service, but might also be shared with other users in real time. Furthermore, other things than just the position might be shared with the position receiver making things such as recommender services possible. This makes it interesting to categorize LBSs in relation to location privacy, and thereafter place the existing location privacy methods using this categorization.

The contribution of this paper is twofold. The first contribution is to provide an overview of how existing location privacy methods relate to different types of LBSs, hence aiding the developer in the choice of privacy method. This is done using a two-dimensional classification scheme with *type of LBS* on one axis and *high level location privacy method* on the other. The existing work is then placed in this categorization, and hence a developer can consult it to choose an appropriate method for his location enabled app. The second contribution of this paper is to provide the research community with a road-map for research in location privacy. This is done by analyzing the above mentioned overview to reveal gaps in research. It will then be considered whether the location privacy methods of the classification can solve the gaps, and if this it is the case that a category has issues that cannot be solved with existing methods, a new method will be proposed.

Several other papers have addressed the problem of surveying and classifying location privacy methods. Krumm [25] identifies a number of open research questions in location privacy by identifying location privacy methods, attacks on these, and by surveying the results of empirical studies. Scipioni and Langheinrich [34] recognize the need for further research to be done in relation to location privacy in the newer LBS category of Social Networking (SN) services, and they propose a categorization of LBSs based on the multiplicity between sender and receiver of location. Christin et. al [8] survey the entire area of privacy in participatory sensing including location privacy. However, the three mentioned papers lack a way to make the coupling between existing methods and how they can be applied to different categories of LBSs.

The rest of the paper is structured as follows. Section 2 and Section 3 describe the two dimensions of the classification. Section 4 places the existing methods in the classification. Section 5 covers open challenges and Section 6 provides a conclusion.

2   Categories of Methods for Location Privacy

In the following we present our categorization of location privacy methods. This is based one a categorization proposed by Andersen [3], which builds on the work of Duckham and Kulik [12]. In this paper we divide privacy methods into the five categories of: *Anonymity*, *Classical Security*, *Spatial Obfuscation*, *Temporal Obfuscation*, and *Protocol*. We elaborate on these categories in the following:

Anonymity methods obtain privacy by hiding the identity of the user when providing the location. It is therefore possible to see the exact location, but impossible to tie any user to the location. A sub-category of anonymity is *pseudonymity* where the user's real identity is replaced by a pseudonym, and the idea is then that it should be impossible for an adversary to use this pseudonym to identify the user's real identity.

Classical Security methods provide privacy using classical security methods. This can be either *cryptography* or *security policies*. In cryptography the position can be encrypted using either a secret or public key encryption scheme (usually public key), so that only the provider and consumer of the position will be able to read the contents, hiding it from adversaries. When using security policies it can be expressed who can and cannot gain access, similar to access control lists in file systems.

Spatial Obfuscation methods obtain privacy by obfuscation the position of the user in space. This means that rather than providing a single point as the location an area A is provided to the position receiver.

Temporal Obfuscation methods provide privacy by obfuscating the position of the user in time. This means that instead of providing the user position in real time, the location is provided at an obfuscated position in time by adding Δt.

Protocol Privacy is obtained by having a custom protocol to enhance the privacy. This is usually used in combination with anonymity or spatial obfuscation to either hide the user identity or aid in obfuscating the position.

3   Categories of Location Based Services

In this section we will provide a categorization of LBSs. The categorization is defined in relation to relevant properties of location privacy methods. This is partly inspired by Andersen [3] who proposes LBS categories and Scipioni and

Langheinrich [34] who divide SN services into categories based on multiplicity between sender and receiver. It is our claim that the latter applies to a broader range of LBSs than just SN. Besides that we include details about the position sensitivity, importance of ID, and whether the position is shared in real time. We use this to emphasize what differs between the types of LBS that we identified. The interesting properties are:

Receiver. Who is receiving the position? This can either be a *service* which is running on a server or it can be *peers* where other users will use the position. A last option would be the case where the service runs locally, as it is the case in most car navigation devices. However, if everything runs locally the privacy concerns change. If the phone is stolen it is suddenly a threat to the privacy if sensitive information is located on the phone. This is, however, not in the scope of the privacy of intended sharing of positions and is therefore omitted.

Number of Receivers. The number of users which will receive the position. Can be 1 or n.

Number of Users. The number of users which need to provide their position in order for the LBS to make sense. Can be 1 or n.

ID Importance. How important is it for the LBS to know the true identity of the user. Can be *High*, *Medium*, or *Low*. High means very important, medium means that it depends on the specific application, and low means that it is not needed.

Spatial Sensitivity. How important is it to place the user in an exact point rather than an area. Can be *High*, *Medium*, or *Low*. High means that exact position is needed, medium means that it depends on the specific application, and low means that an area can be provided instead.

Temporal Sensitivity. How important is it that the user is placed in time. Can be *High*, *Medium*, or *Low*. High means that the LBS needs the time, medium means that it depends on the specific application, and low means that time is never essential.

Sharing Phase. Is the data shared in real time, or at a later stage. Referred to as *online* (real time) and *offline* phases.

In our categorization of LBSs, we will call the simple request-reply applications *Point-of-Interest* (POI), everything concerned with social networks *Social Networking* (SN), and participatory sensing *Collaborative Sensing* (CS) as we in the CS category focus on the type of LBSs where users share data with everybody. Furthermore, none of the three mentioned categories cover an emerging type of LBS, namely *Route Tracing* (RT). In this category of LBSs, instead of sharing a single position, the user shares a trace of coherent positions. The four categories are explained in detail in the following. Table 1 lists the important properties in relation to location privacy for the four mentioned categories.

Table 1. Important location privacy properties of the four categories of LBSs

	POI	SN	CS	RT
Receiver	Service	Peers	Service	Peers or Service
# Receivers	1	n	n	n
# Users	1	1	n	1
ID Importance	High	High	Low	Medium
Spatial Sen.	High	Medium	High	Medium
Temporal Sen.	High	High	High	Medium
Sharing Ph.	Online	Online	Online or Offline	Offline

Point-of-Interest. POI services are the first LBSs which appeared. Here a user sends a request to a server for nearest POI. This can e.g. be gas stations or the local weather forecast, and the service then replies with a set of coordinates, localized information, or possibly a route direction to the POI. In POI services, a single user queries a server to find the nearest POI. I.e. we have a 1 to 1 relationship between users and receivers. As the server needs to know who to send the reply to, ID has high importance. POI services are highly spatial sensitive as the precision of the reply depends on it. When the user is moving, POI services are, furthermore, very sensitive in regards to temporal aspects. POI services are only relevant in an online phase.

Social Network Services. SN services have become popular over the last few years with the wide adaption of Facebook Places[2], Google Latitude[3] etc. In these services, users share locations (and optionally meta-data) with friends, which are considered *peers*. SN services have a 1 to n relationship between providers and consumers, as the provider wants to share his data with a well defined (sharing with all is also considered well defined) set of receivers. As SN services are in nature self-promoting, the ID of the user is very important. Spatially, the sensitivity is of medium importance, as it is only important to tie the user to a place which might be defined as an overall area, e.g., in Facebook places where the user's location might be a building complex. Temporal sensitivity is also high as it is not interesting for receivers to know that the user at some point was at a concert if the receivers are trying to meet up with the person. SN services are interesting in an online phase.

Collaborative Sensing. In CS services, the users collect data and provide them for a service and potentially all other users. An example of this is a traffic monitoring system such as the one provided by Google Maps[4]. CS services have an n to n relationship between sender and receivers as it is vital that all the users participate for the service to make sense, and that everybody can access the data. The ID of the individual user is of low importance as it is rather the

---

[2] http://www.facebook.com/places

[3] http://www.google.com/latitude

[4] http://maps.google.com

data he provides that is relevant to the service. Spatially and temporally the sensitivity is high as the exact position is needed as well as the position in time is important. CS services are interesting in both online and offline cases. This is illustrated by the traffic monitoring example. Here the data can be used to get a real time image of the traffic at a certain point, but the data can also be used for analysis of areas often prone to congestion.

Route Tracing. The above categories cover all LBSs where a position is shared in real-time, or in an *online* phase. However, if we want to share a trace of positions collected earlier, in an *offline* phase, we have another set of privacy challenges. In RT the users collect a trace of positions linked in time rather than a single position. An example is sharing exercises such as running routes in systems such as Endomondo[5] where users then can compete on the same routes and distance and analyze performance. Furthermore, RT is becoming widely adapted by insurance companies offering usage-based insurance. An example of this is Alkabox[6] where a box records the GPS position in conjunction with acceleration data and calculates insurance based on these in case of an accident. RT is a relatively new type of LBS but is very important as not only are people sharing exercise routes, but companies are starting to record data about their customers. Furthermore, it has been proposed to use RT for road pricing [11] and hence the government might be able to track citizens leading to a big brother scenario. It is therefore the opinion of the authors that the area of RT is of high importance. That RT should be a category on its own has not yet been proposed in the literature, but as it has different properties than the rest of the categories proposed, it is indicated that RT is not covered by any of the other categories.

In RT, the trace is shared with peers or a service, and the multiplicity between senders and receivers is 1 to n. ID in itself has medium importance depending on the specific application domain. In insurance it is necessary for the insurer to know the ID, but in exercise sharing it is less important to know the exact ID of the user. Here, characteristics of the user might be enough. Spatially, the precision needed is medium as the appropriate accuracy of the position depends on the application area. Temporally, the sensitivity is also medium as it is important to be able to place the individual positions in relation to each other. However, the positions might not need to be placed in time of day. RT is done in an offline phase.

4   Classification of Existing Methods

In the following section, we will classify the existing location privacy methods with respect to the two above mentioned dimensions. Thereafter, we will analyze the contents of the table focusing on empty or close to empty cells and reason about whether the gap has a logical explanation or it is an open area needing more research. The result of the classification can be found in Table 2.

---

[5] http://www.endomondo.com
[6] http://www.alkabox.dk

A challenge for the classification is that some methods combine several types of privacy methods. An example is CacheCloak [29] which is a combination of anonymity and temporal obfuscation. The papers where this is the case, are placed in the category where they fit the best by the authors judgment. In the case of CacheCloak this is anonymity. To discuss the result of the classification we start out with the filled cells:

Table 2. Classification of existing location privacy methods to high level location privacy methods and categories of LBSs

	Point-of-interest	Social Networking	Collaborative Sensing	Route Tracing
Anonymity	Mix Zones[6] k-anonymity[15] CacheCloak[29] CliqueCloak[14] Distributed Anonymity[18] Pseudonymity[33]		AnonySense[9] Traffic Monitoring[19] HitchHiking[35]	
Security	P3P Inspired[1] Confab[22] Dynamic Privacy Management[21] LocServ[32]	Loccacino[10]		
Spatial Ob.	LBAC[4] SpaceTwist[36] Grid-based[16] KNN[23] Source Simulation[28] Louis, Lester and Pierre[38] ILRQ[7] New Casper[30] Obfuscation[13] Path Confusion[20]	Proximity Queries[27]		Gaussian Noise [24] Spatial Rounding [24] Selective Hiding [31]
Temporal Ob.	Temporal Ob.[17]			
Protocol	MIST[2] Geographic Routing[37]			

A lot of work has been done on anonymization in POI [6,15,29,14,18,33]. An example is k-anonymity [15] where the user is indistinguishable among $k - 1$ other users. Classical security in POI is also well covered [1,22,21,32]. An example is Confab [22] which is a framework providing basic security mechanisms for controlling access to data. Spatial obfuscation has also been a main area of interest in POI [4,36,16,23,28,38,7,30,13,20,27]. The New Casper [30] is an example where the user is placed in a grid structure rather than in a single point. Though, not a lot of work has been done in temporal obfuscation, Gruteser and Grunwald [17] have made comments on how such a method should work. Finally, in POI work has been done in creating custom privacy enabling protocols [2,37]. An example is MIST [2] where the routing of the data makes it very difficult to track the origin of data.

In classical security for SN, some work has been done in the Loccacino project [10]. Here user controllable privacy has been tested, mainly with the use of access control lists. Within SN there has also been work in spatial obfuscation with proximity queries [27] where a threshold is used to obfuscate the position of the user.

Some work has been done in anonymization for CS [9,35,19]. An example of this is Hitchhiking [35] where the user's ID is hidden.

Lastly, there has been some work done on spatial obfuscation for RT [24,31]. An example of this is adding Gaussian Noise to a trace, hence rendering it impossible to distinguish the actual positions from the added noise [24].

Next, we will comment on the obvious empty cells in the table. One of the first things to notice is that close to no work has been done in temporal obfuscation for any category. With Table 1 in mind, this is explainable with the fact that all LBSs have high or medium temporal sensitivity, and hence the method is not well suited for LBSs. The next thing to notice in the table is that the POI category is well covered in all location method categories, and hence it should be easy for a developer to choose an appropriate method for any kind of application within this LBS category. Moreover, it seems that this area is well researched, as a large variety of methods have been proposed.

In relation to SN services, not that many methods have been proposed. Here the anonymization category is empty. In relation to our definition of SN services, this makes sense, as the purpose is for the user to share some information about himself. If the data was anonymized it would be impossible to tie this information to a user. The fact that there has only been done work in the categories of security and spatial obfuscation indicates that these categories fit well to SN, but protocol seems to be an unexplored area with possibilities.

In the CS category, there has only been published anonymization location privacy methods. This is due to the fact that when data is anonymized it is difficult to infer a specific user, and since these applications cover LBSs where user ID is irrelevant, this make sense. Sometimes it might, however, make sense to apply some of the other methods to further enhance the privacy of the participating user. This could e.g. be in a weather sensing application where an area rather than a point might be enough. Hence, CS also has unexplored areas.

Lastly, we see that RT only has work done in spatial obfuscation [24,31]. This works fine for some applications of RT, but for the applications mentioned earlier in Section 3 these methods have limited applicability. This is e.g. the case for usage based insurance. Snapping to a grid, as done in Spatial Rounding, might hide the fact that the user has driven in a certain high-risk area which would increase the insurance (depending on the insurance policy and resolution of the grid). In adding Gaussian noise there might be the problem that the insurance company would charge the user for being in all positions (including the noise), and hence this has a potentially huge disadvantage for the user. Lastly, using selective hiding the user could choose to always hide a specific high-risk area in his trace.

As mentioned earlier, RT is becoming more and more used, and considering the mentioned possible applications it is very important to develop privacy methods which cover these as well. An observation is that other categories of LBSs are concerned with sharing a single position and RT is concerned with sharing an entire trace of positions. This observation suggests that it might be a good idea to do some research in an entirely new high level method for location privacy.

5   Open Challenges

As identified in this paper there are still a lot of open challenges in the area of location privacy. We see challenges in three main areas: *Location Privacy Methods*, *Software Engineering*, and *User Awareness*.

Location Privacy Methods require more exploration of protocol and temporal obfuscation for SN services; spatial and temporal obfuscation, protocol, and classical security for CS; and all areas of RT. Moreover, we suggest that emphasis is put on developing a new category for RT as RT has many features that differ from the other categories of LBSs. This is mainly due to the fact that a trace rather than a single position is shared. It is a challenge that for some domains of RT spatial rounding, adding noise, or using selective hiding are not applicable.

Software Engineering calls for further examination of how application developers can be aided in adding location privacy to applications. The categorization presented in this paper is the first step, but currently no tools or frameworks that can aid the developer in adding location privacy to LBSs exist. The ones that do exist are only concerned with very specific types of LBSs in mind. It would be interesting to examine the effects of providing application developers with such a tool or framework, and see if it has an impact of how often location privacy methods would be used.

User Awareness is problematic as users are not all that concerned about sharing their location with others. This is the case, even though research has shown the potential dangers of doing so. Futhermore, research needs to be done in how we make people aware of the possible dangers of sharing location data. It seems that a demand from users could drive the developers to care more.

6   Conclusion

In this paper we presented a two-dimensional classification of location privacy methods in relation to types of LBSs. In this classification we placed the existing privacy methods proposed by the research community. This will serve as a reference for LBS developers wanting to add privacy support to applications. Furthermore, the classification had the purpose of pointing out open areas in location privacy research. The results were that POI is fully covered and less research should be focused on this area. However, there are open issues in the areas of SN and CS services where more privacy methods should be explored. Moreover, the classification showed that the area of RT, though important, is close to unexplored, and that the methods proposed do not cover all applications of RT, suggesting that none of the high level location privacy methods fits the specific purpose. It is concluded that a new category of location privacy methods is needed for this RT.

References

1. Ackerman, M.S.: Privacy in pervasive environments: next generation labeling protocols. Personal Ubiquitous Comput. 8, 430–439 (2004)
2. Al-Muhtadi, J., Campbell, R., Kapadia, A., Mickunas, M.D., Yi, S.: Routing through the mist: privacy preserving communication in ubiquitous computing environments. In: Proc. 22nd Int. Conference on Distributed Computing Systems, 2002, pp. 74–83 (2002)
3. Andersen, M.S.: On limitations of existing methods for location privacy. In: 3rd International Workshop on Security and Privacy in Spontaneous Interaction and Mobile Phone Use (2011)
4. Ardagna, C.A., Cremonini, M., Damiani, E., De Capitani di Vimercati, S., Samarati, P.: Location Privacy Protection Through Obfuscation-Based Techniques. In: Barker, S., Ahn, G.-J. (eds.) Data and Applications Security 2007. LNCS, vol. 4602, pp. 47–60. Springer, Heidelberg (2007)
5. Bellotti, V., Sellen, A.: Design for privacy in ubiquitous computing environments. In: Proc. of the 3rd conf. on European Conference on Computer-Supported Cooperative Work, pp. 77–92. Kluwer Academic Publishers, Norwell (1993)
6. Beresford, A.R., Stajano, F.: Location privacy in pervasive computing. IEEE Pervasive Computing 2(1), 46–55 (2003)
7. Cheng, R., Zhang, Y., Bertino, E., Prabhakar, S.: Preserving user location privacy in mobile data management infrastructures (2006)
8. Christin, D., Reinhardt, A., Kanhere, S., Hollick, M.: A survey on privacy in mobile participatory sensing applications. Journal of Systems and Software (2011) (in Press) (accepted manuscript)
9. Cornelius, C., Kapadia, A., Kotz, D., Peebles, D., Shin, M., Triandopoulos, N.: Anonysense: privacy-aware people-centric sensing. In: Proc. of the 6th Int. Conf. on Mobile Systems, Applications, and Services, MobiSys 2008, pp. 211–224. ACM, New York (2008)
10. Cornwell, J., Fette, I., Hsieh, G., Prabaker, M., Rao, J., Tang, K., Vaniea, K., Bauer, L., Cranor, L., Hong, J., McLaren, B., Reiter, M., Sadeh, N.: User-controllable security and privacy for pervasive computing. In: Proc. of the 8th IEEE Workshop on Mobile Computing Systems and Applications (2007)
11. Coroama, V.: The Smart Tachograph – Individual Accounting of Traffic Costs and Its Implications. In: Fishkin, K.P., Schiele, B., Nixon, P., Quigley, A. (eds.) PERVASIVE 2006. LNCS, vol. 3968, pp. 135–152. Springer, Heidelberg (2006)
12. Duckham, M., Kulik, L.: In: Drummond, J. (ed.) Dynamic & mobile GIS: investigating change in space and time. CRC (2006)

13. Duckham, M., Kulik, L.: A Formal Model of Obfuscation and Negotiation for Location Privacy. In: Gellersen, H.-W., Want, R., Schmidt, A. (eds.) PERVASIVE 2005. LNCS, vol. 3468, pp. 152–170. Springer, Heidelberg (2005)
14. Gedik, B., Liu, L.: Location privacy in mobile systems: A personalized anonymization model. In: Proc. of the 25th IEEE Int. Conf on Distributed Computing Systems, pp. 620–629 (2005)
15. Gedik, B., Liu, L.: A customizable k-anonymity model for protecting location privacy. In: ICDCS, pp. 620–629 (2004)
16. Gidofalvi, G., Huang, X., Pedersen, T.B.: Privacy-preserving data mining on moving object trajectories. In: 2007 Int. Conf. on Mobile Data Management (2007)
17. Gruteser, M., Grunwald, D.: Anonymous usage of location-based services through spatial and temporal cloaking. In: Proceedings of the 1st International Conference on Mobile Systems, Applications and Services, MobiSys 2003, pp. 31–42. ACM, New York (2003)
18. Gruteser, M., Schelle, G., Jain, A., Han, R., Grunwald, D.: Privacy-aware location sensor networks. In: Proc. of the 9th Conf. on Hot Topics in Operating Systems, vol. 9 (2003)
19. Hoh, B., Gruteser, M., Xiong, H., Alrabady, A.: Enhancing security and privacy in traffic-monitoring systems. IEEE Pervasive Computing 5(4), 38–46 (2006)
20. Hoh, B., Gruteser, M.: Protecting location privacy through path confusion. In: 1st Int. Conf. on Security and Privacy for Emerging Areas in Communications Networks (2005)
21. Hong, D., Yuan, M., Shen, V.Y.: Dynamic privacy management: a plug-in service for the middleware in pervasive computing. In: Proc. of the 7th Int. Conf. on Human Computer Interaction with Mobile Devices & Services (2005)
22. Hong, J.I., Landay, J.A.: An architecture for privacy-sensitive ubiquitous computing. In: Proceedings of the 2nd International Conference on Mobile Systems, Applications, and Services, MobiSys 2004, pp. 177–189. ACM, New York (2004)
23. Khoshgozaran, A., Shahabi, C.: Blind Evaluation of Nearest Neighbor Queries Using Space Transformation to Preserve Location Privacy. In: Papadias, D., Zhang, D., Kollios, G. (eds.) SSTD 2007. LNCS, vol. 4605, pp. 239–257. Springer, Heidelberg (2007)
24. Krumm, J.: Inference Attacks on Location Tracks. In: LaMarca, A., Langheinrich, M., Truong, K.N. (eds.) Pervasive 2007. LNCS, vol. 4480, pp. 127–143. Springer, Heidelberg (2007)
25. Krumm, J.: A survey of computational location privacy. Personal Ubiquitous Comput. 13, 391–399 (2009)
26. Langheinrich, M.: Privacy by Design - Principles of Privacy-Aware Ubiquitous Systems. In: Abowd, G.D., Brumitt, B., Shafer, S. (eds.) UbiComp 2001. LNCS, vol. 2201, pp. 273–291. Springer, Heidelberg (2001)
27. Mascetti, S., Bettini, C., Freni, D., Sean Wang, X., Jajodia, S.: Privacy-aware proximity based services. In: Proc. of the 10th Int. Conf. on Mobile Data Management: Systems, Services and Middleware (2009)
28. Mehta, K., Liu, D., Wright, M.: Location privacy in sensor networks against a global eavesdropper. In: IEEE Int. Conf. on Network Protocols (2007)
29. Meyerowitz, J., Choudhury, R.R.: Hiding stars with fireworks: location privacy through camouflage. In: Proc. of the 15th Annual Int. Conf. on Mobile Computing and Networking (2009)
30. Mokbel, M.F., Chow, C.-Y., Aref, W.G.: The new casper: query processing for location services without compromising privacy. In: Proc. of the 32nd Int. Conf. on Very Large Data Bases (2006)

31. Mun, M., Reddy, S., Shilton, K., Yau, N., Burke, J., Estrin, D., Hansen, M., Howard, E., West, R., Boda, P.: Peir, the personal environmental impact report, as a platform for participatory sensing systems research. In: Proc. of the 7th Int. Conf. on Mobile Systems, Applications, and Services

32. Myles, G., Friday, A., Davies, N.: Preserving privacy in environments with location-based applications. IEEE Pervasive Computing 2, 56–64 (2003)

33. Pfitzmann, A., Köhntopp, M.: Anonymity, Unobservability, and Pseudonymity - A Proposal for Terminology. In: Federrath, H. (ed.) Anonymity 2000. LNCS, vol. 2009, pp. 1–9. Springer, Heidelberg (2001)

34. Scipioni, M.P., Langheinrich, M.: I'm here! privacy challenges in mobile location sharing. In: 2nd Int. Workshop on Security and Privacy in Spontaneous Interaction and Mobile Phone Use (2010)

35. Tang, K.P., Keyani, P., Fogarty, J., Hong, J.I.: Putting people in their place: an anonymous and privacy-sensitive approach to collecting sensed data in location-based applications. In: Proc. of the SIGCHI Conf. on Human Factors in Computing Systems (2006)

36. Yiu, M.L., Jensen, C.S., Huang, X., Lu, H.: Spacetwist: Managing the trade-offs among location privacy, query performance, and query accuracy in mobile services. In: IEEE 24th Int. Conf. on Data Engineering (2008)

37. Zhi, Z., Choong, Y.K.: Anonymizing geographic ad hoc routing for preserving location privacy. In: 25th IEEE Int. Conf. on Distributed Computing Systems Workshops (2005)

38. Zhong, G., Goldberg, I., Hengartner, U.: Louis, Lester and Pierre: Three Protocols for Location Privacy. In: Borisov, N., Golle, P. (eds.) PET 2007. LNCS, vol. 4776, pp. 62–76. Springer, Heidelberg (2007)

A Simulation Model for Evaluating Distributed Storage Services for Smart Product Systems

Markus Miche[1], Kai Baumann[1], Jerome Golenzer[2], and Marc Brogle[1]

[1] SAP Research Switzerland,
Kreuzplatz 20, 8008 Zurich, Switzerland
{markus.miche,kai.baumann,marc.brogle}@sap.com
[2] EADS Innovation Works,
Rue Marius Terce 18, 31300 Toulouse, France
jerome.golenzer@eads.net

Abstract. While subsets of the functionality of intelligent physical objects such as context awareness or integration with backend systems can be analyzed and assessed using small-scale experiments, the evaluation of most distributed services such as content replication and placement strategies requires dedicated simulation environments. Despite the availability of various related simulation frameworks for analyzing P2P overlay networks, WSNs, or RFID technology, there is no simulation model that reflects the characteristics of *smart* products with embedded computing, storage, and networking functionality. This paper proposes a simulation model that facilitates simulation of distributed storage services of smart products based on P2P overlay networks. In order to exemplify the suitability of the proposed simulation model, it is applied to the industry application scenario *smart aircraft manufacturing* as envisaged by EADS Innovation Works.

Keywords: Smart Products, Simulation, Distributed Storage, P2P, Aircraft Manufacturing.

1 Introduction

In diverse domains such as manufacturing, retail, or logistics, one can encounter an increasing number of intelligent physical objects that enhance business processes by means of real-time data or context-aware and personalized user guidance. This ranges from objects being equipped with smart labels such as RFID or NFC tags to so-called *smart* products with embedded computing, storage, and networking capabilities. Smart products are able to build ad-hoc networks as well as to self-organize in scalable Peer-to-Peer (P2P) overlay networks that facilitate efficient communication without relying on central entities. Moreover, smart products make use of distributed process models in order to assist and interact with their users as well as to autonomously collaborate to fulfill their tasks. For this purpose, smart products operate complex distributed services such as distributed process execution services or distributed storage services including content replication and placement strategies.

A. Puiatti et al. (Eds.): MobiQuitous 2011, LNICST 104, pp. 162–173, 2012.

However, even though smart products represent high-class intelligent physical objects, they typically only possess limited on-board storage and computing resources. Moreover, due to their mobility and usage in different environments with varying environmental conditions, smart products are subject to regular disconnections. This characteristic is further affected by the usage of energy-efficient communication modules, which automatically deactivate themselves after a certain period of inactivity [1].

While functionality such as context awareness or integration with backend systems can be analyzed and assessed by means of small-scale experiments, the evaluation of complex distributed services requires extensive test environments. Especially in early development phases, the installation of large test beds is not appropriate and simulation environments reflecting characteristics of smart products appear to be the approach of choice. Simulation environments can be classified into *network simulators* and *overlay simulators*. Network simulators such as NS-3[1] or OMNeT++[2] facilitate packet-level simulation of network protocols and can be utilized for analyzing wireless sensor networks or RFID systems. Overlay simulators such as OverSim[3] or PlanetSim[4] abstract from network details and focus on overlay network routing protocols and services (see survey presented in [2]). However, to the knowledge of the authors, while both kinds of simulators could be used as basis for simulating and evaluating distributed storage services of smart products, there is no simulation model that fully reflects the characteristics of smart product systems.

This paper presents an extended overlay simulation model that facilitates simulation of distributed storage services of smart products being organized in P2P overlay networks. It reflects the characteristics of smart products including their heterogeneity, resource limitation, mobility, as well as their process-based operations. As opposed to common overlay simulators that assume simplified topologies, the proposed model enables consideration of underlay networks with realistic topologies in order to enable accurate simulations. Even further, the paper presents a detailed analysis and modeling of the smart products industry scenario *smart aircraft manufacturing* as envisaged by EADS Innovation Works using the proposed simulation model. This shows not only the suitability of the latter but moreover a potential procedure for analyzing and modeling simulations of distributed storage services of smart products.

The remainder of the paper is structured as follows: Section 2 presents the proposed simulation model for smart products. This includes the conceptual structure of the model, simulation events, product and content properties, as well as underlay network configuration options. Thereafter, the smart products industry scenario *smart aircraft manufacturing* as well as a detailed modeling of the latter using the proposed simulation model are presented in Section 3. The paper concludes in Section 4 with an outlook on future work.

---

[1] http://www.nsnam.org/

[2] http://www.omnetpp.org/

[3] http://www.oversim.org/

[4] http://projects-deim.urv.cat/trac/planetsim/

2   Conceptual Simulation Model

2.1   Conceptual Structure of the Simulation Model

The proposed extended overlay simulation model for distributed storage services of smart products consists of four logical layers. The underlay network layer is used to model basic underlay networks with realistic topologies in order to enable accurate simulations and analyses of distributed services. This includes node distribution and clustering, bandwidth allocation, as well as communication delays. Due to the purpose of the simulation model, i.e., the simulation of distributed storage services of smart products being organized in P2P overlay networks, additional underlay network properties such as packet delay variation or packet loss are not considered. This way, quality attributes of distributed storage services such as average content access latencies or content access hit rates given that messages are assigned pre-defined timeouts can be evaluated with much higher accuracy compared to simulation models that purely rely on virtual random topologies. The second layer, overlay network, encapsulates all functionality of P2P content location and routing substrates.

While most simulation models solely consider a single application layer, the proposed model distinguishes between overlay services, i.e., distributed services that directly operate on the P2P overlay network, and the actual application logic that utilizes functionality of the overlay service layer. Finally, the simulation model applies the Common API (CAPI) as defined by [3] in order to ease simulation of different overlay networks and overlay services. The layered structure of the simulation model as well as an exemplary instantiation is presented in Fig. 1.

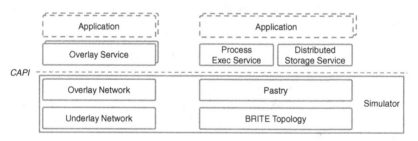

Fig. 1. Conceptual Structure of the Simulation Model

The simulation model is designed for discrete event simulators and follows the two phases and the control flow defined by [4]. While events scheduled and processed by the simulation engine affect all layers of the simulation model (see Section 2.2), only the two lower layers are actually controlled by the simulation engine and require simulator-specific implementations. In contrast, applications as well as overlay services that comply with the CAPI can directly be deployed in the simulation environment without requiring adaptations. This simplifies simulation of distributed services of smart products and is especially valuable, if simulation is used in early development phases and complemented by test-bed experiments.

2.2   Simulation Events

The dynamics of smart product systems is modeled by events that are scheduled and processed by the simulator. On the underlay and overlay network layer, the simulation model supports node *join*, node *fail* and *leave*, as well as node *move* events. Joining nodes are integrated into the underlay network, in which they are associated with unassigned underlay nodes that reflect their capabilities. Moreover, they self-organize into the overlay structure according to the means of the concrete overlay network implementation. Node *fail* events are used to model ungraceful leaves of nodes, i.e., nodes that suddenly disappear (e.g., because they run out of energy or loose connectivity). This behavior is complemented by node *leave* events, which are used to model graceful leaves of nodes that explicitly announce their leave to enable other nodes to react accordingly (e.g., by triggering content handover). Finally, node *move* events trigger node position changes, which are fully covered by the underlay network layer (see Section 2.3).

In addition to the typical events for simulating node churn, the simulation model covers overlay service events for simulating distributed storage services. This includes content *get* as well as *put* events, which reflect queries for content objects and explicit content storage, respectively. Replication or caching strategies are not covered by *put* events and must be separately estimated in order to determine the expected overall load generated during simulation runs. As described in [5], the simulation model moreover includes *process execution* events that trigger process operations and – indirectly – distributed storage service events for collecting content required during process executing as well as for persisting process results (an example is presented in Section 3.1).

The distribution functions of node *join* and *move* events as well as content *get* and *put* events are configured as described in [6, 7]. Node *leave* and *fail* events adopt the lifetime churn model defined by the simulation framework OverSim.[5] Finally, node *process execution* events are scheduled based on a normal distribution (see Table 1).

Table 1. Simulation Events

Event	Distribution Function
Node join	$t_{join} := Poisson(\lambda)$
Node fail	$t_{fail} := Weibull(\alpha, \beta)$
	$P(fail) = \delta$
Node leave	$t_{leave} := Weibull(\alpha, \beta)$
	$P(leave) = 1 - P(fail) = 1 - \delta$
Node move	$t_{move} := Normal(\mu, \sigma^2)$
Get request	$t_{get} := Poisson(\lambda)$
Put request	$t_{put} := Poisson(\lambda)$
Node process execution	$t_{process} := Normal(\mu, \sigma^2)$

Both overlay network and overlay service events are scheduled according to a node-centric event scheduling approach. Hence, instead of having the simulator randomly assigning events to nodes, nodes are responsible for scheduling their events. As depicted in the simulation event graph illustrated in Fig. 2, node *join* events are

---

[5] http://www.oversim.org/wiki/OverSimChurn

scheduled during simulation initialization in order to prepare a basis network structure. *Join* events schedule node-specific *move, put, get,* and *process execution* events as well as themselves to enable new nodes joining the network. Each of these events reschedules itself in order to simulate node-specific activities according to the distribution functions defined above. Finally, since nodes may either fail or leave the network, node *fail* and *leave* events are assigned probabilities that are evaluated during the scheduling phase of the node join event routine.

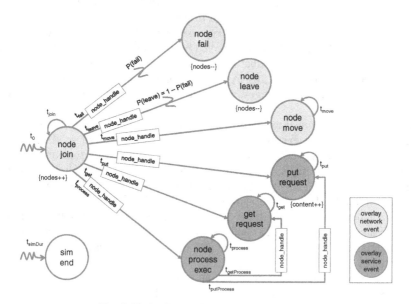

Fig. 2. Node-Centric Simulation Event Graph

2.3   Simulation Parameter

In addition to simulation events, the proposed simulation model includes node- and content-related simulation parameters that reflect the specifics of smart products. This enables modeling of heterogeneous node classes, which differ in the configuration of the distribution functions presented in Table 1 as well as regarding their on-board storage capacity. Heterogeneous communication capabilities are modeled by associating node classes with matching underlay nodes, i.e., nodes with few resources are assigned to underlay nodes with low-bandwidth communication links. Moreover, multiple content classes can be modeled and assigned to node classes, with each content class consisting of content objects of different size. This is required, because smart products with limited resources typically generate and request content of relatively smaller size than powerful smart products.

In order to facilitate simulations with high numbers of nodes and content objects, both storage capacity and content size are defined in virtual storage units (e.g., Integer values). Finally, for each content class, access popularity is configured using a Zipf-like distribution function [7].

Table 2. Simulation Parameter

Simulation Parameter	Distribution Function
Node storage capacity	$Finite - range\ discrete\ distribution$
Content size	$Finite - range\ discrete\ distribution$
Content access popularity	$Zipf - like\ distribution\ (exponent < 1)$
Underlay hierarchy	$2 - layer\ hierarchy$
Underlay cluster positioning	$Randomly$
Underlay intra-cluster node positioning	$Heavy\ tailed$
Underlay cluster topology	$Scale - free\ network$
Underlay intra-cluster topology	$Star\ topology$
Underlay node bandwidth	$Uniform\ distribution$
Underlay link delay	$Assigned\ by\ topology\ generator$
Underlay node movement	$Intra -\ and\ inter -\ cluster\ movements$

The underlay network used within the proposed simulation model requires at least as much underlay nodes as the maximum amount of nodes that may join the network during simulation (see Table 1). Nodes are organized in multiple autonomous systems (AS), which are used to model node clustering. This reflects the typical spatial clustering of smart products known from most envisaged application scenarios. Each AS consists of at least one AS-router that enables intra- as well as inter-AS communication and is assigned a configurable upper bound of participating nodes. To enable inter-AS communication given node churn and movement, inter-AS topology is realized as a scale-free network using the topology generation model introduced by Barabási and Albert [8]. Underlay nodes within an AS are arranged in a star topology, with the AS-router representing the central node. While AS are randomly placed on a virtual map, intra-AS distribution of underlay nodes follows a heavy-tailed distribution. Hence, inter-AS communication passes at least two AS-routers, namely the local AS and the remote AS-router. Communication between two underlay nodes of the same AS is always routed via the local AS-routers. This is reasonable, because the simulation model solely considers smart products being organized in P2P overlay networks; ad-hoc connections between products is out of scope.

Delivery time of route messages sent in the underlay network is affected by link delays and the smallest bandwidth available on the path between sender and receiver. While the former mainly affects delivery time of small messages (e.g., *get* request), the latter has an impact on messages with large content objects (e.g., *get* response). Since the main purpose of the underlay network layer is the realization of an accurate simulation of overlay networks and services, it only makes use of a static delay and bandwidth matrix, which is created before the actual simulation. This way, the delay and the minimal available bandwidth of a path between any two nodes are statically available and do not need to be calculated lazily. While this reduces simulation accuracy, it clearly enhances simulation execution.

Finally, node movement is realized by absolute changes of nodes' underlay position (as opposed to considering node traces). This is reasonable, since distributed storage service likely don't consider any small location change but focus on complete movements after which nodes remain stable for a certain period of time (e.g., for triggering content replacement). The simulation model supports local and remote position changes to enable intra-AS and inter-AS node movement, respectively. Note that instead of keeping idle underlay nodes for node *move, fail,* and *leave* events to enable proper communication failure handling, the simulation model maintains an internal mapping between overlay nodes and underlay nodes (both idle and active). This reduces the overall number of underlay nodes required to reflect a certain scenario with mobile products.

3   Smart Aircraft Manufacturing

3.1   Application Scenario Description

Today's aircraft manufacturing processes are characterized by paper-based process descriptions that have to be carried by blue-collar workers as well as manual tracking of assembly results. Obviously, the integration of smart products such as smart torque wrenches has great potential for enhancing efficiency of aircraft manufacturing processes. This includes automation of process steps such as tool configuration, maintenance of results of single process steps, as well as accumulation and aggregation of assembly results in order to obtain (real-time) information about aircrafts' manufacturing status.

Fig. 3 provides an overview of a future *smart aircraft manufacturing* scenario as envisaged by EADS Innovation Works [9]. The illustration shows the different kinds of smart products used in the scenario as well as their organizational interrelation.

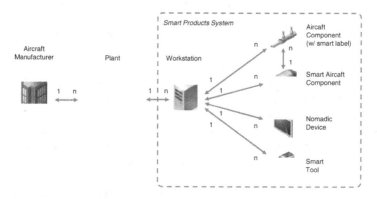

Fig. 3. Smart Aircraft Manufacturing

As described in [10], instance-level aircraft manufacturing process descriptions are distributed from the aircraft manufacturer to the different plants, in which they are further dispatched to the corresponding smart aircraft components and/or workstations at which manufacturing is accomplished. Plants consist of several workstations with multiple blue-collar workers per workstation. Each blue-collar worker carries a nomadic device, which is used to display instructions of manufacturing processes as well as to annotate corresponding results. In addition, each blue-collar worker makes use of smart tools (e.g., smart torque wrench, smart drill) that are automatically configured based on extended manufacturing process descriptions and capable of delivering results (e.g., torque and angle) to nomadic devices. Even further, while most components such as bolts are merely identifiable via smart labels, certain (compound) aircraft components also play the role of smart products. This way, they are able to maintain digital representations of their manufacturing status as well as open manufacturing processes that are to be accomplished (see [11]). Eventually, the component-level information maintained by smart aircraft components and workstations is delivered to and aggregated by the aircraft manufacturer in order to realize digital representations of entire aircrafts as being manufactured [9].

From a technical perspective, the smart products of the smart aircraft manufacturing scenario, i.e., nomadic device, smart tool, smart aircraft component, as well as workstations, are interconnected in a structured, multi-level P2P overlay network. Due to the limited storage capacity of smart products and the incomplete network coverage in plants [10], a distributed storage service is employed as overlay service with dedicated content replication and placement strategies. This services aims at maintaining a high-level of user-perceived performance as well as at enhancing content availability and durability in order to ensure complete digital representations of aircrafts as manufactured that can be used in subsequent phases of the product lifecycle [5].

3.2   Simulation Modeling

In order to enable evaluation of different overlay networks and services as well as the overall benefit of the envisaged smart aircraft manufacturing scenario, the latter has been modeled using the proposed simulation model.[6] The model simulates 3 shifts à 8 hours in a single plant.[7] This plant is assumed to consist of 10 workstations with a maximum number of 100 blue-collar workers per workstation. Each worker is assumed to carry 1 nomadic device as well as up to 3 smart tools. To simplify simulation modeling, workstations are assumed to be used to assemble one smart aircraft component at the same time (sequential production). Non-smart aircraft components are not explicitly modeled as they are assumed to not being capable of participating in the overlay network (e.g., due to resource and processing limitations). Instead, they use other smart products as proxies for submitting *put/get* requests. These requests are indirectly considered by adapting the request rate of the associated smart aircraft components. Finally, it is assumed that the assembly of smart aircraft components lasts 2 hours on average; the storage unit used to model storage capacity of smart products as well as content size represents 0,1 MB.

In order to determine the scale of one simulation step, multiple simulation runs with an average content size of 10 storage units (1 MB) and different underlay network configurations (e.g., different network size and node positioning) were performed and analyzed. This resulted in an average roundtrip time of 20 simulation steps for a *get*

---

[6] Since there is no prototype of the presented scenario available so far, the configuration of most parameters is based on assumptions that reflect the current status of work.

[7] Limiting the scope to a single plant is valid, because the focus of the simulation is on the extent to which smart products enhance performance of aircraft manufacturing processes.

request. Based on the assumption of an average delivery time of 10 seconds for a message with a payload of 1 MB, a simulation step is scaled to 0,5 seconds. Consequently, the simulation of 3 shifts à 8 hours lasts 172.800 simulation steps.

Simulation Events and Parameter. First, workstations are modeled as stable nodes that join during simulation initialization phase; they neither fail nor leave the network, nor do they change position. Workstations possess an average storage capacity of **127.500** MB. Second, based on the assumption of an average number of **90** blue-collar workers per workstation with each worker carrying **1** nomadic device, the simulation model consists of **900** nomadic devices on average. Nomadic devices possess on-board storage with an average storage capacity of **5.400** MB and have an average lifetime (in terms of network participation) of **4** hours, which reflects a single break per shift. Third, due to the assumption of sequential production, the simulation model includes **10** aircraft components on average (one per workstation). As described above, aircraft components have an average lifetime of **2** hours and an average storage capacity of **32,5** MB. Finally, based on the assumption of each blue-collar work carrying **2** smart tools on average, there is an average number of **1.800** smart tools with an average storage capacity of **1,6** MB. Due to their limited resources, smart tools have an average lifetime of **35** minutes. This reflects the fact that smart tools tend to deactivate communication in order to save energy in case they are not actively used (e.g., after completion of a process they have been used for).

Since all activities in the above-described smart aircraft manufacturing scenario are based on well-defined process models, the determination of *put/get* request rates per node class is derived from the process execution configuration. It is assumed that processes consist of 8 steps with each step requiring the usage of 2 smart tools (average values). As presented in Table 4, the average execution time of processes is defined as 30 minutes. Processes are solely started by nomadic devices and each nomadic device is only capable of starting a single process at the same time. Moreover, it is assumed that each blue-collar worker performs 3 processes during the assembly of an aircraft component. While smart tools store results of each process step, nomadic devices, workstations, as well as aircraft components only store results of completed processes.

Consequently, because smart tools have an average lifetime of roughly one process duration, they submit 8 *get* requests (step-related configuration) and 8 *put* requests (storage of step result) on average. Nomadic devices are alive for approximately the assembly of 2 aircraft components. Since they store both processes as well as corresponding results they have an average *put/get* request rate of 12. Due to an average number of 90 blue-collar workers per workstation with each worker performing 3 processes to assembly an aircraft component, the latter has an average *put* request rate of 270 per lifetime. Moreover, since it is assumed that aircraft components know not only their manufacturing status but also open processes to be accomplished, their average *get* request rate equals their average *put* request rate. Finally, workstations have an average *put/get* request rate of 3.240. On the one hand, they provide nomadic devices and/or aircraft components with processes to be accomplished. On the other hand, they accumulate and aggregate results of all local processes in order to obtain digital representations of aircrafts as being manufactured. The detailed modeling of content class and node classes is presented in Table 3 and Table 4, respectively.

Table 3. Modeling of Content Classes in Storage Units (* indicates assumptions)

	Values (Portion)	Average Content Size
Content Class A*	2 (0,4), 5 (0,3), 10 (0,2), 50 (0,1)	9,3
Content Class B*	2 (0,8), 5 (0,2)	2,6

Table 4. Modeling of Node Classes (* indicates assumptions)

	Workstation	Nomadic Device	Aircraft Component	Smart Tool
#Nodes (average)*	10	900	10	1.800
Storage capacity*	750.000 (0,3) 1.500.000 (0,7)	20.000 (0,2) 50.000 (0,6) 100.000 (0,2)	250 (0,7) 500 (0,3)	10 (0,7) 20 (0,2) 50 (0,1)
Node join*	*Join during simulation initialization*	*Poisson(28.800)*	*Poisson(14.400)*	*Poisson(3.600)*
Node fail*	*Stable*	*Weibull(15; 28.800) P(fail) = 0,02*	*Weibull(10; 14.400) P(fail) = 0,05*	*Weibull(4; 4.200) P(fail) = 0,1*
Node leave*	*Stable*	*Weibull(15; 28.800) P(leave) = 0,98*	*Weibull(10; 14.400) P(leave) = 0,95*	*Weibull(4; 4.200) P(leave) = 0,9*
Node move*	*Stable*	*Normal(7.200; 100)*	*Stable*	*Normal(3.600; 100)*
Put request[8]	*Poisson(53,3) content class A*	*Poisson(2.384) content class A*	*Poisson(52,6) content class B*	*Poisson(425) content class B*
Get request	*Poisson(53,3) content class A*	*Poisson(2.384) content class A*	*Poisson(52,6) content class B*	*Poisson(425) content class B*
Node process execution*	–	*Normal(3.600; 100)*	–	–

Underlay Configuration. To determine the required total amount of underlay nodes, it has to be taken into account both the maximum number of products and a buffer to perform node movement. As mentioned before, the network of a single plant consists of **2.720** smart products on average with **20** products (workstation, aircraft component) being non-moving. Due to the variance of the selected distribution functions (see Table 1), the maximum number of nodes participating in the network is **5.420**. To ensure that intra- and inter-AS node movement can also be performed during peak phases, the total amount of underlay nodes is incremented to **6.000**.

---

[8] In order to ensure overlay stabilization up to a certain degree before submitting *put/get* requests, the latter are not submitted but after an initial delay of 200 simulation steps. This value results from analyses of multiple simulation runs and has to be adapted depending on overlay network properties.

According to the number of workstations, the underlay network is organized in 10 ASs. Each AS has a maximum number of 600 nodes. This includes up to 599 underlay nodes with one of them playing the role of a workstation and at least one AS-router. The bandwidth of inter-AS and intra-AS communication links is configured using a constant bandwidth of 1.000 MBits/s and a uniform distribution between 11MBits/ and 54MBits/s, respectively.

The smart aircraft manufacturing scenario has been modeled using the topology generator BRITE [12] with the parameters shown in Table 5 and Table 6. While most attributes can be directly realized using BRITE, the star topology used to interconnect underlay nodes with local AS-routers cannot be modeled by default. This has been approached by a modified delay and bandwidth matrix, which includes links between each underlay node and its local AS-router. Links that are not part of the generated topology are added using the minimum bandwidth and the sum of all delays along the shortest path between the underlay node and its local AS-router.

Table 5. BRITE Underlay Configuration

	BRITE Underlay Configuration
Topology type	$Top - Down, 2\ layer\ hierarchy$
AS connection model	$Smallest\ k - degree\ (k = 25)$
Topology generation model	$Barab\acute{a}si, Albert\ (incremental\ growth, preferential\ connectivity)$

Table 6. BRITE Underlay Node Configuration

	AS Layer	Node layer
Size main plane	1.000	100
Size inner plane	100	10
Number of nodes	10	600
Node placement	$Random$	$Heavy\ tailed$
Min number of links per node	9	2
Bandwidth distribution	$Constant\ (1.000)$	$Uniform\ (min = 11, max = 54)$

4   Conclusion and Outlook

This paper proposes a discrete, event-based simulation model that enables accurate simulation and evaluation of distributed storage services of smart products. For this purpose, it extends common overlay simulators and includes underlay network configurations in order to enable modeling of realistic topologies. Moreover, by complying with the Common API, the model eases the simulation of different P2P content location and routing substrates as well as overlay services. Being tailored to the simulation of distributed storage services, the simulation model provides overlay network and overlay service events, which are scheduled according to a node-centric scheduling approach. Moreover, in order to account for the characteristics of smart products, the simulation model contains simulation parameter that enable modeling of heterogeneous node and content classes as well as proper underlay network configurations. Finally, the paper presents an application of the proposed simulation model to the smart products industry scenario *smart aircraft manufacturing* as envisaged by EADS Innovation Works. This includes a description of the scenario as well as detailed modeling of simulation events and parameters, and illustrates the suitability of the simulation model.

Based on the simulation model and the presented instantiation, which are currently both being implemented, future work focuses on simulation and evaluation of distributed storage services and P2P content location and routing substrates of smart products. Amongst others, this includes the replication strategy presented in [5] as well as the hybrid overlay network outlined in [10]. Moreover, the described scenario is currently being realized in a simplified version in the course of the research project SmartProducts. Results of experiments conducted with this prototype will be used to verify and enhance the presented configuration of the simulation model.

Acknowledgments. Part of this research has been funded under the EC 7th Framework Programme, in the context of the SmartProducts project (231204).

References

[1] Mühlhäuser, M.: Smart Products: An Introduction. In: Mühlhäuser, M., et al. (eds.) AmI 2007 Workshops. CCIS, vol. 11, pp. 158–164. Springer, Heidelberg (2008)

[2] Ahulló, J.P., López, P.G., Artigas, M.S., Arias, M.A., Aixalà, G.P., Bruchmann, M.: PlanetSim: An extensible framework for overlay network and services simulations. Architecture and Telematic Services Research Group, Technical Report DEIM-RR-08-002 (2008)

[3] Dabek, F., Zhao, B., Druschel, P., Kubiatowicz, J., Stoica, I.: Towards a Common API for Structured Peer-to-Peer Overlays. In: Kaashoek, M.F., Stoica, I. (eds.) IPTPS 2003. LNCS, vol. 2735, pp. 33–44. Springer, Heidelberg (2003)

[4] Law, A.M.: Simulation Modeling and Analysis, 4th edn. Mcgraw-Hill Professional (2006)

[5] Miche, M., Ständer, M., Brogle, M.: Leveraging Process Models to Optimize Content Placement - An Active Replication Strategy for Smart Products. In: 5th ERCIM Workshop on eMobility, Vilanova i la Geltrú, Spain, pp. 27–38 (2011)

[6] Kangasharju, J., Schmidt, U., Bradler, D., Schröder-Bernhardi, J.: ChunkSim: simulating peer-to-peer content distribution. In: Proceedings of the 2007 Spring Simulation Multiconference, Norfolk, Virginia, vol. 1, pp. 25–32 (2007)

[7] Steinmetz, R., Wehrle, K.: Peer-to-Peer Systems and Applications. Springer-Verlag New York, Inc. (2005)

[8] Barabási, A.L., Albert, R.: Emergence of scaling in random networks. Science 286(5439), 509 (1999)

[9] Hugues, P., Golenzer, J.: A Virtual Plane to Build and Maintain Real Ones. SmartProducts Whitepaper (March 2010)

[10] Miche, M., Erlenbusch, V., Allocca, C., Nikolov, A., Mascolo, J.E., Golenzer, J.: D4.1.3: Final Concept for Storing, Distributing, and Maintaining Proactive Knowledge Securely. EU FP7 SmartProducts, Deliverable (2011)

[11] Kröner, A., Haupert, J., Brandherm, B., Miche, M., Barthel, R.: Towards a Model of Object Memory Links. In: International Workshop on Networking and Object Memories for the Internet of Things, Beijing, China (2011)

[12] Medina, A., Lakhina, A., Matta, I., Byers, J.: BRITE: An approach to universal topology generation. In: MASCOTS, p. 0346 (2001)

Instance-Informed Information Systems: A Pre-requisite for Energy-Efficient and Green Information Systems

Kary Främling[1], Jan Nyman[2], André Kaustell[3], and Jan Holmström[4]

[1] School of Science, Aalto University, P.O. Box 15500, FIN-00076 Aalto, Finland
Kary.Framling@aalto.fi,
[2] ControlThings Oy, Råbackavägen 7, FIN-06650 Hammars, Finland
Jan.Nyman@controlthings.fi
[3] Posintra Oy, Electrical Building Services Centre, Gnistvägen 1,
FIN-06150 Borgå, Finland
Andre.Kaustell@posintra.fi
[4] School of Science, Aalto University, P.O. Box 15500, FIN-00076 Aalto, Finland
Jan.Holmstrom@aalto.fi

Abstract. In order to create energy-efficient, ubiquitous and green information systems, it will be necessary to exchange information and co-ordinate action between systems that have traditionally not been interoperable. Providing such interoperability is a major challenge unless the underlying information systems are implemented in a way that allows for the collection of relevant information, such as (near) real-time sensor readings and higher-level events, as well as and the ability to take proper actions based on that information. The paper shows how and why instance-informed information systems are a requirement for implementing energy-efficient and green information systems, as well as showing how such information systems have been implemented in several real-world applications.

Keywords: Instance-informed, agent processing, Green IS, energy informatics.

1 Introduction

Climate action and reducing greenhouse gases has become a top topic in EU and all over the world. Transports and living, i.e. the heating and cooling of buildings, both play a major role for the CO_2 emissions in the world. In this paper, we present solutions for local and remote monitoring of the energy usage of buildings and vehicles. We also show how relevant information can be collected and presented to the users and owners of buildings and vehicles that allows them to identify the most efficient ways to reduce their energy usage if they want to do so.

Information systems (IS) tracking consumption on the level of the individual artefact, or what we in this paper term *instance* are a cornerstone for achieving

A. Puiatti et al. (Eds.): MobiQuitous 2011, LNICST 104, pp. 174–185, 2012.

energy efficiency. In this paper we propose instance-informed information systems as a platform for the collection and analysis of energy data sets to support the continuous optimization of energy efficiency while promoting 'green' values.

A context where instance-informed IS has already resulted in considerable improvements of energy efficiency in the past, and still continuing today, are the computerized engine control systems of motor vehicles introduced since the 1980's. Initially the control systems were introduced to reduce pollution but were later also used to reduce fuel-consumption. Computerized engine control systems are instance-informed because they continuously adjust and adapt the control parameters of the engine depending on the individual tear and wear of the engine, as well as on the current atmospheric conditions. When such instance-informed vehicles become internet-connected, the possibility to gather information from fleets of vehicles will make it possible to further optimize engine design and tuning, as well as optimizing the usage of vehicle fleets, and improving the behaviour of drivers.

It is important to make a clear distinction between Green information technology (IT) and Green IS [1]. Green IT is more focused on how to make computing infrastructure more energy efficient, whereas an information system is the combination of people, processes, and technologies that enables the processing of digitized information [2]. In this paper we focus on Green IS, which in [1] is defined to be a design and implementation of information systems that contribute to sustainable business processes. In this paper, we furthermore focus on *energy informatics* in particular, which is defined as [3]:

Energy informatics is concerned with analyzing, designing, and implementing systems to increase the efficiency of energy demand and supply systems. This requires collection and analysis of energy data sets to support optimization of energy distribution and consumption networks.

Because the scope of Green IS extends far beyond a single organisation, the required IS must also be able to reach across multiple organisations. One domain that has similar requirements on multi-organisational information exchange is the Internet of Things (IoT) [4][5]. The information system architecture presented in this paper, and in use in many of the case applications, was originally developed mainly for the IoT and product lifecycle information management [6]. Due to the similarity of requirements we can introduce instance-informed IS as a platform to fulfil the requirements of energy informatics, as well as Green IS in general.

After this introduction, the paper provides the basic theory and building blocks behind instance-informed IS. Then we show how such instance-informed IS have been implemented in several Green IS-related applications and why instance-informedness is necessary for a successful implementation of such information systems, followed by conclusions.

2   Instance-Informed Information Systems

Our work on instance-informed IS was initiated as an IoT design. Several definitions and views exist on the IoT but they all include the need to represent and handle unique instances of products and 'Things' in general. A manufactured Thing becomes a unique instance at the latest when it enters its usage phase. A product in use exits the realm of conventional product-type based product life-cycle management. The product lifecycle information management concept [6] was developed as a cradle-to-cradle approach to extend product lifecycle man-agement from the design and manufacturing phases to the usage and end-of-life phase of a manufactured product's instance-specific lifecycle [7], not forgetting the possible refurbishing and recycling of the Thing or parts of it.

Most needs and applications considered here are related to the product usage phase. In the rest of this section we will define instance-informed IS, present the main building blocks and theoretical implications of them and describe how such a system has been implemented.

2.1   Building Blocks of Instance-Informed IS

The need for instance-informed IS was initially identified when attempting to model objects in the real world that all had individual properties and possibly also different functions that can be performed on them, which lead to the creation of object-oriented languages. The first truly object-oriented language, Simula 67 [8], was developed for system description and simulation programming that corresponded to real-world objects such as industrial plants. The number of properties and relationships between different objects grew too big and complex to handle by existing procedural languages. A great breakthrough happened in the 1980's when graphical user interfaces were developed at the Rank Xerox Palo Alto Centre. The object-oriented language Smalltalk was developed at the same time [9] for making it easier to manage the properties of a multitude of visual elements on the screen as well as the relations between them. Most of the current popular programming languages such as Java, C++ and C# can be considered to be derivatives of Smalltalk.

When creating information systems for the IoT we are essentially facing sim-ilar challenges as the designers of object-oriented languages, i.e. how to manage instance-specific information. The new challenge in the IoT context is that the information systems that produce, store and process that information tend to be distributed over different computing devices that may belong to different organ-isations and where Things may be mobile. Mobility creates technical challenges due to intermittent network connectivity, but also creates new challenges regard-ing e.g. security and privacy. Furthermore, with the increasing use of embedded computing in real-world products, we are also facing challenges in managing in-formation collected by millions of embedded computers regarding the physical product that they are mounted on. On the minimal level, the embedded com-puter can be just an identification device such as a barcode, RFID tag, magnetic stripe or similar, which means that much of the information about the instance needs to be stored remotely. Product lifecycle information management is a do-main where information about the usage of every product instance needs to be stored and communicated when needed and where it is needed. Design and manufacturing information are also relevant. The challenge is that all the differ-ent pieces of information tend to be distributed over company servers, service company computers as well as the embedded computers of the instances.

Instance-informed IS make the identification of instances, and the tracking and handling of instances over long time-spans and many locations the basis of the design. The design makes it possible to track changes of any property of any instance, such as location and age. This approach to managing information about product instances has been presented under different names in the past, such as product-centric information management [10], item-centric information management [11] and intelligent products [12][13][14].

An instance is unique. This means that it has a set of properties that have unique values at any moment in time. A car has a certain colour, a certain number of horse powers etc. at any given moment in time. The number of properties can easily become huge when going down to all the details of any product instance. However, different organizations and individuals may use different views that contain different sets of the instance's properties, as well as different names, units, languages etc. for them. This often becomes a practical challenge because it gives interoperability issues when exchanging the information. Standards for messaging interfaces and information representation are usually the best way of overcoming such interoperability issues. In practice, there are many domains where such standards do not exist. IoT is one of those domains, where the EPC Information Services (EPCIS) [15] and related standards attempt to provide a universal and standardized way of finding and exchanging Thing-related information. So far, EPCIS is defined and used almost exclusively for supply chain management applications. Therefore, EPCIS is not a universal information exchange standard for the IoT.

Another challenge for handling instance-specific information is when database and IS designs either explicitly or implicitly assume that all instances must belong to a class, as is often the case according to the extensive survey of systems engineering literature in [16]. Parsons and Wand claim that the assumption of inherent classification, which is due to the human cognitive way of processing, represents a major obstacle to evolution and innovation. This solution design is not a technical necessity but based on the IS designer's assumption of inherent classification of instances. The assumption means that Things can be referred to only as instances of classes. In the context of operations management the assumption of inherent classification of materials means that all product items must be assigned to a material type. The tendency to manage material flows as transfers between stocks that only modify the count of identical products in different places, rather than tracking movements of instances, follows from this general preference for classification over identification. This type of approach makes it difficult to deal with instances that are heterogeneous and changing. For dealing with heterogeneous and changing instances there is a need for an inter-organizational tracking solution that is loosely coupled and not tightly linked to any particular locations or actors.

Parsons and Wand propose to overcome these challenges by introducing the two-layered architecture illustrated in Fig. 1. The first layer represents unique instances with their unique properties, independent of any classes to which the instances may belong. The second layer consists of views based on sets of

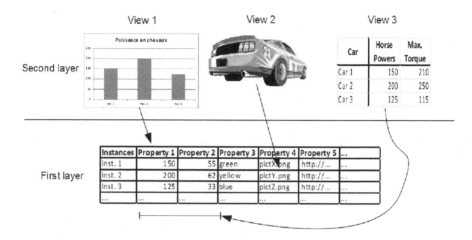

Fig. 1. Example of two-layered architecture, with unique instances but several possible views on them, e.g. as a bar in a graph, as a picture or as as a row in a table with selected properties

properties that are relevant for a particular purpose, organisation or user. Such views may be created, removed or modified at any time without affecting the instances in the first layer.

In practice, the digital representation of instance property values, i.e. the first-layer values, are typically stored in the instance's embedded computer or in a database (or possibly even several databases). In addition to instance property values, relations between different instances and other information entities should preferably be handled as first-layer information because organisation-dependent vocabularies used for representing such relations easily become a major obstacle for interoperability. From a data consistency point of view it would be desirable that these first-layer values would be stored in one single database. Access to that database should always be done through a software component that takes care of the consistency of the first-layer instance information, such as the Product Agent approach proposed in [17]. Such a Product Agent can then provide different views to the instance information by implementing different communication protocols, messaging interfaces or even graphical user interfaces [18][19].

2.2   Instance-Informed Information Processing

In the theory of information technology proposed in [20], p. 280 the representation and manipulation/processing are distinguished as the two aspects always present in an IS. In the definition of sensor networks in [3], terms used such as 'reports the status', 'can be analyzed' etc. are clearly information manipulation and processing actions. Multi-agent systems and agent processing [21] are one model for implementing instance-informed information processing.

Two-layer architectures consisting of instances and contingent aggregation are effective because the architectures create environments where interactive agents can effectively harness information provided by the environment [18]. The responses of interactive agents are not anticipated or pre-designed but formulated based on sensing the environment and interaction with other agents [22]. Actions performed by agents are typically e.g. data filtering, rule-based processing, neural net-based detection of events, event generation etc. [23].

In order to enable agents to do processing of information from different organisations, the agents must be able to access and understand the information in a uniform way. In object-oriented programming, the Design Pattern concept [24] is commonly used for defining 'good' designs that combine recommendations for information storage and for information processing. The extension of design patterns to instance-informed IS has been proposed e.g. in [25]. A major challenge in instance-informed IS compared to ordinary object-oriented programming is that universal access to information requires standardised interfaces to run the typically multi-organisational applications envisioned, of which the IoT is probably the most universal one. There is currently a lack of such universally accepted standardised interfaces, even though some standardisation initiatives exist, such as the already mentioned EPCIS standard, as well as the Quantum Lifecycle Management workgroup of The Open Group (www.opengroup.org/qlm/).

2.3   Implementation of Instance-Informed IS

Instance-informed IS can be implemented in many ways while respecting the principles of a two-layered view and processing based on design pattern principles. One example of such an IS is the open-source DIALOG platform (http://dialog.hut.fi), which was from the beginning developed for the requirements of IoT in 2001 [10].

DIALOG is generic software in the sense that it provides protocol- and interface-neutral messaging mechanisms with message persistence functionality, security mechanisms, and so forth, which are separated from the business logic itself, which is implemented by agents. Fig. 2 illustrates the internal architecture of a DIALOG node. We see that the components involved in sending and receiving messages are separated from agents who consume and produce messages; each has its own classes with a common interface, i.e., the receive and the send handlers. Different protocols and messaging interfaces can be easily supported. DIALOG supports e.g. a Java remote method invocation (RMI) interface, a Web Service interface using the Simple Object Access Protocol (SOAP) and an interface using HTTP POST messages. Implementing a new interface or 'view' only requires adding corresponding receiver and sender classes. The DIALOG node contains a configurable mapping mechanism that defines what messages go to which agent(s) and what sender to use for which messages.

DIALOG has been used as the platform for implementing the remote monitoring systems of vehicles described in the next section. Remote monitoring and control of energy consumption have been implemented following similar principles. However, the actual interfaces, communication protocols etc. have been selected based on the current state of the art technology in the building automation domain.

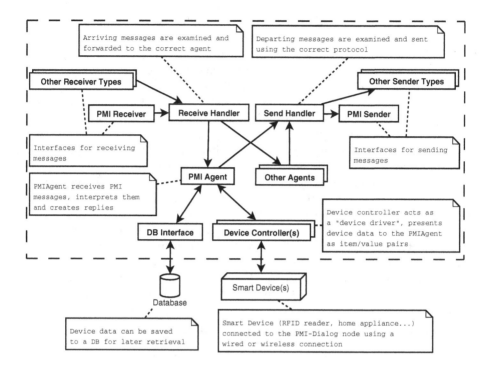

Fig. 2. The Dialog architecture. The dashed line shows the node boundary. The Dialog architecture can support many different interfaces for receiving and delivering messages using e.g. the PMI (PROMISE Messaging Interface) protocol.

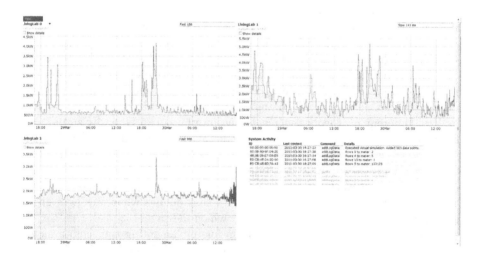

Fig. 3. Visualisation of energy consumption from three living lab targets, including status information

3 Remote Monitoring and Control of Energy Consumption in Buildings and Vehicles

An energy monitoring system that visualizes the actual energy consumption of a house or a flat in real time has been developed at the Electrical Building Services Centre in Porvoo, Finland (www.stok.fi/eng). A resident may instantly 'see' his or her energy consumption as a constantly updating graph on a web page, as shown in Fig. 3. The graph makes it possible to visualize the effect of various energy savings measures. One instantly gets feedback on how energy consumption is affected by switching on and off electrical devices, for instance a television set. The users of the system can also write blog-type comments, and share them with other users.

Fig. 4. Electricity consumption monitoring hardware

The system itself is flexible and cheap. It is a stand-alone, plug-and-play type of solution, based on off-the-shelf consumer hardware supplemented by software created in the project (see Fig. 4). The system reads data from an electricity meter, channels it through the Internet using the residences broadband connection, and stores the data in a database.

This energy monitoring system will be used to monitor energy usage in Finland in Porvoo's new Skaftkärr housing area (http://www.skaftkarr.fi/en), where this system is being set-up in residences, or LivingLabs. Currently we are in the initial testing phase with half a dozen LivingLabs. The residences are inhabited by real families, so that we can get user-centered experiences on the usability of the system we are developing. In the future, energy monitoring will also include district heating and energy produced locally by solar panels.

An example of an instance-informed smart appliance has been implemented for air handling units (AHU) with heat recovery. AHUs usually include heating and cooling aggregates that allow them to have total control of the base-level inside temperature. AHUs are the most significant piece of equipment regarding the energy efficiency of modern low-energy houses. Such houses are built with thick insulation and with as little air leakage as possible, which signifies that the ventilation system has to ensure that the indoor air remains at a good quality. A good air quality can only be obtained by a sufficient ventilation, which sets high requirements on the heat recovery systems used in AHUs.

Remote monitoring of AHUs provides Green IS benefits such as remote condition monitoring, optimization of maintenance operations etc. In addition to these, it is possible to continuously monitor and adapt the control of the AHU for optimal heat recovery efficiency in all conditions (Fig. 5). The optimal control parameters to use in the control IS depend on outdoor and indoor temperatures, humidity and other environmental factors. The dynamics of the building itself and the behavior of other systems in the building also have an influence on how to maintain the best compromise between temperature, humidity, air quality and other factors while keeping the inhabitants satisfied and optimizing the total energy-efficiency.

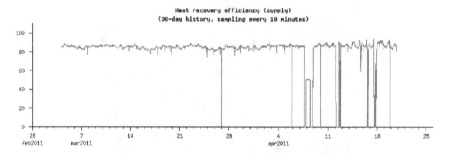

Fig. 5. Information collected about AHU efficiency at the end of heating period

Instance-informed systems have also been implemented in projects performed together with industrial partners in the automotive domain. In the automotive domain, remote monitoring of vehicles can give substantial savings in maintenance and repair costs, reliability, re-sale value, improvement in driver behaviour and optimisation of fleets of vehicles, such as the airport vehicles monitored in Fig. 6. All these benefits are also important from a Green IS point of view.

Especially when an increasing number of vehicles will be powered by electricity, such vehicle fleet management capabilities may also turn out to be crucial for Green IS applications. Benefits can be expected from monitoring the current energy consumption, estimating the remaining kilometers to go with the current charge, as well as when and where to go and re-charge. However, from the Green IS point of view, the fleet management aspect may be even more important because it could give an information in real time about the charging capacity available depending on the location, as well as the total need for charging in the near future. Both the knowledge about the available energy storage capacity and the knowledge about the charging needs might be important for optimizing energy production and usage.

Fig. 6. Partial view of airport vehicles, where the shape indicates the type of vehicle and the colors indicate the status of the vehicle, e.g. 'in use', 'engine is on' etc

The presented systems show that there is a clear need for managing instance-specific information on the device (AHU and vehicle), aggregate (house) as well as fleet level (fleets of vehicles). In principle, every instance manages its own information. However, in many Smart Grid applications, it may be necessary to collect information from many different instances. Depending on the application, the needed information may change. This is where the two-layered model provides basic principles for disconnecting the actual information and the way it is structured from the views or interfaces provided to it. When those interfaces are structured according to design pattern principles, it is possible to creat such loosely-coupled applications that are necessary in Smart Grid applications, where different organisations, individuals, products etc. have to interact and act together.

4   Conclusion

The requirements on information interoperability and co-ordinated action for Green IS are a challenge for many current information systems that are developed for organisation-specific needs and that are usually not inter-operable. Furthermore, such systems are not designed for storing, managing and processing information about instances such as houses, vehicles, building automation equipment etc.

In this paper, we have shown how instance-informed IS can enable the collection of information from a multitude of heterogeneous information sources that are relevant for energy informatics. We claim that any Green IS will have to be instance-informed in order to enable a holistic control and optimisation of all the elements of the system.

Acknowledgment. This work has been financed by industrial partners, the Finnish Funding Agency for Technology and Innovation (Tekes) and the AsEMo project financed by the European Regional Development Fund.

References

1. Watson, R.T., Boudreau, M.-C., Chen, A., Huber, M.H.: Green is: Building sustainable business practices (2008)
2. Melville, N.: Information systems innovation for environmental sustainability. MIS Quarterly 34(1), 1–21 (2010)
3. Watson, R., Boudreau, M., Chen, A.: Information systems and environmentally sustainable development: Energy informatics and new directions for the is community. MIS Quarterly 34(1), 23–38 (2010)
4. Ashton, K.: Internet things - mit, embedded technology and the next internet revolution. In: Tag 2000, 25.5.2000, Baltic Conventions, The Commonwealth Conference and Events Centre, London (2000)
5. Gershenfeld, N.: When Things Start to Think. Owl books (2000)
6. Främling, K., Harrison, M., Brusey, J., Petrow, J.: Requirements on unique identifiers for managing product lifecycle information - comparison of alternative approaches. International Journal of Computer Integrated Manufacturing 20(7), 715–726 (2007)
7. Jun, H.-B., Shin, J., Kiritsis, D., Xirouchakis, P.: System architecture for closed-loop plm. International Journal of Computer Integrated Manufacturing 20(7), 684–698 (2007)
8. Nygaard, K., Dahl, O.-J.: The development of the simula languages. ACM SIGPLAN Notices 13(8), 245–272 (1978)
9. Goldberg, A., Robson, D.: Smalltalk-80: The language and its Implementation. Addison-Wesley Publishing Company, Reading (1983)
10. Kärkkäinen, M., Ala-Risku, T., Främling, K.: The product centric approach: a solution to supply network information management problems? Computers in Industry 52(2), 147–159 (2003)
11. Rönkkö, M., Kärkkäinen, M., Holmström, J.: Benefits of an item-centric enterprise-data model in logistics service: a case study. Computers in Industry 58(8), 814–822 (2007)
12. Kärkkäinen, M., Holmström, J., Främling, K., Artto, K.: Intelligent products - a step towards a more effective project delivery chain. Computers in Industry 50(2), 141–151 (2003)
13. Främling, K., McFarlane, D.: Editorial for special issue on intelligent products. Computers in Industry 60(3), 135–136 (2009)
14. Meyer, G., Främling, K., Holmström, J.: Intelligent products: A survey. Computers in Industry 60(3), 137–148 (2009)
15. EPCglobal, Epc information services (epcis) version 1.0.1 specification (2007), http://www.gs1.org/gsmp/kc/epcglobal/epcis/ epcis_1_0_1-standard-20070921.pdf (accessed August 29, 2011)
16. Parsons, J., Wand, Y.: Emancipating instances from the tyranny of classes in information modeling. ACM Transactions on Database Systems 25(2), 228–268 (2000)

17. Främling, K., Ala-Risku, T., Kärkkäinen, M., Holmström, J.: Agent-based model for managing composite product information. Computers in Industry 57(1) (2006)
18. Wegner, P.: Why interaction is more powerful than algorithms. Communications of the ACM 40(5), 80–91 (1997)
19. Petrie, C., Bussler, C.: Service agents and virtual enterprises: A survey. IEEE Internet Computing 7(4), 68–78 (2003)
20. Beynon-Davies, P.: Formated technology and informated action: The nature of information technology. International Journal of Information Management 29(4), 272–282 (2009)
21. Wooldridge, M., Jennings, N.: Intelligent agents: Theory and practice. Knowledge Engineering Review 10(2), 115–152 (1995)
22. Holland, J.: Hidden order: how adaptation builds complexity. Addison Wesley Longman Publishing Co., Inc. (1995)
23. Luckham, D.: The Power of Events. Addison-Wesley, Boston (2002)
24. Gamma, E., Helm, R., Johnson, R., Vlissides, J.: Design Patterns – Elements of Reusable Object-Oriented Software. Addison Wesley, Reading (1995)
25. Främling, K., Ala-Risku, T., Kärkkäinen, M., Holmström, J.: Design patterns for managing product life cycle information. Communications of the ACM 50(6), 75–79 (2007)

SenseBox – A Generic Sensor Platform
for the Web of Things

Arne Bröring[1,2,3], Albert Remke[1,3], and Damian Lasnia[1]

[1] Institute for Geoinformatics, University of Münster,
Weseler Str. 253, Münster, Germany
{arneb,a.remke,d.lasnia}@uni-muenster.de
http://swsl.uni-muenster.de
[2] ITC Faculty, University of Twente,
Enschede, The Netherlands
[3] 52°North Initiative for Geospatial Open Source Software GmbH,
Martin-Luther-King-Weg 24, Münster, Germany

Abstract. Applications of the Web of Things reach from smart shoes posting your running performance online, over the localization of goods in the production chain, to computing the insurance cost of cars based on the actually driven kilometers. Thereby, Web of Things applications follow the REST paradigm, i.e. access to things and their properties is offered via REST APIs. This allows an easy meshing of web-enabled things into existing Web applications. This work introduces the Sense-Box, a small computing device equipped (1) with different sensors to perceive its environment and (2) with a Web server and an according REST API which makes it available as a first class citizen on the Web. In an example use case of this generic sensor platform, the SenseBox is deployed next to a road and its in-built ultra sonic sensor is used to detect the number of bypassing cars and eventually determine the traffic density.

Keywords: Web of Things, Geosensors, Sensor Integration.

1 Introduction

The Web of Things (WoT) is about connecting real world objects to the Web. These objects have an identity represented by a URI and they are able to communicate with people, machines or other objects, e.g. by responding to an http GET request. They have a memory as to store and to provide information both about themselves and about the context they are living within.

Objects may have additional capabilities. They may act as sensors, taking up certain stimuli and transform them into useful observations. Or they are able to do something, e.g. open and close valves or move to a certain location. Depending on the degree of control by operators these objects act more or less autonomously. All activities require a certain amount of intelligence, i.e. some kind of situational awareness, the ability to conclude and to solve problems. This general pattern of an intelligent object is depicted in Figure 1.

A. Puiatti et al. (Eds.): MobiQuitous 2011, LNICST 104, pp. 186–196, 2012.

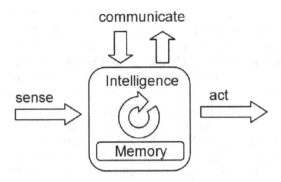

Fig. 1. The intelligent object patten

We are particularly interested in web enabled sensor objects, which are able to provide aggregated spatiotemporal information about some environmental phenomena. The deduced research question is: Does the WoT paradigm facilitate the provision and use of spatiotemporal sensor data?

The SenseBox project investigates certain real world use cases for web enabled sensor objects as to explore interaction patterns and practical requirements. Aim is to develop a generic sensor platform which is easily deployable in an on-the-fly manner and available as a thing on the Web. After introducing the concept of the Web of Things and the research field of integrating sensors with the Web (Section 2) this paper outlines the Traffic SenseBox case study (Section 3) and describes in detail the SenseBox architecture and its communication interface (Section 4). In Section 5, we compare the developed approach to related work. The paper ends with conclusion and an outlook to future work (Section 6).

2   Background

The vision of the two related research fields of Internet of Things [1] and Web of Things [2] is on integrating general, real-world things with the Internet or Web, respectively. Examples for such things are household appliances, embedded and mobile devices, but also smart sensing devices. Often, the user interaction takes place through a cell phone acting as the mediator within the triangle of human, thing, and Internet / Web. The application fields of the Internet of Things are influenced by the idea of ubiquitous computing [3]. They reach from smart shoes posting your running performance online, over management of logistics (e.g., localization of goods in the production chain), to insurance (e.g., car insurance costs based on the actually driven kilometres).

For technically realizing the Internet of Things, research topics include protocol stacks for the Internet Protocol (IP) standard optimized for smart things (e.g., IPv6, 6LoWPAN) [4], naming services for things [5], or the unique identification of objects (e.g., RFID). The Web of Things can be seen as an evolvement of the Internet of Things. It leverages existing Web protocols as a common language for real objects to interact with each other. HTTP is used as an application protocol rather than a transport protocol as it is generally the case in web service infrastructures. Things are addressed by URLs and their functionality is accessed through the well-defined HTTP operations (GET, POST, PUT, etc.). Hence, Web of Things applications follow the REST paradigm [6]. Specific frameworks (e.g. [7], or [8]) offer REST APIs to enable access to things and their properties as resources. These REST APIs may not only be used to interact with a thing via the Web, also website representations of things may be provided to display dynamically generated visualizations of data gathered by the thing. Then, the mash-up paradigm and tools from the Web 2.0 realm can be applied to easily build new applications. An example application may use Twitter to announce the status of a washing machine or may let a fridge post to an Atom feed to declare which groceries are about to run out.

An already established approach for integrating sensors with the Web is the Sensor Web Enablement (SWE) framework defined by the Open Geospatial Consortium (OGC); its current state is described in [9]. SWE specifications are very generic and powerful since intended use cases are broad and often complex (e.g. disaster management or early warning systems). However, use cases, which do not need the full functionality on data filtering, sensor discovery, tasking and event handling as provided by SWE, may be easier to realize with the Web of Things approach by considering sensor objects as things. Hence, this work investigates the application of Web of Things principles to a simple sensor platform – the SenseBox.

3   The *Traffic* SenseBox Case Study

Strassen.NRW[1] is a state government enterprise, which is responsible for the construction and maintenance of about 20,000 kilometers of the road network in North-Rhine Westfalia, Germany. One of its tasks is the traffic management, i.e. monitoring, forecasting, and controlling the traffic flow as to assure mobility and safety on its road network. Strassen.NRW maintains a comprehensive telematics infrastructure as to gather real time information on e.g. traffic density and weather conditions and to control special devices such as electronic road signs or route guiding displays. The metering of traffic flow is based mainly on the use of statically mounted induction loops, which count the passing vehicles. But this sensor network is not dense enough for real time monitoring of the traffic situation in case of accidents and daily moving road works. That is the reason why Strassen.NRW is interested in additional means for collecting real time information on the traffic flow. Thus, we evaluate the following use case:

A specialized Traffic SenseBox is mounted to the safety truck securing mobile road works (e.g. for maintaining batters and guardrails). This SenseBox is able to count passing vehicles by utilizing an ultrasonic sensing unit capable of

---

[1] http://strassen.nrw.de

measuring distances to objects in front of it (Figure 2). Once switched on, the preconfigured SenseBox automatically connects through the mobile communication network to the Web. Once available on the Web, it can register as a new traffic sensor at the registry of the telematics infrastructure of Strassen.NRW.

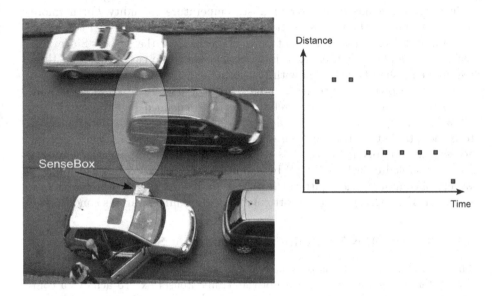

Fig. 2. The Traffic SenseBox test environment

The squad leader of the mobile road work has than the option to access the SenseBox through his mobile device, e.g. to check if it is working properly. He may even add further information on the situational context (e.g. the type of mobile road work, operator of the SenseBox). At the same time the operator of the Strassen.NRW traffic management system notices a new sensor item popping up on his map display, symbolizing the type of sensor and the current traffic flow. He is able to select this item to get further information such as the number of vehicles currently passing by. Also, Police cars could be equipped with Traffic SenseBoxes. In case of an accident, SenseBoxes could be placed together with warning signs in a certain distance to the accident location.

The organization, which owns a Traffic SenseBox decides about granting access to this device and thus about sharing its capabilities. Configuring and tasking sensors will be handled restrictively. Requesting information from sensors may be open to other institutions such as local authorities, automobile associations or private companies, which maintain their own traffic information systems. It has to be investigated in further detail, if direct access to sensors is valuable enough or if aggregated and quality assured information is preferred, which would be rather a service of the sensor owning organization.

4   The SenseBox - Requirements and Design

The technical design of the SenseBox needs to be generic and flexible so that it can be utilized in different use cases. Outdoor deployments, e.g. the detection of traffic density (Section 3), require the SenseBox to be robust against external influences such as mechanical stress, dust, temperature, humidity. Furthermore, it needs to make reliable observations under varying environmental conditions concerning for example weather, traffic, or position of the sensor. Since non-technicians deploy a SenseBox, this process needs to be easy. Together, those requirements shall be achieved with low costs.

The SenseBox is conceptualized as a physically and logically autonomous unit. As to be discoverable it has to self-register at predefined registries. It has to allow for changes both to its configuration and to its resource/data model as to be adaptable to various use cases. As for supporting privacy issues securing access is mandatory for most of the use cases. While the application protocol for web enabled objects is HTTP by definition, the SenseBox has to support a variety of communication patterns (e.g. pull, push) and low level protocols (e.g. UMTS, IEEE 802.11) as to support communication under various conditions.

4.1   The SenseBox Hardware and Deployment Setup

The SenseBox prototype is designed to operate on 12V and 24V batteries or car lighter sockets, as used in case of the Traffic SenseBox. To achieve a compact design a Mini-ITX low-power motherboard[2] is chosen which allows an integration of the needed hardware components within 15x15x15 centimeters. The motherboard is equipped with a 1.66 GHz Intel Atom processor, 2GB RAM and 8GB CompactFlash mass storage for data processing, data storage and as web server platform. The web connectivity is established by a UMTS/3G USB device so that all collected and processed data is available on the web in real time.

The web accessible data within our prototype setup is mostly derived from the two sensor outputs, GPS and ultrasonic sensor. The Arduino framework[3], consisting of microcontroller board hardware and the firmware programming language, is utilized to integrate the sensor components with the web enabled computing component. The Arduino Uno microcontroller board provides the capability to connect and configure a variety of different sensors in an easy way, and to preprocess the sensor outputs and send them to the main computing module. The ultrasonic range finder is configured to measure the distance between the near side lane and passing vehicles while the GPS component provides location and time awareness, e.g., to georeference the other sensor's outputs. Figure 3 shows the assembled SenseBox hardware prototype which has been tested in the car counting scenario as shown in Figure 2.

---

[2] http://www.mini-itx.com/
[3] http://www.arduino.cc/

Fig. 3. The SenseBox hardware prototype

4.2   The SenseBox Software Architecture

The design of the SenseBox software architecture is shown in Figure 4. In its center, the integrator component triggering sub-components to provide communication interfaces as well as interfaces to sensors and the database. The interface to sensors is established by a well-defined and generic message protocol for data coming from the Arduino board to which the sensors are connected. The transformator component retrieves these raw sensor data and is able to translate them to observations with more descriptive metadata (e.g. unit of measure or links to definitions of observed phenomena). Further, the transformator can apply specialized processing steps to certain incoming sensor streams to derive higher-level information. For example in the use case of this work (Section 3), the number of cars passing by the SenseBox is calculated from the distances measured by the ultrasonic sensor. Once assessed, this event of a new observation is broadcasted to the other components of the business logic; among them, the database handler receives the event and stores the observation in a database. Henceforth, the observation can be accessed via the REST interface as described in the following (Section 4.3).

4.3   A REST API for SenseBoxes

In order to provide data gathered by the SenseBox to other Web applications, a REST API for accessing measured observations is designed based on previous work we have done on meaningful URI schemes for sensor data [10].

A representation of a SenseBox can be accessed by following the URI *http://my.authority.org/boxes/<id>*. A list of observations gathered by the sensors of this SenseBox can be retrieved by appending the URI segment */observations*. To represent single observations as XML we rely on the established Observations & Measurements standard [11]. Single observations are accessed by following the URI scheme *http://my.authority.org/boxes/<id>/observations/ <observation id>*.

When dealing with sensor data for different thematic properties which are varying over time and space, it is important to offer according filter mechanisms to enable the retrieval of certain data subsets. For example, a reference to all car count observations of a SenseBox is given by appending an according query selecting this property filter: *http://my.authority.org/boxes/7/observations ?property=car_count*. Multiple property identifiers can be appended. By adhering to the proposal of [12] for a sound URI scheme, these multiple identifiers are separated by semicolons, as their order does not matter.

To refer to observations from a particular time instant or period, the time query token can be appended to the URI followed by two comma-separated time strings encoded according to the ISO 8601 specification [13]. For example, the URI *http://my.authority.org/boxes/7/observations ?time=2011-01-10T14:00, 2011-02-11T16:00 &property=car_count* points to the observation collection with all car count observations taken by SenseBox '7' from January 1st 2011 at 2pm until February at 4pm. The first time string represents the start date of the time period for which observation should be returned, the second indicates the end of the time period. The second time string can also be omitted when a link to observations of a particular time instant has to be specified.

As a spatial filter, a bounding box can be appended to the URI. We use commas to separate the ordered parameters forming a bounding box. The first four values are the coordinates defining a two dimensional rectangle, while the fifth value is the identifier of their coordinate reference system: *<minCoord1>, <minCoord2>,<maxCoord1>,<maxCoord2>,<crsURI>*. This spatial filter is either applied to the last position of the SenseBox or if the time parameter is specified as well, is applied to the position of the SenseBox at the defined time. An example of a URI using a bounding box filter is specified as follows: *http://my.authority.org/ boxes/7/observations ?bbox=3,6,23,36, urn:ogc:def:crs: EPSG:6.5:4326*.

5   Related Work

Already in 2002, Delin [14] defined a concept with similar characteristics to the Web of Things paradigm, the so-called Sensor Web, a heterogeneous pool of distributed web accessible sensor nodes. His approach described a set of micro-power, micro-bandwidth, and micro-cost sensor pods that are inter-connected and designed and manufactured along well-defined use cases. Today, these characteristics are provided by mainstream wireless sensing networks utilizing the *Motes* concept. Motes are small-sized sensor nodes with limited computing capabilities and able to connect with each other within a certain connectivity range to monitor phenomena of interest. Recent research and manufacturing activities focused on the advancement of such sensor network technology by enhancing intelligent nodes that are equipped with more processing-power [15]. For example, Oracle offers a ready-to-use development kit consisting of hardware and software components for sensor nodes, called *Sun Spots*[4], with a 10 meter connectivity range. These generic nodes are capable of transforming Wireless Sensor Networks to Wireless Sensor Actuator Networks, because their nodes are able to change the behavior of the observing system [16], while former sensor networks were primarily designed to solely monitor their environment [17].

The SenseBox is similar to the approaches above; however, the hardware design is not primarily addressing bandwidth or processing limitations, hence, more expensive computations and storing capabilities (e.g., database for long-term sensor data storing) are available. Further, the SenseBox focuses on completely embedded web functionality and therefore provides a well-defined REST API offering a light-weight sensor data access protocol based on HTTP. This is for example contrary to the approach designed by Resch [15] that utilizes OGC's Sensor Web Enablement standards. Those standards [9] are richer in functionality but also more complex and hence more difficult to integrate with client applications.

Although, the Traffic SenseBox, as a first use case, has been primarily served as an example to demonstrate the generic SenseBox concept, related approaches for traffic control shall also be compared here. Table 1 gives an overview and comparison of traffic control systems currently in use. Besides object tracking based solutions which make use of the smartphone capabilities of car drivers, such as Waze[5], systems exist that need an additional physical infrastructure in form of sensor platforms mounted beyond or next to the street network. The latter once are either based on subsurface sensors (e.g. Canoga[6]) or are camera-based traffic control systems (e.g. Sensor Technologies[7]). Compared to those systems, the current design of the Traffic SenseBox with its single ultrasonic sensor has a clear drawback of poor measurement detail; it can only count cars, while the other systems are able to observe speed at all lanes simultaneously. However, due to the generic design of the SenseBox, future designs may include additional sensors (e.g. a second ultrasonic sensor) which would allow determining the speed of by-passing cars.

The SenseBox approach has advantages in terms of flexibile control over the deployed infrastructure. Road network administrators can decide in an ad-hoc manner where new SenseBoxes need to be deployed, e.g. in case of an accident or construction. This is not the case for subsurface sensor systems and also cameras are usually persistently mounted. Vehicle tracking via Web connected mobile phones and associated GPS sensors appears on first sight as the best solution. However, it lacks flexibility since road network managers have no control over the underlying infrastructure and are dependent on users who provide their

---

[4] http://www.sunspotworld.com
[5] http://world.waze.com/
[6] http://www.gtt.com/Products/CanogaTrafficSensingSystem
[7] http://www.sensor-tech.eu/sensor_tv_en.htm?Lang=EN

positional data. In addition, such object (or human) tracking based approaches are critical in terms of privacy, just like camera based approaches are. Thus, the Traffic SenseBox can be seen as a flexible and privacy-aware real time traffic control system.

Table 1. Comparsion of real time traffic control systems

	Physical Infrastructure needed	Measurement detail	Flexible control over infrastructure	Privacy
Object tracking (GSM, GPS)	Reusable (+)	+	o	-
Subsurface sensors	Yes (-)	+	-	+
Camera-based	Yes (-)	+	o	-
SenseBox	Yes (-)	-	+	+

6   Conclusions and Outlook

This work presents the SenseBox - a generic sensor platform focusing on an easy accessibility via the Web by following the Web of Things approach. The SenseBox's REST interface enables its integration as a first class citizen on the Web and includes thematic, spatial, as well as temporal filtering of observations gathered by its sensors. By utilizing the Observations & Measurements standard from OGC's SWE framework, we showed that the WoT approach can be integrated with the Sensor Web concept. We can conclude that the integration of sensors is facilitated by following the WoT paradigm, since HTTP is utilized by many applications. However, most of the logic is decentralized, meaning that sensors need to become rich in functionality - which is realizable for platforms such as the SenseBox, as it is particularly designed for those tasks.

Applying the SenseBox in the described use case of determining the traffic density by counting cars with an ultrasonic sensor has already shown satisfying results. However, the restricted range of the chosen ultrasonic sensor allows only counting cars on the nearby lane. In future, this use case setup will be refined, but also other use cases will be investigated (e.g., precision agriculture, air pollution monitoring, or noise assessment) to prove the genericness of the SenseBox. The full benefit of the SenseBox concept can be achieved as soon as such sensor resources are shared across organizations (e.g. Strassen.NRW, municipalities, or automobile clubs). Whether this is practically possible concerning political policies, business models, trust, etc. has to be investigated.

In future, we plan to evolve the SenseBox design by separating the platform logic from the specific sensor interfaces. To achieve this, the SenseBox will be combined with our previously developed Sensor Interface Descriptor concept [18] which allows the declarative description of sensor protocols to enable plug & play of sensors [19]. Furthermore, the REST interface will be extended in future so that the configuration of the SenseBox via HTTP PUT will be possible as well as a push-based observation delivery. Also, other representations of observation resources shall be supported, such as the RDF format to make SenseBoxes available on the Linked Data Cloud [20], similar to our previous work on a RESTful proxy [21] for the Sensor Observation Service [22]. Another direction of research to be tackled is the inter-communication between SenseBoxes for more reliable observations. Based on the on-board GPS sensor, near SenseBoxes may be identified autonomously for initiating interaction via the Web.

Acknowledgment. This work is financially supported by the project *Flexible and Efficient Integration of Sensors and Sensor Web Services* funded by the ERDF program (grant N 114/2008) of the European Union, as well as the 52°North Sensor Web community (http://52north.org/sensorWeb) which envisions a real time integration of heterogeneous sensors into a coherent information infrastructure. Further, the authors thank the students of the University of Muenster who have contributed to the development of the SenseBox project: Dustin Demuth, Kristina Knoppe, Maurin Radtke, Arthur Rohrbach, Raimund Schnürer, Christopher Stephan, Umut Tas, and Jan Wirwahn.

References

1. Gershenfeld, N., Krikorian, R., Cohen, D.: The Internet of Things. Scientific American 291(4), 76–81 (2004)
2. Guinard, D., Trifa, V.: Towards the Web of Things: Web Mashups for Embedded Devices. In: International World Wide Web Conference. ACM, Madrid (2009)
3. Weiser, M.: The Computer for the 21st Century. Scientific American 265(9), 94–104 (1991)
4. Hui, J.W., Culler, D.E.: IP is Dead, Long Live IP for Wireless Sensor Networks. In: SenSys 2008: Proceedings of the 6th ACM Conference on Embedded Network Sensor Systems, pp. 15–28. ACM, New York (2008)
5. EPCglobal: EPCglobal Object Name Service (ONS) 1.0.1. EPCglobal Inc. (2008)
6. Fielding, R.T., Taylor, R.N.: Principled Design of the Modern Web Architecture. ACM Transactions on Internet Technology 2(2), 115–150 (2002)
7. Pinto, J., Martins, R., Sousa, J.: Towards a REST-style Architecture for Networked Vehicles and Sensors. In: 8th IEEE International Conference on Pervasive Computing and Communications Workshops (PERCOM Workshops), pp. 745–750. IEEE, Mannheim (2010)
8. Ostermaier, B., Schlup, F., Romer, K.: WebPlug: A Framework for the Web of Things. In: 8th IEEE International Conference on Pervasive Computing and Communications Workshops (PERCOM Workshops), pp. 690–695. IEEE, Mannheim (2010)
9. Bröring, A., Echterhoff, J., Jirka, S., Simonis, I., Everding, T., Stasch, C., Liang, S., Lemmens, R.: New Generation Sensor Web Enablement. Sensors 11(3), 2652–2699 (2011)
10. Janowicz, K., Bröring, A., Stasch, C., Everding, T.: Towards Meaningful URIs for Linked Sensor Data. In: Devaraju, A., Llaves, A., Maue, P., Kessler, C. (eds.) Towards Digital Earth: Search, Discover and Share Geospatial Data, Workshop at Future Internet Symposium, vol. 640. CEUR-WS, Berlin (2010)

11. Cox, S.: OGC Implementation Specification 07-022r1: Observations and Measurements - Part 1 - Observation schema. Open Geospatial Consortium, Wayland, MA, USA (2007)
12. Richardson, L., Ruby, S.: RESTful Web Services. O'Reilly Media, Inc. (2007)
13. ISO: ISO 8601:2004 - Data elements and interchange formats - Information interchange - Representation of dates and times. International Organization for Standardization (ISO), Geneva, Switzerland (2004)
14. Delin, K.: The Sensor Web: A Macro-Instrument for Coordinated Sensing. Sensors 2, 270–285 (2001)
15. Resch, B., Mittlboeck, M., Lippautz, M.: Pervasive Monitoring - An Intelligent Sensor Pod Approach for Standardised Measurement Infrastructures. Sensors 10(12), 11440–11467 (2010)
16. Xia, F., Tian, Y., Li, Y., Sung, Y.: Wireless sensor/actuator network design for mobile control applications. Sensors 7(10), 2157–2173 (2007)
17. Heidemann, J., Govindan, R.: Embedded sensor networks. In: Handbook of Networked and Embedded Control Systems, pp. 721–738 (2005)
18. Bröring, A., Below, S., Foerster, T.: Declarative Sensor Interface Descriptors for the Sensor Web. In: Brovelli, M., Dragicevic, S., Li, S., Veenendaal, B. (eds.) WebMGS 2010: 1st International Workshop on Pervasive Web Mapping, Geoprocessing and Services, vol. 38. ISPRS, Como (2010)
19. Bröring, A., Maué, P., Janowicz, K., Nüst, D., Malewski, C.: Semantically-enabled Sensor Plug & Play for the Sensor Web. Sensors 11(8), 7568–7605 (2011)
20. Bizer, C., Heath, T., Berners-Lee, T.: Linked Data - The Story so far. Journal on Semantic Web and Information Systems 5(3), 1–22 (2009)
21. Janowicz, K., Bröring, A., Stasch, C., Schade, S., Everding, T., Llaves, A.: A RESTful Proxy and Data Model for Linked Sensor Data. International Journal of Digital Earth (2011) (in press)
22. Bröring, A., Stasch, C., Echterhoff, J.: OGC Interface Standard 10-037: Sensor Observation Service (SOS) 2.0 Interface Standard. Open Geospatial Consortium, Wayland, MA, USA (2010) (candidate standard)

Analysis of Data from a Taxi Cab Participatory Sensor Network

Raghu Ganti, Iqbal Mohomed, Ramya Raghavendra, and Anand Ranganathan

IBM T. J. Watson Research Center,
19 Skyline Dr, Hawthorne, NY, USA

Abstract. Mobile *participatory* sensing applications are becoming quite popular, where individuals with mobile sensing devices such as smartphones, music players, and in-car GPS devices collect sensor data and share it with an external entity to compute statistics of mutual interest or map common phenomena. In this paper, we present an analysis of the data from a real-world city-scale mobile participatory sensor network comprised of about two thousand taxi cabs. Our analysis spans data collected from the taxi cab sensor network over the course of a year and we use it to make inferences about life in the city. The large scale data collection (size and time) from these taxi cabs allows us to examine various aspects about life in a city such as busy "party" times in the city, peak taxi usage (space and time), most traveled streets, and travel patterns on holidays. We also provide a summary of lessons learned from our analysis that can aid similar city-scale deployments and their analyses in the future.

1 Introduction

Participatory sensing applications [5,6,8,12,14,18,22] have become quite popular recently. Participatory sensing applications [3] rely on voluntary data collection and sharing within a community towards a common goal such as measurement or mapping of a common phenomenon. A large number of these applications [6,8,12,22] rely on data collected from mobile devices (e.g. in-car sensing devices, mobile GPS devices). For example, CarTel [12] collects location information from GPS sensors in cars to infer traffic conditions. GreenGPS [8] computes fuel-optimal routes from OBD-II sensors installed in cars. Such mobile sensor data sets are a rich source of information, that can be used to measure various global phenomena. For example, location and speed information from moving cars can be used to infer traffic conditions, air pollution levels at large scales can be collectively measured using individual measurements from cars, and potholes on roads can be detected using moving vehicles.

However, as we move from academic studies into real-world deployment and usage, the participatory system becomes more complex as it provides an end-to-end service. In such systems, not only does data get collected in near real-time, it must also be processed by applications expediently. Furthermore, real-world systems will not always be perfectly scalable, either due to architechtural limitations

A. Puiatti et al. (Eds.): MobiQuitous 2011, LNICST 104, pp. 197–208, 2012.

or lack of resources for overprovisoning. Thus, the vagaries of the real-world will affect the absolute number and mobility of nodes in the sensing network over time, and this leads to variation in the operational characteristics of the processing network.

In this paper, we present an analysis of data from a large scale participatory sensing deployment of GPS devices on a fleet of about two thousand taxi cabs in the city of Stockholm, Sweden. These cabs collect and relay periodic location information over the course of a year. We examined about 100 million data points (each point is a location sample from a particular cab) over the course of a year. In this paper, we take the first step of analyzing a large participatory sensing dataset to understand the implications on system deployment, urban management and city dwellers. In particular, we use this testbed to analyze taxi cab availability patterns and draw interesting life-in-a-city inferences from this rich data set.

We also consider the matter of spatio-temporal coverage of taxi cabs - a key issue if additional environmental sensors were installed in these vehicles. In this paper, we show that taxi cabs provide an excellent platform for mobile sensor data collection. They are wide spread, especially in large cities, and are constantly available (there are taxi cabs at any given time of the day, which we will show later). They can be used to determine patterns in the daily lives of people, for example we will show later that Thursday-Saturday is a peak taxi cab usage period, from which we can infer that there is a significant increase in traffic in this city on weekends.

The rest of the paper is divided as follows, we will begin by describing the system architecture and the implementation details in Section 2. We will then provide a detailed analysis of the data from our deployment in Section 3. We discuss the lessons learned and future research directions pertaining to our large scale deployment in Section 4. Related work is presented in Section 5 and the conclusions are summarized in Section 6.

2   System Description

The deployment described in this paper was carried out over time by a large number of individuals as part of a pilot project by the city government of Stockholm. One of the key goals of the deployment was to gain the capability to be able to do real-time analysis of traffic conditions in the city.

We now provide a description of the entire system for data collection, processing, and analyzing the sensor data collected from the taxi based participatory sensor network. This system comprises of three main components, (i) mobile GPS devices equipped with cellular network connectivity installed in taxis, (ii) centralized data collection server, and (iii) IBM InfoSphere Streams [13] for data analysis. Our architecture is a layered one, depicted in Figure 1, which illustrates the various components of our system.

Taxi cabs (participating in our deployment) are installed with GPS devices that can upload acquired samples to the backend via a cellular data network. Due

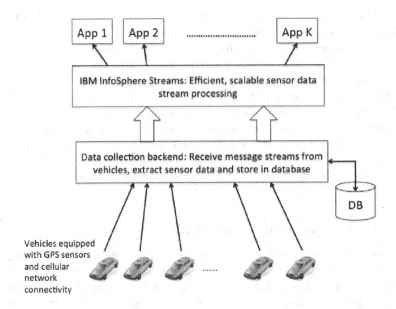

Fig. 1. Architectural components of data collection and processing

to privacy constraints, these devices acquire GPS samples only when a passenger is not present in the taxi cab. Although, in our deployment, specialized GPS devices were used for data collection, we envision that future deployments will simply use smartphones such as the Apple iPhone, Google Nexus S, which are equipped with GPS sensors as well as cellular data networks.

The backend is composed of a data broker and a post processing module. The data broker receives data streams from mobile GPS devices installed in taxis and sends the received messages to the post processing module, which extracts the sensor data from the received stream and then stores it in a database.

The data analysis layer, IBM InfoSphere Streams, interacts with the database to analyze the aggregate sensor data to compute aggregate statistics or phenomena of common interest. Application developers use InfoSphere Streams and the corresponding tools to develop applications. In this paper, we do not use the online fast stream processing capabilities of Infosphere streams (in our previous work [2], we show the scalable and fast processing capabilities of Infosphere streams and use it for implementing a real-time traffic analysis application). We use Infosphere streams to analyze the data collected in an offline manner.

3   Analysis

This section describes and analyzes the sensor data collected from the experimental deployment. The goal of this analysis is to provide insights along two different dimensions: 1) utilize the data collected to infer societal scale phenomena and 2) utilize the data collected to showcase a taxi finding application. The sheer scale of this system enables us to draw meaningful conclusions about data collection and processing as well as societal phenomena.

Before we dive into the detailed analysis, we will provide the reader with some details about the data we analyzed. The GPS data traces obtained are for about two thousand taxis for the entire year of 2008. In total, there were about 100 million GPS probe points for the whole year. We plot the number of vehicles collecting sensor data on a given day for a month in Figure 2(a). We observe from Figure 2(a) that the total number of taxicabs collecting sensor data on a given day varies between about 1400 and 1800. Further, we also observed a periodic pattern in the number of vehicles (not shown here) corresponding to the day of the week. A similar observation was made for other months of the year.

3.1 Societal Phenomena: Life in a City

Large scale participatory sensing systems are a platform for providing insights into interesting societal phenomena. In this section, we provide such insights into aggregate phenomena at a societal scale for this particular metropolitan city (with a note that these phenomena will differ based on the city and could change for this city over time). We plot the average number of cabs on a given day of the week for *all* the data of the entire year in Figure 2(b). We observe from Figure 2(b) that the cab traffic is the highest closer to the weekend (Thursday to Saturday). This suggests that there is an increased cab usage (e.g. people traveling to train stations or partying and getting back home) starting Thursday and all the way to Saturday. Further, we also observe that the traffic starts to decrease starting Sunday, with the minimum being on Tuesdays.

In order to understand the "times" when people are out on the streets in this large metropolitan city, we plot the average number of taxi cabs at a given hour of the day for the entire year in Figure 2(c). We also compare the historical average with that of the weekday and weekend averages. We observe from Figure 2(c) that the number of taxi cabs are least late in the night and early in the morning (00:00 to 05:00 hours) and peak at about 10:00 hours and remain more or less constant until 16:00 hours), this pattern is consistent on both weekdays and weekends. We note that the number of cabs is significantly higher on weekends compared to weekdays by a factor of about 1.5. Another observation is that the number of cabs on weekends is slightly lower during the late night/early morning hours (00:00 to 05:00 hours) when compared to weekdays.

Another aspect of the life in a city that we would like to highlight are the holidays and the traffic on these days. We plot the average number of cabs for a given hour of the day across our entire data set and compare it with the average number of cabs on three major holidays in this city, December 24th, December 25th, and December 31st. We make some interesting observations during the holiday times in this city. First, we observe from Figure 2(d) that on December 31st, the number of cabs are lesser than the average until 16:00 hours and it then increases over the next eight hours by a factor of 1.5. A similar observation is made for Christmas eve. On the other hand, the Christmas day itself has a

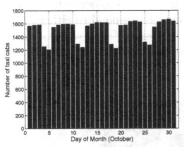

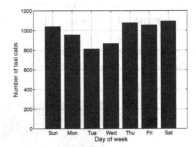

(a) Number of taxi cabs on a given day for a month

(b) Average number of taxi cabs on a given day of the week for the entire year

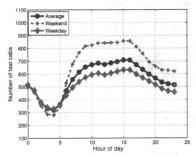

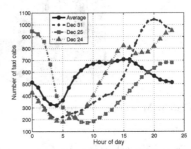

(c) Number of taxi cabs at a given hour of the day

(d) Average number of taxi cabs on three major holidays at a given hour of the day

Fig. 2. Perspectives on taxi cab availability

significant dip starting at 05:00 hours and the number of cabs are lesser by about factor of 1/3. We conclude that a participatory sensing system consisting of taxi cabs is likely to have uneven coverage. Such historical aggregate data can be used by taxi dispatching companies to efficiently manage their fleet by estimating the number of vehicles to dispatch and the time of dispatch as well. Further, they can be used to determine *hotspots*, where an individual can hail a taxi cab with a high probability (we will illustrate this aspect in the next section).

In what follows, we will provide some insights into the cab drivers lives. The GPS location samples acquired from the taxi cabs are map matched using a simple algorithm. The map matching algorithm does the following, it finds a few candidate nearest links (on the map) to a point, then for each of the points, it finds the shortest path from the previous point to the current point and verifies if the speed of travel from the previous point to the current point is within a certain threshold. We are aware of more sophisticated map matching algorithms [21,16], which we plan on incorporating in future analyses of the data from our deployments. We plot the top one hundred frequently traveled roads (based on the map matched data) for a month across all the cabs in Figure 3 within the downtown area of the metropolitan city. We observe from Figure 3 that the majority of roads used by the taxi cabs correspond to either highways or major arterial roads (which we verified by comparing against the actual map of the city). We conclude that taxi cab drivers adapt their behavior based on the customer demand they expect.

Fig. 3. Most traveled roads by taxi cabs in the downtown area of the city

3.2 Taxi Distribution in Geographical Space and Time

Many taxi cab customers have long wait times, especially at peak times and high passenger traffic areas (e.g. train stations, airports). For example, a taxi cab wait time survey [20] shows that the wait times for cabs at a major junction can be as high as 60 minutes. A useful application to taxi cab customers would be one that provides a spatio-temporal heatmap of available taxis, such that they can determine the closest junction to which they can walk towards. We built one such application using InfoSphere Streams and illustrate a few results. Figure 4 plots the taxi cab availability at different times of the day and the day of the week near a major train station in the big city. The availability is color coded with green being the least number of cabs and white being the most number of cabs (red indicates a fairly reasonable number of cabs). We observe from Figure 4 that the train station is a hotspot for taxi cabs at any time of the day or day of the week.

We plot a similar map for a predominantly residential neighborhood near the downtown. The hotspot pattern in this neighborhood is quite different from the one near the train station. For example, we observe that the weekday evenings and nights are better times to get cabs in residential neighborhoods as opposed to weekday mornings or weekend mornings (at around 07:00 hours). Real-time hotspot availabilities can be provided by this application (when receiving real-time GPS streams) and thus enable customers to find taxi cabs efficiently (in space and time).

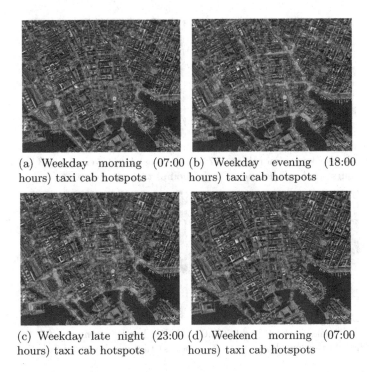

(a) Weekday morning (07:00 hours) taxi cab hotspots

(b) Weekday evening (18:00 hours) taxi cab hotspots

(c) Weekday late night (23:00 hours) taxi cab hotspots

(d) Weekend morning (07:00 hours) taxi cab hotspots

Fig. 4. Taxi hotspots near the main train station for one day

4   Lessons Learned

In the course of our analysis of the data from the deployment, we gleaned insights into several potential challenges that would be relevant to similar deployments in the future. We are currently exploring solutions to these problems and provide a research roadmap for the deployment (data collection, processing, and analysis) of large scale participatory sensing applications.

4.1   Taxi Cabs as a Deployment Platform

While the taxi cabs in our deployment only consist of GPS location sensors, additional sensors can be placed in the taxi cabs. For instance, previous research projects have demonstrated the benefits of placing accelerometers in vehicles in order to detect pot holes on roads [12]. We also postulate that air quality sensors placed in vehicles would provide important data for researchers. The benefit of placing such environmental sensors on taxi cabs is that the constantly moving taxi cabs would provide wide geographical coverage.

Our analysis in Section 3 suggest that there is significant unevenness in the spatial distribution of taxi cabs. We observed persistent "coverage" at major transit hubs (train stations, airports, etc.) and highways, while some neighborhoods (upscale residential areas, for instance) exhibit significant variability over

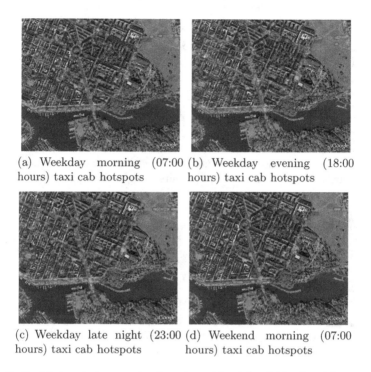

(a) Weekday morning (07:00 hours) taxi cab hotspots

(b) Weekday evening (18:00 hours) taxi cab hotspots

(c) Weekday late night (23:00 hours) taxi cab hotspots

(d) Weekend morning (07:00 hours) taxi cab hotspots

Fig. 5. Taxi hotspots in a predominantly residential neighborhood for one day

time. The basis for this variability is that taxi cabs go to where they expect their customers to be.

A trivial application we considered was whether the data received from cabs in a given hour of one day could be used to plot the major arteries of the city? Figure 6 shows the resulting image for 4 hours: three hours on a weekday and one hour on a weekend. We had assumed that if we considered normal hours when taxicabs would be used, we would be able to see a clear picture. We can see this in panels (b) and (c) of the figure. We also plot the road network map of Stockholm in Figure 6(e), which acts as a baseline for comparison.

However, our intuition was that if we looked at very early hours (4am on a weekday and 7am on a weekend - shown in (a) and (d) panels of the figure), we would not be able to make out much. We were surprised to see that this was not the case. First off, even early in the day, there are a significant number of cabs in operation. Second, these cabs are moving (at car speeds, no less) during this hour, which means that the number of geographical points we collect as well as their spatial coverage will be significant. This is a somewhat special feature of building a sensing platform from taxicabs - a sensing system built on top of private cars or pedestrians may not share this feature.

An application that requires coverage in spatial regions where there is none, could attain this by directing an empty taxi cab to go to a particular address. Such an arrangement would be agreeable to taxi cab drivers as they would still get paid. The benefit for the application creators is that they would have to pay drivers only when there happens to be no opportunistic coverage of a neighborhood. This raises a number of interesting questions, such as what address to pick

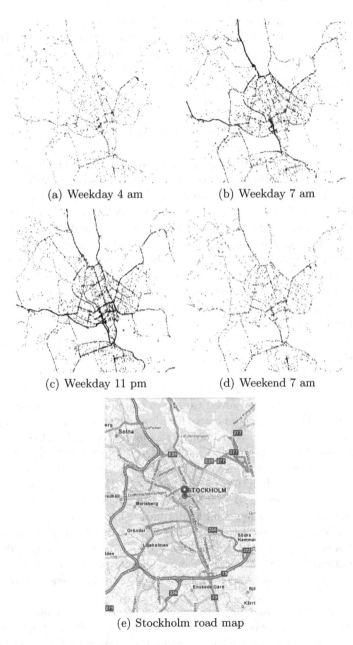

(a) Weekday 4 am   (b) Weekday 7 am

(c) Weekday 11 pm   (d) Weekend 7 am

(e) Stockholm road map

Fig. 6. Taxi presence for one day

to minimize cost for the application creator while maximizing coverage, etc. We plan to explore this matter in future work.

4.2   Server Provisioning

In recent years, the idea of elastic computing (dynamically scaling the number of processing nodes based on demand) has received considerable positive attention. As the sensing applications built on top of the taxicab network process data as soon as it is received, the computational resources required by these applications directly depends on the amount of sensor data flowing into the system. Of course, this is a function of the number of taxicabs in operation at that time. We also observed that the average number of taxicabs varies across the day. This suggests an opportunity for savings if we reduce machines during early morning hours. Additionally, our data tells us that there are far more cabs in the city on weekends (Figure 2(c)). As such we may want to have more machines on these days.

An interesting observation we make from our data was that special days, such as holidays, will drastically change the number of cabs being driven around. For instance, Figure 2(d) shows a peak around new years eve and very significant drops at other times. Clearly, occasions such as holidays and special events (e.g. concerts) must be taken into account if we start scaling the number of machines based on history. Another observation is that a steep ebb in the number of taxicabs occurs just before the peaks. We see this pattern on each of the three special days we considered. This is somewhat intuitive because cab drivers may decide to shift their working hours based on the occasion in order to improve their incomes.

5   Related Work

In this section, we describe related work. CarTel [4,7,12] is a participatory sensing deployment where twenty seven cars were equipped with in-vehicle sensors (e.g. GPS, OBD-II) and collected traces for about 290 hours. The CarTel project developed a system to collect continuously streaming sensor data from in-vehicle sensors using WiFi hotspots. They developed traffic prediction, pothole detection, and automotive diagnostics applications using the data collected. Further, algorithms for map matching were also developed [21]. The movement of about fifteen thousand taxis over a 21 month period in Singapore was analyzed in [1]. The paper focused on obtaining traffic information from the deployment. In [23], taxi cab mobility data is used to detect flawed "urban planning" by identifying traffic bottlenecks. In contrast to the above deployments, our paper describes a generic system for data collection from a mobile participatory sensing system and provides analysis of societal phenomena and discusses various lessons learned.

The Berkeley mobile millenium project [11] deployed GPS enabled cell phones on one hundred cars and collected location data on a ten mile stretch near Union city, California for eight hours. The collected data was used for extensive traffic analysis including traffic prediction. Other traffic analysis applications such as [9,17] focus on privacy issues when sharing location data within a community. Nericell [15] uses mobile phones for monitoring traffic flows in cities of the developing regions, where the traffic tends to be more chaotic and there are a large number of vehicles including 2-wheelers, 3-wheelers, cars, and buses. The StarTrack [10] system provides a scalable middleware and API for building continuous tracking application. The location data that is collected from users can be leveraged by multiple applications via a high-level API that aggregates individual location samples into "tracks". A cooperative transit tracking application using GPS enabled smartphones where individuals share GPS samples from their daily bus rides to track in-transit buses was developed in [22]. GreenGPS, a participatory sensing application that predicts fuel efficient routes is presented in [8]. In the paper, the authors deploy GPS and OBD-II sensors on sixteen personal cars and collect fuel consumption sensor data tagged with location data. These data are then used to construct fuel consumption models to predict the fuel efficient route. Our goal in this paper is to analyze data from a taxi cab participatory sensor network and provide insights into lessons learned and societal phenomena.

We are also aware of an iPhone application called *Cab Sense* [19] that provides the user with the best corner to catch a taxi in New York City. As far as we are aware, we do not know of any related publication. In this paper, we analyze the data collected and present various insights and claim no novelty in regard to the application itself.

6   Conclusions

In this paper, we analyzed data from a real-word deployment of a system that continuously collects and processes GPS data from taxicabs. We made several observations pertaining to the system's operational characteristics. For instance, we found that processing delays in this system are a function of the number of taxi cabs that are actively collecting data at that time. We also made use of the data to examine societal phenomenon and taxi distributions across geographical space and time. Finally, we presented operational insights gleaned from our analyses and suggested avenues for future research.

References

1. Balan, R.K., Nguyen, K.X., Jiang, L.: Real-time trip information service for a large taxi fleet. In: Proc. of ACM MobiSys, pp. 99–112 (2011)
2. Biem, A., et al.: Ibm infosphere streams for scalable, real-time, intelligent transportation services. In: Proc. of ACM SIGMOD, pp. 1093–1104 (2010)
3. Burke, J., et al.: Participatory sensing. Workshop on World-Sensor-Web, co-located with ACM SenSys (2006)
4. Bychkovsky, V., et al.: A measurement study of vehicular internet access using in situ wi-fi networks. In: Proc. of ACM MobiCom, pp. 50–61 (2006)
5. Davis, M., et al.: Mmm2: Mobile media metadata for media sharing. In: CHI Extended Abstracts on Human Factors in Computing Systems, pp. 1335–1338 (2005)

6. Eisenman, S.B., et al.: The bikenet mobile sensing system for cyclist experience mapping. In: Proc. of SenSys (November 2007)

7. Eriksson, J., et al.: The pothole patrol: Using a mobile sensor network for road surface monitoring. In: Proc. of ACM MobiSys, pp. 29–39 (2008)

8. Ganti, R.K., et al.: GreenGPS: A participatory sensing fuel-efficient maps application. In: Proc. of ACM MobiSys, pp. 151–164 (2010)

9. Ganti, R.K., Pham, N., Tsai, Y.-E., Abdelzaher, T.F.: Poolview: Stream privacy for grassroots participatory sensing. In: Proc. of SenSys 2008, pp. 281–294 (2008)

10. Haridasan, M., Mohomed, I., Terry, D., Thekkath, C.A., Zhang, L.: Startrack next generation: A scalable infrastructure for track-based applications. In: Proc. of OSDI, pp. 409–422 (2010)

11. Herrera, J.C., et al.: Evaluation of traffic data obtained via gps-enabled mobile phones. Transport Research, Part C 18(4), 568–583 (2009)

12. Hull, B., et al.: Cartel: a distributed mobile sensor computing system. In: Proc. of SenSys, pp. 125–138 (2006)

13. IBM. Infosphere streams, http://www.ibm.com/software/data/infosphere/streams/

14. Lu, H., et al.: Soundsense: Scalable sound sensing for people-centric applications on mobile phones. In: Proc. of ACM MobiSys, pp. 165-178 (2009)

15. Mohan, P., Padmanabhan, V.N., Ramjee, R.: Nericell: Rich monitoring of road and traffic conditions using mobile smartphones. In: Proc. of ACM SenSys, pp. 323–336 (2008)

16. Newson, P., Krumm, J.: Hidden markov map matching through noise and sparseness. In: ACM SIGSPATIAL International Conference on Advances in Geographic Information Systems, pp. 336–343 (2009)

17. Pham, N., Ganti, R.K., Uddin, Y.S., Nath, S., Abdelzaher, T.: Privacy-Preserving Reconstruction of Multidimensional Data Maps in Vehicular Participatory Sensing. In: Silva, J.S., Krishnamachari, B., Boavida, F. (eds.) EWSN 2010. LNCS, vol. 5970, pp. 114–130. Springer, Heidelberg (2010)

18. Reddy, S., et al.: Image browsing, processing, and clustering for participatory sensing: Lessons from a dietsense prototype. In: Proc of EmNets, pp. 13-17 (2007)

19. Sense Networks. Cab sense, http://www.cabsense.com/

20. Singapore Government. Average hourly passenger wait time for taxi cabs, http://www.lta.gov.sg/public_transport/doc/Website-Feb11.pdf

21. Thiagarajan, A., et al.: Vtrack: Accurate, energy-aware traffic delay estimation using mobile phones. In: Proc. of ACM SenSys, pp. 85–98 (2009)

22. Thiagarajan, A., et al.: Cooperative transit tracking using smart-phones. In: Proc. of ACM SenSys, pp. 85–98 (2010)

23. Zheng, Y., Liu, Y., Yuan, J., Xie, X.: Urban computing with taxicabs. In: Proc. of ACM UbiComp (2011)

POSTER
Adaptive OSGi-Based Context Modeling for Android

Darren Carlson and Andreas Schrader

Institute of Telematics (Ambient Computing Group), University of Lübeck,
Ratzeburger Allee 160, 23538 Lübeck, Germany
{carlson,schrader}@itm.uni-luebeck.de

Abstract. Although contextual information is recognized as a foundation of self-adapting software, context modeling middleware is often prohibitively complex and limited to small-scale deployments. To mitigate this complexity, we are developing Dynamix, a wide-area context modeling approach for Android. Dynamix simplifies context-aware application development through an extensible, OSGi-based framework that runs as a background service on a user's Android-based device, modeling context information from the environment using the device itself as a sensing, processing and communications platform. Context modeling is performed by a tailored set of plug-ins, which are dynamically provisioned to the device over-the-air during runtime. User privacy is maintained by a user-configurable context firewall. This poster introduces Dynamix's OSGI-based context modeling approach.

Keywords: Ubiquitous computing, Context-awareness, Middleware, OSGi, Android, Component integration, Reusability, Over-the-air provisioning.

1   Introduction

The rapid adoption of smart-phones, tablet computers and net-books has paralleled a dramatic increase in the usage of mobile data applications (or "apps"). As apps become unmoored from the preconceptions of conventional desktop computing, mobile users expect them to adapt intelligently and fluidly across a broad range of everyday situations, execution environments and device platforms. However, although contextual information is widely recognized as an essential foundation of self-adapting software, context modeling and management middleware is often prohibitively complex and limited to small-scale deployments [1, 2]. As a consequence, mobile app developers transitioning from enterprise and desktop scenarios face significant (and often prohibitive) complexity when creating context-aware apps.

Over the last decade, a variety of approaches have been devised to help insulate developers from the demands of context modeling and management [3]. Recently, interest in wide-area context-awareness has generated a variety of techniques that model *preexisting* sources of environmental information using the capabilities of the user's mobile device [4]. In such scenarios, adaptive middleware is often used to provide various functionality [5], including sensor abstraction; context modeling and representation; service discovery and binding; and others. Unfortunately, existing

A. Puiatti et al. (Eds.): MobiQuitous 2011, LNICST 104, pp. 209–213, 2012.

adaptive middleware technologies (e.g., OSGi [6]) have been difficult to deploy on most mobile platforms.

The explosive rise of Google's Android platform is providing a foundation for domain-specific mobile middleware based on OSGi. Briefly, OSGi defines a comprehensive dynamic module system for Java, whereby software functionality is encapsulated within distinct logical units – called *Bundles* – that contain both executable software and metadata. In an OSGi-based application, Bundles are dynamically woven together at runtime using an OSGi Framework implementation (OSGi container). In terms of OSGi deployment, Android overcomes previous mobile platform limitations though a software stack that supports multitasking (including long-lived background processes), a comprehensive inter-process communication model and broad Java compatibility. Several recent projects [7-9] have demonstrated that Android can be effectively used as the foundation of context-aware applications. These projects benefit from Android's broad device support and extensive user base; however, Android developers still lack comprehensive, wide-area support for sensing, modeling, representing and provisioning context information.

Towards this end, we're developing a wide-area context modeling approach for Android, called Dynamix. The foundation of Dynamix is an extensible middleware framework, which runs as a background service on a user's device, modeling context information from the environment using the device itself as a sensing, processing and communications platform. Context modeling is performed by a tailored set of plug-ins, which are packaged as OSGi Bundles and provisioned to the device over-the-air (OTA) during runtime. Context plug-ins are used to insulate app developers from the complexities of context modeling, which often involve specialized domain knowledge. Figure 1 provides a high level overview of the Dynamix infrastructure.

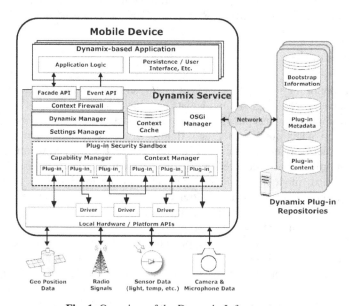

Fig. 1. Overview of the Dynamix Infrastructure

As shown in Figure 1, a Dynamix Framework instance (Dynamix Service) is situated between the host device's low-level capabilities (local hardware and platform APIs) and a set of Dynamix-based applications, which execute in their own runtime processes. Context modeling is performed on behalf of requesting apps using a tailored set of context plug-ins, which execute within an embedded OSGi container hosted by the Dynamix Service. Context plug-ins interact directly with a device's underlying hardware, platform APIs and communications facilities within a Plug-in Security Sandbox, which provides secured access to system resources, user data and Android services.

Within the Dynamix Service, an embedded OSGi container (Apache Felix) is managed by a custom OSGi Manger, which provides Dynamix-specific features, such as plug-in installation and updates; event services (e.g., plug-in installed or updated notifications); and integrated class-path management (to support plug-in access to bundled resources, such as images). The OSGi Manager works in tandem with the Capability Manager to actively prevent the loading of incompatible plug-ins (e.g., plug-ins that require unavailable hardware). A multithreaded Bundle installer was also developed to support parallel plug-in installations, progress notifications and Bundle verification. Plug-in Bundles can be provisioned from a customizable set of plug-in repositories. Plug-ins can be manually installed into a Dynamix Service, or deployed automatically in the background in response to app requests. Figure 2 shows the Dynamix Service's Home tab (left) and the Plug-ins tab (right) during a parallel plug-in installation process.

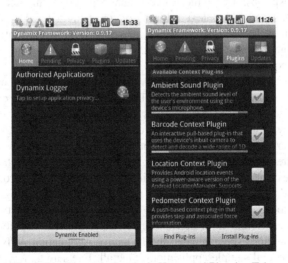

Fig. 2. The Dynamix Service's Home and Plug-ins Tabs

Dynamix apps are defined as standard Android applications that incorporate extra context modeling functionality provided by a local Dynamix Service. Dynamix apps communicate with the Dynamix Service using an Android Service Connection, which is a core component of the Android IPC model. Communication is facilitated through two Dynamix interfaces, which provide a simple way for Android apps to interact with the Dynamix Service. The Facade API enables apps to request context modeling support. The Event API enables apps to receive system notifications and context events from the Dynamix Service.

Dynamix mediates the flow of context events (from plug-ins to applications) using a configurable Context Firewall, which enables users to precisely manage the privacy risk level of the contextual information available to each app. Users define a Context Firewall policy for each app using preconfigured Privacy Policies and custom settings. A Privacy Policy assigns an overall trust level to an application, ranging from blocked (no trust) to highest trust. A trust level determines the privacy risk level of the context information that it is allowed to flow from plug-ins to an application. Users can tap on each context plug-in in the Dynamix Service's user interface to view a detailed description of the supported privacy risk levels.

After an app has been granted security authorization by the Context Firewall, it requests context support by creating *context subscriptions* using the Facade API. A context subscription is a registration made by a specific Dynamix listener indicating that it wishes to receive context events of a particular type. During a context subscription registration, the requested context type is checked against the plug-ins installed in a Dynamix Service. If the Dynamix Service is able to support the context subscription type (i.e., it has a compatible context plug-in installed), it sets up the subscription, initiates context modeling, and informs the app using the Event API. If context support is not available locally, the Dynamix Service will attempt to dynamically discover and install compatible context plug-ins using its configured set of plug-in repositories. Once the context subscription is initiated, the Dynamix Service sends discovered context information to its registered listeners using an extensible Context Event object, which contains both event data (i.e., context information) and event metadata (e.g., context type, event source, string representation, expiration information).

As a proof of concept, we created and evaluated a prototype implementation of the Dynamix infrastructure shown in Figure 1. The prototype includes an embedded OSGi container (Apache Felix 3.2.2) and was tested on several Motorola Milestone, Samsung Galaxy Tab, and HTC Hero devices. We evaluated the framework's abstractions by creating eight example context plug-ins, which ranged in complexity from simple extensions of existing Android sensor services, to relatively complex integrations of externally developed proprietary and open-source projects. Prototype context plug-in functionality includes physiological monitoring; radio signal detection; geo-location detection; social network profile extraction; orientation primitives; ambient sound level detection; step detection and step force calculation; and bar-code scanning. We evaluated the Dynamix Application APIs by developing and evaluating several sample applications. Overall, five sample Dynamix apps were developed by several participants. The apps included a range of functionality, including context event logging; product pricing and reviews; virtual information space management; health monitoring; social network interaction; and third party framework integration. Integration of the Dynamix Framework was not observed to be overly complex, even for developers with little or no Android experience.

Moreover, the diversity of these initial apps provides encouraging indications that Dynamix can be used in a variety of wide-area scenarios.

Dynamix (formerly Aladdin) is developed within an Ambient Assisted Living project supported by the Federal Ministry of Education and Research (BMBF), Germany. ID: 16KT0942. For more information, please see http://www.smartassist.de [10] and http://dynamixframework.org.

References

1. Want, R., Pering, T.: System challenges for ubiquitous & pervasive computing. In: Proceedings of the 27th International Conference on Software Engineering, St. Louis, MO, USA (2005)
2. Davies, N., Gellersen, H.-W.: Beyond Prototypes: Challenges in Deploying Ubiquitous Systems. Pervasive Computing 1(1), 26–35 (2002)
3. Baldauf, M., Dustdar, S., Rosenberg, F.: A survey on context-aware systems. International Journal of Ad Hoc and Ubiquitous Computing 2(4), 263–277 (2007)
4. Carlson, D., Schrader, A., Busch, D.: Modular framework support for context-aware mobile cinema. Personal and Ubiquitous Computing 12(4), 299–306 (2008)
5. Endres, C., Butz, A., MacWilliams, A.: A Survey of Software Infrastructures and Frameworks for Ubiquitous Computing. Mobile Information Systems 1(1), 41–80 (2005)
6. OSGi Service Platform Release 4,
   http://www.osgi.org/Specifications/HomePage
7. van Wissen, B., Palmer, N., Kemp, R., Kielmann, T., Bal, H.: ContextDroid: an expression-based context framework for Android. In: Proceedings of PhoneSense (2010)
8. IST-MUSIC Consortium. IST-MUSIC: Context-aware self-adaptive platform for mobile applications, http://ist-music.berlios.de
9. Appeltauer, M., Hirschfeld, R., Rho, T.: Dedicated Programming Support for Context-Aware Ubiquitous Applications. In: Proceedings of the International Conference on Mobile Ubiquitous Computing, Systems, Services and Technologies, Valencia, Spain (2008)
10. Schrader, A., Carlson, D., Rothenpieler, P.: SmartAssist - Wireless Sensor Networks for Unobtrusive Health Monitoring. In: Proceedings of the 5th Behaviour Monitoring and Interpretation Workshop at the 33rd German Conference on Artificial Intelligence (KI 2010), Karlsruhe, Germany (2010)

POSTER
Towards Proactive Adaptation in Pervasive Environments

Sebastian VanSyckel, Gregor Schiele, and Christian Becker

Universität Mannheim, 68131 Mannheim, Germany
{sebastian.vansyckel,gregor.schiele,christian.becker}@uni-mannheim.de
http://proactive.bwl.uni-mannheim.de

Abstract. Pervasive computing applications can adjust their behavior to a multitude of information deemed to be relevant for their situation, their so-called context. Thus far, however, adaptation in such context-aware systems is reactive and limited to the application itself. These restrictions inevitably delay adjustments to events. They cause frequent reconfigurations, and may result in inferior overall system configurations. To remedy these shortcomings, we propose a framework for proactive adaptation that supports applications in preparing for, or counteracting, upcoming context events. The framework consists of (i) a context management component with prediction capabilities, (ii) an application model for calculating adaptation alternatives, and (iii) a pool of adaptation strategies for decision-making.

Keywords: Proactive Adaptation, Context-aware Computing, Pervasive Computing.

1 Introduction

Today, context-aware pervasive computing applications detect the current state of their environment – their so-called context – and adapt themselves to it, dynamically. To do so, a multitude of sensors are deployed, measuring conditions like user location and speed, light level, and temperature. When a predefined context event occurs, the application reacts to this, e.g. by adapting its deployment or behavior. However, this *reactive adaptation approach* has a number of important shortcomings. First, adaptation can only happen after the event has occurred. This leads to inevitable delays before an application can adapt, e.g. due to the complexity of computing the best adaptation. During this time, the application may act inappropriately, annoying users or even causing system failures. More importantly, in some cases, it might not be acceptable for a given context event to occur at all. A reactive system can never prevent specific context events. It can only try to minimize the damage. In addition to this, reactive adaptation can only optimize for the current application context. It has no knowledge about the development of future context states. Therefore, an adaptation decision might later on turn out to be

A. Puiatti et al. (Eds.): MobiQuitous 2011, LNICST 104, pp. 214–218, 2012.

suboptimal or even invalid. In dynamic environments, this may lead to numerous reconfigurations over a short period of time.

We believe that *proactive adaptation* can resolve these shortcomings. In a proactive system, applications can prepare themselves to future context events, e.g. by precomputing the best adaptations. In addition, they can optimize for series of future context events, e.g. minimizing the number of necessary reconfigurations. Finally, unacceptable context events can be avoided by adapting the chain of events leading to them. In our work we examine how to realize such proactive pervasive computing systems. To do so, we develop a conceptual framework for proactive adaptation that identifies all necessary components and algorithms, and integrates them in a single system.

In this paper we identify three main components, namely *context prediction management*, *application model* and *adaptation strategies*. We analyze the challenges resulting from proactivity for each of these components and propose how to address them.

2   Proactive Framework

Figure 1 shows our approach to proactive adaptation, which is based on a trisection of the research question. The *context prediction management* (CPM, Section 2.1) is responsible for providing suitable access to context information as well as predicting context, whereas the *application model* (AM, Section 2.2) is responsible for finding all possible configurations based on the provided context and the set of context requirements posed by the application. Finally, the *adaptation strategies* (AS, Section 2.3) can determine the best chain of adaptations by applying their predefined policy. In the following, we describe the three components in more detail.

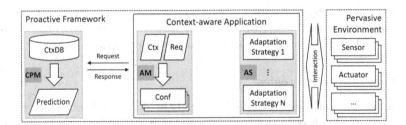

Fig. 1. A Framework for Proactive Adaptation

2.1   Context Prediction Management

Context management – acquisition, representation, preprocessing, and provision of context – is key for any context-aware system, as it provides the data on which the system adapts. In the case of proactive adaptation, this data includes context predictions. There exist a multitude of context prediction approaches. However, none is suitable for all forms of context, e.g. numerical vs. symbolic. For a generic framework, this results in the challenge of integrating several prediction methods into a single *context-aware prediction* approach.

Predictions are never certain. Research questions posed by this are: (i) how to efficiently manage chains of interdependent predictions, especially in the case of a wrong prediction, (ii) how to support a range of application-specific prediction requirements (QoS), such as false positive/ negative tolerance, and (iii) how can the system in general handle wrong predictions, especially in the case of a malicious adaptation due to false information. A basic recovery approach for malicious adaptations is a fallback to the reactive scheme. Therefore, the context management must also provide current context information to the application.

In summary, the context management provides both current and predicted context, following QoS parameters, to the application model, which we describe next.

2.2   Application Model

The application model is responsible for calculating and rating all possible adaptation alternatives given one context, current or future, and the applications requirements towards its context. In contrast to reactive systems, it is not sufficient to find one functioning adaptation, as the greatest benefits of proactive adaptation lie in the optimization of an adaptation series. The optimization is then done by the adaptation strategies (Section 2.3). This subdivision enables the framework to support reactive adaptation by simply omitting the last step.

Challenges, in addition to developing a feasible approach to the above mentioned search problem, are: (i) how to specify the application's requirements and model their importance, e.g. environment conditions and remote resources, as well as *must-have* and *nice to have*, (ii) how to calculate ratings of possible adaptations, e.g. goodness, reconfiguration costs and duration, and cost to benefit ratio, and (iii) the implications of enabling applications to alter their context via actuators. Expanding adaptation from an application to the entire environment dramatically increases the search space of adaptation alternatives and puts forth further questions, such as adaptation coordination.

2.3   Adaptation Strategies

The adaptation strategies calculate the best chain of adaptations, considering an application's goals, situation and current condition, the alternatives provided by the application model, and its predefined policy. Exemplary strategies may be energy efficiency or service consistency. A mobile application, for instance, should be cautious about its resources, whereas a stationary service should perform at its highest level.

These goals, situations and conditions may also interfere, increasing the complexity of finding a viable solution. A further challenge is how to factor in the uncertainty of predictions. As mentioned before, false predictions may lead to malicious adaptations. The risk of this to happen may outweigh an inferior configuration, leading to the question of how to calculate risk and model risk aversion.

3   Related Work

Various adaptive frameworks, such as Gaia [4], iROS [3], and PCOM [1], have been developed over the past decade. They enable mobile applications to adapt their behavior at runtime, as well as incorporate remote resources and services. Hereby, the underlying adaptation strategies, especially the distribution of responsibilities throughout the system, reside on a spectrum between *laissez-faire*, i.e. application-initiated, and *application-transparent*, i.e. system-initiated, adaptation [5]. In any case, adaptation in the above mentioned systems is reactive, i.e. executed after the triggering event. The framework Aura [2] is an exception in the sense that it anticipates proactive adaptation for some aspects of the system, such as network load and data distribution. Further work on this topic, however, has not yet been published.

4   Current and Future Work

The presented framework constitutes our approach to a proactive system on the level of the components' tasks. Currently, we are designing the system architecture and developing a middleware-based prototype. Within, the context management is realized as a centralized service that – next to providing access to current and predicted context – acts as a mediator between the applications and the pervasive environment. To achieve this, we created an additional abstraction using context variables. This allows an application to request any context service without knowledge of the providing device.

The next step will be the development of the application model, before we implement a small set of adaptation strategies. With the completion of the prototype, we expect to show significant improvements over reactive adaptation, such as increased energy efficiency and service quality.

5   Conclusion

We have presented a framework that enables context-aware applications to prepare for their future context based on prediction, requirement satisfaction, and strategic adaptation. This not only reduces delays caused by the reactive nature of traditional systems, but also allows applications to run in an optimal configuration with regard to a series of context events. Following one of several strategies, a proactively adapting application can, amongst others, save resources and provide a consistent level of service.

References

1. Becker, C., Handte, M., Schiele, G., Rothermel, K.: PCOM - A Component System for Pervasive Computing. In: IEEE Proc. Pervasive Computing and Communications (PerCom), pp. 67–76 (2004)

2. Garlan, D., Siewiorek, D., Smailagic, A., Steenkiste, P.: Project Aura: Toward Distraction-free Pervasive Computing. IEEE Pervasive Computing 1(2), 22–31 (2002)
3. Johanson, B., Fox, A., Winograd, T.: The Interactive Workspaces Project: Experiences with Ubiquitous Computing Rooms. IEEE Pervasive Computing 1(2), 67–74 (2002)
4. Roman, M., Hess, C., Cerqueira, R., Ranganathan, A., Campbell, R., Nahrstedt, K.: A Middleware Infrastructure for Active Spaces. IEEE Pervasive Computing 1(4), 74–83 (2002)
5. Satyanarayanan, M.: Mobile Computing: Where's the Tofu? ACM SIGMOBILE Mobile Computing and Communications Review 1, 17–21 (1997)

POSTER
Zero-Configuration Path Loss Model-Based Indoor Localization

Ryangsoo Kim, Wooyeol Choi, Hyuk Lim, and Jae-Hyung Jang

Department of Information and Communications
Gwangju Institute of Science and Technology (GIST)
Gwangju 500-712, Republic of Korea
hlim@gist.ac.kr

Abstract. In received signal strength (RSS)-based indoor localizations, the localization accuracy of a target node highly depends on the accuracy of estimated distances relative to anchors having a known location. Because RSS measurements are translated into distances by the path loss model (PLM), the accurate and prompt characterization of PLM parameters is crucial for improving the localization performance, especially as the wireless channel environment dynamically varies over time. Here, we propose a *zero-configuration* method based on inter-anchor measurements in order to accurately characterize PLM parameters with no offline onsite measurements. We then describe and compare two different approaches for converting the RSS measurements to the corresponding distances.

Keywords: Zero-configuration, localization, received signal strength, path loss model.

1 Introduction

With the advent of ubiquitous computing environments, received signal strength (RSS)-based indoor localization techniques have received considerable attention because of their advantage of easy implementation on existing wireless local area network (WLAN) infrastructure. In this paper, we consider a WLAN comprised of *anchors* with known locations and target nodes to be localized. For example, the access points (APs) of IEEE 802.11 WLAN deployment can serve as anchors in an indoor environment. Each anchor node periodically broadcasts beacons tagged with its ID, and records the RSS of beacon broadcasts. When a target node broadcasts a localization request packet, the anchor nodes measure the RSS of the request packet and estimates the location of the target node by using the path loss model (PLM), which characterizes the mapping between the RSS measure and the geographic distance.

A. Puiatti et al. (Eds.): MobiQuitous 2011, LNICST 104, pp. 219–223, 2012.
© Institute for Computer Sciences, Social Informatics and Telecommunications Engineering 2012

2 Proposed Localization Algorithm

2.1 Zero-Configuration Localization

In this paper, we propose a *zero-configuration* method [1] based on inter-anchor measurements, which periodically performs RSS measurements among the anchor nodes within the transmission range of each other, to realize the fully automated and online calibration of RSSs in the time and spatial domains. Because the RSS measure is susceptible to the physical characteristics of wireless networks, such as multi-path fading and signal attenuation due to the changes in temperature, humidity, and object mobility, parameters of the PLM change over time, such as the pass loss exponent and received power at a reference distance. Nevertheless, their accurate characterization is crucial for achieving an accurate localization. As the proposed localization method updates the PLM *online* with no offline onsite measurements, it can capture (in real-time) the effects of dynamic environmental changes and thereby improve the localization accuracy.

2.2 PLM Construction

We construct a simplified PLM based on inter-anchor RSS measurements. We first make the assumption that the signal strength is inversely proportional to d^α, where d is the geographical distance between the nodes and α is the path loss coefficient. Based on this assumption, the PLM can be approximately characterized by parameters α and β as follows:

$$p \, [\text{dBm}] = \beta - 10\alpha \log_{10}(d) + n, \tag{1}$$

where p is the received power at the receiver, and n is the Gaussian random noise with zero mean and variance σ^2. In this case, the first step in constructing such a path loss model is to instruct each anchor node to periodically transmit beacon packets, to measure RSSs from the other nodes, and to estimate the parameters that characterize the PLM. Let $\mathbf{p}(b)$ denote a RSS measurement vector, whose element is the RSS measurement gathered in dBm by a beacon node b, and $\mathbf{d}(b)$ denote the corresponding distance vector. Then, for the RSS measurements, the PLM in (1) is represented as the linear system $\mathbf{p} = \beta \mathbb{1}_\ell - 10\alpha \log_{10}(\mathbf{d}) + \mathbf{n}$, where $\ell = |\mathbf{p}|$, $\mathbb{1}_\ell \in \mathbb{R}^\ell$ is the 1's column vector. The two parameters α and β are then given by the least square solution of the linear system, i.e.,

$$\begin{bmatrix} \alpha \\ \beta \end{bmatrix} = (\mathbf{A}^T \mathbf{A})^{-1} \mathbf{A}^T \mathbf{p}, \tag{2}$$

where $\mathbf{A} = [-10 \log(\mathbf{d}) \ \mathbb{1}_\ell]$. This PLM is periodically updated by taking a weighted moving average of the RSS measurement whenever the anchor node receives a new sample of RSS measurement from its neighboring nodes.

2.3 Converting RSS to Distance

Once the PLM is obtained, the distances from the target node to the anchor nodes can be computed by inverting the PLM given in (1). Here, we consider two approaches for computing the distance corresponding to the measured RSS values. The first approach is to take the time average of the RSS values recorded for a certain time interval; the distance (denoted by d_a) is given by a function of the average RSS as follows:

$$d_a(\mathbb{E}[p]) = 10^{\frac{\beta - \mathbb{E}[p]}{10\alpha}}. \tag{3}$$

The other approach is to compute the distance for each RSS measurement using (1), and to use the average of the distances computed for a certain period as the final estimated distance. In this case, let d_i denote the distance for each RSS measurement, d_i is then given by $d_i(p) = 10^{\frac{\beta - p + n}{10\alpha}}$. However, the expectation of d_i is different from the actual distance d that can be obtained when $n = 0$ in (1) because it is biased, as was addressed in [2]. Here, the expectation of d_i is given by

$$\mathbb{E}[d_i] = d \cdot \mathbb{E}[10^{\frac{n}{10\alpha}}] = d \cdot \gamma(\alpha, \sigma), \tag{4}$$

where $\gamma(\alpha, \sigma) = e^{\left(\frac{\sigma \ln 10}{10\sqrt{2}\alpha}\right)^2}$. This relation implies that when the estimated distance is obtained by taking the average of d_i, it is equal to the actual distance scaled by γ. Therefore, the actual distance can be accurately estimated by compensating for the bias of $\mathbb{E}[d_i]$ as follows:

$$d_c = \frac{\mathbb{E}[d_i]}{\gamma(\alpha, \sigma)}. \tag{5}$$

Once the distances to the anchor nodes are estimated, the geographic location of the target node can be determined using lateration algorithms [3–5].

3 Experiments

In this section, we evaluate the performance of the PLM parameter estimation and localization accuracy by using MATLAB in conjunction with an empirical RSS measurement data set obtained from the SPAN laboratory at the University of Utah [6]. The RSS measurement was obtained from 44 wireless devices in a 14 m x 13 m office area.

In order to characterize the PLM parameters, we randomly selected N nodes from among 44 wireless devices and computed α and β in (2) using their pairwise RSS measurements. Fig. 1 shows the estimated path loss exponent α with respect to N. In the figure, the mean value of α is approximately 2 regardless of the number of the selected nodes, which implies that the nodes are deployed under a line-of-sight channel environment. We can also see that the standard deviation is relatively high when N is small, due to the spatial diversity of wireless channel environments.

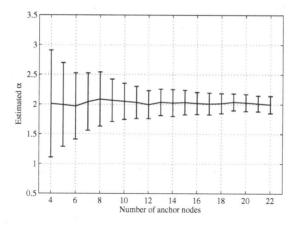

Fig. 1. Mean and standard deviation of the estimated path loss exponent α

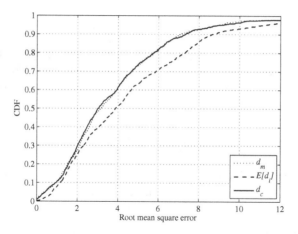

Fig. 2. Cumulative distribution of position errors for d_a, $\mathbb{E}(d_i)$, and d_c

We chose the five anchor nodes and then randomly selected the target nodes. The distances between the anchor nodes and the selected target nodes were obtained using (3)–(5), and the location of the target node was computed by the linear least square (LLS) approach in [7]. Note that the standard deviation of the measured RSS value was reported to be 3.92 (dBm) in [6]. Fig. 2 shows the cumulative distribution of the root mean square errors (RMSEs) of the target node location. We found that the localization obtained using the compensated distance (d_c) was approximately 30% more accurate than that with no bias compensation ($d_i(\mathbb{E}[p])$), and was almost same as that obtained by d_a in (3).

4   Conclusion

In this paper, we proposed a zero-configuration method for the fully automated and online calibration of PLM parameters in order to cope with the temporal and spatial variation of wireless channel environments, and subsequently described two approaches for converting RSS measurements to the corresponding distances. The experimental results showed that if the distance estimate obtained by each RSS measurement is averaged over time, it is biased, which results in a poor estimation accuracy, though this can be accurately compensated for by using an appropriate scaling factor.

Acknowledgement. This research was partially supported by the UTRC program funded by DAPA and ADD, Leading Foreign Research Institute Recruitment Program through NRF funded by MEST (K20903001804-11E0100-00910), and the Center for Distributed Sensor Network at GIST.

References

1. Lim, H., Kung, L.-C., Hou, J.C., Luo, H.: Zero-configuration indoor localization over ieee 802.11 wireless infrastructure. Springer Wireless Networks 53(7), 405–420 (2010)
2. Zanca, G., Zorzi, F., Zanella, A., Zorzi, M.: Experimental comparison of RSSI-based localization algorithms for indoor wireless sensor networks. In: The ACM Workshop on Real-World Wireless Sensor Networks (2008)
3. Niculescu, D., Nath, B.: Ad hoc positioning system. In: IEEE Globecom (2001)
4. Nagpal, R., Shrobe, H., Bachrach, J.: Organizing a Global Coordinate System from Local Information on an Ad Hoc Sensor Network. In: Zhao, F., Guibas, L.J. (eds.) IPSN 2003. LNCS, vol. 2634, pp. 333–348. Springer, Heidelberg (2003)
5. Savvides, A., Han, C.-C., Strivastava, M.B.: Dynamic fine-grained localization in ad-hoc networks of sensors. In: ACM MobiCom (2001)
6. Patwari, N., Hero, A.O., Perkins, M., Correal, N.S., O'Dea, R.J.: Relative location estimation in wireless sensor networks. IEEE Trans. on Signal Processing 51(8), 2137–2148 (2003)
7. Yang, J., Chen, Y.: Indoor localization using improved rss-based lateration methods. In: IEEE Globecom (2009)

POSTER
Towards a Privacy – Respectful Telematic Verification System for Vehicle and Driver Authorizations*

Ana I. González-Tablas, Almudena Alcaide, Guillermo Suarez-Tangil,
José M. de Fuentes, and Israel Barroso-Perez

Computer Science and Engineering Department, Universidad Carlos III de Madrid,
Avda. de la Universidad 30, 28911 Leganés, Spain
{aigonzal,aalcaide,jfuentes,ibperez}@inf.uc3m.es, gtangil@pa.uc3m.es

Abstract. The use of ubiquitous technologies to implement a telematic on-the-road verification of driver and vehicle authorizations would provide significant benefits regarding road safety, economic costs and convenience. Privacy-aware digital credentials would enable such a service although some challenges exist. The goal of this on-going work is to address these challenges. The first contribution herein presented is an enhanced data model of driver and vehicle authorizations. Secondly, we provide an analysis of existing privacy-aware digital credential systems that may support the implementation of the system.

Keywords: Digital credential, Privacy, Vehicle, Driver, Enforcement, Intelligent Transportation Systems.

1 Introduction

Nowadays, improving road safety is one of the major challenges in developed countries. Valid and up-to-date credentials attesting the conditions of vehicles and drivers are required to prove the suitability of a circulating vehicle from the road safety point of view. Enforcement of this requirement is usually done by human patrols deployed on road stretches. Agents stop vehicles and visually inspect the credentials, most of which are currently issued in paper form. The effectiveness of this procedure to decrease the number or the seriousness of traffic fatalities is related to the intensity of controls. Enforcement systems built on electronic credentials and Intelligent Transportation System (ITS) technologies would enable a more convenient, frequent and effective enforcement. However, some problems must be overcome to develop such a system. Firstly, the current set of driver and vehicle authorizations constitutes an inefficient and complex data model to operate with, in the digital world. Secondly, critical privacy issues

---

* The authors acknowledge the financial support granted by the *Comunidad de Madrid* under CCG10-UC3M/TIC-5174.

A. Puiatti et al. (Eds.): MobiQuitous 2011, LNICST 104, pp. 224–227, 2012.

Table 1. Summary of the main characteristics of current Spanish credentials

Semantic meaning		Credential	Holder	Issuer	Expiration date	Revocability	Verified facts and attributes
Authorizes the vehicle (VIN/ Registration Number) to circulate	Authorizes the vehicle to circulate from a technical point of view	Technical inspection card	Vehicle	Manufacturer / Regional Industry Department	Never	No. Compulsory renewal if attributes change	Holdership, authenticity, authorized issuer.
		Technical inspection report, record (in technical inspection card) and sticker	Vehicle	Technical Inspection Station	Specific number of years		Holdership, authenticity, authorized issuer, up-to-date.
	Authorizes the vehicle to circulate from an administrative point of view	Vehicle registration certificate and registration plate	Vehicle & Keeper	Road Traffic Authority	Never	Yes (documents are usually retained)	Holdership, authenticity, authorized issuer, not revoked.
		Proof of tax payment	Vehicle & Keeper	Local Tax Administration / Bank	Annuity Payment	No	Holdership, authenticity, authorized issuer, up-to-date.
		Proof of compulsory insurance payment	Vehicle & Owner / Keeper	Insurance Company / Bank	Annuity Payment		Holdership, authenticity, authorized issuer, up to date.
Authorizes a person (ID) to drive a vehicle	Authorizes the driver to circulate with a certain type of vehicle	Driving license	Person	Road Traffic Authority	Specific number of years	Yes	Holdership, authenticity, authorized issuer, up to date, not revoked.

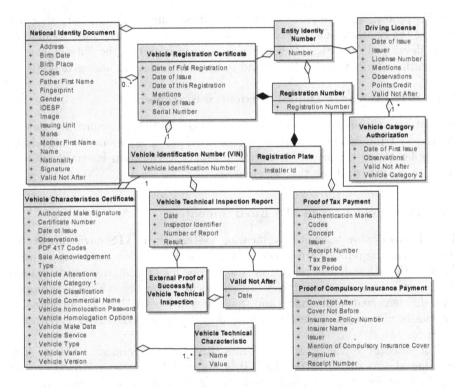

Fig. 1. Improved credential data model

arise concerning the traceability and surveillance of drivers and vehicles. Thirdly, the restrictions imposed by ITS environments must be considered. The final goal of this on-going research is to build a privacy-respectful telematic enforcement system for the verification of vehicle and driver authorizations.

Table 2. Summary of the properties analyzed in the schemes. An entity is described by β attributes and wants to unlinkably perform α different verification·procedures each one δ times.

	Brands [2]	Kwon [4]	Chameleon [5]	Camenish [3]	Verheul [6]
No. of Certificates	$\alpha\delta$	$\alpha\delta$	1	α	α
Workload	$O(\beta)$	$O(\beta)$	$O(\beta)$	$O(\beta)$	$O(\beta)$
Accept Non Predefined Control Policies?	✓	✓	✓	✗	✗
Commercial Implementation	U-prove	✗	✗	Idemix	✗
Unlinkability (Pseudonyms Changes)	✗	✗	✗	✗	
PKI Standard Compliance	✗	✓	✓	✗	✗
Anonymous Credential Acquirance	✓	✓	✓	✓	✓

2 Proposed Vehicle and Driver Authorizations System

2.1 Improved Credential Model

In this poster, we summarize the first results of our research. First, after analyzing the Spanish legislation (see Table 1), a new credential data model has been developed (see Fig. 1), which significantly improves the current one by eliminating attribute redundancy, and unnecessary relations and credentials.

2.2 Privacy-Aware Digital Credential Systems

Second, we have analyzed current credential systems that allow proving the credentials' attributes anonymously (see Table 2). These schemes are the candidates for implementing the privacy-respectful telematic verification system for vehicle and driver authorizations that we envision.

2.3 Deployment on an ITS Environment

In order to deploy telematic verification system on an ITS environment, we assume that the vehicle carries its credentials on the vehicle's Hardware Security Module (HSM) and that the driver also carries his credential set in a secured device such as a smart card. We further assume that the vehicle is equipped with different credential readers and that the vehicle's OBU/HSM will act as an intermediary between credentials verification system and the driver's credential platform.

If it is assumed that Road Side Units (RSU) act as verifiers, a vehicle (circulating at 120 km/h) covers the RSU's range (1 km) in 30 s. Therefore, the feasibility of deploying a system such as the envisioned one on ITS environments will strongly depend on the specific scheme or schemes selected to implement the designed set of credentials (see Fig. 1) or others that summarize the attributes that must be verified. Results in [1] throw promising figures as the holdership verification process of a Camenisch credential is said to take around 10.45 s in a Java card.

References

1. Bichsel, P., Camenisch, J., Groß, T., Shoup, V.: Anonymous credentials on a standard java card. In: Proc. of the 16th ACM Conf. on Computer and Communications Security, CCS 2009, pp. 600–610. ACM, New York (2009)
2. Brands, S.: Rethinking Public Key Infrastructures and Digital Certificates; Building in Privacy. MIT Press (2000)
3. Camenisch, J., Sommer, D., Zimmermann, R.: A General Certification Framework with Applications to Privacy-Enhancing Certificate Infrastructures. In: Fischer-Hübner, S., Rannenberg, K., Yngström, L., Lindskog, S. (eds.) Security and Privacy in Dynamic Environments. IFIP AICT, vol. 201, pp. 25–37. Springer, Boston (2006)
4. Kwon, T.: Privacy preservation with x.509 standard certificates. Information Sciences, 47–53 (2011), doi:10.1016/j.ins.2011.02.016 Key: citeulike:8971918
5. Persiano, G., Visconti, I.: An Efficient and Usable Multi-show Non-transferable Anonymous Credential System. In: Juels, A. (ed.) FC 2004. LNCS, vol. 3110, pp. 196–211. Springer, Heidelberg (2004)
6. Verheul, E.R.: Self-Blindable Credential Certificates from the Weil Pairing. In: Boyd, C. (ed.) ASIACRYPT 2001. LNCS, vol. 2248, pp. 533–551. Springer, Heidelberg (2001)

POSTER
IPS: A Ubiquitous Indoor Positioning System

Moustafa Alzantot, Reem Elkhouly,
Amal Lotfy, and Moustafa Youssef

Egypt-Japan University of Science and Technology (E-JUST),
Alexandria, Egypt
{moustafa.alzantot,reem.elkhouly,
amal.youssef,moustafa.youssef}@ejust.edu.eg

Abstract. Although GPS has been considered a ubiquitous outdoor localization technology, we are still far from a similar technology for indoor environments. While a number of technologies have been proposed for indoor localization, such as WiFi and GSM-based techniques, they are isolated efforts that are way from a true ubiquitous localization system. A ubiquitous indoor positioning system is envisioned to be deployed on a large scale worldwide, with minimum overhead, to work with heterogeneous devices, and to allow users to roam seamlessly from indoor to outdoor environments.

We describe an architecture for the ubiquitous indoor positioning system (IPS)[1]. We then focus on the feasibility of automating the construction of a worldwide indoor floorplan and fingerprint database which, as we believe, is one of the main challenges that limit the existence of a ubiquitous IPS system. Our proof of concept uses a crowd-sourcing approach that leverages the embedded sensors in today's cell phones, such as accelerometers, compasses, and cameras, as a worldwide distributed floorplan generation tool. This includes constructing the floorplans and determining the areas of interest (corridors, offices, stairs, elevators, etc). The cloud computing concepts are also adopted for the processing and storage of the huge amount of data generated and requested by the system users. Our results show the ability of the system to construct an accurate floorplan and identify the area of interest with more than 90% accuracy.

Keywords: Area of interest classification, Automatic floorplan construction, Ubiquitous indoor localization.

1 Introduction

Many indoor location determination technologies have been proposed over the years, including: infrared [1], ultrasonic, and radio frequency (RF) [2]. All these

---

[1] More details can be reached at the project's web page
http://wrc.ejust.edu.eg/IPS.html

A. Puiatti et al. (Eds.): MobiQuitous 2011, LNICST 104, pp. 228–232, 2012.

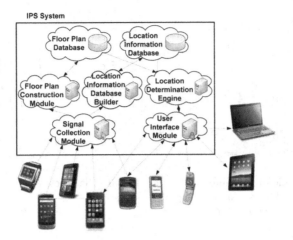

Fig. 1. The IPS system architecture

technologies provide varying levels of accuracy that can support different application needs. However, each of these technologies is designed to be deployed in a certain area, with known floorplans, and some of them require deployment of special hardware and/or require special calibration of the area of interest. We address the problem of realizing a ubiquitous indoor positioning system (IPS). Similar to the outdoor GPS, a ubiquitous indoor positioning system is envisioned to be deployed on a large scale worldwide, with minimum overhead, to work with heterogenous devices, and to allow users to roam seamlessly from indoor to outdoor environments. Such a system will enable a wide set of applications and provide a richer environment for location-aware social networking applications.

We believe that obtaining floorplans for virtually all buildings worldwide is the *main challenge* that limits the existence of a ubiquitous indoor localization system. As an example, although WiFi has been installed in a large number of buildings worldwide and WiFi localization can give meter accuracy [2], it cannot be leveraged as an IPS as there are no floorplans for all WiFi-enabled buildings. This can be due to the lack of building blueprints, as is the case in many developing countries, privacy issues, or to the fact that no one is willing to take the effort to submit the floorplan to a worldwide floorplan database. Even if someone submits the floorplan, there is still a manual effort required to process the floorplan to identify the areas of interest. In addition, constructing a WiFi signal fingerprint for a given area is an expensive, time consuming process that has to be repeated from tim to time to capture changes in the environment. In addition, a floorplan cannot be used for WiFi localization without constructing a fingerprint for the area of interest, which is a time consuming process. Updating the floorplan and the fingerprint is a task that has to be repeated from time to time to capture changes in the environment. Clearly, a true worldwide ubiquitous localization system has to overcome these hurdles.

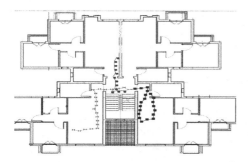

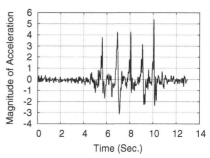

Fig. 2. An example of the different traces generated by the different users using the cell phones' inertial sensors

Fig. 3. The acceleration pattern for five steps

2   System Design

The IPS system we envision is based on leveraging the cell phone as a ubiquitous computing device with a number of internal sensors, such as accelerometers, compasses, and cameras. The cloud computing concepts will be leveraged for the processing and storage of the huge amount of data generated and requested by the system users. Figure 1 gives an overview of an IPS system components. The system consists of five modules.

2.1   Raw Signal Collection Module

This module is responsible for collecting the data from the cell phones sensors. These sensors may produce different signals such as the acceleration, compass readings, gyroscope readings, WiFi information (signal strength and heard APs), GSM information (signal strength and nearby cell towers), camera images, sound signals, outdoor GPS signal, etc. Each signal is associated with a timestamp and is forwarded to other modules for processing.

2.2   FloorPlan Construction Module

This module takes the raw and processed sensor signals from the large number of users who use a building daily and fuse them to estimate the floorplan. It is also responsible for dynamically updating the floorplan. The estimated floorplans are stored in the cloud for later retrieval.

The first step in constructing the floorplan is to construct the user traces inside a building from the raw sensor data (Figure 2) by dead reckoning. To limit the growing error in location estimation using cheap noisy inertial sensors, we decided to track the users location by applying a step detection algorithm to identify the pattern of acceleration during a step. Figure 3 shows the acceleration pattern for five steps.

Once the user traces are constructed, the next step is to construct the floorplan and identify the areas of interest. Our technique is based on dividing the unknown floorplan area into blocks and classifying each block based on the traces that go through it (Figure 4). We have four different classes: Office, corridor, elevator, and stairs. We used the C4.5 tree-based classifier [3] to build a decision tree from a training set. We also use a bootstrap aggregation ensemble learning technique [4], this enables us to parallelize the technique, and hence becomes more suitable for the cloud.

2.3   Location Information Database Builder Module

This module is responsible for constructing the fingerprint database for the location determination system. It populates the fingerprint database, also stored in the cloud, based on the WiFi and GSM information it gets from the cell phones inside the building.

2.4   Location Estimation Engine

This module is responsible for estimating the user location based on the signals it receives in the user query. It consults the fingerprint generated by the Location Information Database Builder Module.

2.5   User Interface Module

This module is responsible for interacting with the system users. It receives a query from the users about their current location. This query may include a variety of sensor information, such as WiFi information, camera image, and other signals. The module then consults its location estimation engine and returns the current estimated user location and possibly the floorplan the user is currently located at.

3   Experiments and Results

As an example of a typical environment for the IPS, our experiment is conducted in a floor plan covering an area of $448m^2$ and covered with an 802.11 network. We have three different users carrying three android phones (two Nexus One phones and one Samsung Galaxy S phone). All phones have the same set of sensors: 3-axis accelerometer, 3-axis magnometer, WiFi and GSM information. Table 1 shows the confusion matrix of classification between different areas of interest inside a building. Although the GPS does not work indoors, we use it as a synchronization point to determine global reference points. In addition, even though the phones contain cameras and microphones, these are not used in our current testbed. Our system has been able to construct an accurate floorplan and identify the area of interest with more than 90% accuracy.

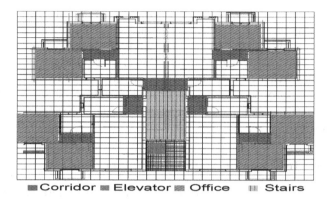

■ Corridor ■ Elevator ▨ Office   ▥ Stairs

Fig. 4. The floorplan used in our evaluation divided into blocks. Note that the entire area is not highlighted for clarity.

Table 1. The confusion matrix for the classifier

Actual	Predicted			
	Stairs	Corridor	Elevator	Office
Stairs	478	23	0	0
Corridor	0	250	0	0
Elevator	0	0	46	0
Office	46	0	0	182

References

1. Want, R., Hopper, A., Falcão, V., Gibbons, J.: The active badge location system. ACM Trans. Inf. Syst. 10(1), 91–102 (1992)
2. Youssef, M., Agrawala, A.: The Horus WLAN location determination system. In: Proceedings of the 3rd International Conference on Mobile Systems, Applications, and Services (MobiSys), pp. 205–218. ACM, New York (2005)
3. Ross Quinlan, J.: C4.5: Programs for Machine Learning. Morgan Kaufmann Publishers Inc., San Francisco (1993)
4. Opitz, D., Maclin, R.: Popular ensemble methods: An empirical study. J. Artificial Intelligence Res., 169–198 (1999)

POSTER
An Embedded Fusion System for Location Management

Eduardo Metola and Ana M. Bernardos

Universidad Politécnica de Madrid, Telecommunications School
Avenida Complutense 30, 28040 Madrid, Spain
{eduardo.metola,abernardos}@grpss.ssr.upm.es

Abstract. This paper presents the design and development of a Fusion System that combines data from different communication and location sensors (WiFi, GPS, Cell-Id) to provide consumer location-based services with the best available position estimate. In practice, this location manager is a light module, designed to run in a mobile device and ready to be used by any application requiring seamless indoor/outdoors positioning information. It automatically manages hand-offs among different localization systems. Its logic is based on a decision tree built on an initial set of Quality of Location parameters.

Keywords: localization system, multisensor data fusion, Quality of Location, mobile applications.

1 Introduction

Recently, mobile services increasingly aim at providing the user with personalized features. In particular, location is a parameter that may enable or enhance the functionalities of e.g. guides, navigators or social networks. Thanks to the number of (communication) technologies that are nowadays available in mobile devices, it is feasible to easily retrieve the user's location. When outdoors, GPS, cell-ID and WiFi network identification fingerprints are the most common technologies; these technologies may be used in a cooperative manner to infer location (e.g. [1] [2]). When indoors, it is usually needed to deploy ad-hoc positioning systems to guarantee availability and accuracy. These positioning systems are often built on technologies commonly available in smartphones, like WiFi [3] or Bluetooth [4]. When better accuracy (centimeter range) is needed, the possible choices include e.g. infrared, ultrasounds or ultrawideband, technologies that can be deployed at different costs in terms of resources and complexity. Additionally, beacon-oriented techniques (based on short-range approaches, e.g. bidimensional codes or NFC) may complement any technology deployed in any setting.

These technologies usually work in an independent manner: no internal system to deal with automated positioning technology selection is actually available in mobile application development kits, so each application using location as input parameter has to handle it at its own risk. As location may be used in simultaneous services, it is reasonable to design a fusion system (FS) layer to handle it, to avoid duplicating internal tasks: ideally, this fusion layer will select the best position estimate while

A. Puiatti et al. (Eds.): MobiQuitous 2011, LNICST 104, pp. 233–237, 2012.
© Institute for Computer Sciences, Social Informatics and Telecommunications Engineering 2012

taking into account the consumer application needs (in terms of accuracy and sampling rate) and the mobile device's resources (in terms of energy and workload). The fusion layer will provide seamless featured location information when the user is moving indoors-outdoors and vice versa, and also when commuting between different indoor positioning systems, handling handoffs and minimizing the time with 'no-location' information.

In order to select the technology to be used in each moment, the fusion layer has to evaluate the Quality of Location coming from the potential options. How to quantify the efficiency and the quality of the estimation has been addressed e.g. in [5][6]: in these works, Quality of Location (QoL) is an aggregated term to analyze the goodness of the estimation, using different features like accuracy, precision, freshness, temporal and spatial resolution. Other approaches try to merge different sources of information when some conflicting situations are detected, as mentioned above in [1] [2](e.g. when not all the sensors are working at the same time) or to develop new algorithms that take advantage of the redundant information [7].

In this paper, we present a preliminary version of the previously mentioned FS, which has been built as a component to be entirely deployed in a smartphone. This component is providing an API, which may be used by any application needing to retrieve seamless location information.

2   Positioning Technologies and Architecture Approach

The FS architecture is designed to run in a mobile device, making use of an external infrastructure only to support indoor localization algorithms that usually rely on local information (e.g. resource maps divided into zones or fingerprints). This local information is stored in a server and is opportunistically downloaded when needed.

For this first implementation of the FS, localization systems based on GPS, Cell-ID and WiFi technology have been integrated, although the fusion system is scalable in number of technologies and algorithms. The system is capable of providing a location estimate whenever any of these technologies are available.

GPS location information is not available when indoors, so in this case, specific localization systems are used:

- *Supervised indoor positioning system*: e.g. in our labs, there is a WiFi network built on four access points (APs), which enables the deployment of received signal strength (RSS) positioning algorithms (fingerprint and propagation channel based ones [8]), each of them providing different accuracy (average 2.5 meters).
- *Legacy unsupervised indoor positioning system*: nowadays, in any office-like environment it is usual to find a good number of different WiFi networks. Thus, we have built an algorithm that takes advantage of the existing infrastructure to match the visible access points with a previously stored fingerprint. The algorithm compares the MAC address of the access points that a device is detecting to a digital map which stores, for a number of selected coordinates, the set of MAC addresses detected in a calibration phase. Obviously, location accuracy depends on the granularity of the calibration phase (how many calibration points have been stored in the database). This algorithm provides a symbolic location (zones), while the previous one provides coordinates.

The decision algorithm logic gives priority to the most accurate technology available in a given moment. When indoor, RSS-based algorithms provides best estimates than MAC-based one. If none of them are available, then the ubiquitous Cell-ID provides its estimate. The accuracy of the estimation is forwarded to the application for it to handle the situation. In this first version of the FS, we have used two features of QoL to choose which source gathers the position estimation from: 1) its accuracy, to put in order each technology in a priority level and 2) the elapsed time since the last measure (availability) for each algorithm, in order to include information about the freshness of the measurement (to decide if an estimation is out of date).

3   Implementation Details

The FS has been developed on an Android smartphone, which includes the necessary sensors for the positioning systems to work. The FS is composed by an activity component, which handles the core algorithm, managing the state of each source of position information (WiFi algorithms, GPS and cell-Id) through four different processes. The core algorithm is also in charge of selecting the most adequate estimate. To that effect, each localization process controls the position estimate that each independent algorithm offers, starting and stopping a service component that represents the sensor access of each technology. In this case, there are three services to gain access to the sensors data.

The four localization processes are qualified depending on their accuracy. The two best ones are GPS when outdoors, which can offer an accuracy from some meters [8] and WiFi RSS fingerprinting when indoors, that can achieve an accuracy of 1,5 meters in best case [9]. If any of these systems are available, the fusion algorithm will not get any other data. Otherwise, WiFi MAC fingerprinting algorithm will be requested to offer its position information. This method can offer a variable accuracy, depending on the separation of the zones where the calibration measurements were taken and, of course, of the stability of the electromagnetic fingerprint (as it is an uncontrolled environment, WiFi networks may appear or disappear without any control). The distance between two zones can cover from few meters up to different floors inside a building. Finally, cell-Id algorithm is the last option, because its accuracy is over several hundreds of meters [10], but available whenever there is cellular coverage.

For demonstration purposes, the activity component representing the FS is composed of several threads. Two of them are continuously running. One of them handles the GUI (Graphical User Interface) - if the FS works as an application -, and the other one launches any algorithm process upon request. It means that, according to what was mentioned in previous paragraph, an algorithm process will start only if it is better qualified. E.g.: if cell-Id is currently giving the position estimation, the processes of the other three algorithms or systems will be active. If, in a given moment, any of them can offer its position estimation, cell-Id process will be stopped, and the new one will keep on running. If the available one is the WiFi MAC algorithm, WiFi RSS algorithm process and GPS process will keep running until they find the position estimation.

Figure 1 summarizes this performance, showing which processes are active and looking for new and recent locations (in rows) depending on the one that is currently offering the estimate (in columns).

		Process giving the location estimate in a given moment				
		GPS	WiFi RSS	WiFi MAC	Cell-Id	None
Active processes, looking for a better estimate	GPS	-	No	Yes	Yes	Yes
	WiFi RSS	No	-	Yes	Yes	Yes
	WiFi MAC	No	No	-	Yes	Yes
	Cell-Id	No	No	No	-	Yes

Fig. 1. Active process depending on the current available location technology

Apart from taking accuracy into consideration, the four processes handle the elapsed time requirement and activate or deactivate a flag, depending on the freshness of the given estimate. For the WiFi RSS algorithm, an extra requirement at signal level has been included: in order to guarantee the correctness of the estimation, this system is only initiated if a sufficient number of access points are visible. In our implementation, we have set this parameter to 3, which is the minimum requested to perform trilateration.

Each process can call each corresponding service, implemented in a new thread. GPS process calls GPS service, cell-Id process calls cell-Id service and both WiFi algorithms call a WiFi service, which makes different tasks depending on the calling process:

- WiFi Service: when this service starts in a new thread, it makes a subscription to the WiFi adapter, demanding an event call when the WiFi sensors scan is finished. Then it stores in a database either the RSS vector coming from the Aps infrastructure (RSS fingerprinting algorithm), or the WiFi MAC vector visible from the smartphone (WiFi MAC fingerprinting algorithm).
- GPS Service: this service makes a subscription to the GPS sensor. This sensor is able to offer the position thanks to the API that Android provides through the SDK.
- Cell-Id Service: in this service, a subscription to cell location changes is enabled. When it occurs, a request to http://opencellid.org is sent in order to get the position of the cell using its identifier.

4   Conclusions

The main purpose of this FS is to provide seamless location information to an application or service, enabling the developer with a single interface to retrieve position data. The adopted approach is light and highly autonomous, capable of minimizing communication needs. It manages handoffs between outdoor-indoor positioning systems, and transitions between supervised and unsupervised indoor positioning systems, aiming at minimizing the commuting time. Together with embedded algorithms for localization, it minimizes the need of performing positioning in infrastructure.

Our current work focuses on enhancing the preliminary model for QoL. The final model should be suitable to optimize resources management in the mobile device (in terms of computation time and energy consumption). Coordinately, we aim at defining an interface for the applications to describe their localization needs. Finally, as the FS is designed to run in the mobile device, it can be part of a system to guarantee privacy control on location information, so how to include some user-centric features to facilitate privacy management is also being considered.

Acknowledgments. This work is being supported by the Government of Madrid under grant S2009/TIC-1485 and the Spanish Ministry for Science and Innovation under grant TIN2008-06742-C02-01.

References

1. Zirari, S., Canalda, P., Spies, F.: WiFi GPS based combined positioning algorithm. In: IEEE Int. Conf. on Wireless Communications, Networking and Information Security, pp. 684–688 (2010)
2. Yeh, S.-C., Hsu, W.-H., Su, M.-Y., Chen, C.-H., Liu, K.-H.: A study on outdoor positioning technology using GPS and WiFi networks. In: International Conference on Networking, Sensing and Control, pp. 597–601 (2009)
3. Kushki, A., Plataniotis, K.N., Venetsanopoulos, A.N.: Kernel-Based Positioning in Wireless Local Area Networks. IEEE Trans. on Mobile Computing 6(6), 689–705 (2007)
4. Cruz, O., Ramos, E., Ramirez, M.: 3D indoor location and navigation system based on Bluetooth. In: Procs. 21st International Conference on Electrical Communications and Computers, pp. 271–277 (2011)
5. Kim, Y., Lee, K.: A Quality Measurement Method of Context Information in Ubiquitous Environments. In: Procs. International Conference on Hybrid Information Technology, vol. 2, pp. 576–581 (2006)
6. Sheikh, K., Wegdam, M., Van Sinderen, M.: Quality-of-context and its use for protecting privacy in context aware systems. Journal of Software 3 (2008)
7. Fang, S.-H., Lin, T.-S.: Cooperative multi-radio localization in heterogeneous wireless networks. Wireless IEEE Tran. on Comm. 9(5), 1547–1551 (2010)
8. Cecchini, J.: Next generation GPS-aided space navigation systems. IEEE Aerospace and Electronic Systems Magazine 17(12), 7–10 (2002)
9. Moreno, C.J., Bernardos, A.M., Casar, J.R.: An indoor location system based on RSS probability distribution estimation. Works. User-Centric Tech. and Applications, Salamanca (2008)
10. Trevisani, E., Vitaletti, A.: Cell-ID location technique, limits and benefits: an experimental study. In: Sixth IEEE Workshop Mobile Computing Systems and Applications, pp. 51–60 (2004)

DEMO
MultiCAMBA: A System to Assist
in the Broadcasting of Sport Events*

Roberto Yus[1], David Antón[2], Eduardo Mena[1],
Sergio Ilarri[1], and Arantza Illarramendi[2]

[1] University of Zaragoza, María de Luna 1, Zaragoza, Spain
{ryus,emena,silarri}@unizar.es
[2] Basque Country University, Manuel de Lardizábal s/n, San Sebastián, Spain
danton004@ikasle.ehu.es, a.illarramendi@ehu.es

Abstract. In this demo paper we present *MultiCAMBA* (*Multi-CAMera Broadcasting Assistant*), a context– and location–aware system that, using a 3D model updated continuously with real-time data retrieved from the scenario, helps technical directors (TDs) in the live broadcasting task. They can indicate in run-time their interest in certain moving objects or geographic areas, and the system is in charge of selecting the cameras that can provide the kind of view required. To achieve this task, the system continuously recreates the views of the cameras in a 3D scenario, considering possible occlusions among the objects.

Keywords: Location-aware system, Multiple camera management.

1 Introduction

Nowadays, the broadcasting industry is demanding new software systems that facilitate the broadcasting task. On the one hand, these systems should help increase the richness of live content production. On the other hand, they should contribute to decrease the production costs, mainly by reducing the need of highly specialized human resources to produce (create, edit, and distribute) audiovisual content. In that direction, we have developed the MultiCAMBA system, that enables TDs to quickly select, among many cameras (some of them can be static and others be attached to moving objects), the one that fulfills his/her requirements and whose view should be broadcasted.

The key features of MultiCAMBA, which supports the processing of location-dependent queries [3] about moving objects and cameras, are briefly highlighted as follows:

- It allows TDs to query about cameras viewing a target object/area and even obtaining a specific kind of view (front, top, rear and covering 50% of the target, etc.), through an *easy-to-use interface that recreates the real scenario using Google Earth technology.*

---

* This work has been supported by the CICYT project TIN2010-21387-C02.

A. Puiatti et al. (Eds.): MobiQuitous 2011, LNICST 104, pp. 238–242, 2012.

- *It ranks the cameras* obtained as a result according to different criteria: the time needed to view the target object/area, the distance to the target, the percentage of the object viewed, the percentage of the shot occupied by the target object, and/or the distance to the target.
- *It offers advanced functionalities.* For example, it estimates the time needed to view a target object by considering the cameras features. Besides, it analyzes the view of a camera taking into account occlusions among objects.

Other works also address the problem of multi-camera management (e.g., [1,2]). However, they only consider static cameras (i.e., at fixed locations). On the contrary, the cameras considered in our proposal can be static or attached to moving objects. Moreover, we are not aware of any system that has applied an architecture for processing location-dependent queries in the context of live content production to retrieve a list of cameras providing views that fulfill certain requirements.

In the following we explain the two main components of MultiCAMBA: 1) the *query processor*, that executes the TD queries about interesting objects/areas to obtain the cameras fulfilling his/her requirements; and 2) the *Graphical User Interface*, that allows the TD to define these queries and visualize their results. Additional details can be obtained from the Web page of MultiCAMBA (http://sid.cps.unizar.es/MultiCAMBA).

2 Query Processor

The query processor is the component in charge of managing the queries submitted by the TD. These location-dependent queries are continuously evaluated (every second) in order to provide accurate and up-to-date results to him/her.

For example, the following interesting queries, among others, are supported by the query processor:

- Cameras that can view a certain object.
- Cameras that capture a side view of a certain object.
- Cameras that can view a certain percentage of an object in a defined area.

The query processor implements the functions defined in [4] and the 3D techniques in [6] to obtain the cameras that are fulfilling (or would be able to fulfill in the near future) the specified requirements of the TD. To compute a certain camera view (and for example to obtain the percentage of an object covered by it), a 3D engine (specifically, *JMonkeyEngine*) has been used. Due to space limitations, we refer the interested reader to the aforementioned papers for further information about how these tasks are performed.

Testing MultiCAMBA in a scenario involving real moving objects and cameras is very costly and it would be difficult to design repeatable experiments. So, we have developed a simulator that enables the accurate simulation of these scenarios by using stored *real* samples (obtained every second) of the location and direction of objects and cameras. So far, we have evaluated our system in the context of the popular rowing races of San Sebastian, using real data corresponding to the competition of September 2010. Performance tests in this scenario show that the system can achieve an average refreshment period of 0.085 seconds (see [6]), so MultiCAMBA can be used for live broadcasting.

3   Graphical User Interface

The Graphical User Interface (GUI) has been developed as a Web page where the TD can define queries about interesting objects, visualize the results to his/her queries, define areas of interest, etc. It is clear and easy to use, as its appearance is similar to the usual workplace of a TD, where there are several input sources to select and a screen where the next source to be aired can be previewed. The main components of the GUI (see Figure 1) are:

- The *query interface*, that facilitates the definition and submission of queries and shows the results in tables.
- The *overview map*, a Google Earth plugin that supports navigating through the scenario, defining interesting areas, and visualizing the results of the queries submitted.
- The *camera inputs*, two windows where the user can preview the video stream of the selected cameras before broadcasting them.

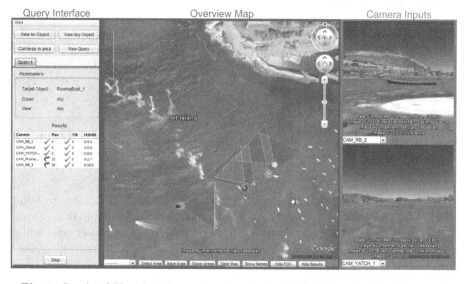

Fig. 1. Graphical User Interface using Google Earth plugins to simulate cameras

We use Google Earth to show to the TD a 3D up-to-date overview of the moving objects and cameras in the scenario and the results to his/her queries. This is a user-friendly way of displaying the results and allows an easy interaction with the system. If no real video stream is available for the camera inputs, then the camera view is also recreated by using GE (as in [5]).

Different colors and shapes are used to clearly represent different important elements in the scenario: the target object (denoted by a yellow star), the cameras currently fulfilling the query constraints (green hexagons), the cameras that would be able to fulfill the requirements in a few seconds (blue hexagons), and the cameras that cannot fulfill the requirements (red hexagons). Figure 1 shows an example where the results of a query and the field-of-view (brown triangles) of the cameras are displayed on the overview map.

The GUI enables the TD to create his/her queries by selecting the target object or a specific camera (among the objects and cameras in the scenario), the area of interest where the target has to be located, the kind of view to obtain of the target (front, rear, side, etc.), the amount of the target that the camera has to cover (complete, any, or a certain percentage), etc. The TD can also define the ranking criterion to be applied to the answer set: 1) the time needed to obtain the required view (cameras that can provide the view right now could be more interesting); 2) the distance to the target (a shorter distance could lead to a more detailed shot); 3) the percentage of the target being viewed (TDs could want to view at least 80% or 100% of the target object); and/or 4) the amount of space that the target occupies in the shot (the more space occupied by the target the smaller the amount of space with other uninteresting objects). Once a query is defined, it can be submitted and/or stored to be loaded later.

4   Conclusions and Future Work

In summary, MultiCAMBA is a context– and location–aware system that gives a step forward in the development of software that allows to increase the efficiency in the broadcasting task by: 1) reducing the human effort required for live production (thanks to the friendly user interface provided) and 2) giving the opportunity to obtain richer content productions (due to the advanced features supported by the query processor).

As future work, we plan to consider more scenarios where the system can be helpful. For example, it can be used for other sport events such as cycling, where a distributed approach is needed due to the specific environment (long distances between objects, mountain landscape, etc.). Moreover, the features of Multi-CAMBA could be also exploited in other non-sport scenarios (e.g., emergency management) involving moving objects and videocameras.

References

1. Aliaga, D.G., Xu, Y., Popescu, V.: Lag camera: A moving multi-camera array for scene-acquisition. Journal of Virtual Reality and Broadcasting 3(10) (December 2006)
2. Du, W., Hayet, J.-B., Piater, J., Verly, J.: Collaborative multi-camera tracking of athletes in team sports. In: Workshop on Computer Vision Based Analysis in Sport Environments, CVBASE 2006 (May 2006)

3. Ilarri, S., Mena, E., Illarramendi, A.: Location-dependent query processing: Where we are and where we are heading. ACM Computing Surveys 42(3), 12:1–12:73 (2010) ISSN 0360-0300
4. Ilarri, S., Mena, E., Illarramendi, A., Yus, R., Laka, M., Marcos, G.: A Friendly Location-Aware System to Facilitate the Work of Technical Directors When Broadcasting Sport Events. Mobile Information Systems 8(1), 17–43 (2012) ISSN 1574-017X
5. Michaelsen, E., Jaeger, K.: A Google-Earth based test bed for structural image-based UAV navigation. In: 12th International Conference on Information Fusion (FUSION 2009), pp. 340–346 (July 2009)
6. Yus, R., Mena, E., Bernad, J., Ilarri, S., Illarramendi, A.: Location-Aware System Based on a Dynamic 3D Model to Help in Live Broadcasting of Sport Events. In: 19th ACM International Conference on Multimedia (ACMMM 2011), Scottsdale, Arizona (USA), pp. 1005–1008. ACM Press (November 2011) ISBN 978-1-4503-0616-4

DEMO
Classroom7: Please, Make Sure Your Phones Are Switched On!

Moustafa Alzantot, Muhammad Hataba, and Moustafa Youssef

Egypt-Japan University of Science and Technology (E-JUST),
Alexandria, Egypt
{moustafa.alzantot,mohamed.hataba,moustafa.youssef}@ejust.edu.eg

Abstract. Nowadays, mobile phones are becoming ubiquitous computing devices. They are widely used by people with different ages and in virtually all places on Earth, even in developing countries. However, there are still some concerns about performing heavy computations on mobile devices due to their limited resources. The emerging growth of cloud computing and wireless communication offers a chance for creating a new generation of mobile applications that benefit from both mobile phones and cloud computing. In this demo, we present Classroom7 as an example of cloud-empowered feature-rich mobile applications that can be used to ameliorate the education process. Classroom7 attempts to increase the interaction between students and their teacher and to allow them to create and access educational contents in a new attractive way. We utilize the sensors, e.g. cameras and microphones embedded in the phone, as a method for data input, where the required heavy computations, e.g. optical character recognition, speech-to-text and other processing algorithms, are offloaded to the cloud. Moreover, we show how mobile phones can help a teacher to easily track and assess the skills of each individual student with minimal effort.

We foresee that instead of considering mobile phones a source of distraction in classrooms, it will be considered an important tool in the education process in the near future. Teachers would ask their students to make sure that their mobile phones are switched on during a lecture.

1   Introduction

Classrooms are typically crowded with a large number of students. This hinders the interaction between students and their teacher and presents a challenge for the teacher to assess and evaluate the skills of each individual student adequately. Also, due to financial limitations, it may not be possible to provide modern digital interactive learning tools like smart boards, interactive response systems, or even provide a computer for each student. Therefore, many schools, especially in developing countries, depend only on classic white-boards and traditional textbooks to provide the learning materials to students. However, those tools are becoming less effective for teaching and learning, as they do not offer a

A. Puiatti et al. (Eds.): MobiQuitous 2011, LNICST 104, pp. 243–247, 2012.

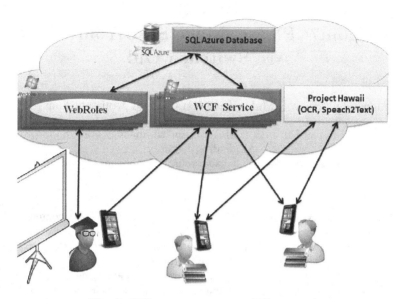

Fig. 1. Different components of Classroom7

method for interaction between students and their teacher and also they can only provide static contents which falls a step behind in the current rich-media revolution era.

With mobile phones becoming truly ubiquitous computing devices, they offer an opportunity for providing an affordable and highly effective learning system. However, major limitations of mobile phones are their processing speed, small storage, and limited battery power. Hence, there is a great benefit from offloading the storage and computationally intensive parts of the system to the cloud. This way the amount of processing required to run on the phone Cpu can be dramatically reduced to increase the battery lifetime.

In this demo, we introduce Classroom7 as an example of cloud-empowered mobile applications that makes use of both mobile phones and cloud computing to provide a number of functionalities aiming for enhancing the education process in classrooms.

Classroom7 can be used from anywhere by students to access the learning contents and so it satisfies the mobility needs of students who spend much of their time traveling [3]. Also, Classroom7 does not require any dedicated infrastructure to be installed in classrooms for its operation. Moreover, it can be used with a minimal administration effort. Figure 1 gives an overview of the different components of Classroom7.

With Classroom7, we envision that rather than asking students to switch their phones off at the beginning of a lecture, the teacher might start a lecture with saying:" Please make sure your phones are switched on!".

Fig. 2. Using Classroom7 to review the virtually stuck notes

2   Goals

In this demo, we present the different functionalities offered by Classroom7 as an example of a cloud empowered mobile application. The offered functionalities include: virtual sticky notes, mobile interactive book, and students lounge. Those functionalities are covered in details in sections 2.1, 2.2, and 2.3 respectively. The operation of those functions depend on a number of cloud-hosted services like OCR, Speech-to-Text, and cloud storage.

2.1   Virtual Sticky Notes

Typically students like to take notes or transcribe a lecture. Usually, those notes are written in the margins of the textbook or in a notebook. Classroom7 allows students to take notes or perform lectures transcription in an annotative way using their mobile phones. A student may type a note on his/her mobile or alternatively record a section of the lecture using the microphone of his/her mobile. The recorded part will be converted into text using the Microsoft Project Hawaii Speech-to-Text service running on the cloud [1]. The student will also have a chance to edit the converted text. The notes generated either by typing or recording will be virtually stuck to a page in the text book using the camera of the mobile phone. The student can specify which page he wants the note to be stuck onto by taking a camera shot of that page. An algorithm for identifying the page based on OCR is run on the cloud. Both the note and a page identifier are saved on the cloud.Reviewing previously taken notes can be easily done just by taking a camera shot for the same page. The page identification algorithm will identify the page and all previously stuck notes associated with this page will be displayed on the students mobile. The action of using Classroom7 to review notes virtually stuck to page in the textbook is shown in Figure 2. The student will also be able to share his/her notes with other colleagues.

2.2   Mobile Interactive Book

The "Mobile Interactive Book" feature offered by Classroom7 is a method for linking the static contents in the traditional textbooks to their corresponding

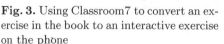

Fig. 3. Using Classroom7 to convert an exercise in the book to an interactive exercise on the phone

Fig. 4. Using Classroom7 to convert a static figure in the textbook to a video on the phone

more interactive versions. Classic textbooks are limited to contain only static contents (e.g. text, figures, and images). Those type of contents do not interact with a student actions (for example: the user cannot submit his/her answer to an exercise by pressing one of the answer choices in his/her textbook). Also the contents offered in textbooks are limited in terms of the information they can present compared to currently available rich contents media (like videos and interactive maps).

Classroom7 allows a student to view an interactive version related to the static content he/she might find in his/her textbook. The student can ask for the interactive content corresponding to certain annotated in the textbook by using the camera of his mobile to take a shot of this part. The image taken by the camera will be then submitted to our cloud service, where a content identification algorithm using the OCR service is run. Based on the identified content, a more interactive version will be displayed on the mobile phone of the student. The current version of Classroom7 prototype supports three types of interactive contents: exercises, videos, and maps.

Interactive Exercises. If a student takes a camera shot of a page in his/her textbook containing an exercise, he/she will be provided with an electronic version of the same exercise on his/her mobile phone. The questions and answer choices will be rendered in a randomly shuffled order for each student. The student can submit his/her answers to the exercise trough his/her phone. The submitted answers will be saved in the cloud, and automatically graded. Both the teacher and the student are able to have an instantaneous access to the score report (Figure 3).

Interactive Maps. If a student takes a camera shot of a map drawn in his textbook, he/she will be able to view an interactive map of the same region on his/her mobile phone. This map can be zoomed in/out, and may contain landmarks and annotations.

Educational Videos. If a student takes a camera shot of a static figure drawn in his textbook, he/she will be able to view an educational video corresponding to that figure. The action of using Classroom7 to convert a static figure in the textbook to a video on the user's mobile is shown in Figure 4.

2.3   Students' Lounge

Classroom7 offers the "Students' Lounge" feature which is a virtual place where students and their teachers can be engaged into discussions. This service aims at encouraging students to be more collaborative and socially active with each other. Students can share announcements and discussions with each other and also with their teacher.

More demonstration scenarios and videos can be found on our Classroom7 web site [2].

3   Implementation

The current prototype of Classroom7 is implemented using C# and Microsoft SilverLight for Windows Phone 7 devices and depends on Microsoft Windows Azure and SQLAzure as the cloud backend for computation and storage respectively. We employed a number of cloud hosted services like Optical Character Recognition (OCR), Speech-to-Text and Storage on the cloud offered as a part of Microsoft Research Project Hawaii [1]. The demo uses the following equipment:

– HTC HD7 mobile phones.
– Lenovo ThinkPad T41 laptop used to access the management portal.

4   Conclusion

The Classroom7 demo shows how mobile applications can be empowered by using cloud services. As an example, we show how the modern mobile phones can be leveraged in a number of attractive and innovative scenarios to increase the interaction between students and their teacher and how they can be used to augment the classic textbooks by allowing students to stick virtual notes and extract more interactive relevant learning materials. We believe that such an application can be utilized in enhancing the education process.

Acknowledgment. This project was supported in a part by a grant from Microsoft Research Project Hawaii.

References

1. Microsoft Research Project Hawaii,
   http://research.microsoft.com/en-us/um/redmond/projects/hawaii
2. Classroom7 Web Site, http://classroom7.co.cc
3. Masters, K.: Low-key m-learning: a realistic introduction of m-learning to developing countries. In: Sixth Conference on Communications in the 21st Century: Seeing, Understanding, Learning in the Mobile Age, Budapest (2005)

ZigBee-Assisted WiFi Transmission for Multi-interface Mobile Devices

Hua Qin, Yanfei Wang, and Wensheng Zhang

Iowa State University, USA

Abstract. It has been common for a mobile device to have WiFi and Bluetooth interfaces. As the ZigBee technology becomes more mature, it will not be surprising to see the ZigBee interface commonly embedded in mobile devices together with WiFi and other interfaces in the near future. To leverage the ZigBee interface for improving the communication performance of a mobile device, we propose a ZigBee-assisted WiFi transmission system where the ZigBee is used to coordinate the communication activities of WiFi to reduce contention and collision. A prototype of the proposed system and a detailed simulator of it have been implemented; extensive experiments and simulations have been conducted. The results show that, the proposed system can achieve significantly higher throughput and energy efficiency than the IEEE 802.11 protocol.

Keywords: ZigBee, WiFi, IEEE 802.11, throughput.

1 Introduction

Recently, mobile devices are increasingly equipped with multiple network interfaces [1–3]. It has been common for a mobile device, such as smart phone, PDA and laptop, to have both WiFi and Bluetooth interfaces. As the ZigBee technology becomes more and more mature, embedded ZigBee interfaces have emerged and the size is becoming smaller and smaller [4,5]. It will not be surprising to see the ZigBee interface commonly embedded in mobile devices together with WiFi and Bluetooth interfaces in the near future. With ZigBee interfaces, mobile devices can communicate with various electrical and electronic appliances to realize the smart home entertainment and control, home awareness, mobile services, commercial building and smart industrial plants [6].

The WiFi interface perhaps is the most common interface found in mobile devices for data transfer as it provides good combination of throughout, range and power efficiency. However, the WiFi interface may have to consume a large amount of bandwidth and energy for contention and combating collision, especially when mobile devices located in a small area (e.g., conference room, library, stadium, etc.) all have heavy traffic to transmit. To reduce contention, many protocols have been proposed. However, most of them (e.g., Overlay MAC [7], TDM MAC [8], token-passing MAC [9], etc.) require to either modify the underlying MAC protocol or introduce extra control overhead.

A. Puiatti et al. (Eds.): MobiQuitous 2011, LNICST 104, pp. 248–259, 2012.

The co-existence of the ZigBee and the WiFi interfaces in the same mobile device inspires us to develop new techniques to address the above issue. The key idea is that nearby mobile devices use their ZigBee interfaces to coordinate their communication activities to reduce contention and collision. The rationales behind the idea are as follows. The ZigBee interface and the WiFi interface can use different channels, and hence the coordination using ZigBee interfaces will not consume the WiFi bandwidth. As the WiFi transmission has higher rate and energy consumption than ZigBee transmission, the utilization of WiFi for large-size data transmission and ZigBee for small-size control message transmission presents an ideal, efficient resource allocation pattern. Such collaboration is possible because ZigBee may not be used frequently in the places, such as conference room, library and stadium, where WiFi traffic could be very heavy.

In this paper, we propose a simple yet effective ZigBee-assisted WiFi transmission system for the *high traffic density* scenario. In this system, mobile devices leverage ZigBee communication to form clusters where each cluster has a cluster head and multiple cluster members that can directly communicate with the head via the ZigBee interface. According to the communication demands of individual mobile devices, members in the same cluster collaboratively run a TDMA-like protocol with the ideal goal that, at any moment only one of them attempts to use the WiFi channel so as to eliminate or greatly reduce the contention within a cluster and thus mitigate the contention in the whole network.

The rest of the paper is organized as follows. Section 2 presents the system model. Section 3 elaborates our proposed design. The results of comprehensive simulation and prototype implementation are reported in Section 4 and 5, respectively. Section 6 summarizes related work, and finally Section 7 concludes the paper.

2   System Model

To run our proposed system, each network node (e.g., laptop) has two wireless interfaces: ZigBee (IEEE 802.15.4) and WiFi (IEEE 802.11). We call such nodes **Z-WiFi** nodes. The WiFi interface is for data transmission while the ZigBee interface is for coordinating node transmission activities. Due to current popularity of the IEEE 802.11 protocol, Z-WiFi nodes may co-exist with the nodes that do not have or use ZigBee but use the Standard IEEE 802.11 protocol. We call such nodes **S-WiFi** nodes.

Our design targets mainly at the scenarios where data traffic is heavy due to high node density and/or high packet transmission rate per node. The design objectives are as follows.

- *High Throughput*: By using the information gathered by ZigBee interfaces to carefully schedule the data transmission of WiFi interfaces, our design should reduce the contention among nodes and thereby increase the throughput.
- *Energy Efficiency*: Through reducing the contention experienced by the WiFi interfaces, our design should also decrease the power consumption of nodes.

- *Compatibility*: On one hand, our system should not demand changes in the existing WiFi and ZigBee standards. On the other hand, Z-WiFi and S-WiFi nodes should not harm each other, but should be in the win-win status when co-exist.
- *Fairness*: Our design should organize data transmission of WiFi interfaces in a way that the shared channel is shared relatively fairly among all nodes.

3   Proposed Design

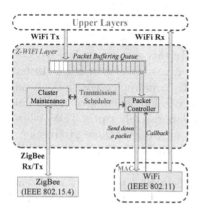

Fig. 1. System architecture

Fig. 1 depicts the architecture of our proposed Z-WiFi system, which is built atop WiFi and ZigBee. Thus, it is transparent to and independent of these standards. The *cluster maintenance* component works through communication over the ZigBee interface. A *packet buffering queue* is used to temporarily buffer packets from the upper layer. Through monitoring the status of the queue, packet arrival rate can be inferred, based on which the *transmission scheduler* dynamically computes the TDMA-like schedule for WiFi transmission within a cluster. The schedule is executed by the *packet controller* component which controls the timing and speed for passing packets in the *packet buffering queue* down to the underlying IEEE 802.11 MAC layer.

In the section, we present the deign details of our proposed Z-WiFi network. Briefly, we first present the cluster formation scheme. Then, the intra-cluster and the inter-cluster coordination are elaborated, respectively. After that, heuristics is designed to deal with practical issues.

3.1   Cluster Formation

To facilitate the coordination of WiFi transmission for reduced contention, we propose to organize nodes that have potential need for contention into a single cluster through ZigBee communication. Based on existing cluster formation protocols [13], we propose a cluster formation scheme efficient for the scheduling of WiFi transmission.

Initially, each node marks itself as a free node (denoted as **FN**). To obtain information about neighboring nodes, each node periodically broadcasts a *beacon message*, defined as $\langle Node\_id, CH\_id, i, r_i \rangle$, via its ZigBee interface. Here, $Node\_id$ is the network-wise unique id of the sender, CH_id is the node id of its cluster head (denoted as **CH**) if the sender has joined a cluster (otherwise it is empty), and i is a cluster-wide unique *index* of the sender, assigned by the corresponding CH, when it joins the cluster. Besides, r_i is its current packet arrival rate (in the unit of *bits/second*) of the node with index i, estimated through monitoring the status of its packet buffering queue. Note that, if the sender is a cluster member (denoted as **CM**) or a FN, r_i is the packet arrival rate of its own; if it is a CH, r_i is the sum of packet rates of all nodes in its cluster. The usage of r_i and i is to be detailed later.

Based on beacon exchange, each node can maintain a neighbor information list to record the most recent information about its neighbors. If a FN has heard a beacon from one or multiple CHs, it chooses the one whose cluster has the *smallest* packet arrival rate to join. Otherwise, if a FN does not find any CH after a certain rounds of beacon exchange, it announces itself as a CH candidate by broadcasting a *formation* packet piggybacking the number of FNs in its neighborhood. When a node that is not a CH candidate first receives the formation packet, it waits for a certain period of time to overhear other possible formation packets; when the backoff expires, the candidate CH having the largest number of FNs is chosen as its CH and a *registration* packet is sent back to the candidate to join. Upon receiving a registration packet, the candidate node becomes a new CH. In response to each registration from a new CM, the CH sends back an *index* packet, in which a cluster-wide unique index i (i is a positive integer) is assigned to the CM. Note that, the index of a CH is 0.

3.2   Intra-cluster Coordination for WiFi Transmission

Based on the cluster structure, WiFi transmissions of nodes within the same cluster between CH and CMs for reduced contention are coordinated. Each CM is time-synchronized with its CH.

Besides, each node measures the packet arrival rate (i.e., r_i) at its packet buffering queue, rather than at application layer. When packet buffering queue is full, any incoming packet from upper layer is dropped, which imposes a limit on the value of r_i. Hence, r_i cannot be infinitely large.

With the synchronized time reference, time is divided into frames and each frame is further sliced into slots of equal length. The length of a slot, denoted as τ_w, is the empirical time needed to send a packet through WiFi interface. The CH assigns the slots in each frame to the nodes in its cluster, according to their packet arrival rates. In the following, we show how the CH computes the WiFi transmission schedule (i.e., the slots to transmit), how it is represented and how the CH updates the schedule to its CMs by using the ZigBee interfaces.

A WiFi transmission schedule is represented and sent as a sequence of binary bits, which can be contained in the payload of a single ZigBee packet. A sequence consists of many sub-sequences of 0(s) separated by a 1. For example, sequence

$$00000110000100010010001000100 \cdots 0$$

represents that a WiFi transmission schedule, where each frame has 17 slots, nodes with indices 0, 1, 2, 3, 4 and 5 are assigned with 5, 0, 4, 3, 2 and 3 slots, respectively. Node 0 (i.e., the CH) can perform WiFi transmission during the first 5 slots of each frame, node 1 may not exist or has no packet to send, node

2 can perform WiFi transmission during the 6th to the 9th slot of each frame, and so on and so forth. WiFi transmission schedule periodically is updated and broadcasted by the CH via its ZigBee interface as the packet arrival rate may change in each node.

Particularly, in our experiments, we set the payload size to 28 bytes, which is the default payload size used by TinyOS. Once the payload size is determined, the maximum number of slots in a frame is also determined. We denote the maximum number of slots in a frame as f_w^{max}. Also, we use r_i to denote the packet rate of node with index i $(i = 0, \cdots, N-1)$ in the cluster, recalling that each node is assigned a unique index. Let δ $(0 < \delta \leq 1)$ be a predetermined system parameter. The number of slots allocated to each node i (denoted as n_i) and the actual number of slots composing a frame (denoted as f_w) is computed as follows:

$$n_i = \left\lfloor \min\left\{\delta \cdot \frac{r_i}{B \cdot \tau_w}, f_w^{max} \cdot \frac{r_i}{\sum_{j=0}^{N-1} r_j}\right\}\right\rfloor > 0, \tag{1}$$

$$f_w = \sum_{i=0}^{N-1} n_i \leq f_w^{max}, \tag{2}$$

where B is the WiFi bandwidth. Thus, $r_i/B\tau_w$ represents the expected number of packets sent by node i. The rationale behind the slot computation is of three folds:

- For the sake of fairness, the number of slots allocated to a node is proportional to the packet arrival rate of the node while the total number of slots composing a frame should not exceed f_w^{max}.
- The ratio between the number of slots and the packet arrival rate is determined by system parameter δ. The larger is δ, the longer is a frame and the larger number of consecutive slots a node can use for WiFi transmission, and vice versa. Through our experiments, increasing δ leads to decrease in energy consumption and increase in packet delay, and vice versa. To balance energy consumption, δ is set to 0.2.
- Based on Eq. (1), the *clustering condition* can be defined as follows: *a FN node can join or form a cluster only if for any node i (including itself) in the resulted cluster $n_i > 0$ can be satisfied*. On one hand, a node with very few packets to send do not need to join or form a cluster and it can just use the IEEE 802.11 protocol as a FN. On the other hand, a node with a high packet rate should not be allowed to join a cluster if its joining makes any existing node in the cluster have *zero* slot to transmit. Thus, after a certain period of time, it will attempt to form a new cluster.

Ideally, each node transmits data through its WiFi interface only during the slots assigned to it, and one packet uses one slot time (i.e., τ_w) to be transmitted. It follows that n_i packets should be sent down to the underlying 802.11 MAC layer in each frame. However, in practice, this is hardly true.

To make full use of each slot, we propose to use the *callback* (i.e., notification of the completion of a packet transmission) from the underlying MAC layer to control the timing for passing packets downwards, as illustrated in Fig. 1. Specifically, when the scheduled transmission time (i.e.,$n_i\tau_w$) begins, the packet buffering queue delivers a packet to the MAC layer. As long as the scheduled time does not run out and there is an available packet for transmission, a packet will be pushed down to the MAC layer once the callback of previous packet is received.

3.3   Inter-cluster Dynamics for Dealing with Mobility

Due to mobility, a CM may move out the range of its CH and join another cluster; a FN may discover a CH and join the cluster headed by that CH; a CH may move into the range of another CH and their clusters may be merged to reduce the number of co-existing clusters and hence inter-cluster contention.

Cluster Switching. When a CM with index i finds it has moved out of the ZigBee communication range of its CH, i.e., failing to receive beacon from its CH for a certain time, it attempts to discover nearby CHs by overhearing beacons. If it finds some CHs, it joins the cluster that has the lowest overall packet arrival rate. If no CH is found in vicinity, it becomes a FN, which can either join another cluster, or form its own cluster. Note that, if a CH fails or is turned off, its CMs will not be able to receive beacon messages from it, in which case they will react as if they have moved out of the communication range of the CH and perform cluster switching as depicted above.

Cluster Joining. When a CM or CH becomes a FN, it first tries to join other cluster by turning on its ZigBee and listening for a certain time. If it finds some CHs in the vicinity, a registration packet is sent. Upon receiving the registration packet, the CH acknowledges that node by replying an *index packet* containing a unique index (typically the *smallest unused* index in the cluster) assigned to that node, if the clustering condition (See Eq. (1)) can be satisfied. Once the index packet is successfully received by the FN, it becomes a CM of that cluster. If no CH is found, it starts the cluster formation process as described in Section 3.1, if the clustering condition can be satisfied.

Cluster Merging. To dynamically minimize the cluster density and hence reduce inter-cluster contention, cluster merging is proposed as follows. As CHs are always awake, they may overhear WiFi transmission schedule packets from nearby clusters. When a CH (CH1) overhears a schedule packet from another CH (CH2), it checks if it can cover more than half of CMs of CH2. If so, merging process will be conducted through the negotiation between these two CHs. As a results, the nodes that are in the cluster of CH2 and covered by CH1 are merged into the cluster of CH1, while the rest of CMs become FNs, which with either join other clusters or form a new cluster later.

3.4   Practical Issues

Turning on/off ZigBee Our system is designed mainly to improve WiFi performance in high-contention scenarios, and the IEEE 802.11 protocol can already achieve the optimal throughput when the contention is low. To avoid unnecessary control overhead, we propose a simple heuristic parameter γ for turning off ZigBee interfaces of Z-WiFi nodes when the contention is low and turning on them when the contention is high. The nodes without using ZigBee interface run the IEEE 802.11 protocol.

Specifically, each node records transmission time (i.e., duration from the arrival of a packet to the reception of corresponding ACK) of the most recent outgoing packets. Let T_{pkt} be average transmission time, then

- ZigBee is turned off, if $T_{pkt} < 0.5 \times \gamma\tau_w$;
- ZigBee is turned on, if $T_{pkt} > 1.5 \times \gamma\tau_w$.

$\gamma\tau_w$ represents the expected packet delivery delay when system throughput is saturated. The selection of γ is to be studied in Section 4.1.

Co-existence of Z-WiFi and S-WiFi. In practice, Z-WiFi and S-WiFi nodes may co-exist in a small area. Since they run different protocols for data transmission, the resulting performance is different. Generally, S-WiFi nodes can achieve better performance than Z-WiFi nodes, because S-WiFi nodes can contend for channel occupation all the time while Z-WiFi nodes are only allowed to access the channel within their scheduled time slots. To address this practical issue, we propose to dynamically tune the contention window of Z-WiFi nodes so as to achieve a win-win status, in which both types of node can achieve throughput improvement and good fairness. Due to space limit, the detailed design is presented in [20].

4   Simulation

To evaluate our proposed system in a large-scale network, we simulate the system with ns2 simulator. In the simulation, the following major metrics are studied:

- *Network throughput* (Mb/s) is the total amount of data successfully transmitted (i.e., ACKed at sender side) in the network. To measure the throughput, each node runs an application which keeps sending UDP packets and by default totally all these nodes generate the data input with an average rate of 20.4Mb/s (i.e., 22 packets/s at each node on average). All the packets have maximum payload size.

- *Energy consumption* (J/Mb) is computed as the total amount of energy consumed by all network interfaces of all nodes divided by the number of Mbs of data that has been successfully transmitted. The energy consumed by the WiFi interface is measured according to the specified power consumption rate of SX-SDWAG 802.11g wireless module [16] (i.e., 1047mW for transmission, 513mW for reception and 420mW for being idle) and the power consumed by the ZigBee interface is measured according to the specified power consumption of CC2420 RF transceiver [17] (i.e., 52.2mW for transmission, 56.4mW for reception, 1.28mW for being idle, 0.06μW for sleeping and 0.06mW for transition).

- *Throughput fairness* is measured with respect to the fairness index (FI) [18], which is defined as $FI_{tp} = \frac{\mu(\chi)}{\mu(\chi)+\sigma(\chi)}$, where $\mu(\chi)$ and $\sigma(\chi)$ are the mean and the standard deviation of χ at all network nodes. χ is the ratio of throughput to input. Obvious, FI_{tp} is between 0 and 1. The more closer FI_{tp} approaches 1, the better is the fairness.

Unless otherwise specified, our simulation use the settings shown in the table below. Also, we adopt the random waypoint mobility model, where the pause time is fixed to 20s and the maximum speed is 2m/s. Besides collision-caused drops, each node intentionally drops 2% incoming packets on ZigBee communication to simulate the packet loss due to interference from WiFi. The default IEEE 802.11g protocol is used.

Number of nodes	50	Network scale	100m × 100m
Range of WiFi (R_w)	120m	Range of ZigBee (R_z)	60m
Simulation time	1 hour	WiFi slot length (τ_w)	0.001s
ZigBee on/off parameter (γ)	15	Packet buffer size	50 packets

4.1 Comparing with S-WiFi System and Studying Parameter γ

To find the best time to turn on ZigBee so as to maximize the performance, we compare Z-WiFi system, configured with four different values of γ (i.e., 1, 5, 15 and 25), with S-WiFi system.

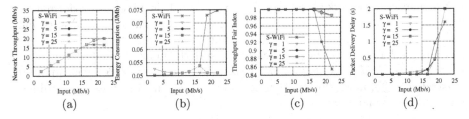

Fig. 2. Choosing parameter γ by comparing with S-WiFi

From Fig. 2a, we can see that when network input is below 17Mb/s, S-WiFi system can almost deliver all incoming packets. When input is beyond 17Mb/s, S-WiFi nodes reach the maximum throughput. At this time, ZigBee interface of Z-WiFi nodes should be turned on to assist WiFi transmission. As shown in Fig. 2a and 2c, $\gamma = 5, 15$ or 25 can precisely render ZigBee turned on at the right time. This is because, due to accumulated waiting delay in the packet buffer queue, packet transmission delay rises up drastically (from less than one millisecond to more than hundreds of milliseconds) once S-WiFi system gets saturated. Thus, large values of γ (e.g., $\gamma > 5$) can work appropriately. Particularly, when ZigBee interface is turned on (i.e., input exceeds 17Mb/s), energy consumption drops rapidly, as shown in Fig. 2b, which shows that our proposed system can save energy.

When $\gamma = 1$, ZigBee interface is turned on when network input (i.e., contention) is low. At this time, our protocol cannot help, as the S-WiFi system has already achieve the optimal throughput. Hence, the overhead introduced for ZigBee communication makes Z-WiFi systems consume more energy.

In addition, we also measure average packet delivery delay from application layer, as illustrated in Fig. 2d. From the results, setting γ to 15 or 25 can guarantee that Z-WiFi system can achieve no longer packet delivery delay than S-WiFi system when input is below 21Mb/s. When input is above 21Mb/s, our system also becomes saturated and thereby packet delivery delay increases. Note that the packet delivery delay of Z-WiFi system is longer than that of S-WiFi system only when the throughput of Z-WiFi is higher than S-WiFi.

To summarize from the above results, *our proposed system can improve the network throughput by 18%, reduce the energy consumption by 32% and provide much better fairness, when the network traffic density is high.*

4.2 Performance with Different Network Scale

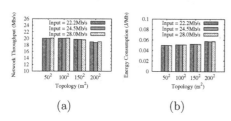

(a)   (b)

Fig. 3. Impact of network scale on performance

Fig. 3 shows how our system works with different network scale. Generally, the throughput slightly decreases as the scale of the network becomes larger, due to the number of clusters increasing. When the number of clusters within WiFi transmission range increases, contention gets more severe, which degrades the performance. However, the number of clusters will not become too large, since cluster merging mechanism is applied, which can ensure the number of interfering clusters close to $\lceil R_w^2/R_z^2 \rceil$ (e.g. 4 under our simulation). For energy consumption illustrated in 3b, more clusters consume more energy in transmission coordination and cluster maintenance.

4.3 Impact of ZigBee Packet Loss on Performance

Apart from random collision-caused packet loss, we also study the packet loss due to other environmental phenomena (e.g., interference, obstacle, multipath, etc.). Thus, we conduct a simulation by varying packet loss ratio from 2% to 20%. As shown in Fig. 4, our performance degrades slightly as loss ratio gets larger. For throughput, it is because of the insufficient utilization of channel caused by increasing delay or error in updating WiFi transmission schedule. The energy consumption increases mainly because of the increased energy consumption for contention caused by schedule inconsistencies, resulted from packet loss.

5   Implementation

5.1   Prototyping

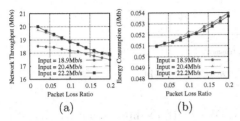

Fig. 4. Impact of ZigBee packet loss on performance

As a proof of concept, we implement a prototype of our proposed system. We build a testbed with 10 DELL D-Series laptops (called *nodes* hereafter), each running the Ubuntu Linux 8.10 (kernel 2.6.27-17-generic). Each node is also equipped with a D-Link WNA-2330 Wireless G Notebook Adapter (108Mbps, 802.11g, Atheros chipset, PCMCIA) and a Crossbow telosB mote (i.e., ZigBee interface). Note that *the wireless adapter is built with the state-of-the-art technology, which can deliver higher throughput than standard 802.11g devices.* The scheduling of WiFi transmission is implemented upon MadWiFi [19], an open-source driver for Atheros chipset-based 802.11 Wireless LAN devices. The prototyped ZigBee communication is implemented upon TinyOS 2.1.1 platform, where 10 nodes form a cluster. The WiFi interfaces of all nodes run in the ad hoc model and are tuned to Channel 3, and the ZigBee interfaces are tuned to Channel 26; thus, the interference between them is small. Besides, the implementation of transmission scheduling is based on *software timer* provided by Linux kernel, which can allow a minimum granularity of $1\mu s$.

Experiments have been conducted on the prototyped system to evaluate the feasibility and the performance of our designed system. For comparison, two sets of experiments are conducted by running the IEEE 802.11 protocol and our proposed system, respectively. Through the experiments, we measure the maximum network throughput as the number of nodes increases from 2 to 10. To measure the maximum throughput, each node generates UDP traffic of 34.8 Mb/s. Each packet has a payload of 1450 bytes, which makes the overall packet to exactly fit into a single MAC-layer frame. The duration of each experiment run is 5 minutes. The experiment is conducted three times. Besides, $n_i = 10$ and $\tau_w = 0.001$s.

5.2   Experiment Results

The experiment results are shown in Fig. 5. In general, compared with the IEEE 802.11 protocol, our proposed system can improve the network throughput significantly. Particularly, when the number of involved nodes reaches 10, the improvement of throughput can be as high as 49.1%. As expected, our proposed system outperforms the IEEE 802.11 protocol when the number of transmitters is large (e.g., more than 4 nodes in our experiment). As that number keeps increasing, the difference becomes more significant because the IEEE 802.11 protocol suffers from severe contention and the throughput drops fast.

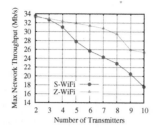

Fig. 5. Maximum Network Throughput

Moreover, the standard deviation (STDV) of throughput among different nodes is also measured, as shown in the table below. From the results, we can see that using our proposed system introduces much lower throughput STDV, which indicates better throughput fairness.

# of transmitters	Throughput STDV of S-WiFi	Throughput STDV of Z-WiFi
4	1.1016	0.1780
6	0.8016	0.1281
8	0.7698	0.1775

Through the experiments, our proposed system has been shown to be able to improve throughput significantly and provide fair sharing of bandwidth.

6   Related Work

Recently, some research has conducted to investigate co-located interfaces for improving the performance of IEEE 802.11 network. One of the first work is Blue-Fi [1], which brings forth the idea of using other co-located interface to assist WiFi transmission. It uses the co-located Bluetooth to predict the availability of the WiFi connectivity by using user's trend of repeatedly encountering the same set of bluetooth devices and cell-towers. Different from Blue-Fi, our system uses ZigBee interface, which has a much longer communication range. Thus, it can provide a better communication capability under the mobile environment. Our proposed system is motivated by this feature. Because of using different hardware and methodologies, the accomplishment of Blue-Fi and Z-WiFi are also different. Besides, ZiFi [2] utilizes ZigBee radios to identify the existence of WiFi networks through WiFi beacons, while WiZi-Cloud protocols [3] have been proposed to use WiFi-ZigBee radios on mobile phones and Access Points to achieve ubiquitous connectivity, high energy efficiency, real time intra-device/inter-AP handover. Unlike those work, our work focuses on improving the performance WiFi transmission under the DCF through reducing contention. In general, the previous work targets on saving energy, but our work aims to improve the throughput, power efficiency and fairness.

7   Conclusion

In this paper, we have proposed a simple yet effective system for ZigBee-assisted WiFi transmission. Mobile devices form clusters. Coordinated through ZigBee interfaces, members in each cluster take turns to transmit, resulting in reduced contention and collision. Results of experiment and simulation have verified our design by showing that, the throughput, power consumption and fairness can be improved.

Acknowledgments. This work is supported partly by the NSF under Grants CNS-0834593 and CNS-0831874, and by the ONR under Grant N00014-09-1-0748.

References

1. Ananthanarayanan, G., Stoica, I.: Blue-Fi: Enhancing Wi-Fi performance using Bluetooth signals. In: MobiSys (2009)
2. Zhou, R., Xiong, Y., Xing, G., Sun, L., Ma, J.: ZiFi: Wireless LAN Discovery via ZigBee Interference Signatures. In: MobiCom (2010)
3. Jin, T., Noubir, G., Sheng, B.: WiZi-Cloud: Application-transparent Dual ZigBee-WiFi Radios for Low Power Internet Access. In: InfoCom (2011)
4. One RF Technology, Short Range RF, http://www.one-rf.com
5. LS Research, LLC., ZigBee ProFLEX Module, http://www.lsr.com
6. Wikimedia, ZigBee, http://www.wikipedia.org/wiki/Zigbee
7. Rao, A., Stoica, I.: An overlay MAC layer for 802.11 networks. In: MobiSys (2005)
8. Koutsonikolas, D., Salonidis, T., et al.: TDM MAC Protocol Design and Implementation for Wireless Mesh Networks. In: CoNEXT (2008)
9. Liu, I., Takawira, F., Xu, H.: A Hybrid Token-CDMA MAC Protocol for Wireless Ad Hoc Networks. In: TMC (2008)
10. Kim, S.M., Chong, J., Jung, C., et al.: Experiments on Interference and Coexistence between Zigbee and WLAN Devices Operating in the 2.4GHz ISM band. In: NGPC (2005)
11. Shuaib, K., Boulmalf, M., Sallabi, F., Lakas, A.: Co-existence of Zigbee and WLAN: A performance study. In: Proc. IEEE/IFIP Int. Conf. Wireless & Optical Communications Networks (2006)
12. Wikimedia, IEEE 802.11, http://en.wikipedia.org/wiki/802.11
13. Wan, J., Yuan, D., Xu, X.: A review of cluster formation mechanism for clustering routing protocols. In: ICCT (2008)
14. Wu, H., Peng, Y., Long, K., Cheng, S., Ma, J.: Performance of Reliable Transport Protocol over IEEE 802.11 Wireless LAN: Analysis And Enhancement. In: InfoCom (2002)
15. Ni, Q., Li, T., Turletti, T., Xiao, Y.: Saturation throughput analysis of error-prone 802.11 wireless. In: JWCMC (2005)
16. Silex Wireless Modules, http://www.silexamerica.com
17. CC2420 RF transceiver, http://www.chipcon.com
18. Qiao, D., Shin, K.G.: Achieving Efficient Channel Utilization and Weighted Fairness for Data Communications in IEEE 802.11 WLAN under the DCF. In: IWQoS (2002)
19. MadWifi, http://madwifi-project.org
20. Qin, H., Wang, Y., Zhang, W.: ZigBee-Assisted WiFi Transmission for Multi-Interface Mobile Devices. Technical Report (2011), http://www.cs.iastate.edu/~qinhua/papers/zwifi.pdf

A Dynamic and Distributed Addressing and Routing Protocol for Wireless Sensor Networks

Tomás Sánchez López[1] and Gonzalo Huerta-Canepa[2]

[1] EADS UK Innovation Works, Newport NP10 8FZ, UK
tomas.sanchezlopez@eads.com
[2] Korean Advanced Institute of Science and Technology, Daejeon 305-701, S. Korea
gonzalo@huerta.cl

Abstract. Wireless Sensor Networks (WSNs) have traditionally had static topologies that require little or no maintenance from their addressing mechanisms. New research directions have introduced additional scenarios where WSNs should adapt to the environment and network conditions. This shift in requirements also means that the addressing schemes should evolve dynamically, providing a distributed and lightweight way of assigning addresses to the sensor nodes. In addition, the routing protocols, which drive the information exchange within the network, must leverage the addressing properties in order to function efficiently. In this paper, we present Sequence Chain (SC) as a lightweight tree-based addressing mechanism for Wireless Sensor Networks. SC offers distributed and dynamic address allocation together with optimized tree routing. We compare our work with the de-facto industry standard, ZigBee, and show how SC improves the formation of addressing trees and yields up to three and a half times shorter multi-hop routes.

Keywords: Wireless Sensor Networks, Addressing, Smart Objects.

1 Introduction

Mobile and Ad-hoc Networks (MANETs) are mobile networks of computing devices that are able to communicate amongst each other without the use of an infrastructure. MANETs devices run typically on batteries and use wireless communication. Unlike wired networks, which lack strong power and infrastructure constraints, MANETs must optimize their operation and keep the connectivity even when unexpected topology changes occur. Wireless Sensor Networks are similar to MANETs in that they are formed by wireless devices which must communicate among themselves without the use of an infrastructure. However, traditional WSNs do not consider mobility among their sensor nodes but rather assume static topologies that remain after deployment for all the network lifetime. Furthermore, WSNs are also traditionally centralized in the sense that a Base Station collects all the sensor readings from the network members.

Dynamic address allocation is a common problem for MANETs where mobile nodes constantly join and leave the network. Most of the approaches are based on the Internet Protocol (IP). Node mobility is typically handled by the IP

A. Puiatti et al. (Eds.): MobiQuitous 2011, LNICST 104, pp. 260–272, 2012.
© Institute for Computer Sciences, Social Informatics and Telecommunications Engineering 2012

standards themselves, whose objective is to provide transparent routing allowing nodes to conserve their original address while moving around different subnetworks. Automatic address allocation, however, poses additional challenges. A number of approaches rely on centralized agents that assign new addresses according to a pool of available alternatives [5,13]. Other approaches allow decentralized address assignment but require Duplicate Address Detection (DAD) techniques in order to ensure unique addresses [12,9].

Recent developments on Wireless Sensor Networks [7,2] make the inclusion of dynamic address allocation a desirable feature. However, the dynamic addressing techniques used in MANETs are inappropriate for WSNs due to their specially scarce resources. Typical WSNs node limitations include limited RAM and Flash memories, slow processing, short radio ranges and short-lived batteries. IP addressing is generally unsuitable for WSNs due to the excessive overhead of the IP protocol stack. Furthermore, centralized sensor node agents are also inappropriate since the sensor nodes's energy is easily exhausted. Finally, approaches that use DAD should also be avoided because of the message overhead caused by the search for duplicate addresses throughout the network.

In this paper, we propose a lightweight addressing scheme that provides excellent dynamic properties while minimizing the overhead of the assignment process. Our addressing scheme, called Sequence Chain (SC), assigns addresses in a hierarchical manner, additionally enabling simple and efficient routing among the network nodes. In this paper, we prove that both the functionality and the performance of SC are superior to any other related work, including the de-facto industry standard for Wireless Personal Area Networks (WPAN) ZigBee [16].

The rest of this paper is organised as follows. Section 2 reviews the related work in the area. Section 3 and 4 introduces our proposed scheme. Section 5 compares SC with ZigBee as part of our evaluation. Finally section 6 concludes the paper.

2 Related Work

Address allocation in ad-hoc and wireless networks has been extensively discussed over the last years. Many protocols have been proposed that try to address the problems of this type of networks, such as mobility, node joining and separation, network merge, etc. Although the specific constraints of WSNs restrict even more the protocol design, very little work has been done in the area. Besides few exceptions, most existing WSNs architectures just provide static addresses or assume that generic protocols designed for ad-hoc wireless networks would fit into the sensor nodes. We have reviewed those existing approaches that are more relevant to our work, and we present a summary of them on table 1. Although due to spece restriction we can not provide a detailed discussion on the related work, the following list describes the criteria that we followed to comparing and reviewing them. As the table shows, with the support of mobility and the splitting and merging of networks, Sequence Chain is the only protocol that fully considers dynamic WSNs.

- *WSN:* If the scheme was developed specifically for WSNs. This characteristics indicates that more concern was put on the constraints of the nodes.
- *Mobility:* If mobility of nodes is specifically considered.
- *Split/Merge:* If network split or network merger are supported.
- *Unique:* If the result of the address assignment is a unique address, without the need of any additional protocol such as DAD.
- *Concatenation:* If the assigned addresses are a result of concatenating local identifiers. This is the technique followed by our proposal.
- *Distributed:* If the assignment process is distributed (no centralized agents).
- *Overhead:* The stimated overhead of the address assignment process, including duplicate address detection and address look-up costs when applicable.

Table 1. Comparison of relevant addressing protocols

Scheme	WSN	Mob.	S/M	Unique	Conc.	Dist.	Overhead
MANETconf [9]	No	No	Yes	No	No	Yes	$O(n)$
DACP [5]	No	Yes	Yes	No	No	Yes	$O(n)$
PACMAN [12]	No	No	No	No	No	Yes	$O(1) + F(P)$‡
DART [6]	No	Yes	Yes	Yes	No	Yes	$O(logn), O(n)$†
L$^+$ [3]	No	Yes	No	Yes	Yes	No	$O(1), O(logn)$†
Yao and Dressler [14]	Yes	No	No	No	No	No	$F(P) + O(n)$‡
Bhatti and Yue[1]	Yes	No	No	Yes*	No	Yes	$O(1) + O(n)$
ZigBee [16]	Yes	No	No	Yes	No	Yes	$O(1)$
Zheng & Lee [15]	Yes	No	No	Yes	No	Yes	$O(1)$
Sequence Chain	Yes	Yes	Yes	Yes	Yes	Yes	$O(1)$

† Address assignment overhead, Address look-up overhead
‡ $F(P)$ is a function of the probability that the selected address is not duplicated dependent on the destination agent

3   The Sequence Chain Addressing Scheme

In our previous work [10][11], we proposed an architecture and a set of protocols that drive the formation of Smart Object (SO) networks. Wireless sensor nodes were attached to the objects to implement those protocols and to represent the objects in the architecture. As a requirement, SOs should be able to leave or join a network at any time, and so the SO network protocols need to support mobility tailored for the constrained WSNs.

Distributed addressing schemes such as ZigBee [16] or LEADS [8], fix their address space to a number of bits. Starting from this fixed address space, they assign addresses by, for example, allowing parents to distribute portions of the space to their children. This assures global unique addresses and fairness in the assignment. However, portions of the address space become easily exhausted, causing the rejection of new nodes while other portions of the space remain free. Furthermore, even if a low number of nodes are part of the network, their addresses still occupy the full number of bits, wasting memory in packets and routing tables and also processing time in address comparison and others.

In SC, rather than partitioning a fixed address space we construct addresses by attaching locally unique identifiers to build a global unique address. Each parent assigns its children a sequence number that distinguishes it locally from its siblings. This sequence number is then attached to the address of the parent to form the final child's address. This way, any node will be assigned a unique address in a simple, distributed, hierarchical way. The simplicity of the address assignment allows SC to provide advanced functionality with relatively low cost. The proposed addressing scheme has the following properties:

- *Hierarchical*: Nodes receive addresses organized in a tree structure. The node from the network that accepts a joining request of a new node becomes a parent. Hence, senders of joining requests become children.
- *Distributed and unique*: Each node is responsible for assigning addresses only to its children. The address that a child receives is derived from its parent address in a way that makes that address unique for the network.
- *Scalable*: If a node leaves a network, its address becomes automatically available for any other node joining with the same parent. The addresses increase in size as the network becomes bigger. Network merges reassign the addresses of the network with the smallest number of nodes.
- *Low overhead*: A parent only needs to know its immediate children to assign addresses in a unique manner. The addressing scheme provides routing along the tree with nearly no cost. A node can know how many hops it is away from any destination by just analyzing the destination address, and parents can route packets following the tree by just comparing their address with the packet's destination address. Additionally, parents can provide shortcuts to the destination by routing packets to neighbors that are closer to the destination than following the tree.

3.1   Node Join and Network Merge

As described in our previous work [10], Smart Objects periodically send request packets to discover other SOs and networks. One of the purposes of those discovery packets is to trigger an address allocation process. When the process is over, the SO that received the advertisement packet will become the *parent*, and the SO that sent the advertisement packet will become a new *child* of that parent. This parent/children relationship creates a hierarchical relationship among all the nodes of a network, resulting in a *tree* structure. Every parent but the root of the tree (the first node of a network) assigns local identifiers to its children in a sequentially increasing order, starting from 0. The root of the tree assigns itself the address 0, which is both a local and a global tree address. For this reason, a root starts assigning addresses to its children from 1. To form a global unique address, a child attaches its local address to the address of its parent. As a result, the address of every node of a network contains all the addresses of its parents from its immediate parent to the tree's root. Since it is not possible to specify the separation of parent-child portion within the address, the number of bits used for each child address must be equal in order to ensure that addresses are unique. This number is a network-wide value and is called bits-per-level

(BPL). For example, two bits will provide four children per parent, three bits eight children, etc. Figure 1 shows an example with two BPL and node addresses displayed in binary format.

Sequence Chain does not fix the address space but allows addresses to grow in length as needed (i.e. as the number of the levels of the tree grows), effectively providing a dynamic address space. An address length (i.e number of bits) is determined by the level (i.e depth) of the node holding the address and the BPL variable ($length = depth * BPL$). Thus each node in the network can know the length of its own address and the length of the addresses of its parent and children. Additionally, given any address a node can know the address' node depth since the BPL variable is known network wide. Addresses can also be found in packets, as source and destination end-points, and in neighbour tables (see section 4). In order to be able to determine the length of arbitrary addresses and thus be able to extract and process them adequately, the level of the node to which each address belongs is included together with the addresses. Although the size of this *level* field would depend on the maximum desired depth for a network, 5 or 6 bits (32 and 64 levels respectively) would be enough to fulfil the needs of networks of millions of nodes while giving enough flexibility for unequal tree growth. For an evaluation on the SC address lengths please see section 5.2.

Algorithm 1. JoinAdvRequest reception

Input: JoinAdvRequest
Output: JoinAdvResponse
HAL = HighestSOnet#($ListOfRequests + Myself$) ;
if *(NetworkID ϵ HAL)* **then**
    $SOnet\#$ = $SOnet\#$ + Sum(List of $AssociationRequest.SOnet\#$) ;
    $SOtree\#$ = $SOtree\#$ + Sum(List of $AssociationRequest.SOnet\#$) - 1;
    Store(List of $AssociationRequest.SOtree\#$) ;
    send JoinAdvResponse($NetworkID$, $SOnet\#$, ComputeAddress($Address$), Address, NoReverse) **to** $ListOfRequests$ & children ;
end

Algorithm 2. JoinAdvResponse reception

Input: JoinAdvResponse($NewNetID,SumSOnet\#$, $NewAddress,ParentAdd,NoReverse$)
Output: JoinAdvResponse
$NetworkID=NewNetID$;
$Parent\_address=ParentAdd$;
$Address=NewAddress$;
$SOnet\#$ = $SOnet\#$ + $SumSOnet\#$;
if *(Reverse)* **then**
    MakeChildParent ;
end
if *(HaveChildren)* **then**
    JoinAdvResponse($NewNetID$, $SOnet\#$, ComputeAddress($NewAddress$), Address, NoReverse) **to** children ;
end
if *(HaveParent)* **then**
    MakeParentChild ;
    send JoinAdvResponse($NewNetID$, $SOnet\#$, ComputeAddress($NewAddress$), Address, Reverse) **to** parent ;
end

Network merging is supported by re-assigning the addresses of the network with the *least* number of nodes (i.e. the merged network). The number of nodes of each network is calculated in a distributed way and requires no global knowledge. The network merging process is very similar to joining individual nodes, and every new child's address is computed entirely by its parent according to its own address and the sequence of the child. The node from the merged network that serves as the bridge for the merge (i.e. the node that sent the request packet - JoinAdvRequest) will obtain its new address from its new parent, the same way as if it was a single node. Once its new address is computed, it will propagate a re-assignment command to its children, which in turn will propagate it to their own children. This process will continue until all the nodes of the merged network are assigned a new address. Join requests may be sent and received by nodes which are not the root of the tree. As a result, network merging often incurs in a parent-child misplacement, where links from the merged network must be reversed in order to keep the hierarchical structure of the tree.

Algorithms 1 and 2 detail the process involved in the joining and merging of networks. The same algorithm is utilized for both single node joining and network merge, since a single node is considered as a network which contains only one node. Sequence Chain also supports the joining of several networks simultaneously. The `ListofRequests` variable contains all the requests that were received by this node in a particular request period.

When a merge occurs, a new network ID must be elected in order to represent the new network. The election of a new network ID is influenced by the number of nodes in a network. As mentioned before, the number of nodes also dictates which one of the networks that are merging will change its addresses. The *SOnet#* and *SOtree#* variables store the total number of nodes of the network and the number of descendants of a given node respectively. The *SOtree#* will be used in section 3.2 in order to update the *SOnet#* variable when a subtree leaves the network. The algorithm generates a `JoinAdvResponse`, that is sent to the requesting nodes with the addresses computed as described earlier. Upon reception, the node receiving the `JoinAdvResponse` should first proceed with the changes indicated in the packet: update its Network ID information, its own address and the address of its parent. The *Reverse* and *NoReverse* arguments indicate if the child-parent relationship among the node that sends the `JoinAdvResponse` packet and the node that receives it should be reversed, as explained earlier. Finally, the changes reported by the `JoinAdvResponse` packet should also be transmitted to the rest of the nodes of the merged networks. The algorithm achieves that by sending `JoinAdvResponse` in a recursive manner until all the members are notified.

3.2   Node Leave and Network Split

When a network leave occurs, a tree link is broken, in which one of the ends was a parent and the other one was a child. We assume that both parent and child become aware of their broken bond in a reasonably low amount of time. Algorithm 3 depicts what is the procedure when either child or parent notices the broken link. Children that find their parent missing will attempt to find a new parent from the same network, choosing the parent with the shortest address. A parent that finds one of its children missing, will first wait for any *orphan* node to request to rejoin the network. The algorithm also elects a new network identifier when needed and updates the node count of both the network and each node's subtree. Note how all the procedure is distributed and does not depend on any node warning about its departure, but just on nodes noticing that their parent or children are not responding.

Algorithm 3. *Leaving* procedure

```
if (Parent missing) then
    AnswerList=SearchNewParent(NetworkID) ;
    if (AnswerList ≠ null) then
        NewParent=SelectShortestAddress(AnswerList);
        MakeParent(NewParent) ;
        rejoin=True ;
        SOnet#=(SOtree#+1)+NewParent.SOnet# ;
    else
        rejoin=False; Address=rootAddress; SOnet#=SOtree# + 1;
    end
    UpdateChildren(Address, SOnet#); CheckNetIDleft() ;
end
if (Child missing) then
    SOnet#=SOnet# - (Child.SOtree# + 1) ;
    SOtree#=SOtree# - (Child.SOtree# + 1) ;
    ListOfOrphans=wait(OrphansToJoin) ;
    if (ListOfOrphans = null) then
        CheckNetIDleft() ;
    else
        SOnet#=SOnet#+(Orphan.SOtree# + 1);
        SOtree#=SOtree#+(Orphan.SOtree# + 1) ;
    end
    UpdateTree(SOnet#,Difference(SOtree#)) ;
end
```

---

4   Sequence Chain Routing

The Sequence Chain addressing scheme provides tree routing by simple comparison of addresses. This is possible due to two simple properties:

- Any node's address contains the addresses of all its parents towards the root.
- The number of maximum children for each parent is fixed network-wide. This means that the number of address BPL is fixed.

Let dest be the destination address of a packet and destL the length of that address. In a similar way, let router be the address of the node that receives the packet and is asked to route it to the destination, and routerL the length of that address. Let nbits be the number of BPL and '×' and '*' the concatenation and arithmetic multiplication operations respectively. Fundamental properties of Sequence Chain are:

1. $destL = nbits * n$, where $\mathbf{n} \in \mathbb{N}$. In a similar way, $routerL = nbits * m$, where $\mathbf{m} \in \mathbb{N}$.
2. if $dest = x \times k$ and $router = x \times j$, where $k \neq j$, then $\frac{length(k)+length(j)}{nbits}$ is the number of hops from the router node to the destination. This is also true if $length(x) = 0$.
3. if $dest = router \times y$, then the destination is one of the children in **router**'s subtree
4. if $dest = router \times y$, and $y = z \times v$, $router \times z$ is the next hop to $dest$, where $length(z) = nbits$ and z is the local address of one of the children of $router$.

In the previous properties, x, k, j, y, z and v are portions of addresses and their length also follow property 1.

The general tree routing operation is then as follows: When a node **router** receives a packet and is asked to route it to **dest**, it first checks if its address **router** is contained in the destination address **dest**. If so, it means that the destination is in its subtree, and the next hop is computed as in property 4. If its address is partially contained or not contained at all, the packet must be sent to its parent.

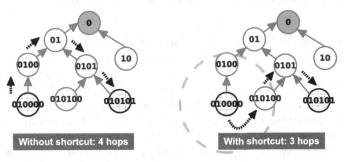

Fig. 1. Example of routing in Sequence Chain. BPL=2.

It is possible to provide shortcuts to the destination by analyzing the addresses of the neighbour nodes before proceeding with the general tree-routing. Neighbour addresses can easily be obtained by overhearing packets at node joining time, routing or link health checking, and storing them in a neighbour table. Figure 1 shows an simple example of how one routing hop can be saved by analysing the address of the neighbouring nodes of the origin node of a packet. Note that this technique can be applied at any point on a routing chain, every time a routing decision has to be made.

It also worth noting that networks built using the SC addressing scheme can also benefit from the addressing properties outlined earlier even if tree routing is not used. For example, in many mesh routing mechanisms, such as AODV or DSR [4], the initial effects of flooding for routing discovery can be mitigated by limiting the number of hops that the broadcast will be propagated. In SC networks, this number can be set to the number of hops between source and destination nodes if the SC tree routing was used.

5   Evaluation

According to section 2, ZigBee is the most similar related work to Sequence Chain as well as being a widely used industrial standard for WSNs. Therefore, in this section we will analyse a number of metrics aiming to demonstrate that our proposed addressing mechanism is superior to ZigBee. The rationale behind each one of the metrics is detailed on each of the subsections below. The simulator introduced in [10] was used to obtain all the evaluation results presented in the following sections. Common parameters of all the simulation scenarios include:

- A square deployment area of 500x500 meters.
- A Sequence Chain BPL of two. This limits the maximum number of direct children per node to four.
- ZigBee parameters of $nwkMaxChildren=4$ and $nwkMaxRouters=4$. In this way, the maximum number of children is the same as SC, and all the children are capable of having other children (i.e. being *routers*) in the same way as SC. Since the $nwkMaxDepth$ variable very much affects the results, it will be varied throughout our simulations
- For each simulation scenario, 100 repetitions with randomized node locations.

The method adopted for the simulations was the following: the programmed disconnected nodes were positioned randomly in the deployment area, and the node closest to the center of such area was identified. This node was assigned the address '0' and made part of the tree (root and initiator of the network). For each other node in an increasing distance from the initiator, a parent node was selected, which was 1) in the transmission range of the node 2) already part of the tree and 3) had an available child address. For all the potential parents meeting these requirements, the parent which was in the lowest level (least depth) in the tree was selected. After a parent was chosen for a node, the following node was selected and the process repeated until all the nodes in the deployment area had searched for a parent.

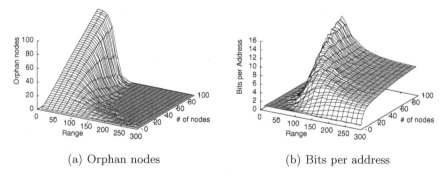

(a) Orphan nodes   (b) Bits per address

Fig. 2. Average orphan nodes and maximum depth resulting from simulations of SC

5.1   Orphan Nodes

Those nodes that are unable to find a parent are considered *orphan*. Orphan nodes may appear for two main reasons: no parent was found in the transmission range of the selected node, or parents were found but they were unable to accept more children. As a general rule, the smaller the number of orphans that appear in a random deployment scenario, the better the addresses are being assigned.

Graph 2(a) shows how the average orphan nodes from the SC simulations vary when both the number of nodes in the simulation and their transmission range varies. As the graph shows, when the number of nodes increases, the number of orphan nodes tends to decrease since the density of deployed nodes allows more nodes to find an available parent. At the same time, the number of orphan nodes decreases as the transmission range increases, since the chances of finding available parent nodes also increases. For ZigBee, instead of showing one graph for each value of *nwkMaxDepth*, table 2 shows how often the number of orphan nodes resulting from the SC simulations are higher than, lower than or equal to those of the ZigBee simulations for each simulated value of *nwkMaxDepth*. From Table 2, we see that SC obtains a lower number of orphan nodes for almost any value of *nwkMaxDepth*, and that the improvement of SC is lower in the middle values of *nwkMaxDepth*.

Table 2. Comparison percentages of orphan nodes between SC and ZigBee

nwkMaxDepth → ↓ Orphan nodes	1	2	3	4	5	6	7	8	9	10	11	12	13	14
$SC > ZigBee$	0%	1%	2%	4%	7%	9%	11%	0%	1%	1%	1%	0%	0%	1%
$SC < ZigBee$	81%	75%	53%	23%	16%	10%	9%	13%	32%	40%	45%	49%	52%	55%
$SC = ZigBee$	19%	24%	45%	73%	77%	81%	80%	87%	67%	59%	54%	51%	48%	44%

5.2   Bits Per Address

ZigBee uses fixed 16 bit network addresses and so can accommodate a maximum of 65536 nodes per network. The address assignment mechanism uses chunks of the 16 bit address space that are assigned by a parent to its children. As a consequence, children are allocated addresses according to the potential descendants that they may have. Previously it was shown that random joins tend to produce more orphan nodes in ZigBee, which fixes its addressing space for each child. Also, if the number of nodes per network is not very high, fixed large addresses waste valuable memory space both in the nodes themselves (e.g. in neighbour tables) and in the protocols that use the addresses for communication (e.g. message exchange). SC allows the increase of address lengths on demand when the number of nodes increases, as long as the number of BPL is respected. This strategy not only produces shorter addresses, but also provides more flexibility by not limiting the maximum number of nodes in any part of the addressing tree.

Graph 2(b) shows the variation of the number of address bits as both the number of nodes and their transmission range are varied. Results show that the Sequence Chain addressing scheme always produces shorter addresses than ZigBee (i.e under 16 bits). Addresses are longer for high number of nodes and relatively low ranges. These conditions coincide with the location of the deepest trees, and therefore with the longest routes (Graph 3(a)). Only 19% of the addresses generated by SC are longer than 8 bits, which would be beneficial even in case of memory restrictions (for example if a byte is the minimum addressable memory portion). Note that even if we consider the 5 or 6 bit `level` field needed to calculate an address length as part of its bit count (as mentioned in section 3.1), the resulting address lengths are still 25 to 30 per cent shorter than those of ZigBee.

5.3   Tree Depth and Routing

Nodes looking for parents to join the tree always choose the candidate which is located in the lowest level of the addressing hierarchy. However, depending on the addressing scheme, the list of candidates may differ and the trees depth might grow in different ways. Trees with larger maximum depths are potentially less efficient, since messages have to traverse longer distances from the origin to the destination if the addressing tree is followed for routing. We analyzed the performance of tree routing between Sequence Chain and ZigBee by measuring the number of hops between origin and destination nodes on randomized communication scenarios. For each deployment scenario, addressing trees were formed for both Sequence Chain and ZigBee addressing schemes. Finally, origin and destination were randomly chosen and communication simulated between them. This last step was repeated fifty times, and the average number of hops was recorded for those repetitions.

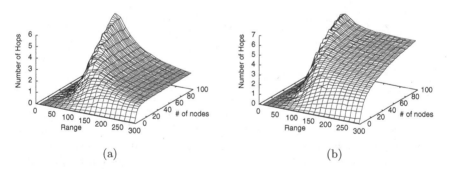

(a)   (b)

Fig. 3. Average number of hops with randomized routing scenarios using the SC with shortcut 3(a) and ZigBee 3(b)

Table 3. Distribution of simulated average route lengths for different tree depths

nwkMaxDepth → ↓ Average n°of hops	1	2	3	4	5	6	7	8	9	10	11	12	13	14
$SCshortcut > ZigBee$	89%	36%	23%	15%	12%	9%	10%	4%	15%	23%	25%	26%	26%	27%
$SCshortcut < ZigBee$	8%	61%	74%	82%	85%	88%	87%	92%	82%	74%	72%	71%	71%	70%
$SCshortcut = ZigBee$	3%	3%	3%	3%	3%	3%	3%	4%	3%	3%	3%	3%	3%	3%

Figure 3(a) shows the results obtained by using the Sequence Chain addressing and routing with the shortcut mechanism. Figure 3(b) show the results using the ZigBee tree routing. In order to compare these differences with different values of *nwkMaxDepth*, Table 3 presents a percentage comparison among these 2 routing algorithms. Sequence Chain with the shortcut mechanism obtains significantly shorter routes as compared with ZigBee. We have recorded differences of up to 3.8 hops for some scenarios, which is 3.5 times shorter than ZigBee.

6 Conclusion

In this paper, we present the tree-based Sequence Chain addressing mechanism for Wireless Sensor Networks. SC proposes a simple and distributed way of assigning addresses to nodes inside a WSN, and supports all the features required by dynamic and mobile environments such as node join and leave or network split and merge, as well as mechanisms for avoiding address space exhaustion problems. By means of the hierarchical way in which addresses are assigned, SC can provide extremely simple and efficient routing along the tree. We demonstrate that SC provides notable benefits in tree formation and routing, and generally produces more stable networks than ZigBee, in which the number of orphan nodes and tree depths is balanced and does not depend on protocol variables or deployment scenarios. We conclude that the Sequence Chain addressing mechanism is adequate for dynamic and mobile WSNs, and that it provides excellent performance both in tree formation and in tree routing. Additional results and an overview of the conclusions on the context of a Smart Objects architecture can be found in [11].

References

1. Bhatti, G., Yue, G.: A structured addressing scheme for wireless multi-hop networks. Tech. rep., Mitsubishi Electric Research Labs Tech. Report (2002)
2. Butler, Z., Rus, D.: Event-based motion control for mobile-sensor networks. IEEE Pervasive Computing 2, 34–42 (2003)
3. Chen, B., Morris, R.: : Scalable landmark routing and address lookup for multi-hop wireless networksl^+. Tech. rep., MIT LCS Technical Report 837 (2002)
4. Johnson, D., Hu, Y., Maltz, D.: RFC 4728: The Dynamic Source Routing Protocol (DSR) for Mobile Ad Hoc Networks for IPv4. The IETF Trust (2007)
5. Elizabeth, Y.S., Sun, Y., Belding-Royer, E.M.: Dynamic address configuration in mobile ad hoc networks. Tech. rep., Computer Science, UCSB, Tech. Rep (2003)
6. Eriksson, J., Faloutsos, M., Krishnamurthy, S.V.: Dart: Dynamic address routing for scalable ad hoc and mesh networks. IEEE/ACM Transactions on Networking 15(1), 119–132 (2007)
7. Heo, N., Varshney, P.: A distributed self spreading algorithm for mobile wireless sensor networks. In: 2003 IEEE Wireless Communications and Networking, WCNC 2003, vol. 3, pp. 1597–1602 (2003)
8. Lu, J.L., Valois, F., Barthel, D., Dohler, M.: Low-energy address allocation scheme for wireless sensor networks. In: IEEE 18th International Symposium on Personal, Indoor and Mobile Radio Communications, PIMRC 2007, pp. 1–5 (2007)

9. Mesargi, S., Prakash, R.: Manetconf: Configuration of hosts in a mobile ad hoc network. In: Proc. of INFOCOM 2002, New Yok, NA, pp. 1059–1068 (2002)

10. Sánchez López, T., Kim, D., Huerta Canepa, G., Koumadi, K.: Integrating wireless sensors and rfid tags into energy-efficient and dynamic context networks. The Computer Journal 52(2), 240–267 (2008)

11. Sánchez López, T., Ranasinghe, D., Harrison, M., McFarlane, D.: Adding sense to the internet of things. Personal and Ubiquitous Computing, 1–18 (2011)

12. Weniger, K.: Pacman: Passive autoconfiguration for mobile ad hoc networks. IEEE Journal on Selected Areas in Communications 23(3), 507–519 (2005)

13. Weniger, K., Zitterbart, M.: Ipv6 autoconfiguration in large scale mobile ad-hoc networks. In: Proceedings of European Wireless 2002, pp. 142–148 (2002)

14. Yao, Z., Dressler, F.: Dynamic address allocation for management and control in wireless sensor networks. In: Proc. of HICSS 2007, p. 292b (2007)

15. Zheng, J., Lee, M.J.: A resource-efficient and scalable wireless mesh routing protocol. Ad Hoc Networks 5, 704–718 (2007)

16. ZigBee Alliance: ZigBee Specification. ZigBee Alliance (2008)

Neuron Inspired Collaborative Transmission in Wireless Sensor Networks

Stephan Sigg[1], Predrag Jakimovski[2], Florian Becker[2], Hedda R. Schmidtke[2],
Alexander Neumann[2], Yusheng Ji[1], and Michael Beigl[2]

[1] National Institute of Informatics (NII), Tokyo, Japan
{sigg,kei}@nii.ac.jp
[2] Karlsruhe Institute of Technology (KIT), Pervasive Computing Systems, TecO,
Germany
{jakimov,becker,neumann,schmidtke,michael}@teco.edu

Abstract. We establish a wireless sensor network that emulates biological neuronal structures for the purpose of creating smart spaces. Two different types of wireless nodes working together are used to mimic the behaviour of a neuron consisting of dendrites, soma and synapses. The transmission among nodes that establish such a neuron structure is established by distributed beamforming techniques to enable simultaneous information transmission among neurons. Through superposition of transmission signals, data from neighbouring nodes is perceived as background noise and does not interfere. In this way we show that beamforming and computation on the channel can be powerful tools to establish intelligent sensing systems even with minimal computational power.

Keywords: computational neuroscience, neuronal networks (NN), distributed adaptive beamforming, artificial intelligence (AI), collaborative communication, superimposed signals, context recognition.

1   Introduction

Smart spaces are spaces equipped with sensing systems consisting of sensor nodes of different types linked in a wireless sensor network, which collaboratively provides intelligent systems applications. For installing smart spaces, it is essential to address questions of scalability and cost reduction. One idea is to use lightweight sensor node platforms and employ algorithms for self-organization of sensor networks. In particular, bio-inspired solutions are promising candidates, as many biological systems are able to produce complex global behaviour from simple only locally interacting identical components. Smart spaces fit this description very well: they consist of a large number of low-cost computing nodes enabled to sense environmental parameters and to communicate locally so as to keep transmission power low.

While the number of required nodes can be huge for scenarios such as the massive deployment of RFID tags for item level tagging, the limited computing power and physical constraints to the transmission reduce the amount of useful

A. Puiatti et al. (Eds.): MobiQuitous 2011, LNICST 104, pp. 273–284, 2012.
© Institute for Computer Sciences, Social Informatics and Telecommunications Engineering 2012

computation feasible in such scenario. In particular, the constrained communication and computational power of individual nodes lower the employment of algorithms that can be executed on the nodes directly. In addition, the available low power hinders long distanced transmission and thus the far-range exchange of information in larger areas.

A biological system that matches these constraints is the nervous system of the brain. Neurons communicate "wirelessly" locally. Through a complex electrochemical process the synapse of a neuron bridges the gap to the dendrites of other neurons. Each dendrite in turn is connected to a main cell body, the soma, where the neuron performs a single, very simple computational task: an addition of the weighted input signals from all dendrites. The result is sent, through the axon, a possibly far distance to the synapse of the neuron, where again it is transmitted to the dendrites of other neurons. This very simple distributed sensing and processing platform is able to perform astonishingly complex computational tasks in a wide range of biological systems. In this paper, we explore whether an extremely cost efficient WSN would be able to perform the basic steps of this process: the transmission from synapse to dendrite, the addition of weighted signals, and the transmission of the result from soma to synapse.

Our system consists of two types of sensor nodes, which we call dendrite nodes and synapse nodes. A neuron is a distributed system. It consists of several dedrite nodes and one synapse node. The dendrite nodes of a neuron obtain signals from their immediate surroundings and send them collaboratively, using a technique called beamforming, to the synapse node of the neuron. Beamforming can bridge farther distances and the overlay of signals at the receiving synapse can be used to compute the addition function [3].

We thus extended the understanding of smart spaces by considering the space itself as "alive", i. e. the installed wireless sensor network including sensory information processing is functioning as a biological neural system cooperating with the user.

After discussing the related work in section 4, we detail this structure in section 2 and explain how neuronal structures can evolve in wireless networks. Section 3 verifies it in mathematical simulations. In section 5 we draw our conclusion.

2   From Collaborative Transmission to Neuronal Structures

The following sections briefly introduce the biological neuron system, distributed adaptive transmit beamforming and their joint application to wireless sensor networks.

2.1   Biological Neuron Systems

The fundamental processor units of a central nervous system represent biological neurons interlinked together in a complex manner and providing a biological

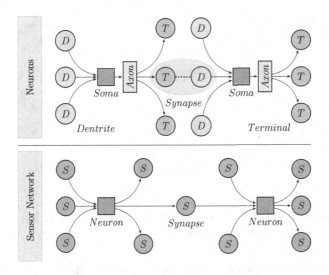

Fig. 1. Schematic representation of neuronal structures into WSN

organism with cognitive capabilities. The communication between neurons and thus the information processing of, for instance, a sensed environment is accomplished by permanently sending out electrical pulses called action potentials or spikes. The form of an action potential has no encoding information because all emitted pulses show the same shape. The information is rather encoded in the number and firing time points of the action potentials. A series of pulses emitted consecutively by a neuron is called a spike train. The spiking neurons interact in a dynamic way, so that the degree of firing pulses depends on exciting or inhibiting the neuron by its connected adjacent neurons. The physiology of a neuron is divided into three inherent components: dendrites, soma and axon (cf. figure 1). The dendrites collect signals sent out from other neurons. These signals pass through to the soma, the cell body containing the cell nucleus, where the processing of the signals take place. The output signal of the intrinsic processing consisting of an emitting spike train is relayed along the axon to other neurons. The connection between two neurons is called synapse which describes an actual gap, also known as the synaptic cleft. Here, the signal transmission is carried out in a complex manner, whereby the pre-synaptic neuron is exciting a post-synaptic neuron electro-chemically.

For mapping biological neuronal structures onto wireless sensor networks in order to create smart spaces we adapted wireless communication to neuronal functioning phenomenologically. Two types of transceiver nodes[1] α and β are working together to emulate the functioning of a neuron and neural networks, respectively. In particular, neuronal components such as dendrites are realized by nodes of type α and for the functioning of synapses the nodes of type β are used. Through collaborative transmission of signals between different types of

---

[1] Applied for different tasks although they feature the same functionality.

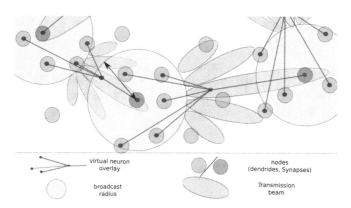

Fig. 2. Schematic illustration of a neuron overlay in a network of wireless nodes utilising distributed adaptive beamforming techniques

nodes, the soma and axon of a neuron are recreated implicitly. In the modeling of smart spaces the nodes of type α have the function primarily of sensing and transmitting the sensory information to an assigned node of type β, which in turn can transmit a processed information to further nodes. Based on our previous work in [3] sensor values and other entities can be assigned to binary sequences initialised randomly, and transmitted to an associated receiver node. In terms of neuronal encoding the randomly drawn binary sequences correspond to spike trains a neuron is emitting. The simultaneous transmission of binary sequences and thus the occurring superposition of signals on the channel corresponds to behaviour of the dendrites and soma. For extracting the data in superimposed signals refer to [3]. The characterization so far, a neuronal network can be engineered to achieve reasoning in a spatial distributed sensor network.

2.2 Distributed Adaptive Beamforming for Neuron Overlays

To create a neuron overlay in a wireless sensor network, we map the structures described above for the neuron system to wireless nodes. As described above, it generally suffices to identify two types of nodes as α-nodes and β-nodes. With these nodes we model the information transfer from dendrites.

Generally, we assume that each type β node (synapses) is associated with a group of type α nodes (dendrites) as depicted in figure 2.

These dendrites are located in the proximity of other type β nodes. Information in this network can then be disseminated from type β nodes to nearby type α nodes associated with other synapses. The dendrites then forward these stimuli to their synapses which are possibly activated by this process and then further disseminate information to activate other synapses over their dendrites.

Information dissemination from type β nodes to dendrites in close proximity can be interpreted as normal omnidirectional broadcast transmission. A problem that might occur for the information transfer from dendrites to their respective synapses in this scheme, however, is that due to the omnidirectional information

transfer among wireless nodes and since dendrites likely transmit simultaneously, collisions will occur during transmission. Also, we would have to employ
a sophisticated protocol to identify the correct synapses for each transmission.

However, we can overcome both problems elegantly by utilising distributed
beamforming transmission. When dendrites associated with specific synapses are
synchronised for their carrier phase and frequency, they can act as a distributed
beamformer in their transmission. A signal received from a distributed beamformer has an improved signal strength at a specific spatial location but fades
into background noise at most other locations [6]. The reason for this property
is that the identical signals transmitted from various transmitters constructively
overlay only at a spatially sharply restricted region since signal path lengths are
mostly unique from the various locations of distributed transmitters. At most
other locations the signals interfere destructively and fade to background noise
provided that a sufficient count of signals is transmitted simultaneously.

We propose to utilise an iterative distributed adaptive beamforming mechanism for wireless sensor networks which was discussed in [6,8,14] to establish the
connection between dendrites and their respective synapses.

Generally, in order to establish a transmission beam from a set of distributed
devices to a remote receiver, carrier phases of transmit signals have to be synchronised with respect to the receiver location and the phase and frequency
offset of the distributed local oscillators. After synchronisation, a message $m(t)$
is transmitted simultaneously by all transmit devices $i \in [1..n]$ as

$$\zeta_i(t) = \Re\left(m(t)e^{j(2\pi(f_c+f_i)t+\gamma_i)}\right) \qquad (1)$$

so that the receiver observes the superimposed signal

$$\zeta_{\text{sum}}(t) + \zeta_{\text{noise}}(t) =$$
$$\Re\left(m(t)e^{j2\pi f_c t}\sum_{i=1}^{n}\text{RSS}_i e^{j(\gamma_i+\phi_i+\psi_i)}\right) + \zeta_{\text{noise}}(t) \qquad (2)$$

with minimum phase offset between carrier signals:

$$\min\left(|(\gamma_i + \phi_i + \psi_i) - (\gamma_j + \phi_j + \psi_j)|\right) \qquad (3)$$
$$\forall i, j \in [1..n], i \neq j.$$

In equation (1) and equation (2), f_i denotes the frequency offset of device i to
a common carrier frequency f_c. The values γ_i, ϕ_i and ψ_i represent the carrier
phase offset of node i as well as the phase offset in the received signal component due to the offset in the local oscillators of nodes (ϕ_i) and due to distinct
signal propagation times (ψ_i). $\zeta_{\text{noise}}(t)$ denotes the noise and interference in the
received sum signal. We assume additive white Gaussian noise (AWGN) here.
With RSS_i we describe the received signal strength of device i.

3   Results

To show the feasibility of the proposed neuronal overlay, we utilised a matlab-
based numerical simulation environment in which collaborative nodes are

synchronised for their phase and simultaneous transmission of various neighbouring and interleaved neuron structures is demonstrated.

In these simulations, 180, 240, 300 or 500 type α transmit nodes are placed
uniformly at random on a $30m \times 30m$ square area. These nodes are randomly
allocated to 2, 3, 4 or 5 type β receiver nodes – the synapses – which are additionally placed in this area. Receiver and transmit nodes are stationary. Frequency
and phase stability are considered perfect.

In these simulations, the groups of nodes first synchronise their carrier phase
in 6000 iterations to their synapses with the iterative carrier synchronisation described in [6,8,14]. Afterwards, the nodes simultaneously transmit an amplitude
modulated binary sequence. Although all sequences are then superimposed at
the type β nodes, we can show that due to the beamforming transmission the
signal designated for a specific type β node is dominant at this node while the
superimposition of other signals results in less dominant background noise.

Nodes transmit at a base band frequency of $f_{base} = 2.4$ GHz with a transmit
power of $P_{tx} = 1$ mW and a transmission gain of $G_{tx} = 0$ dB. The type β nodes
have an antenna gain of $G_{rx} = 0$ dB. Random noise power was -103 dBm as
proposed in [1]. For the pathloss between transmit and receive nodes we utlised
the Friis free space equation [10]

$$P_{tx} \left(\frac{\lambda}{4\pi d} \right)^2 G_{tx} G_{rx}. \tag{4}$$

We derived the median and standard deviation from 10 identical simulation
runs for each distinct configuration. Signal quality is measured by the Root of
the Mean Square Error (RMSE) of the received signal to an expected optimum
signal as

$$RMSE = \sqrt{\sum_{t=0}^{\tau} \frac{\left(\zeta_{\text{sum}} + \zeta_{\text{noise}} - \zeta_{\text{opt}} \right)^2}{n}}. \tag{5}$$

Here, τ is chosen to cover several signal periods.

The optimum signal is calculated as a perfectly aligned and properly phase
shifted received sum signal from all transmit sources. For the optimum signal,
noise is disregarded. In the following sections we detail the impact of several
environmental parameters on the performance of the transmission.

3.1   Count of Neurons

We altered the count of type β nodes utilised in the simulations from 2 over
3 and 4 to 5 nodes. Figure 3 illustrates the relative BER for changing number
of neuron overlay groups. The figure depicts the improvement of the median
BER normalised on the lowest BER achieved in the simulations with only two
synapses. The value 1 represents the lowest BER transmission achieved. We observe that the beamforming transmission quality gradually deteriorates with increasing number of neurons. This is not surprising since for each neuron overlay,

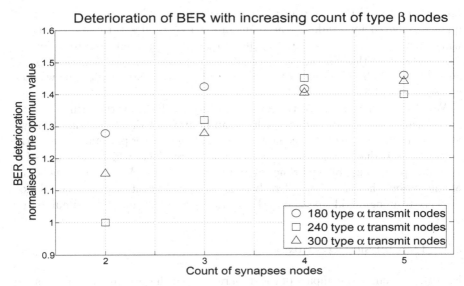

Fig. 3. Relative improvement of the median BER for increasing count of neuron groups

a distinct signal sequence is modulated onto the mobile carrier. With increasing count of synapses nodes, therefore the count of different signals which are superimposed rises. Similarly, the interference rises at all respective synapses nodes.

3.2 Count of Transmit Nodes

Also, we altered the count of transmit nodes. Generally, we expect that the BER decreases with increasing node count, since then more interference signals are superimposed from an increased count of locations so that potentially the superimposed sum signal ζ_{sum} better approximates random noise. Figure 4 depicts the results from these simulations. The figure depicts the situation for three type β nodes with 180, 240, 300 and 500 type α transmit nodes. For this scenario we could not observe a significant trend with the count of nodes utilised. This means that already groups of about 60 nodes are sufficient to significantly perturb the superimposed sum signal at non-correlated receive nodes in order to allow simultaneous transmission of neuron overlays.

3.3 Location of Receivers

The location of receivers might impact the signal quality for simultaneous transmission. Since type α transmit nodes are synchronised in phase to achieve the most coherent superimposition in the proximity of the respective type β node, the interference also increases for nearby nodes. We study the impact of this property on the BER of the transmitted signal sequences by comparing the signal quality achieved for random placement of synapses nodes with simulations in which the synapses nodes are spatially maximally separated. Figure 5 depicts the results from this simulation. We altered the count of type β nodes from 2 over 3 and 4 to 5. The count of transmit nodes in distinct simulations was set to 180, 240 and 300 respectively.

We observe that generally, the normalised median BER for the scenarios with fixed locations of synapses nodes achieve an improved BER. Occasionally, however, the performance in the scenarios with random receiver placement is slightly better. This is due to the random positioning of receivers which also allows for optimum positioning of type β nodes and receiver nodes. With increasing count of simulations, however, this effect becomes less significant. We can see this for instance from figure 5d that shows the average performance over all simulations.

3.4 Transmission Data Rate

Finally, we studied the impact of the data rate at which the symbol sequences are modulated onto the wireless carrier by transmit nodes. Naturally, we expect the BER to rise with increasing data rate [13]. Figure 6 confirms this expectation. The figure shows the normalised median BER for various data rates with respect to the count of transmit nodes or the count of neuron overlays. In both cases we observe that the BER increases with increasing data rate. Consequently, it is possible to counter an increasing BER due to other environmental effects by decreasing the transmission data rate.

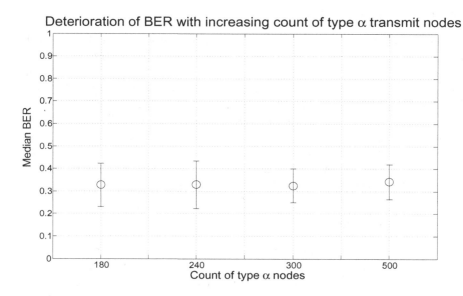

Fig. 4. BER for increasing node count

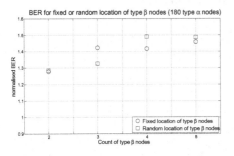

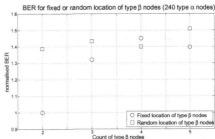

(a) BER for different count of neuron over-lays; 180 transmit nodes.

(b) BER for different count of neuron over-lays; 240 transmit nodes.

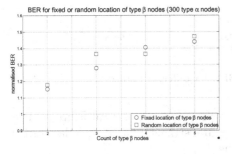

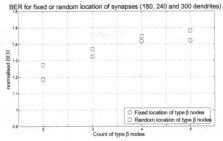

(c) BER for different count of neuron over-lays; 300 transmit nodes.

(d) BER for different count of neuron overlays; average of all counts of transmit nodes.

Fig. 5. BER for different count of neuron overlays for deterministic and randomly placed synapses nodes and various counts of transmit nodes

4 Related Work

Traditional neural models are distinguished mainly into three different generations [4], i. e. the McCullouch-Pitts neurons referred also as perceptrons or threshold gates (first generation), the feedforward and recurrent sigmoidal neural nets assigned to the second generation and the spiking neural networks (SNN) termed as the third generation. While the first generation of neural models features binary input and output signals, and calculate every boolean function, the neural models of the second generation are able to compute beside arbitrary boolean functions, as well to approximate any continuous mathematical function. In addition, these kind of neural networks are characterized by employing learning algorithms such as the backpropagation. The third class of neuronal models represent spiking neural networks, which simulate real biological neural systems. The common feature of all described generations is that all neuron models are applied on computer hardware of the von Neumann architecture. In contrast, we simulated biological neuronal structures in wireless sensor networks

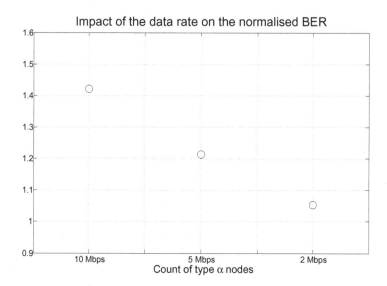

Fig. 6. Normalised median BER for different data rates

using simple transceiver nodes to emulate behavior of biological neurons. The communication and processing of spiking neural signals is based on collaborative transmission and simple on-off-shift-keying.

Algorithms for distributed adaptive beamforming are distinguished by closed-loop phase synchronisation and open-loop phase synchronisation techniques [6]. Closed-loop carrier synchronisation can be achieved by a master-slave approach [15]. Transmit nodes then send a synchronisation sequence simultaneously on code-divisioned channels to a destination node. The destination calculates the relative phase offset of the received signals and broadcasts this information to all transmitters that adapt their carrier signals accordingly.

Due to the high computational complexity burden for the source node to derive the relative phase offset of all received signals, this implementation is not suggestive in some applications for wireless sensor nodes.

Alternatively, a Master-slave-open-loop synchronisation can be applied [5]. In this method, however, the generally high complexity for the nodes is shifted from the receiver node to one of the transmit nodes. Therefore, this approach also suffers from its high computational load.

A simpler and less resource demanding transmit beamforming scheme to synchronise carrier signal components in phase and frequency was proposed in [9]. This computationally cheap carrier synchronisation utilises a one-bit feedback on the achieved synchronisation quality that is transmitted in each iteration from a remote receiver [6,7]. The central optimisation procedure of this process consists of n devices $i \in [1, \ldots, n]$ randomly altering the phases γ_i of their carrier signal $\zeta_i(t)$ in each iteration. The carrier synchronisation process for distributed adaptive transmit beamforming is then generally described by a random search method [8,11,12]. Since a decreasing signal quality is never accepted the method eventually converges to the optimum with probability 1 [8]. The authors of [11] demonstrated in a case study that the method is feasible to synchronise frequency as well as phase of carrier signal components. In [8] it was determined that the expected optimisation time of this approach for a network of n transmit nodes is linear in n when in each iteration the optimum probability distribution is chosen for the random decision taken by the nodes. For a fixed uniform distribution over the whole optimisation process, a sharp asymptotic bound of $\Theta(n \cdot k \cdot \log n)$ was derived for the expected optimisation time [14]. Here, k denotes the maximum number of distinct phase offsets a physical transmitter can generate.

5   Conclusion

We presented a method to build a neural network overlay over a wireless sensor network. In particular, we utilised an iterative, computationally cheap method for carrier synchronisation among distributed nodes to establish a synchronised transmission beam among nodes allocated to one neuron in the neural network overlay. Due to beamforming, communication can be established simultaneously in several neurons in the overlay network. With this construction we are able to establish smart spaces capable of executing complex computations on computationally limited wireless nodes. In mathematical simulations, we demonstrated how a cost efficient wireless sensor network is able to perform the transmission from synapse to dendrite, the addition of weighted signals and the transmission of the result from the soma to synapse. In particular, the impact of the count of synapses, the count of dendrites, the location of dendrites and the transmission data rate impacts the bit error rate of the simultaneous superimposed transmission from dendrites to several respective synapses.

Acknowledgements. This work was supported by a fellowship within the Postdoc-Programme of the German Academic Exchange Service (DAAD) We further acknowledge funding for the project Polytos, in the BMBF-funded excellence cluster "Printed Organic Circuits and Chips", and also by the Deutsche Forschungsgemeinschaft (DFG) in the project "SenseCast: Kontextprognose zur Optimierung von Netzwerkparametern in drahtlosen Sensornetzen" (BE4319/1).

References

1. 3GPP. 3rd generation partnership project; technical specification group radio access networks; 3g home nodeb study item technical report (release 8). Technical Report 3GPP TR 25.820 V8.0.0 (March 2008)
2. Bucklew, J.A., Sethares, W.A.: Convergence of a class of decentralised beamforming algorithms. IEEE Transactions on Signal Processing 56(6), 2280–2288 (2008)
3. Jakimovski, P., Becker, F., Sigg, S., Schmidtke, H.R., Beigl, M.: Collective communication in dense sensing environments. In: The 7th International Conference on Intelligent Environments - IE 2011, Nottingham Trent University, United Kingdom (July 2011)

4. Maass, W.: Networks of spiking neurons: the third generation of neural network models. Neural Networks 10, 1659–1671 (1997)

5. Mudumbai, R., Barriac, G., Madhow, U.: On the feasibility of distributed beamforming in wireless networks. IEEE Transactions on Wireless communications 6, 1754–1763 (2007)

6. Mudumbai, R., Brown, D.R., Madhow, U., Poor, H.V.: Distributed transmit beamforming: Challenges and recent progress. IEEE Communications Magazine, 102–110 (February 2009)

7. Mudumbai, R., Hespanha, J., Madhow, U., Barriac, G.: Scalable feedback control for distributed beamforming in sensor networks. In: Proceedings of the IEEE International Symposium on Information Theory, pp. 137–141 (2005)

8. Mudumbai, R., Hespanha, J., Madhow, U., Barriac, G.: Distributed transmit beamforming using feedback control. IEEE Transactions on Information Theory 56(1) (January 2010)

9. Mudumbai, R., Wild, B., Madhow, U., Ramchandran, K.: Distributed beamforming using 1 bit feedback: from concept to realization. In: Proceedings of the 44th Allerton Conference on Communication, Control and Computation, pp. 1020–1027 (2006)

10. Rappaport, T.: Wireless Communications: Principles and Practice. Prentice Hall (2002)

11. Seo, M., Rodwell, M., Madhow, U.: A feedback-based distributed phased array technique and its application to 60-ghz wireless sensor network. In: IEEE MTT-S International Microwave Symposium Digest, pp. 683–686 (2008)

12. Sigg, S., Beigl, M.: Collaborative transmission in WSNs by a (1+1)-ea. In: Proceedings of the 8th International Workshop on Applications and Services in Wireless Networks, ASWN 2008 (2008)

13. Sigg, S., Beigl, M., Banitalebi, B.: Organic Computing - A Paradigm Shift for Complex Systems. In: Efficient Adaptive Communication From Multiple Resource Restricted Transmitters. Autonomic Systems Series, ch. 5.4. Springer (2011)

14. Sigg, S., El Masri, R.M., Beigl, M.: A sharp asymptotic bound for feedback based closed-loop distributed adaptive beamforming in wireless sensor networks. Transactions on Mobile Computing (2011)

15. Tu, Y., Pottie, G.: Coherent cooperative transmission from multiple adjacent antennas to a distant stationary antenna through awgn channels. In: Proceedings of the IEEE Vehicular Technology Conference, pp. 130–134 (2002)

Minimizing the Side Effect of Context Inconsistency Resolution for Ubiquitous Computing

Chang Xu, Xiaoxing Ma, Chun Cao, and Jian Lu

State Key Laboratory for Novel Software Technology, Nanjing University
Department of Computer Science and Technology, Nanjing University
Nanjing, Jiangsu, China
{changxu,xxm,lj}@nju.edu.cn, caochun@gmail.com

Abstract. Applications in ubiquitous computing adapt their behavior based on contexts. The adaptation can be faulty if the contexts are subject to inconsistency. Various techniques have been proposed to identify key contexts from inconsistencies. By removing these contexts, an application is expected to run with inconsistencies resolved. However, existing practice largely overlooks an application's internal requirements on using these contexts for adaptation. It may lead to unexpected side effect from inconsistency resolution. This paper studies a novel way of resolving context inconsistency with the aim of minimizing such side effect for an application. We model and analyze the side effect for rule-based ubiquitous applications, and experimentally measure and compare it for various inconsistency resolution strategies. We confirm the significance of such side effect if not controlled, and present an efficient framework to minimize it during context inconsistency resolution.

Keywords: Context inconsistency resolution, side effect, ubiquitous computing.

1 Introduction

Ubiquitous computing applications keep emerging. These applications adapt their behavior based on contexts perceived from environments. A good example is Android and iOS applications developed in recent years. They perceive environmental conditions (or *contexts*), and make continual adaptations for delivering smart services.

Unfortunately, contexts from environments usually contain uncontrolled noises. Even with data filtering [14][16], contexts may still be subject to inconsistency (or *context inconsistency*) [25][27][28]. It behaves as an application's contexts conflicting with each other by violating physical laws or application-specific rules. The application's adaptation can thus be faulty, e.g., one adaptation cancels the effect of the other, or an unexpected adaptation occurs at a wrong time or a wrong place.

Context inconsistency detection is therefore receiving attention in recent years [12] [17][21][28]. While the detection is straightforward, how to effectively resolve detected context inconsistencies is non-trivial. The contexts involved in an inconsistency are called *inconsistent contexts*. Which of them actually caused this inconsistency is usually unknown. Various techniques have proposed formulating heuristic rules, do-

A. Puiatti et al. (Eds.): MobiQuitous 2011, LNICST 104, pp. 285–297, 2012.

main knowledge, or user intentions [1][4][13][25][26] to identify key contexts from these inconsistent ones. By removing these key contexts, an application is expected to no longer suffer from context inconsistency. However, existing practice largely overlooks every application's internal requirements on using these contexts for its adaptation. Directly removing these contexts may change an application's behavior unexpectedly, especially when these contexts are identified without knowing how they are to be used in this application. We call such unexpected consequences the *side effect* of context inconsistency resolution.

As an extreme example, an application may remove all accessible contexts to resolve inconsistency. This will definitely change this application's behavior drastically. Therefore, an intuitive idea is to minimize the loss of contexts during inconsistency resolution. However, simply reducing the number of removed contexts may not work as expected, since these removed contexts may play an important role in this application. Therefore, a reasonable idea is to minimize the side effect of context inconsistency resolution according to each application's individual specification.

Our later evaluation discloses that significant side effect (over 44.0%) can result from existing inconsistency resolution techniques, and this forms a practical challenge to effective context management for ubiquitous computing. In this paper, we are interested in understanding, measuring, and minimizing such side effect according each application's individual requirements, as well as addressing challenges in doing so.

The remainder of this paper is organized as follows. Section 2 presents a running example to illustrate the side effect of context inconsistency resolution, and introduces background knowledge. Section 3 proposes our side effect measurement framework. Section 4 explains the realization of our framework and its use for measuring the side effect of context inconsistency resolution. Section 5 compares the side effect of various inconsistency resolution strategies, and shows how our framework minimizes such side effect dynamically. Finally, Section 6 presents related work and Section 7 concludes this paper.

2   Context Inconsistency Resolution and Its Side Effect

2.1   Side Effect: A Running Example

Unlike fixing traditional inconsistency in UML models [8][18] or data structures [6], resolving context inconsistency changes contexts as well as an application's behavior due to its adaptation based on the changed contexts. Since such consequences are inevitable, then *what one should protect in context inconsistency resolution?* The answer would vary with the application nature.

Consider a stock tracking application [28], in which a forklift transports stock items from the loading bay of a warehouse to its storage bay. RFID technology (RFID stands for radio frequency identification) is used to track each transported item. For safety, a rule is set up to ensure the nonexistence of missing RFID reads: *Any item detected at the loading bay should be detected again later at the storage bay.* This rule helps guard the completeness of inventory records. Context inconsistency resolution, if having to change contexts, should *protect such rules from being violated.* Besides, if context inconsistency can be resolved by *removing irrelevant contexts*, e.g., other forklift's location contexts, that would be even preferred. This is because useful contexts (this forklift's RFID contexts) can be thus protected from being destroyed.

This example illustrates the importance of protecting *useful properties* (e.g., safety rules) and *useful contexts* (e.g., RFID contexts). Based on this, we argue two requirements for context inconsistency resolution in ubiquitous computing:

(1) Identify key contexts from inconsistent contexts such that after removing these key contexts, the remaining contexts are inconsistency-free.
(2) If there are multiple options fulfilling the first requirement, then select the one that protect useful properties and useful contexts as many as possible.

Existing inconsistency resolution techniques have focused on the first requirement. Since they already form such "multiple options", we focus on the second requirement in this work. We use *side effect* to model how these properties and contexts are affected by inconsistency resolution, and propose to minimize it at runtime along with inconsistency resolution. To facilitate our discussions, we brief background knowledge about context inconsistency resolution below.

2.2   Context Inconsistency Resolution Techniques and Strategies

Context inconsistency stems from several reasons. A major one is noisy data. For example, RFID read rate can drop to 60-70% in real-life deployment [14]; GPS errors are often tens of meters; for GSM cellphone network, field tests can result in errors of 187-287 meters [24]. People have proposed various filter and threshold techniques to smooth these noisy data [14], or measured them probabilistically with uncertainty levels [16]. Still, data-level techniques cannot completely prevent a ubiquitous computing application from suffering context inconsistency.

Context inconsistency may also come from the failure of synchronizing all contexts [22] or the absence of a global consistency of all environmental conditions [19]. Due to such complexity, context inconsistency is receiving growing attention in recent years. There are roughly three categories of existing work on addressing context inconsistency or inconsistent contexts.

One category takes an *application-specific* approach based on context type or application nature. For example, Deshpande et al. [7] proposed smoothing location contexts by interpolation techniques; Jeffery et al. [14] proposed adjusting sensing window size to retrieve missing RFID contexts. These pieces of work use geometry knowledge or probabilistic models to preprocess contexts, e.g., making location contexts form an expected curve or RFID contexts statistically follow a distribution. They are not generally applicable to other types of contexts or applications.

The second category targets at more applications by *heuristic rules*. These rules are formulated by domain experts or from empirical experiments. They suggest key contexts for removal in order to make resulting contexts inconsistency-free. Such rules can be conservative by removing all inconsistent contexts [1], or optimistic by denying the latest contexts in inconsistent ones from being accessible to applications [4]. The selection of such key contexts can also be random [4] or follow some criterion, e.g., minimizing the number of all removed contexts [26].

The third category follows user's *preferences or priorities*. They can be statically decided in advance [13][20][25], or calls for user's participation at runtime to best fit user's intentions dynamically [23].

While these techniques vary in their formulation and effectiveness, their consequences on resulting contexts are similar, behaving as some key contexts are removed and remaining ones are accessible to applications. Therefore, we classify these techniques according to their consequences on resulting contexts. Our classification includes the following four strategies that cover the aforementioned techniques (these four strategies are to be used in our later evaluation):

(1) ALL: Removing all inconsistent contexts;
(2) LATEST: Removing the latest context (a representative of those fixed criteria);
(3) RANDOM: Removing a random context (a representative of random criteria);
(4) FEWER: Minimizing the number of all removed contexts.

3   Side Effect Measurement Framework

Side effect measurement concerns how contexts are being used in an application in order to calculate how useful properties and contexts are affected. In the following, we first explain the concept of context, application specification, and side effect, and then present a framework to measure the side effect at runtime.

3.1   Context and Application Specification

In ubiquitous computing, new contexts characterizing environmental conditions keep emerging. Usually only a subset of recent contexts is accessible to applications. They are called *available contexts*.

Available contexts are used in an application according to this application's design logic. A large body of ubiquitous computing applications has their logics formulated by *adaptation rules*, which specify what to do under what conditions [11][20][22]. The set of such rules is called *application specification*. An application specification includes information about interesting contexts and the conditions under which adaptation should take place. They are important clues about useful contexts and properties concerned by this application.

Such rule-based applications are being widely used and supported by many context middleware or frameworks [20][25], and they are our focus in the paper.

3.2   Context Use and Side Effect

If available contexts are already inconsistency-free, they are safe for using by an application specification. The process of evaluating contexts according to an application specification is called *context evaluation*. For example, the aforementioned stock tracking application checks whether available contexts indicate the forklift has arrived at the storage bay so that it can unload transported items. This checking process is an example of context evaluation. Let available contexts be A, application specification be S, and context evaluation be $\otimes_E$. Fig. 1 abstracts this context use scenario.

Fig. 1. Context use in an application (*without* context inconsistency resolution)

Fig. 2. Context use in an application (*with* context inconsistency resolution)

If available contexts contain any inconsistency, then the inconsistency should be resolved. Fig. 2 illustrates how available contexts A are first processed for resolving inconsistency I. Then resolved contexts A' are used for context evaluation by application specification S. $\otimes_R$ represents the process of context inconsistency resolution.

We note that R in Fig. 1 and R' in Fig. 2 are two different context evaluation results. Their comparison discloses the side effect of context inconsistency resolution. As different resolution strategies correspond to different processes of context inconsistency resolution, n strategies can lead to n different evaluation results R_1, R_2, ..., R_n. Then the side effect can be measured by comparing these R_1, R_2, ..., R_n to a base value R_{base}. In practice, R_{base} can be set to R, which represents the context evaluation result without any inconsistency resolution. If one finally selects a resolution strategy k ($1 \le k \le n$) that *minimizes* the difference between R_k and R, it implies the effort of: (1) first resolving context inconsistency, and then (2) making the application behave as *similar* as no context inconsistency resolution occurred. This effort is reasonable and makes sense in most cases.

The comparison between R_k and R also concerns what metric to measure. It is decided by what one plans to protect in context inconsistency resolution. To protect useful contexts, the *number or types of contexts* that are referred to in evaluation result R_k can be calculated as the side effect metric for comparison. If an application specification also contains useful properties like safety rules, the *number of instances satisfying these properties* can also be calculated from R_k as the side effect metric.

3.3   Side Effect Measurement

Side effect measurement seems straightforward but actually not. The major issue is the complexity caused by multiple context evaluations. Given n resolution strategies to compare, context evaluation has to be conducted n times, with n *different* sets of resolved contexts A_k ($1 \le k \le n$). Fig. 3 (left) illustrates the whole picture, and the part in the dashed rectangle is what one has to complete in order to compare n evaluation results. This part has to be completed *efficiently* as it works at runtime.

We address this challenge using our incremental measurement idea. From Fig. 3 (left), n context evaluations differ only at n inputted sets of resolved contexts A_k ($1 \le k \le n$). These sets of resolved contexts come from the same available contexts A and same context inconsistencies I, but with a different resolution process $\otimes_{R_k}$ ($1 \le k \le n$). If one detects context inconsistency in short periods or incrementally [28], the number of context inconsistencies in each period would be a *small constant*. Then the n sets of resolved contexts A_1, A_2, ..., A_n would be similar to each other. This motivates us to share the computation across n context evaluations with little cost.

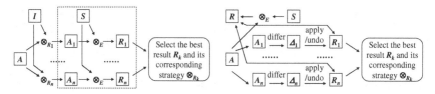

Fig. 3. Side effect measurement framework (left: direct; right: incremental)

We brief our incremental side effect measurement idea below for Fig. 3 (right):

(1) Conduct context evaluation on available contexts A and application specification S, and obtain result R for later reference.

(2) For each resolution process $\otimes_{R_k}$, calculate the difference Δ_k between resolved contexts A_k and available contexts A. Then apply Δ_k to reference result R to obtain updated result R_k.

(3) Undo Δ_k to restore R_k back to R.

(4) Repeat Steps (2)-(3) for all n resolution processes, and finally select the best one that minimizes the given side effect metric (subject to user's choice).

The novelty of this idea is that one does not have to conduct n *complete* context evaluations. Instead, one only needs to conduct it *once*, and later *update* it n times for different results. The benefits include reduced computation time (almost down to $1/n$ time) as well as reduced space cost (no need to store n intermediate evaluation results). However, the key to success is how one can *efficiently* update reference result R to obtain required result R_k and later restore it back to R. This concerns underlying data structures and operations, and we present one realization for them below.

4   Realization of the Framework

In this section, we discuss the realization of our incremental side effect measurement framework. We start with basic blocks of context, pattern, and rule in an application specification, and explain key data structures for supporting efficient context evaluation and its result update and restoration.

4.1   Context, Pattern, and Rule

Context. Context is represented as a tuple with multiple fields, each of which is a name-value pair. This is comparable to many pieces of existing work on context modeling [13][20][21] in order to be representative. For example, an RFID context can be represented as ((type, "RFID"), (subject, "tag 0327"), (predicate, "detected by"), (object, "reader a"), (time, "10:20:05am")).

Pattern. Pattern is used to select interesting contexts satisfying predefined conditions in this pattern. For example, pattern ((type, "RFID"), (subject, "tag 0327")) select all RFID contexts about tag 0327, i.e., this tag is being continually tracked by this pattern. When context c satisfies the conditions in pattern P, we say that c matches P, represented as $c \in P$.

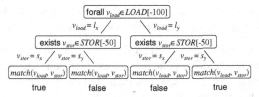

Fig. 4. Context evaluation tree for the safety rule in the stocking tracking application

Rule. A modeling language is used to specify rules in an application specification. It is based on first-order logic with timing constraints. Its expressive power is comparable to existing work on specifying adaptation rules [16][20][22][25]:

$f ::=$ forall $v \in P[t]$ (f) | exists $v \in P[t]$ (f) | (f) and (f) | (f) or (f) |
$\quad (f)$ implies (f) | not (f) | $bfunc(v, \ldots, v)$.

The above syntax follows their traditional first-order logic interpretations. $P[t]$ refers to a pattern P that selects contexts restricted by a period of t. Terminal $bfunc$ refers to any application-specific function that returns a Boolean value.

An application specification can contain multiple rules, each of which is constructed by recursively using the above syntax. For example, the following rule specifies the aforementioned safety rule in the stock tracking application:

forall $v_{load} \in LOAD[-100]$ (exists $v_{stor} \in STOR[-50]$ $(match(v_{load}, v_{stor})))$.

This rule specifies that each RFID context perceived at the loading bay (in the past 100s) should be able to find its matched RFID context at the storage bay later within a specified period (in the past 50s), implying the nonexistence of missing RFID reads.

4.2   Context Evaluation Tree

We use *context evaluation tree* (CET) to represent how context evaluation is conducted for a rule in the application specification. Each rule owns such a tree. By this tree, we can: (1) efficiently update it for a new context evaluation, and (2) measure the aforementioned side effect metrics for useful contexts and properties.

Suppose $LOAD[-100] = \{l_x, l_y\}$ and $STOR[-50] = \{s_x, s_y\}$. Then the CET of the safety rule can be constructed as Fig. 4 shows. The construction naturally follows the rule's syntactic hierarchy. From this CET, the *number of useful contexts* can be easily calculated (4), as a total of four contexts have participated in the context evaluation of this rule. Besides, the *number of instances satisfying the safety rule* can also be derived (2), as two pairs of contexts $((l_x, s_x)$ and $(l_y, s_y))$ satisfy the *match* function. We next explain how a CET can be efficiently updated for computation reuse (reuse for n context evaluations in comparing n resolution strategies).

4.3   CET Update

We first explain efficient construction of a CET. As a CET is based on available contexts A and application specification S, it can be seen as the result of applying a series of *context changes* (constituting A) to an empty CET (following a rule's syntactic hierarchy in S). These context changes include the following two types:

New Context. When a new context emerges from environment, a relevant CET can be *incrementally* updated to incorporate this context. For example, if $STOR[-50]$ has a new context s_z, then two "exists $v_{stor} \in STOR[-50]$" nodes should be attached with a new branch corresponding to this new context s_z as existing contexts s_x, s_y.

Expired Context. If a previous context expires due to its timing constraint, a relevant CET can also be *incrementally* updated to incorporate this change. For example, if $LOAD[-100]$'s previous context l_x expires, then the branch corresponding to context l_x (with three nodes) should be removed from the tree.

Therefore, the reference result R required in Step (1) of the side effect measurement framework can be efficiently calculated without reconstructing whole CETs when any context change occurs. For the side effect comparison in Steps (2)-(3), we note that R should also be efficiently updated to obtain R_k ($1 \le k \le n$) for n resolution strategies. This can be done by updating relevant CETs to incorporate the following two change types from resolution strategies:

Removed Context. When a resolution strategy needs to remove a context for resolving inconsistency in Step (2), we *temporarily* remove branches corresponding to this context from relevant CETs (similar to "expired context"). However, these branches are kept in a buffer. Later when the framework needs to undo this resolution strategy in Step (3), we restore these branches to their original places.

Added Context. We also support some rare resolution strategies that add new contexts to resolve inconsistency. This can be done by *temporarily* adding corresponding branches to relevant CETs (similar to "new context"). These branches are removed later to undo the effect of a resolution strategy.

Therefore, applying and undoing a resolution strategy can also be *incrementally* realized without reconstructing whole CETs.

4.4   Efficiency Analysis

Due to space limitation, we only brief our efficiency analysis results below. Let the height of a CET be h and its node number be d. We have:

(1) Handling a "new context"/"added context" change takes $O(h) - O(d)$ time;
(2) Handling an "expired context"/"removed context" change takes $O(h)$ time;
(3) Undoing an "added context"/"removed context" change takes $O(1)$ time.

In our side effect measurement framework, each resolution strategy takes a limited number of steps to resolve context inconsistency detected in small periods. Let the number be restricted by a constant l (usually 0.3-0.5 in our experiments). We have:

Step (2): Applying n resolution strategies takes $O(n \cdot l \cdot h) - O(n \cdot l \cdot d)$ time;
Step (3): Undoing n resolution strategies takes $O(n \cdot l \cdot h)$ time.

Consider that l is a small constant, h is fixed (also a constant), and almost all resolution strategies remove selected inconsistent contexts only (factor d can thus be removed). Then Steps (2) and (3) take $O(n)$ time, which implies that *the whole framework takes $O(1)$ time to measure the side effect for each resolution strategy* (Step (1) is incrementally conducted as explained and can be merged into later steps). This guarantees the framework to be *efficient* and *scalable* at runtime.

A buffer needs to be maintained for keeping temporarily removed branches, but at the same time, the same size of space is released from relevant CETs. Therefore, there is no extra space cost in addition to what is required by CETs themselves.

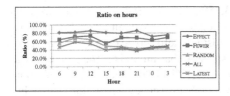

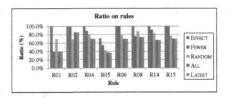

Fig. 5. Side effect comparison (hour-based)   **Fig. 6.** Side effect comparison (rule-based)

5   Experimentation

We use an open-source context simulator Siafu (http://siafusimulator. sourceforge.net/) to measure and compare the side effect of different context inconsistency resolution strategies. Siafu loads the data of a realistic town of Leimen in Germany. It ran for a continuous 24-hour day and generated a total of 288,000 contexts. These contexts contain a controlled error rate of 15% and were checked against 12 consistency constraints for inconsistency. The contexts and detected inconsistencies were used for our experiments.

To measure the side effect of context inconsistency resolution on ubiquitous applications, we studied Active Campus [9], Gaia [20][21], Socam [10], CARISMA [2], Egospaces [15], and Runes [5]. From them, we formulated 16 rules as the application specification for our experiments. The specification contains varying requirements of using contexts for adaptation. Its mixed nature helps alleviate possible bias caused by any single application.

The experiments were conducted on a machine with Intel Core 2 Duo 2.13GHz CPU and 1GB RAM. Software includes Windows XP Professional SP3 and Oracle/Sun JRE 1.6. The side effect is measured by the ratio between R_k and R on a metric that combines both the number of useful contexts and number of instances satisfying useful properties, with an equal weight for experimental purposes.

Fig. 5 compares the side effect of five resolution strategies based on different *hours* (starting at 6am). These strategies include FEWER, RANDOM, ALL, and LATEST discussed earlier in Section 2. A new strategy is EFFECT, which compares the above four strategies at runtime and always selects the one that minimizes the side effect (by highest ratios). From Fig. 5, all strategies caused side effect. RANDOM, ALL, and LATEST are most severe with a ratio of 38.0-68.8% (31.2-62.0% side effect). FEWER is better with a ratio of 55.8-73.5% (26.5-44.2% side effect). EFFECT's ratio is highest (72.1-85.7%), implying the least side effect (14.3-27.9%).

Fig. 6 compares the side effect based on different *rules*. Among 16 rules, eight of them (R01-02, R04-06, R08, R14-15) are affected by inconsistent contexts. RANDOM, ALL, and LATEST are most severe with a ratio of 36.6-85.5% (14.5-63.4% side effect). FEWER is better with a ratio of 40.0-100.0% (0.0-60.0% side effect). EFFECT's ratio is still highest (71.1-100.0%), meaning the best control on the side effect (0.0-28.9%).

On average, RANDOM, ALL, and LATEST have a ratio of 56.0%, 49.4%, and 48.5%, which shows *significant* side effect (over 44.0%) resulted from context inconsistency resolution. FEWER behaves better: 67.5% (32.5% side effect), which results from its nature that tries to minimize the number of all removed contexts in resolving inconsistency. This helps protect applications from losing useful contexts and properties to some degree. By dynamically selecting the strategy that minimizes the side effect at runtime, EFFECT improves the average ratio to 81.4% (18.6% side effect). We note that zero side effect may not be possible as inconsistency resolution inevitably changes contexts and an application's behavior. Still, EFFECT makes such attempt and controls context inconsistency resolution with the *least* side effect on applications.

We owe this ability to the framework's runtime efficiency and scalability (negligible experimental time: totally several seconds for all 24-hour contexts). Otherwise, it would have failed to measure and compare the side effect dynamically.

6   Related Work

Ubiquitous computing and context-awareness are receiving increasing attention. Various application frameworks [11][15] and middleware infrastructures [2][10][20][25] have been proposed to support the development of context-aware ubiquitous applications. These applications may be subject to context inconsistency at runtime, and therefore call for efforts to address context inconsistency.

People proposed various techniques to detect context inconsistency efficiently by reusing previous checking results [28], or asynchronously by identifying distributed inconsistency-triggering events that occur concurrently [12]. Detected context inconsistencies can be modeled or analyzed in different forms like application exceptions against normal work routines [17], or semantic conflicts when different terminologies or semantics are mixed [21].

Context inconsistency resolution work like [14][16] focuses on filtering raw contextual data probabilistically and marking remaining ones with uncertainty levels. While this gives useful hints on how likely they are correct, applications still face problems when selecting useful contexts from them without knowing possible consequences by doing so. Domain knowledge or user observations can be formulated as heuristic rules or user preferences [1][4][13][20][23][25][26], but they help little on this issue. As disclosed by our analysis and experimental results, these pieces of work suffer from *uncontrolled* side effect that impairs useful contexts and properties specific to certain applications.

A recent piece of work [3] proposed resolving context inconsistency based on application logics. This shares some observations as ours. However, this work assumes the availability of effect function for each action in an application, and requires error recovery plans to compensate what has been caused by context inconsistency.

Our work is based on our earlier efforts for context inconsistency detection [28] and manual resolution with fixed policies [25]. We later extended the work with heuristic rules to automatically resolve context inconsistency [26]. We identified negative consequences caused by context inconsistency resolution, and experimentally measured them for two applications [27]. Based on our earlier preliminary efforts, in this paper we formulated the side effect issue in context inconsistency resolution, and presented an efficient side effect measurement framework. Our incremental measurement technique enables *runtime* side effect calculation and comparison, allowing the selection of the best resolution strategy with the *least* side effect on applications.

7   Conclusion

The study in this paper measures the *significant side effect* caused by context inconsistency resolution on ubiquitous applications. It shows that side effect can be a *new criterion* for evaluating various inconsistency resolution techniques in addition to their original objectives. It can be further explored what is the most suitable base to which the side effect should be compared, and how the most suitable measurement metric can be selected. The answers should be application-specific. Our framework provides *a systematic way to measure such side effect*, as well as *an efficient realization* to compare different resolution strategies at runtime. This suits for applications whose requirements of using contexts are not static and can evolve dynamically (i.e., context-aware). We are now working on realistic experiments and automated context repair techniques towards better quality guarantee for ubiquitous applications.

Acknowledgments. This research was partially funded by National Science Foundation (grants 60736015, 61021062, 61100038) and 863 program (2011AA010103) of China. Chang Xu was also partially supported by Program for New Century Excellent Talents in University (NCET-10-0486).

References

[1] Bu, Y., Gu, T., Tao, X., Li, J., Chen, S., Lu, J.: Managing Quality of Context in Pervasive Computing. In: 6th Inter. Conf. on Quality Software, Beijing, China, pp. 193–200 (October 2006)

[2] Capra, L., Emmerich, W., Mascolo, C.: CARISMA: Context-aware Reflective Middleware System for Mobile Applications. IEEE Trans. on Software Engineering 29(10), 929–945 (2003)

[3] Chen, C., Ye, C., Jacobsen, H.: Hybrid Context Inconsistency Resolution for Context-aware Services. In: IEEE Inter. Conf. on Pervasive Computing and Communications, Seattle, Washington, USA, pp. 10–19 (March 2011)

[4] Chomicki, J., Lobo, J., Naqvi, S.: Conflict Resolution Using Logic Programming. IEEE Trans. on Knowledge and Data Engineering 15(1), 244–249 (2003)

[5] Costa, P., et al.: The RUNES Middleware for Networked Embedded Systems and Its Application in a Disaster Management Scenario. In: 5th Annual IEEE Inter. Conf. on Pervasive Computing and Communications, White Plains, NY, USA, pp. 69–78 (March 2007)

[6] Demsky, B., Rinard, M.C.: Goal-directed Reasoning for Specification-based Data Structure Repair. IEEE Trans. on Software Engineering 32(12), 931–951 (2006)

[7] Deshpande, A., Guestrin, C., Madden, S.R.: Using Probabilistic Models for Data Management in Acquisitional Environments. In: 2nd Biennial Conf. on Innovative Data Systems Research, Asilomar, California, USA, Article 26, pp. 1–13 (January 2005)

[8] Egyed, A.: Fixing Inconsistencies in UML Design Models. In: 29th Inter. Conf. on Software Engineering, Minneapolis, MN, USA, pp. 292–301 (May 2007)

[9] Griswold, W.G., Boyer, R., Brown, S.W., Tan, M.T.: A Component Architecture for an Extensible, Highly Integrated Context-aware Computing Infrastructure. In: 25th Inter. Conf. on Software Engineering, Portland, USA, pp. 363–372 (May 2003)

[10] Gu, T., Pung, H.K., Zhang, D.Q.: Toward an OSGi-based Infrastructure for Context-aware Applications. In: 2nd IEEE Inter. Conf. on Pervasive Computing and Communications, Orlando, Florida, USA, pp. 66–74 (March 2004)

[11] Henricksen, K., Indulska, J.: A Software Engineering Framework for Context-aware Pervasive Computing. In: 2nd IEEE Conf. on Pervasive Computing and Communications, Orlando, Florida, USA, pp. 77–86 (March 2004)

[12] Huang, Y., Ma, X., Cao, J., Tao, X., Lu, J.: Concurrent Event Detection for Asynchronous Consistency Checking of Pervasive Context. In: 7th Annual IEEE Inter. Conf. on Pervasive Computing and Communications, Galveston, Texas, USA, pp. 131–139 (March 2009)

[13] Insuk, P., Lee, D., Hyun, S.J.: A Dynamic Context-conflict Management Scheme for Group-aware Ubiquitous Computing Environments. In: 29th Annual Inter. Computer Software and Applications Conf., Edinburgh, UK, pp. 359–364 (July 2005)

[14] Jeffery, S.R., Garofalakis, M., Frankin, M.J.: Adaptive Cleaning for RFID Data Streams. In: 32nd Inter. Conf. on Very Large Data Bases, Seoul, Korea, pp. 163–174 (September 2006)

[15] Julien, C., Roman, G.C.: EgoSpaces: Facilitating Rapid Development of Context-aware Mobile Applications. IEEE Trans. on Software Engineering 32(5), 281–298 (2006)

[16] Khoussainova, N., Balazinska, M., Suciu, D.: Towards Correcting Input Data Errors Probabilistically Using Integrity Constraints. In: 5th Inter. ACM Workshop on Data Engineering for Wireless and Mobile Access, Chicago, Illinois, USA, pp. 43–50 (June 2006)

[17] Kulkarni, D., Tripathi, A.: A Framework for Programming Robust Context-aware Applications. IEEE Trans. on Software Engineering 36(2), 184–197 (2010)

[18] Nentwich, C., Emmerich, W., Finkelstein, A.: Consistency Management with Repair Actions. In: 25th Inter. Conf. on Software Engineering, Portland, USA, pp. 455–464 (May 2003)

[19] Rajamani, V., Julien, C.: Blurring Snapshots: Temporal Inference of Missing and Uncertain Data. In: 8th Annual IEEE Inter. Conf. on Pervasive Computing and Communications, Mannheim, Germany, pp. 40–50 (March-April 2010)

[20] Ranganathan, A., Campbell, R.H.: An Infrastructure for Context-awareness Based on First Order Logic. Personal and Ubiquitous Computing 7, 353–364 (2003)

[21] Ranganathan, A., Campbell, R.H., Ravi, A., Mahajan, A.: ConChat: A Context-aware Chat Program. IEEE Pervasive Computing 1(3), 51–57 (2002)

[22] Sama, M., Elbaum, S., Raimondi, F., Rosenblum, D.S., Wang, Z.: Context-aware Adaptive Applications: Fault Patterns and Their Automated Identification. IEEE Trans. on Software Engineering 36(5), 644–661 (2010)

[23] Shin, C., Dey, A.K., Woo, W.: Mixed-initiative Conflict Resolution for Context-aware Applications. In: 10th Inter. Conf. on Ubiquitous Computing, Seoul, Korea, pp. 262–271 (2008)

[24] Wu, Z.L., Li, C.H., Ng, J.K.Y., Leung, K.R.P.H.: Location Estimation via Support Vector Regression. IEEE Trans. on Mobile Computing 6(3), 311–321 (2007)
[25] Xu, C., Cheung, S.C.: Inconsistency Detection and Resolution for Context-aware Middleware Support. In: Joint 10th European Software Engineering Conf. and 13th ACM SIGSOFT Symp. on the Foundations of Software Engineering, Lisbon, Portugal, pp. 336–345 (September 2005)
[26] Xu, C., Cheung, S.C., Chan, W.K., Ye, C.: Heuristics-based Strategies for Resolving Context Inconsistencies in Pervasive Computing Applications. In: 28th Inter. Conf. on Distributed Computing Systems, Beijing, China, pp. 713–721 (June 2008)
[27] Xu, C., Cheung, S.C., Chan, W.K., Ye, C.: On Impact-oriented Automatic Resolution of Pervasive Context Inconsistency. In: 6th Joint Meeting of the European Software Engineering Conf. and the ACM SIGSOFT Symp. on the Foundations of Software Engineering, Dubrovnik, Croatia, pp. 569–572 (September 2007)
[28] Xu, C., Cheung, S.C., Chan, W.K., Ye, C.: Partial Constraint Checking for Context Consistency in Pervasive Computing. ACM Trans. on Software Engineering and Methodology 19(3), Article 9, 1–61 (2010)

Activity-Oriented Context Adaptation in Mobile Applications

Jan D.S. Wischweh and Dirk Bade

University of Hamburg
Hamburg, Germany
mail@wischweh.de, bade@informatik.uni-hamburg.de

Abstract. Although usability of mobile devices increases steadily, use of mobile applications is still inconvenient. Adapting application behavior and functionality to the user's current needs is a promising approach to compensate for limited input capabilities. Despite great effort in research, smart adaptable applications are still rare. With our approach, we build upon existing works and extend them with the notion of *activity context*. Activities are one of the most basic elements of context and are well suited to determine the relevance of context entities in a given situation. Such information can be used to realize more intelligent suggestion mechanisms for input elements in mobile applications. The feasibility of our approach has been proven by a prototype implementation of our *Activity Awareness Architecture* for the Android platform providing activity context for mobile applications and a context-aware calendar on top of it demonstrating the usefulness of activity context.

1 Introduction

Throughout the last decade, the use of mobile phones increased steadily. In particular, smartphones are gaining more and more interest [14] as these offer, beside a wide range of communication capabilities, a platform for a multitude of applications, ranging from entertainment to serious business appliances. Along with the growing market of mobile applications the need for user-friendly interaction attracts more attention, because users tend to get accustomed to accessing data and services whenever and wherever they are.

To ease interaction with mobile devices manufacturers increased screen sizes, made them touchable, and attached small sensors (accelerometers, gyroscopes, etc.). By doing so, the devices are enabled to exploit context to adapt application behavior to the current situation, e.g. adjust screen orientation, provide location-based services or filter ambient noise. Research in this area mainly focused on aspects about the physical environment (e.g. [12]), environmental conditions (e.g. [37]), available resources (e.g. [29]) and the user's social context (e.g. [28]) so far. Information about the user himself, his activities as well as causal and temporal relations between context entities are hardly exploited as a source for adaptation yet. Thereby, knowledge about the user's past, present and future activities is not only suited to ease input by presenting context-based suggestions, but may also

A. Puiatti et al. (Eds.): MobiQuitous 2011, LNICST 104, pp. 298–313, 2012.

be used to help automating recurring activities (i.e. tasks) to establish relations between people, places and objects and to infer the user's focus of attention and his cognitive load.

In this paper we propose to use *activity context*, which is inferred by monitoring the user's activities while he is interacting with a mobile device. This kind of context relates to goal-oriented tasks the user performs and is therefore ideally suited for adapting application behavior.

Section 2 of this paper details an application scenario and infers conceptual requirements for our work. Section 3 introduces the idea of activity context and relates it to context in general. In Section 4 a context model is proposed, which is used as a basis for our *Activity Awareness Architecture*, presented in Section 5. We conclude this paper by providing some details of the middleware and demo application we developed to show the feasibility of our approach in Section 6 and by giving our prospects for future work in Section 7.

2   Application Scenario

Alice and Bob want to conduct a meeting. For this purpose, Alice calls Bob to make an arrangement. Afterwards, she opens the calendar application on her mobile phone to create a new appointment. To ease the input the application makes suggestions for each of the input fields. Hence, Bob as well as other people related to Bob are suggested as participants. The calendar also suggests meeting locations like Bob's office or places Alice and Bob met before. This way, the need for textual input is reduced to two simple selections. Moreover, other applications, e.g. a navigation app, can make use of the provided information and once the time of the meeting approaches the navigation app, considering Alice's current location and the traffic situation, informs her right on time to prepare to leave.

2.1   Scenario Analysis

Usability can be seen as a measure of simplicity to reach a specific goal using certain technology [10]. Concerning software artifacts, it is undoubted that the usage context greatly influences the handling of applications and tools [10]. This holds even more, when considering mobile devices, as their usage context is highly dynamic. To overcome usability problems, an application should be able to adapt its functionality to the current context. Three areas of adaptation can be distinguished: adapting the (i) interaction, (ii) content and (iii) presentation [22]. In our approach, we do not propose adaptation mechanisms, but we want to provide application-level information about the user's (activity) context, so that applications can use this to carry out some adaptation logic. Analyzing the presented scenario, some important aspects that need to be considered when using activity context can be identified:

Temporal Relations. In addition to a user's current activity, also past and future activities are important context information. Past activities constitute the *persistent context* (e.g. places where Alice and Bob met before), whereas future activities are a result of *prediction*.

1ˢᵗ- and 2ⁿᵈ-order Relations. In the given scenario the calendar suggests Bob to be a participant based on the fact that Alice just phoned Bob. This is a 1ˢᵗ-order relation. The suggestion to meet at Bob's office is instead based on a 2ⁿᵈ-order relation. Theoretically, relations are not restricted to just two orders, but while the set of related entities grows exponentially with increasing order the relevance probability decreases drastically.

Restriction of Entity Types. For every application, only certain types of entities are relevant. The calendar app in the given example only deals with persons and locations linked with appointments. A navigation app is interested in locations only. The software in use therefore has to restrict the entities to consider based on their types.

Cooperation of Tools. The scenario shows, how different applications may cooperate using context information. The more applications create and use context information, the higher its value for further usage. The calendar app in the scenario makes use of three different context sources and represents a new context source for the navigation app. Thereby, it is not required that applications know each other, but they should instead be loosely coupled.

Bidirectional Flow of Information. As can be seen, the calendar app not only consumes, but also creates new context information which can be used by other applications (e.g. the navigation app). Therefore, the flow of information between applications, or applications and some mediating instance, needs to be bidirectional.

Now, that the idea of using information about a user's activities to adapt application behavior in order to enhance usability has been introduced, a formal view on activities is presented in the next section.

3   Foundations of Activity Context Adaptation

Schilit at al. coined the term *context aware computing* for mobile computer systems, that are able to automatically adapt themselves to the current situation [35]. Various examples for such adaptation exist [9,29,7,28]. The examples range from transparent adaptation to active context-aware behavior where the exploited aspects of the situation range from location to available resources and the social situation.

Because of this broad spectrum, context is quite an abstract term, thus multitude of definitions exist. An often cited definition by Dey and Abowd [11] states, that *"context is any information that can be used to characterize the situation of an entity. An entity is a person, place or object [...]"*. Several works (e.g. [7,25,17]) criticized this definition due its lack of behavioral factors, e.g. activities. Therefore, we follow a modification of Zimmermann et al. [43], stating that: *"[...] Elements for the description of this context information fall into five categories: individuality, activity, location, time, and relations."*. Activities are not seen as context entities, but rather represent relations between such entities [33]. These relations can be based on joint participation as well as temporal or spatial proximity and can be used to determine the relevancy of entities for a given context [13,15]. Moreover, [13] indicated that context and activities inevitably belong together as context is primarily created by activities.

In computer science different perspectives on *activities* exist. For example, *human engineering* experts observe and analyze human activities while handling software artifacts in order to understand and optimize their interactions [26]. In contrast, autonomous *software agents* pursue their own goals and in doing so execute plans and actions to reach them [5]. In the area of *user modeling* a formal, domain-dependent model of users, their goals and actions is created in order to adapt a system's behavior to the users' needs [22].

Our understanding of activities is based on the *activity theory* which tries to comprehend the course of activities by incorporating external influences as well as the actors themselves [23]. This scientific/philosophical way of thinking, stemming from the area of psychology, is based on several basic principles that allow us to establish an understanding about (i) the different ways to automatically monitor activities by a software system and (ii) what parts are out of the scope of monitoring. In the context of our work one of the most important principles in the activity theory is the object-orientation which states that objects always carry socio-cultural knowledge of what can be done with them and how it can be done. Another principle states that activities are mediated through physical and non-physical tools. For example, language influences the way we think about problems. Last but not least, activities are hierarchically composed of actions which in turn are composed of operations. A corresponding hierarchy of motives, goals and conditions exists linking behavioral levels with levels of purpose. Activities and motives are on the top level, they are conscious and long-lasting. Operations and conditions are at the bottom level. Like actions and goals they are short-term, but unlike them they are unconscious.

As activities are carried out over a longer period of time and are, depending on situations, alternated with other activities the activity theory leads us to the conclusion that it will not be possible to completely assess a user's activities and his motives can only be presumed indirectly at best. Furthermore, we can only observe user actions which are carried out using physical (software-)tools. But activity theory also provides us with a starting point for doing so, as in the light of this theory it seems practical to incorporate means for observing actions directly into the (software-)tools which are used to carry out tasks. This marks a difference to traditional approaches to context-awareness where context is often observed from an outside perspective using some kind of sensors. It also marks a difference to user modeling, as this approach strives to be domain-independent and tries to avoid speculation on a user's motives.

We will therefore present a context model for activity context which holds observable information about actions and afterwards a middleware architecture which interacts with arbitrary software tools to gather information, to infer

Table 1. Evaluation of Context Models [42]

	Key/Value	Markup	OO	Dataflow	Relational	Logic	Ontology
(C1) Lightweightness	++	+	/	−	−	−	−−
(C2) Access Efficiency	/	−	/	/	++	/	/
(C3) Aggregation Support	−−	−−	++	++	/	+	+
(C4) Management of Relations	−	−	/	−−	++	+	/
(C5) Natural Projection	−	−	++	−	+	/	+
(C6) Data Distribution	−	−	−	++	/	−	+
(C7) Unambiguousness	−	++	−	−	−	−	++
(C8) Quality Compensation	−−	−−	/	+	−	−	/
(C9) Inference of Facts	−−	−−	−−	−−	−−	++	++

higher-level activity context information and to provide this for applications as a basis to adapt their behavior to the user's current activity.

4   Context Models and Data Schemes

In literature the term *context model* is often used in different ways. Some authors understand a context model as the set of information, their representation as well as processing rules for a certain context-aware application or domain. For example, in an application which adapts to current weather conditions the fact that temperature is represented in degree Celsius, humidity as relative air humidity in percent as well as a rule that states at which thresholds the weather is considered muggy could make up a context model. Typically, authors who describe concrete context-aware systems [18] use the term in this way. Authors who seek to compare different approaches of modeling context [39,16] use the term context model to describe the generic underlying data structures and available operations. These different meanings correspond to the notions of a *database schema* and *data model* in the terminology of database systems.

Throughout this paper we will use the term context model in the latter sense as we understand a context model as a set of methods and formal languages used to create, represent and interpret a context data schema. We will use this understanding to evaluate several existing context models based on a set of requirements that are presented in the following.

4.1   Evaluation of Context Models

A multitude of context models can be found in literature (cp. surveys by Chen/Kotz [6], Strang/Linnhoff-Popien [39] and Hartman/Austaller [16]). Thereby, different categories of models can be distinguished: key/value models, models based upon markup-languages, graphical models, object-oriented models, logical models, ontology-based models and dataflow models.

All of these classes make use of different methods and methodologies in order to model context. For the purpose of modeling activity context we conducted a requirements analysis based on a set of application scenarios as well as a literature survey in order to evaluate existing models. In the following, a set of criteria is presented that need to be considered when it comes to implementing context awareness on modern smartphones, providing a basis for the following evaluation of context models.

(C1) The infrastructure for realizing a model shall pose as few and low requirements as possible on soft- and hardware. (C2) Access to data shall be efficient. (C3) To ease access to high-level context data for developers, mechanisms for aggregating high-level data from lower-level data are vital. (C4) The model shall allow to easily manage relations between context entities. (C5) Real world concepts shall be naturally projected onto a context model, whereat the mapping shall be simple, direct, immediate and comprehensible. Although not used in the scenarios we addressed, future context-aware systems will likely be distributed. Therefore, (C6) support for distribution of context data is required. (C7) The context data shall be unambiguously interpretable even in heterogeneous systems. (C8) Mechanisms for dealing with incomplete, contradictory or uncertain data should also be considered. And finally, (C9) the ability to infer new facts from acquired data or preexisting world knowledge is desirable.

A summary of the strengths and weaknesses of different models can be seen in Table 1. Simple models like key/value- or markup models are lightweight and relatively efficient, but they lack support for more sophisticated demands. Whereas more complex approaches like logic-based models or ontologies offer good support for reasoning and data distribution at the price of being more heavyweight. As activities are relational in nature (cf. Section 3) and access to a potential large quantity of historical data is required a relational model was chosen to model activity context data. However, the context architectures discussed in Section 5 augment this model with some dataflow-oriented mechanisms. Especially when it comes to terms of distributing data and data sources as well as aggregating them this approach is useful to compensate weaknesses of the relational model.

4.2   A Generic Context Data Schema for Activity Context

Activities are the core of our data schema and our concept has to provide means for representing activities, entities and their relationships. Due to the fact that activities always occur in time and space and can form indirect relationships through spatial or temporal relations such data must be represented in the schema (including information about future events). As our approach should not be limited to a certain domain, activities and entities are modeled in a generic and abstract sense. This results in an open schema, extensible for all kinds of activities, entities, relations and application domains.

A graphical representation of the developed context data schema in the *Context Modeling Language* (CML) [18] can be seen in Figure 1. Activities form direct relations to entities and carry information about the place and time in which they took place. Places are also modeled as entities. Activities are enhanced with meta-data about how the data was gathered (as reported by software tools, measured by sensors, inferred from existing knowledge, other indirect means, or planned to be executed in the future), so the quality and reliability of information can be judged. This is especially useful for dealing with future activities

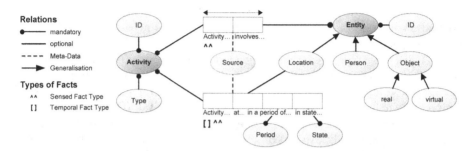

Fig. 1. Core Components of the Context Data Schema

as these are not certain to be carried out. Also, the lifecycle of an activity is modeled, whose abstract states are *ongoing, paused, successfully finished, unsuccessfully finished* or *finished with unknown result*. This information is crucial to infer the goals and needs of a user as a successful operation has other consequences for the goals of a user than an unsuccessful one. Now that we introduced the context data schema the next section will briefly survey existing middleware architectures for context awareness.

5   Architecture and Middleware for Context Awareness

Context data is relatively complex, the retrieval might be cumbersome and its management is not trivial. At the same time, a lot of applications could benefit from using context data and could even contribute context data. The latter is especially true for activity context. To address the difficulties in dealing with context data several approaches for developing middleware architectures for context awareness exist. The general goal of such software systems is to mediate context data between context sources and context consumers (i.e. applications). Typically, such systems are responsible for communicating with sensors, processing context data, supporting context-dependent decisions and for providing a communication infrastructure between the several components of a context-aware system [19].

By analyzing a set of application scenarios as well as existing literature, we found several requirements which apply to any middleware supporting context awareness for mobile devices. Ideally, the middleware should leverage a context model (R1) by being able to hold and manage instances of context data schemes. It should tolerate failures of components (R2), e.g. malfunction of sensors. A generic approach should be flexible and extensible (R3) and would benefit from a separation of basic facts and conclusions (R4) as this not only supports the flexibility, but also would make resources and inference processes more manageable. Compactness and suitability for limited hardware resources (R5), mechanisms for respecting privacy and security needs (R6) and for distributing the constituting components (R7) are other common desires.

Our perspective on activity context reveals additional requirements: In scenarios where activity context is used (cf. Section 2) context-aware applications not only consume context data, but the usage of software tools also directly provides context data. Therefore, the middleware should support activities (R8) by having direct means of reporting them. The more software tools use and provide activity context the greater the potential benefit for the user. As a consequence, such a middleware should be easy to use for application developers (R9). Looking at the scenario analysis presented in Section 2 and the context data schema developed in the previous section it becomes obvious that several traits of data and data structures need to be considered in the design of the middleware, such as: state and event-oriented data (R10.1), relational views (R10.2), time and sequence-oriented pattern analysis (R10.3) as well as hierarchical structures (R10.4). The support for temporal information should be taken into special consideration as there is a need to deal with events expected in the future (R11.1) as well as for recording time series to persist historical data (R11.2).

Besides the well known *Context Toolkit* [34], several other software architectures supporting context awareness have been presented (e.g. [41,19,24,2]). These can be grouped into *service-oriented, agent-oriented* as well as *object-oriented* approaches [42] and are briefly surveyed in the following.

Service-Oriented Approaches. Service-oriented approaches aim at simplifying the use of hardware and network infrastructures for context-aware systems by providing a set of services. Typical services are communication services [27,30,31], services for dealing with geodata and positioning information [27,30,31] and services for local aggregation and storage of context data [27,21,31]. For systems which are meant to be run in a dynamic, fully distributed ubiquitous computing scenario some means for service discovery are usually provided [27,31]. A lot of service-oriented approaches consider the challenges of mobile computing already in their design, several are targeted at smartphones which is why they often shine having a small footprint. The idea of building context-aware services by composing different services is somehow similar to the philosophy of the *Context Toolkit*. However, often these approaches are not based on an explicit context model and the different services lack unity. For instance, the *Context-Phone* platform is a service-oriented approach which provides services to monitor some aspects of user behavior (like messaging or telephony), but is not based on an explicit context model. To gather different kinds of context information, different services have to be queried [30].

Agent-Oriented Approaches. These kinds of approaches use autonomous, cooperative software agents to gather context information. Moreover, the agents are often able to exhibit context-adaptive behavior in order to achieve their goals. They often rely on well-defined context models based on ontologies, such as the *Web Ontology Language* [4], or custom extensions of them. Hence, most of these systems directly support reasoning and inference, but they do not necessarily support pattern detection and analysis. Examples for such approaches are the early work of Schilit [36], Spreitz and Theimer [38] or more recently the *Context Broker Architecture* by Chen et al. [8]. But, hence most existing systems are developed for ubiquitous computing rather than mobile computing they are rather heavy-weight.

Object-Oriented Approaches. In object-oriented approaches context entities are modeled as objects. A supporting middleware provides means for communication between objects, persisting and marshalling and most important observing them as well as notifying other components and entities upon any changes. Examples following this approach are the *Java Context Awareness Framework* [3] and the *DEMAC Context Service* [40]. Object-oriented approaches are very flexible and only make few restrictions. However, as they need to instantiate objects for all context entities they are not very efficient in large-scale scenarios. Moreover, they typically follow the principle of encapsulation and are therefore not well suited for reasoning about context entities, which involves some kind of data mining or pattern analysis. Finally, they can implement a context model, but are not necessarily based on one.

Two recent approaches to support context-aware systems deserve a more detailed explanation as some of their ideas influenced the design of our own middleware to a greater extend.

PACE Middleware. The *Pervasive Autonomic Context-Aware Environments* (PACE) Project [19] developed a middleware to support context data schemes based on a relational context model, along with a formal graphical *Context Modeling Language* (CML) [18] to develop them. The middleware incorporates context repositories holding instances of such data schemes and provides means for managing and discovering them. Repositories support the logging of historical data if needed. Additionally, repositories can be distributed and the middleware manages communication by supporting querying as well as notification mechanisms using content-based message relaying between the loosely coupled components.

Gaia OS. *Gaia OS* was developed as an operating system for context-aware ubiquitous computing applications [32]. It could be described as a service-oriented approach featuring five central services: (i) event management, (ii) context data storage, (iii) a service for detecting the presence of people, hardware, applications and other services, (iv) a service to access properties of such entities, and (v) a context file system. Unlike other service-oriented approaches it features an explicit, logic-based context model. In this model context is represented as four-digit predicate and this structure is closely linked to the mechanisms of the other services. How this works can be illustrated by the example of the *Context File System (CFS)* [20]. By storing a file in the directory /location:/RM2401/situation:/meeting it would be associated with the context "meeting in room RM2401". Listing the content of /situation:/meeting would list all files associated with meetings. Additionally, the special keyword current always expands to the current context. Gaia OS is a good example of leveraging a context model and integrating it with the mechanism of the framework while allowing transparent access by applications. Even applications not having implemented any kind of context awareness could benefit from the CFS and become context-aware (to some degree) without any further development work.

Table 2 gives an overview of our evaluation. Some approaches use activity context to some degree, but none supports generic activities. Furthermore, bidirectional communication between a context-aware application and the enabling middleware in a way that applications not only consume context data, but also provide data is missing in general (R8). Support for temporal information is also generally limited, but some approaches at least provide support for recording and querying historical data (R11.1). Others feature ad-hoc mechanism to query calendar data, but do so without a well-defined model and generic support for future events (R11.2).

Table 2. Evaluation of Architectures for Context Awareness [42]

	Context Toolkit	Service-oriented	Agent-oriented	Object-oriented	PACE	Gaia OS
(R1) Context model	key/value	–	ontology	(object-oriented)	relational	logic
(R2) Fault Tolerance	–	partial	partial	partial	partial	partial
(R3) Extensibility	√	partial	√	√	√	partial
(R4) Separation	√	√	√	√	√	√
(R5) Lightweight	partial	some	–	–	partial	partial
(R6) Privacy	–	some	√	some	√	–
(R7) Distribution	√	√	√	√	√	partial
(R8) Activities	–	–	–	–	–	–
(R9) Ease of Use	partial	partial	partial	partial	partial	partial
(R10) Range of Data Aspects	partial	partial	–	–	–	–
(R11) Temporal Information	partial	partial	partial	partial	partial	–

6 The Activity Awareness Architecture

As existing architectures of context-aware middleware systems do not meet all of the requirements to deal with activity context, we will present our *Activity Awareness Architecture* and describe some of the most important architectural and functional aspects as well as an example for the Android platform.

Support for Activities. To support observing and reporting ongoing activities, the middleware is based on a minimalistic model of activities (cf. Section 4.2). The middleware offers a simple application programming interface (API) to create activities, report lifecycle state changes and assign related entities to them. Such API-calls will automatically trigger the creation and dispatching of events which will inform other endpoints of the system about the ongoing activity.

Modularisation. The basic building blocks of our middleware are loosely coupled modules of two types: *EventSources* generating events and queryable *Repositories* with mixtures of them being possible. An example for an event source would be a sensor which monitors outgoing and incoming phone calls and reports them using the *Activity API*. Repositories are active data containers that are able to process and store data. Multiple repositories may coexist for different tasks or domains. They acquire data by listening for events or querying other sources and are also able to actively engage in event processing by conducting e.g. pattern analysis or infer high-level context from primitive events. To retrieve information afterwards repositories expose simple id-based interfaces for queries, offer path-based interfaces for hierarchical data or SQL-based interfaces for relational data. One example for such a repository is our central module which holds an instance of the context data schema (cf. Section 4.2). Another example is a repository which listens for ongoing activities and provides heuristic-based conclusions which entities are currently relevant for the user.

Communication Infrastructure. The Activity Awareness Architecture uses an event-based publish/ subscribe mechanism as a basic communication infrastructure [1]. Modules and applications declare in which kind of events they are interested by specifying *Filters*. Filters can be based on event types, entity types, ids associated with events or a combination thereof. These filters are registered and managed by our middleware which uses them as a basis for content-based relaying of events. This structure allows for a loose coupling of modules and enables horizontal or vertical data fragmentation which is the basis for distribution later on.

Entities and Context-Dependent, Dynamic Naming Schemes. A special kind of query which repositories may support are context-aware dynamic path-based queries. Assuming that each entity can be identified by its type and its id, it is possible to use a simple path syntax like `/Person/id/5` to query for a certain person or `/Person/id/5/related/Place` to query all places related with the given person. Much like the *Context File System* (cf. Section 5) an entity or a list of entities can be addressed using such dynamic context-based path schemes. But unlike the CFS this mechanism is not limited to files, but can be used for all kinds of entities. The possibility to resolve such path-schemes by using multiple repositories and not being bound to a single central repository is an even more important difference.

Support for Historical Data and Future Events. To deal with future events, like planned activities derived from calendar entries, our event system supports special kinds of events. *InstantEvents* are events taking place at the time they are dispatched and are exactly what traditional events are like. *ScheduledEvents* wrap other events and indicate that something is expected to happen in the future. As future events are not certain to happen they can hold additional meta-information to deal with this uncertainty. If a future event is canceled, for instance because a user deletes a calendar entry, this can be indicated by broadcasting a `CanceledEvent`. In order to query future as well as past events, special *TimelineRepositories* are used. Such repositories hold timelines for events which are managed on the basis of *InstantEvents*, *ScheduledEvents* and *CanceledEvents*. Other modules may not only query, but can also register themselves to be notified some time before future events occur.

6.1 Implementation of a Context-Aware Calendar

We developed a basic implementation of the middleware and a context-aware calendar application for the *Android* platform to prove the feasibility. One of the main reasons for choosing Android, was its application framework, allowing to develop complex applications as a set of specialized, loosely coupled screens. As this concept is close to our understanding of activities it can be easily exploited to monitor the user's activities by injecting proxies between these modules which record what is going on. A similar mechanism can also be used to monitor phone calls.

The different middleware components that enable our context-aware calendar and the data flow between these are depicted in Figure 2. A call sensor monitors incoming and outgoing calls and reports them along with information about the participants using our Activity API. A location sensor monitors the user's whereabouts, tries to translate the position into symbolic location data and creates a `LocationEvent`. All this data is gathered in the *ActivityRepository* which implements the data schema for activity context (cf. Section 4.2). The ActivityRepository in turn is monitored by the *RelevanceRepository* which uses a simple heuristic to estimate which entities are relevant for the user in the near future. The heuristic is based upon the frequency of engaging entities, 1st- and 2nd-order relations between entities, and the temporal proximity of activities in which these entities take part. It is implemented using a bayesian network.

To further ease the use of the Activity Awareness Architecture we developed a generic GUI widget which suggests relevant entities depending on the current context. A path schema can be used as parameter to specify what kind of suggestion should be made. In our demo application we used it to suggest people and places for a calendar entry. Once a calendar entry is created our application will report this using the Activity API. A screenshot of the GUI and the GUI

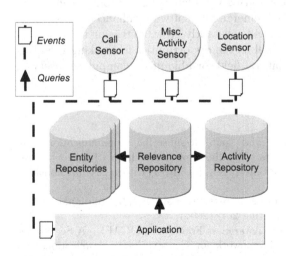

Fig. 2. Middleware Modules and Data Flow   **Fig. 3.** Context-based Calendar App

widget suggesting people to assign with the entry (red bounding box) can be seen in Figure 3.

7   Conclusion

Activities are one of the most basic elements of context and represent goal-directed actions of a user. They are well suited to determine the relevance of context entities in a given situation by establishing relations between them which in turn can be used by applications to adapt their behavior to the user's current needs. In order to do so, a well-defined activity context model as well as a mediating middleware is required. In this paper, we therefore conducted an extensive requirements analysis, evaluated several existing context models and context awareness middleware architectures and concluded that none of the existing approaches is suited for dealing with activity context. Because of this, we presented a generic, domain-independent context data schema which is able to represent activities, the entities taking part as well as relations between these entities. Based upon this data schema, we introduced the *Activity Awareness Architecture*, a middleware for mediating activity context between context sources and context consumers and demonstrated the feasibility of our concepts by presenting an activity-aware calendar application for the Android platform.

As the idea of using activity context in mobile applications is relatively new our prospects for future work include a qualitative evaluation of our heuristic for suggesting related entities in a given context, an analysis in what way our middleware can help to conduct studies about user behavior, to what extent complex event processing techniques can be used to realize notifications about future-directed complex activities and how the activity context data can be distributed among several devices, thereby obeying privacy and security considerations.

In a future where ubiquitous computing will increasingly become reality more and more tools of our daily life will emerge into software-enhanced tools. Thus, the basis for sensing user activities will constantly grow, increasing the potential knowledge of activity context as well as the opportunities for making use of it. Therefore, activity context is a natural field for ubiquitous computing research.

References

1. Aitenbichler, E.: Event-based and publish/subscribe communication. In: Mühlhauser, M., Gurevych, I. (eds.) Handbook of Research on Ubiquitous Computing Technology for Real Time Enterprises, pp. 152–171. Idea Group Publishing (December 2007)
2. Baldauf, M., Dustdar, S.: A survey on context-aware systems. International Journal of Ad Hoc and Ubiquitous Computing 2(4) (2004)
3. Bardram, J.E.: The Java Context Awareness Framework (JCAF) – A Service Infrastructure and Programming Framework for Context-Aware Applications. In: Gellersen, H.-W., Want, R., Schmidt, A. (eds.) PERVASIVE 2005. LNCS, vol. 3468, pp. 98–115. Springer, Heidelberg (2005)

4. Bechhofer, S., van Harmelen, F., Hendler, J., Horrocks, I., McGuinness, D.L., Patel-Schneider, P.F., Stein, L.A.: Owl reference. W3C Recommendation (February 2004) (visited February 5, 2009)
5. Braubach, L.: Architekturen und Methoden zur Entwicklung verteilter agentenorientierter Softwaresysteme. PhD thesis, University of Hamburg (2007)
6. Chen, G., Kotz, D.: A survey of context-aware mobile computing research. Technical Report TR2000-381 (2000)
7. Chen, H.: An Intelligent Broker Architecture for Pervasive Context-Aware Systems. PhD thesis, University of Maryland, Baltimore County (December 2004)
8. Chen, H., Finin, T., Joshi, A.: Using owl in a pervasive computing broker. In: Proceedings of the Workshop on Ontologies in Agent Systems (OAS) (July 2003)
9. Cheverst, K., Mitchell, K., Davies, N.: Design of an object model for a context sensitive tourist guide. Computers and Graphics 23, 24–25 (1999)
10. Coursaris, C.K., Kim, D.J.: A qualitative review of empirical mobile usability studies. In: Proceedings of the Twelfth American Conference on Information Systems, AMCIS (2006)
11. Abowd, G.D., Dey, A.K., Brown, P.J., Davies, N., Smith, M., Steggles, P.: Towards a Better Understanding of Context and Context-Awareness. In: Gellersen, H.-W. (ed.) HUC 1999. LNCS, vol. 1707, pp. 304–307. Springer, Heidelberg (1999)
12. Dix, A., Rodden, T., Davies, N., Trevor, J., Friday, A., Palfreyman, K.: Exploiting space and location as a design framework for interactive mobile systems. ACM Trans. Comput.-Hum. Interact. 7(3), 285–321 (2000)
13. Dourish, P.: What we talk about when we talk about context. Personal and Ubi-Comp 8(1), 19–30 (2004)
14. Gartner, Inc. Market Share: Mobile Communication Devices by Region and Country 2Q11 (August 2011), http://www.gartner.com/it/page.jsp?id=1764714 (visited: August 11, 2011)
15. Greene, S., Finnegan, J.: Usability of mobile devices and intelligently adapting to a user's needs. In: Proceedings of the 1st International Symposium on Information and Communication Technologies, pp. 175–180. Trinity College Dublin, Dublin (2003)
16. Hartmann, M., Austaller, G.: Context models and context awareness. In: Mühlhauser, M., Gurevych, I. (eds.) Handbook of Research on Ubiquitous Computing Technology for Real Time Enterprises, pp. 235–256. Idea Group Publishing (December 2007)
17. Henricksen, K.: A framework for context-aware pervasive computing applications. PhD thesis, University of Queensland (September 2003)
18. Henricksen, K., Indulska, J.: Developing context-aware pervasive computing applications: models and approach. Journal of Pervasive and Mobile Computing 2(1), 37–64 (2005)
19. Henricksen, K., Indulska, J., McFadden, T., Balasubramaniam, S.: Middleware for Distributed Context-Aware Systems. In: Meersman, R. (ed.) OTM 2005, Part I. LNCS, vol. 3760, pp. 846–863. Springer, Heidelberg (2005)
20. Hess, C.K., Campbell, R.H.: A context file system for ubiquitous computing environments. Technical Report UIUCDCS-R-2002-2285 UILU-ENG-2002-1729, Department of Computer Science, University of illinois, Urbana, Illinois (July 2002)
21. Hofer, T., Schwinger, W., Pichler, M., Leonhartsberger, G., Altmann, J., Retschitzegger, W.: Context-awareness on mobile devices - the hydrogen approach. In: Proc. of the 36th Annual Hawaii Int. Conf. on System Sciences (HICSS 2003), p. 292.1. IEEE Computer Society (2003)

22. Jöst, M.: Adapting to the user. In: Mühlhauser, M., Gurevych, I. (eds.) Handbook of Research on Ubiquitous Computing Technology for Real Time Enterprises, pp. 282–295. Idea Group Publishing (December 2007)

23. Kaenampornpan, M., Ay, B.B.: An integrated context model: Bringing activity to context. In: Workshop on Advanced Context Modelling, Reasoning and Management, UbiComp 2004 (2004)

24. Kjær, K.E.: A survey of context-aware middleware. In: Proceedings of the 25th Conference on IASTED International Multi-Conference: Software Engineering, pp. 148–155. ACTA Press, Innsbruck (2007)

25. Kofod-Petersen, A., Cassens, J.: Using Activity Theory to Model Context Awareness. In: Roth-Berghofer, T.R., Schulz, S., Leake, D.B. (eds.) MRC 2005. LNCS (LNAI), vol. 3946, pp. 1–17. Springer, Heidelberg (2006)

26. Kuutti, K.: Activity theory as a potential framework for human-computer interaction research. In: Context and Consciousness: Activity Theory and Human-Computer Interaction, pp. 17–44. MIT Press (1996)

27. Lei, H., Sow, D.M., Davis II, J.S., Banavar, G., Ebling, M.R.: The design and applications of a context service. SIGMOBILE Mob. Comput. Commun. Rev. 6(4), 45–55 (2002)

28. Oulasvirta, A., Raento, M., Tiitta, S.: Contextcontacts: re-designing smartphone's contact book to support mobile awareness and collaboration, pp. 167–174. IEEE Photon. Technol. Lett., Portal (2005)

29. Pham, T.-L., Schneider, G., Goose, S., Pizano, A.: Composite device computing environment: A framework for situated interaction using small screen devices. Personal UbiComp 5, 25–28 (2001)

30. Raento, M., Oulasvirta, A., Petit, R., Toivonen, H.: Contextphone: A prototyping platform for context-aware mobile applications. IEEE Pervasive Computing 4(2), 51–59 (2005)

31. Riekki, J., Davidyuk, O., Forstadius, J., Sun, J., Sauvola, J.: Enabling context-aware services for mobile users. In: Proceedings of IADIS Virtual Multi Conference on Computer Science and Information Systems, pp. 360–369 (April 2005)

32. Román, M., Hess, C., Cerqueira, R., Campbell, R.H., Nahrstedt, K.: Gaia: A middleware infrastructure to enable active spaces. IEEE Pervasive Computing 1, 74–83 (2002)

33. Ryan, C., Gonsalves, A.: The effect of context and application type on mobile usability: an empirical study. In: Proceedings of the Twenty-Eighth Australasian Conference on Computer Science, vol. 38, pp. 115–124. Australian Computer Society, Inc., Newcastle (2005)

34. Salber, D., Dey, A.K., Abowd, G.D.: The context toolkit: aiding the development of context-enabled applications. In: Proceedings of the SIGCHI Conference on Human Factors in Computing Systems: The CHI is the Limit, pp. 434–441. ACM, Pittsburgh (1999)

35. Schilit, B.N., Adams, N., Want, R.: Context-aware computing applications. In: Proceedings of the Workshop on Mobile Computing Systems and Applications, pp. 85–90 (1994)

36. Schilit, W.N.: A System Architecture for Context-aware Mobile Computing. PhD thesis, Columbia University (1995)

37. Schmidt, A.: Implicit human computer interaction through context. Personal and Ubiquitous Computing 4(2), 191–199 (2000)

38. Spreitzer, M., Theimer, M.: Providing location information in a ubiquitous computing environment (panel session). SIGOPS Oper. Syst. Rev. 27(5), 270–283 (1993)

39. Strang, T., Linnhoff-Popien, C.: A context modeling survey. In: Workshop on Advanced Context Modelling, Reasoning and Management, UbiComp 2004 - The Sixth International Conference on Ubiquitous Computing, Nottingham/England (2004)
40. Turjalei, M.: Integration von Context-Awareness in eine Middleware für mobile Systeme. Diplomarbeit, University of Hamburg (June 2006)
41. Winograd, T.: Architectures for context. Hum.-Comput. Interact. 16(2), 401–419 (2001)
42. Wischweh, J.D.S.: Aktivitätsorientierte Kontextadaption in mobilen Anwendungen. Master's thesis, University of Hamburg (July 2009)
43. Zimmermann, A., Lorenz, A., Oppermann, R.: An Operational Definition of Context. In: Kokinov, B., Richardson, D.C., Roth-Berghofer, T.R., Vieu, L. (eds.) CONTEXT 2007. LNCS (LNAI), vol. 4635, pp. 558–571. Springer, Heidelberg (2007)

PINtext: A Framework for Secure Communication Based on Context

Stephan Sigg[1], Dominik Schuermann[2], and Yusheng Ji[1]

[1] National Institute of Informatics, Tokyo, Japan
{sigg,kei}@nii.ac.jp
[2] TU Braunschweig, Braunschweig, Germany
d.schuermann@tu-braunschweig.de

Abstract. We propose a framework for secure device-pairing based on contextual information. In contrast to related work, we utilise fuzzy cryptography schemes to establish a common secret among devices and to account for noise in the contextual features. The framework is implemented for ambient audio and its feasibility is demonstrated in a case study. Additionally, we discuss properties of fingerprints from ambient audio and estimate the entropy of fingerprints in statistical tests.

1 Introduction

With the increased penetration by mobile devices in recent years, security threats and security requirements similarly have multiplied. This orchestration of distinct threats, however, is vague to mobile users. In addition to this, security mechanisms are often perceived as a hassle since they are not unobtrusive and might distract from high-level tasks. Pin, smartcard and password-based schemes are perceived as annoying so that users may even consider to switch off security mechanisms on their device [23]. The requirement that passwords shall be frequently changed, increases the perceived complexity of these systems further. Contemporary mobile communication technologies such as Bluetooth [5] or Near Field Communication (NFC) [17] address this problem differently. While Bluetooth increases the effort of the user, requiring a PIN for device pairing, NFC omits security precautions and rely on the restricted communication range solely.

Is it feasible to provide security that is less obtrusive or even unobtrusive?

In this paper we propose a device-pairing paradigm that is capable of providing unobtrusive security means based on environmental contexts. In particular, mobile devices are equipped with a multitude of sensors that provide them with environmental stimuli such as audio, light, RF temperature or proximity. this data can be exploited in order to derive a classification of a given contextual configuration.

Contextual data is in some respect similar to biometric data. However, in contrast to contextual data, for the use in cryptographic applications, biometric data has some unfavourable properties as detailed in [29].

A. Puiatti et al. (Eds.): MobiQuitous 2011, LNICST 104, pp. 314–325, 2012.

The amount of biometric information is limited: Only   a   restricted
amount of different biometric samples is available.

Biometric data can be stolen: It is generally desired, that biometric information is easily retrieved and verified. On the contrary, biometric information shall be hard to obtain by third parties. This contradiction is frequently
solved in favour of the former requirement. Consequently, as pictures from
a face are easily taken, fingerprints are spread unnoticed and high-quality
photographs of an Iris are feasible from greater distance, the security means
provided by biometric data can be broken by a determined adversary.

Biometric data does not change significantly: In order to increase the
burden for an adversary to break a security system, it is beneficial to periodically change the secret utilised. Since Biometric data never changes
significantly, the seed for cryptographic methods is of limited variability.

We propose to use context as an implicit mechanism to establish a basic level of
security that adapts to current situations. In particular, context information can
be utilised as common secret among devices in the same situation. Observe that
this concept of security is similar to our natural perception of trust. Frequently,
we have an increased level of trust with people that share our context [6]. Classical security mechanism then need only be inferred when activities with higher
security demands are issued.

Despite these benefits, there are also some challenges and concerns that have
to be addressed when contextual information is utilised as the basis of security
means. Similar to biometric information, context data can be considered as noisy
source. This is a hurdle that has to be overcome but it is no principal problem
since it can be addressed by appropriate error correction methods similar to those
utilised for noisy biometric information [29]. Another challenge is to establish a
sufficiently diverse description of context so that the chance of an adversary to
obtain information on this description is low. In particular, the representation
utilised must have a high entropy.

In this work we present a framework for non-interactive, ad-hoc secure communication based on contextual data. The framework will be exemplified for
ambient audio. In a case study, we demonstrate the general feasibility of the
approach and discuss the entropy of secure keys generated from ambient audio.

Unobtrusive security mechanisms enable the implementation of a constant security aura surrounding mobile device. This will increase the burden an attacker
has to overcome.

In section 2, the related work on context-based authentication and security
mechanisms is detailed. Afterwards, in section 3, we propose a framework to
establish security means based on contextual information on a set of devices. The
framework is then exemplary applied for ambient audio. Section 4.1 describes
the generation of audio-fingerprints and discusses their suitability as a seed for
a common secret. In section 4.2, we study the entropy of audio-fingerprints and
show that it is sufficiently high. Section 4.3 details a case study we conducted
to show the feasibility in realistic settings. In Section 5 we draw our conclusion.

2   Related Work

In recent years, increasing interest is expressed in security of mobile devices [24]. The National Institute for Standards and Technology (NIST) summarises many of these considerations regarding device classes, threats and countermeasures in [12]. According to this discussion, generally the threats for mobile devices are comparable to those for stationary computers with additional issues related to the smaller size, the wireless interface and the mobile services provided. The authors also hint that mobile users seldom employ security mechanisms or apply them in a convenient but insecure way as, for instance, by using passwords that are easy to guess. The reason for this behaviour pattern is a general laziness of the mobile user as derived by Nehmadi et al. [23].

Basic requirements of data privacy on mobile phones have been derived by Karlson et al. [13]. Building on these results, De Luca et al. [24] discuss the establishing of context-specific proximity-related security-spheres. In this work, users define which data is accessible in which sphere. The traversal between spheres is established by locations and actions. A work on a context-adaptive mobile device was presented in [25]. The authors present a mechanism for mobile phones to adapt the ringtone volume, vibration and alerts to the current context.

Recently, several authors utilised context as a seed for authentication or the creation of secure keys [22]. Holmquist et al. are probably the first to mention context to establish security [11]. They propose to use context proximity for selective artefact communication. This was later picked up by Gellersen et al. for using identical hand gestures to unlock a credit card [7]. Mayrhofer et al. propose two protocols for secure authentication that utilise accelerometer data in devices which are shaken together [20,21]. In the ShaVe protocol, this information is utilised to verify a Diffie-Hellman key agreement [4]. The ShaCK protocol utilises the extracted feature vectors directly to generate a cryptographic key without further communication between the devices. For sufficient entropy in the generated feature vectors that are utilised as a basis to the key generation, the devices have to be shaken together for a sufficiently long time [19]. This Candidate Key Protocol generates feature sets with identical hash values at both devices and concatenates them to a shared secret key. A similar protocol that utilises rudimentary error correction of binary keys created by shaking processes is introduced by Bichler et al. [1]. They report a false negative rate of more than 11 percent for this approach and for features extracted from accelerometer data [2].

Another popular sensor utilised for authentication is the RF-transceiver. In particular, since the communication channel between two devices is sharply concentrated in time and space but at one time instant unambiguous between two communicating devices [28], authors have utilised the channel impulse response for secret device-pairing [10,16,9]. Although the channel impulse response utilised in these approaches can be considered as a strong cryptographic seed, the approach does not solve the problem of authentication and Man-In-the-Middle attacks. However, some authors have also demonstrated that it is possible to utilise channel information for proximity-restricted protocols [30]. Recently, it

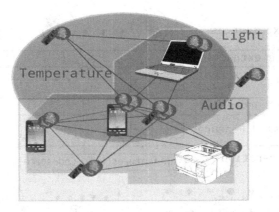

Fig. 1. Illustration of the context-based secure communication scheme with three context classes

was shown that proximity information can accurately be extracted based on recordings of ambient audio. Kunze et al., for instance, demonstrate that the location of a mobile device can be derived by sampling the audio response of its vibration sensor [15]. A discussion on research challenges and opportunities originating from utilising context information for device pairing is found in [26].

Our present work is most related to the work on spontaneous device interaction presented by Mayrhofer et al. in [22,20,21] since we also also propose to utilise context for the creation of a common secret. However, the protocol we describe for our framework is less obtrusive and can even be unobtrusive. The general idea is similar to the approach presented by Bichler et al. but we rely on error correcting codes instead [1]. Very recently, Mathur et al. utilised a similar approach on amplitude and phase data extracted from an RF-channel [18]. Regarding the discussion of the entropy of ambient audio, we recently discussed in [27] the estimation of entropy for contextual information. Similar discussions can be found in [1,22].

3 A Framework for Unobtrusive and Less Obtrusive Secure Device Communication

In this section we propose a framework to establish a secure communication channel based on common but arbitrary contextual information. As depicted in figure 1, we assume that two or more devices which share the same context utilise this information to unobtrusively establish a common secret.

Based on this secret, devices can be paired or a secure communication channel can be established. A device that is not in the same context, however, shall be unlikely able to share the secret. The figure shows devices in three context classes temperature, light and audio. Devices in the same context regarding one or more of these classes are able to utilise contextual information to establish a common secret. For instance, the two mobile phones are in the same audio context and

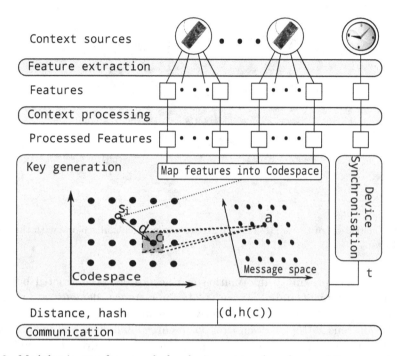

Fig. 2. Modules in our framework for device-pairing based on arbitrary contextual information

are therefore able to establish a secure communication based on this information. The laptop computer is in another audio context and not able to overhear the encrypted communication. It could, however, establish a common secret based on ambient light with the mobile phones. However, in this case, most other devices in the proximity would share the context and therefore the secret.

Establishing of the secure channel can be unobtrusive and non-interactive since it is purely based on the context observed. In order to enable such a communication scheme, features from the context source must be extracted and transformed into a sequence that is sufficiently similar on all devices in the same context but at the same time significantly different for all devices in a different context. This sequence is then utilised as a seed to generate a common secret. For this last step, since features will likely differ slightly also for identical contexts, error correction mechanisms have to be applied.

In the following, we detail general modules that constitute a framework for context-based device authentication. The models are illustrated in figure 2.

Device synchronisation. Due to the frequent fluctuation of context, feature values taken at distinct time will likely not be sufficiently similar to establish a common secret among devices. A synchronisation among devices is required. This module establishes sufficient synchronisation among devices dependent on the accuracy required by the features utilised.

Feature extraction. Any common feature extraction method can be applied. It is important, that the representation of the features is significantly diverse so that it is infeasible for an adversary to test all possible cases in sufficient time.

Context processing. Processing modules such as noise removal, smoothing of features or aggregation can be applied after feature extraction.

Key generation. We expect that the feature vector generated is noisy so that the vectors differ for distinct devices. Therefore, error correction has to be applied in order to achieve a common secret. For this error correction we propose a fuzzy cryptography scheme as described in the following (cf. the corresponding module in figure 2).

For devices i, j and feature representations s_i, s_j from a space $\mathcal{S}$, we utilise error correcting codes to disregard the bias between s_i and s_j. We assume that features are acquired by device i and device j in a sufficiently synchronised manner. We distinguish between a code space $\mathcal{C}$ and a message space $\mathcal{A}$. The message space contains clearly separated messages $a \in \mathcal{A}$. The codespace contains codewords $c \in \mathcal{C}$ that are unambiguously mapped onto the messages $\mathcal{A}$ but additionally contain redundancy. Due to this redundancy, the codespace is sparsely populated with codewords and Δ defines the minimum distance (e.g. Hamming distance) between any two codewords $c, c' \in \mathcal{C}$. In the case that a codeword becomes biased, it is generally possible to correct up to $\lfloor \frac{\Delta}{2} \rfloor$ errors so that the mapping between $\mathcal{A}$ and $\mathcal{C}$ is surjective. The procedure to obtain a common secret is the following.

After extracting feature vectors, these vectors are mapped onto representations in $\mathcal{S}$. The sequences are not necessarily identical to any code word $c \in \mathcal{C}$. We require, however, that $\mathcal{C} \subseteq \mathcal{S}$ and define a distance metric $m : \mathcal{S} \times \mathcal{S} \to \mathbb{R}$. For device i we choose a $c_i \in \mathcal{C}$ randomly and calculate the distance $d = m(s_i, c_i)$ between codeword and context representation on device i. Additionally, the hash of the codeword $(h(c_i))$ can be calculated to allow for verification. When device j now receives $m(s_i, c_i) = d$ and possibly also $h(c_i)$, it will compute c_j so that $m(s_j, c_j) = d = m(s_i, c_i)$ holds. Due to fluctuations in context and in the feature generation process, c_j is not necessarily a valid code word and might differ from c_i so that $d(c_i, c_j) > 0$ holds. By first decoding c_j onto a_j and then encoding a_j back to the message space $\mathcal{C}$, the obtained value $\overline{c_j}$ will equal c_i iff $d(s_i, s_j) < \lfloor \frac{\Delta}{2} \rfloor \Leftrightarrow d(c_i, c_j) < \lfloor \frac{\Delta}{2} \rfloor$. When also $h(c_i)$ is transmitted, device j will assume that a common secret is found when $h(c_i) = h(c_j)$ holds.

Communication. An arbitrary transceiver module is sufficient to provide communication during secret key generation and also for the encrypted communication. Unlike other protocols presented in [22], we do not require a separate trusted communication channel for device-pairing. Since the secret is not transmitted on the channel, a single insecure and noisy communication channel is sufficient.

4   Audio-Based Secure Communication

We implemented this framework with ambient audio as context source [26]. Audio recordings are represented by binary audio-fingerprints based on energy fluctuations [8] in 33 frequency bands over 17 non-overlapping sub-sequences of the recording. For codewords $c \in \mathcal{C}$ with length $|c| = 512$ bits and words $a \in \mathcal{A}$ with length $|a| = 204$ bits we utilised Reed-Solomon codes with $\Delta = \lfloor |c| - |a| \rfloor$. To estimate the entropy of fingerprints, we first discuss properties of the fingerprints in section 4.1 and their entropy in section 4.2. In section 4.3 we briefly demonstrate the performance of this implementation in a realistic environment.

4.1   Properties of Audio-Fingerprints

In a controlled indoor environment we recorded samples with two microphones at various distances. The samples were played back by a single audio source. Microphones were attached to the left and right ports of an audio card with audio cables of equal lengths and placed at 1.5 m, 3 m, 4.5 m and 6 m distance to the audio source. The samples were emitted at quiet ($\approx 10 - 23$dB), medium ($\approx 23 - 33$dB) and loud ($\approx 33 - 45$dB) volume. They consisted of several instances of music, a person clapping her hands, snapping her fingers, speaking and whistling.

We created audio-fingerprints for both microphones and compared their Hamming distance. Overall, 7500 comparisons between fingerprints are conducted in various settings. From these, 300 comparisons are created for simultaneously recorded samples. Figure 3 depicts the median percentage of identical bits in the fingerprints for simultaneously and non-simultaneously recorded samples and several positions of the microphones and loudness levels. The error bars in the figures show the variance in the Hamming distance.

The similarity in the fingerprints is significantly higher for simultaneously sampled audio. Only about 3.8 % of the comparisons from non-matching samples have a similarity of more than 0.58 and only 0.4583 % have a similarity of more than 0.6. Similarly, only 2.33 % of the comparisons of synchronously sampled audio have a similarity of less than 0.7. We observed that the distance of the microphones to the audio source and the loudness level has no impact on the similarity of fingerprints.

The remaining bit errors for synchronously recorded samples can be corrected by error correcting codes (Reed-Solomon in our case) as detailed in section 3.

4.2   Entropy of Fingerprints

Although these results suggest that it is unlikely for a device in another audio context to generate sufficiently similar fingerprints, an active adversary might analyse the fingerprints created to identify and explore a possible weakness in the encryption key. Such a weakness might be repetitions of subsequences in the key or an unequal distribution of symbols. When an adversary overhears a message encrypted with a key biased in such a way, the cypher may leak information about the encrypted message, provided that the adversary is aware of the bias.

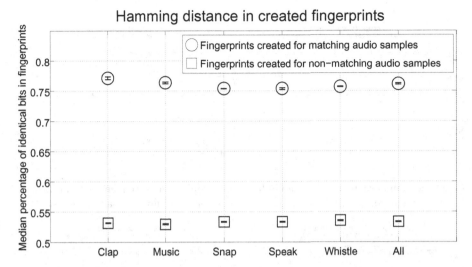

Fig. 3. Median percentage of identical bits in fingerprints created for synchronised and on-synchronised audio recordings over all distances and loudness levels

We tested the entropy of fingerprints generated for audio-sub-sequences. We apply various statistical tests on the distribution of bits in an audio-fingerprint. In particular, we utilise the dieHarder [3] set of statistical tests. This battery of tests calculates the p-value of a given random sequence with respect to several statistical tests. The p-value denotes the probability to obtain an input sequence by a truly random bit generator. We applied all tests to a set of fingerprints of 480 bits length. We utilised the samples obtained in section 4.1 and additionally sampled audio in various outdoor settings (a crowded canteen environment, a heavily trafficked road, an office environment).

In the 7490 test-batches for the fingerprints described in section 4.1 which consisted of 100 repeated applications of one specific test each, only 173 batches, or about 2.31% resulted in a p-value of less than 0.05.[1] Each specific test was repeated at least 70 times. The p-values are calculated according to the statistical test of Kuiper [14].

Figure 4 depicts for all test-series conducted the fraction of tests that did not pass a sequence of 100 consecutive runs at $> 5\%$ for Kuiper KS p-values [14] for all 107 distinct tests in the DieHarder battery of statistical tests.

Generally, we observe that for all test runs conducted, the number of tests that fail is low. It is in all cases within the confidence interval with a confidence value of $\alpha = 0.03$. The confidence interval was calculated for $m = 107$ tests conducted as $1 - \alpha \pm 3 \cdot \sqrt{\frac{(1-\alpha)\cdot\alpha}{m}}$.

Also, we could not observe any distinction between indoor and outdoor settings (cf. figure 4a and figure 4b) so that we conclude that also the increasing

---

[1] All results of the statistical tests are available at http://www.ibr.cs.tu-bs.de/users/sigg/StatisticalTests/TestsFingerprints_110601.tar.gz

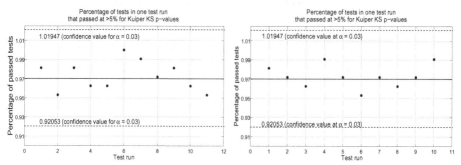

(a) Proportion of sequences from an indoor laboratory environment passing a test

(b) Proportion of sequences from various outdoor environments passing a test

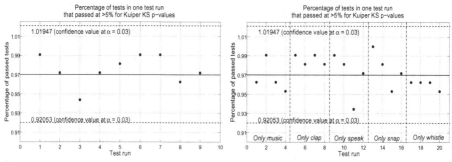

(c) Proportion of sequences from all but music samples passing a test

(d) Proportion of sequences belonging to a specific audio class passing a test

Fig. 4. Illustration of P-Values obtained for the audio-fingerprints from applying the DieHarder battery of statistical tests

noise figure and different hardware utilised [2] does not impact the test results. Since music might represent a special case due to its structured properties and possible repetitions in an audio sequence, we considered it separately from the other samples. We could not identify a significant impact of music on the outcome of the test results (cf. figure 4c).

Additionally, we separated audio samples of one audio class and used them exclusively as input to the statistical tests. Again, there is no significant change for any of the classes (cf. figure 4d).

Summarising, we conclude that we could not observe any bias in fingerprints based on ambient audio. Consequently, the entropy of fingerprints based on ambient audio can be considered as high. An adversary should gain no significant Information from an encrypted message overheard.

---

[2] Overall, the microphones utilised (2 internal, 2 external) were produced by three distinct manufacturers.

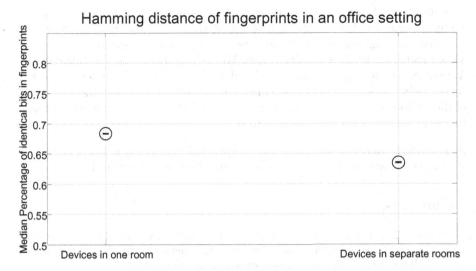

Fig. 5. Median percentage of bit errors in fingerprints from two devices in an office. Audio context was dominated by an FM radio tuned to the same channel.

4.3 Case Study

We consider an environment in which two laptop computers are situated in an office while a third device is located in a neighbouring office. The door to the office was closed but in both rooms we placed two FM-radios, tuned to the same frequency in both rooms. The audio context was dominated by the synchronised music and speech from the FM-radio channel. The distance to the audio source was identical for all devices. The loudness level of the audio source was tuned to about 50 dB in both rooms. Figure 5 depicts the median bit-similarity achieved when the devices were placed in the same room and in different rooms respectively. In both cases the variance in the bit errors achieved is below 0.1 %. When both devices are placed in the same room, the median Hamming distance between fingerprints is only 31.64 %. When the devices are placed in different rooms, the variance in bit error rates is still low with 0.008 %. The median Hamming distance rose in this case to 36.52 %. Consequently, although the dominant audio source in both settings generated identical and synchronised content, the Hamming distance drops significantly when both devices are in an identical room. With sufficient configuration of the error correction method conditioned on the Hamming distance, an eavesdropper can be prevented from stealing the secret key even though some information on the audio context might be leaking.

5 Conclusion

We have proposed a generic framework for device-pairing based on contextual information. The distinct modules of the framework are flexible and can be put into effect by arbitrary implementations. The framework utilises fuzzy cryptography schemes to share a common secret at remote devices without revealing information about the secret. Possible variations in the context samples utilised are corrected by error correcting codes. We demonstrated the feasibility of the framework in an implementation for ambient audio. The implementation was successfully applied in an office setting. Additionally, we analysed the properties of the audio-fingerprints generated and estimated the entropy in statistical tests. In these tests, no bias could be observed.

Acknowledgment. This work was supported by a fellowship within the Postdoc-Programme of the German Academic Exchange Service (DAAD).

References

1. Bichler, D., Stromberg, G., Huemer, M.: Innovative key generation approach to encrypt wireless communication in personal area networks. In: Proceedings of the 50th International Global Communications Conference (2007)
2. Bichler, D., Stromberg, G., Huemer, M., Löw, M.: Key Generation Based on Acceleration Data of Shaking Processes. In: Krumm, J., Abowd, G.D., Seneviratne, A., Strang, T. (eds.) UbiComp 2007. LNCS, vol. 4717, pp. 304–317. Springer, Heidelberg (2007)
3. Brown, R.G.: Dieharder: A random number test suite (2011), http://www.phy.duke.edu/~rgb/General/dieharder.php
4. Diffie, W., Hellman, M.E.: New directions in cryptography. IEEE Transactions on Information Theory IT-22(6), 644–654 (1976)
5. Dunning, J.P.: Taming the blue beast: A survey of Bluetooth based threats. IEEE Security Privacy 8(2), 20–27 (2010)
6. Dupuy, C., Torre, A.: Local Clusters, trust, confidence and proximity, Clusters and Globalisation: The development of urban and regional economies, pp. 175–195 (2006)
7. Gellersen, H.W., Kortuem, G., Schmidt, A., Beigl, M.: Physical prototyping with smart-its. IEEE Pervasive Computing 4(1536-1268), 10–18 (2004)
8. Haitsma, J., Kalker, T.: A Highly Robust Audio Fingerprinting System. Journal of New Music Research 32(2), 211–221 (2003)
9. Ben Hamida, S.T., Pierrot, J.B., Castelluccia, C.: An adaptive quantization algorithm for secret key generation using radio channel measurements. In: Proceedings of the 3rd International Conference on New Technologies, Mobility and Security (2009)
10. Hershey, J., Hassan, A., Yarlagadda, R.: Unconventional cryptographic keying variable management. IEEE Transactions on Communications 43, 3–6 (1995)
11. Holmquist, L.E., Mattern, F., Schiele, B., Alahuhta, P., Beigl, M., Gellersen, H.W.: Smart-Its Friends: A Technique for Users to Easily Establish Connections between Smart Artefacts. In: Abowd, G.D., Brumitt, B., Shafer, S. (eds.) UbiComp 2001. LNCS, vol. 2201, pp. 116–122. Springer, Heidelberg (2001)
12. Jansen, W., Scarfone, K.: Guidelines on cell phone and PDA security. Technical Report SP 800-124, National Institute of Standards and Technology (2008)
13. Karlson, A.K., Brush, A.J.B., Schechter, S.: Can I borrow your phone?: Understanding concerns when sharing mobile phones. In: Proceedings of the 27th International Conference on Human Factors in Computing Systems, CHI 2009 (2010)

14. Kuiper, N.H.: Tests concerning random points on a circle. In: Proceedings of the Koinklijke Nederlandse Akademie van Wetenschappen, vol. 63, pp. 38–47 (1962)
15. Kunze, K., Lukowicz, P.: Symbolic Object Localization Through Active Sampling of Acceleration and Sound Signatures. In: Krumm, J., Abowd, G.D., Seneviratne, A., Strang, T. (eds.) UbiComp 2007. LNCS, vol. 4717, pp. 163–180. Springer, Heidelberg (2007)
16. Madiseh, M.G., McGuire, M.L., Neville, S.S., Cai, L., Horie, M.: Secret key generation and agreement in UWB communication channels. In: Proceedings of the 51st International Global Communications Conference, Globecom (2008)
17. Madlmayr, G., Langer, J., Kantner, C., Scharinger, J.: Nfc devices: Security and privacy. In: Third International Conference on Availability, Reliability and Security (ARES 2008), pp. 642–647 (March 2008)
18. Mathur, S., Miller, R., Varshavsky, A., Trappe, W., Mandayam, N.: Proximate: Proximity-based secure pairing using ambient wireless signals. In: Proceedings of the Ninth International Conference on Mobile Systems, Applications and Services, MobiSys 2011 (2011)
19. Mayrhofer, R.: The Candidate Key Protocol for Generating Secret Shared Keys from Similar Sensor Data Streams. In: Stajano, F., Meadows, C., Capkun, S., Moore, T. (eds.) ESAS 2007. LNCS, vol. 4572, pp. 1–15. Springer, Heidelberg (2007)
20. Mayrhofer, R., Gellersen, H.-W.: Shake Well Before Use: Authentication Based on Accelerometer Data. In: LaMarca, A., Langheinrich, M., Truong, K.N. (eds.) Pervasive 2007. LNCS, vol. 4480, pp. 144–161. Springer, Heidelberg (2007)
21. Mayrhofer, R., Gellersen, H.W.: Shake well before use: Two implementations for implicit context authentication. In: Proceedings of the 9th International Conference on Ubiquitous Computing (UbiComp 2007), pp. 72–75 (2007)
22. Mayrhofer, R., Gellersen, H.W.: Spontaneous mobile device authentication based on sensor data. Information Security Technical Report 13(3), 136–150 (2008)
23. Nehmadi, L., Meyer, J.: A system for studying usability of mobile security. In: Proceedings of the 3rd International Workshop on Security and Privacy in Spontaneous Interaction and Mobile Phone Use (2011)
24. Seifert, J., De Luca, A., Conradi, B., Hussmann, H.: TreasurePhone: Context-Sensitive User Data Protection on Mobile Phones. In: Floréen, P., Krüger, A., Spasojevic, M. (eds.) Pervasive 2010. LNCS, vol. 6030, pp. 130–137. Springer, Heidelberg (2010)
25. Siewiorek, D., Smailagic, A., Furukawa, J., Krause, A., Moraveji, N., Reiger, K., Shaffer, J., Wong, F.L.: Sensay: A context-aware mobile phone. In: Proceedings of the 7th IEEE International Symposium on Wearable Computers
26. Sigg, S.: Context-based security: State of the art, open research topics and a case study. In: Proceedings of the 5th ACM International Workshop on Context-Awareness for Self-Managing Systems, CASEMANS 2011 (2011)
27. Sigg, S., Budde, M., Ji, Y., Beigl, M.: Entropy of Audio Fingerprints for Unobtrusive Device Authentication. In: Beigl, M., Christiansen, H., Roth-Berghofer, T.R., Kofod-Petersen, A., Coventry, K.R., Schmidtke, H.R. (eds.) CONTEXT 2011. LNCS, vol. 6967, pp. 296–299. Springer, Heidelberg (2011)
28. Smith, G.: A direct derivation of a single-antenna reciprocity relation for the time domain. IEEE Transactions on Antennas and Propagation 52, 1568–1577 (2004)
29. Tuyls, P., Skoric, B., Kevenaar, T.: Security with Noisy Data. Springer (2007)
30. Varshavsky, A., Scannell, A., LaMarca, A., de Lara, E.: Amigo: Proximity-based authentication of mobile devices. International Journal of Security and Networks (2009)

In Search of an Internet of Things Service Architecture: REST or WS-*? A Developers' Perspective

Dominique Guinard, Iulia Ion, and Simon Mayer

Institute for Pervasive Computing, ETH Zurich, Switzerland
{dguinard,iulia.ion,simon.mayer}@inf.ethz.ch

Abstract. Current trends inspired from the development of the Web 2.0 advocate designing smart things (e.g., wireless sensors nodes or home appliances) as service platforms. Interoperable services are mainly achieved using two different approaches: WS-* and RESTful Web services. These approaches have previously been compared with respect to performance and features, but no work has been done to elicit the developers' preferences and programming experiences. We conducted a study in which 69 novice developers learned both technologies and implemented mobile phone applications that retrieve sensor data, both through a RESTful and through a WS-* service architecture. The results complement the available technological decision framework when building Internet of Things applications. The results suggest that developers find REST easier to learn than WS-* and consider it more suitable for programming smart things. However, for applications with advanced security and Quality of Service requirements, WS-* Web services are perceived to be better suited.

Keywords: Internet of Things, Web of Things, WSN, Mobile, Web Services, REST, WS-*.

1 Introduction and Related Work

The *Internet of Things* (IoT) explores ways to connect and build upon networks of digitally enhanced, communication-capable objects, such as wireless sensor nodes, mobile phones, and home appliances, generally known as "smart things". Sensor nodes might, for instance, be networked together to create environmental monitoring applications [13].

Home appliances might communicate with each other to offer smarter heating systems or to optimize their energy consumption [5]. However, the development of applications that integrate the functionality of multiple smart things remains a challenging task, because it requires expert knowledge of each platform.

To facilitate this, recent research initiatives tried to provide uniform interfaces that create a loosely coupled ecosystem of services for smart things [5,10]. The goal is to enable a widely distributed platform in which smart things provide services that can be easily composed to create new applications. Two types of

A. Puiatti et al. (Eds.): MobiQuitous 2011, LNICST 104, pp. 326–337, 2012.

service-oriented architectures stand out as potential candidates to enable uniform interfaces to smart objects: the Representational State Transfer (REST) [3] and WS-* [9] Web services:

WS-.* These services declare their functionality and interfaces in a Web Services Description Language (WSDL) file. Client requests and service response objects are encapsulated using the Simple Object Access Protocol (SOAP) and transmitted over the network, usually using the HTTP protocol. Further WS-* standards define concepts such as addressing, security, discovery or service composition. Although WS-* was initially created to achieve interoperability of enterprise applications, work has been done to adapt it to the needs of resource-constrained devices [10,13]. Furthermore, lighter forms of WS-* services, such as the Devices Profile for Web Services (DPWS)[1], were proposed [6].

REST. At the core of a RESTful architecture [3] lie *resources* that are uniquely identified through Uniform Resource Identifiers (URIs). The Web is an implementation of RESTful principles – it uses URLs to identify resources and HTTP as their service interface. Resources can have several representation formats (e.g., HTML, JSON[2]) negotiated at run time using HTTP content negotiation. In a typical REST request, the client discovers the URL of a service it wants to call by browsing or crawling its HTML representation. The client then sends an HTTP call to this URL with a given verb (GET, POST, PUT, etc.), a number of options (e.g., accepted format), and a payload in the negotiated format (e.g., XML or JSON). Several recent research projects implement RESTful Web services for smart things [2] within what has become to be known as the *Web of Things* [5].

While the two architectures share the goal of providing developers with abstractions (i.e., APIs) for interacting with distributed services, they tackle loose coupling and interoperability differently. Consequently, work has been done to evaluate the two approaches. In [8,9], REST and WS-* are compared in terms of re-usability and loose coupling for business applications. The authors suggest that WS-* services should be preferred for "professional enterprise application integration scenarios" and RESTful services for tactical, ad-hoc integration over the Web.

Internet of Things applications pose novel requirements and challenges as neither WS-* nor RESTful Web services were primarily designed to run and be used on smart things, but rather on business or Web servers. This development thus necessitates assessing the suitability of the two approaches for devices with limited capabilities. Yazar et al. [13] analyze the performance of WS-* and RESTful applications when deployed on wireless sensor nodes with limited resources and conclude that REST performs better.

However, evaluating the performance of a system when deployed on a particular platform is not enough to make the architectural decision that will foster adoption and third-party (public) innovation. Indeed, studies like the Technology Acceptance Model [1] and more recent extensions [4] show that the perceived

---

[1] See www.ws4d.org

[2] See www.json.org

ease of use of an IT system is key to its adoption. As many manufacturers of smart things are moving from providing devices with few applications to building devices as platforms with APIs, they increasingly rely on external communities of developers to build innovative services for their hardware (e.g., the Apple App Store or Android Marketplace). An easy to learn API is, therefore, key in fostering a broad community of developers for smart things. Hence, choosing the service architecture that provides the best developer experience is instrumental to the success of the Internet of Things and the Web of Things on a larger scale.

In this paper we complement the decision framework that can be used when picking the right architecture for IoT applications and platforms. We supplement previous work [8,9,13] by evaluating, in a structured way, the actual *developers' experience* when using each architecture in an IoT context. We analyze the perceived ease of use and suitability of WS-* and RESTful Web service architectures for IoT applications. Our study is based on the qualitative feedback and quantitative results from 69 computer science students who developed two applications that accesses temperature and light measurements from wireless sensor nodes. For one of the applications, the participants used a sensor node offering a RESTful Web API. In the second case, they were accessing a sensor node through a WS-* (WSDL + SOAP-based) API.

Our results show that participants almost unanimously found RESTful Web services easier to learn, more intuitive and more suitable for programming IoT applications than WS-*. The main advantages of REST as reported by the participants are *intuitiveness*, *flexibility*, and the fact that it is more *lightweight*. WS-* is perceived to support more advanced *security* requirements and benefits from a clearer *standardization* process.

This paper is structured as follows. Section 2 describes the study methodology. Section 3 presents and analyses the results. Finally, Section 4 discusses the implications of our findings and devises guidelines.

2 Methodology

Our study is based on a programming exercise and the feedback received from a group of 69 computer science students who learned about RESTful and WS-* Web service architectures and implemented, in teams, mobile phone applications that accessed sensor data from different sensor nodes using both approaches. The exercise was part of an assignment in the Distributed Systems course at ETH Zurich[3]. The material used for instructing the students about the two technologies was prepared so as to not introduce a bias[4].

Although we worked on native architectures for both REST and WS-* [5], in order for the results not to be influenced by the performance of the sensors for each architecture, we used two proxies as shown in Figure 1. As a result, the study can focus on the development experience and usability rather than on the architectures' performance that has already been studied by others (e.g., [13]).

---

[3] The assignment is available online: `tinyurl.com/vs-assignment`

[4] All course material is available online: `tinyurl.com/vs-material`

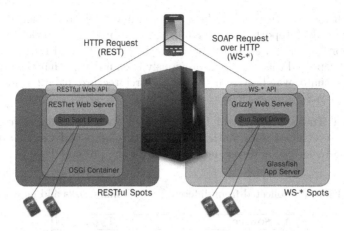

Fig. 1. Setup of the user study. In order not to influence the results, the 4 Sun SPOTs sensor nodes are connected through proxies offering once a RESTful API (left), once a WS-* API (right).

To get and parse the RESTful sensor responses, participants were advised to use the Apache HTTP Client library[5] and JSON.org libraries[6]. To perform the WS-* request, we advised the students to use the *kSoap2* library[7] which offers a set of tools to interact with WS-* services. It is worth noting that while these two libraries are well aligned with the abstractions represented by both architectures and are standard tools for accessing each type of API from a mobile device, the students were free to pick other tools. Averaging over the submissions, the programs had 105 lines of code for the WS-* implementation ($SD = 50.19$, where SD is the Standard Deviation), opposed to 98 lines of code for the REST implementation ($SD = 48.31$).

The two coding tasks were solved in teams of two or three members who were able to freely decide how to split up the tasks amongst team members. The coding tasks were successfully completed by all teams within two weeks. To ensure that every team member had understood the solution of each task, individual structured questionnaires about both technologies had to be submitted. Additionally, we included a voluntary feedback form on the learning process in the study. Students were informed that answers in the feedback form were not part of the assignment, and that responses would be used in a research study. To encourage them to give honest answers about the amount of effort invested in solving both coding tasks, perception, and attitudes towards both technologies, entries in the feedback form were made anonymously. Table 1 summarizes the data collection sources.

Demographics: The participants were from ETH Zurich, in their third or fourth year of Bachelor studies. Teams were formed of two or three members. They were

---

[5] See hc.apache.org

[6] See json.org

[7] See ksoap2.sourceforge.net

taught both technologies for the first time, in a short introduction during the tutorial class. 89% reported not having had any previous knowledge of WS-* and 62% none of REST. From the 35% that had already used REST before the course, half reported that they had previously been unaware that the technology they used actually was based on the REST architecture. 5% (2 students) had programmed WS-* applications.

Additional Tasks: Subsequent tasks involved creating visualization mechanisms for the retrieved data, both locally and through cloud visualization solutions. These tasks are, however, not relevant for the presented study.

Table 1. Data was collected from different programming tasks and questionnaires

Data Source	Type	N
RESTful and WS-* Applications	Team	25
Structured Questionnaire	Individual	69
Voluntary Feedback Form	Anonymous	37

3   Results

In this section, we present our results on the perceived differences, ease of learning, and suitability of the technologies for IoT-related use cases.

3.1   Perceived Differences

Using the structured questionnaire, we collected qualitative data on the perceived advantages of both technologies with respect to each other. While REST was perceived to be *"very easy to understand, learn, and implement,"* lightweight and scalable, WS-* *"allows for more complex operations,"* provides higher security, and a better level of abstraction. Table 2 summarizes the perceived advantages of the two technologies.

3.2   Accessibility and Ease of Learning

In the feedback form, we asked participants to rate on a 5 point Likert scale how easy and how fast it was to learn each technology (1=not easy at all, ..., 5=very easy). As shown in Figure 3, 70% rated REST "easy" or "very easy" to learn. WS-* services, on the other hand, were perceived to be more complex: only 11% respondents rated them easy to learn. Event if all participants were required to learn and explain the concepts of both technologies, compare their advantages, analyze their suitability and explain design decisions, we restricted the sample to participants who reported to have worked on programming both REST and WS-* assignments within their teams (N=19) to avoid bias. We then applied the Wilcoxon signed rank test for the two paired samples to compare the perceived ease of learning for REST and WS-*. Our results show that REST (with an average $M = 3.85$ and a Standard Deviation $SD = 1.09$) was reported

Table 2. Participants felt that WS-* provides more features, but REST is easy to learn and use

REST ($N = 69$)	#
Easy to understand, learn, and implement	36
Lightweight	27
Easy to use for clients	25
More scalable	21
No libraries required	17
Accessible in browser and bookmarkable	14
Reuses HTTP functionality (e.g., caching)	10
WS-* ($N = 69$)	#
WSDL allows to publish a WS-* interface	31
Allows for more complex operations	24
Offers better security	19
Provides higher level of abstraction	11
Has more features	10

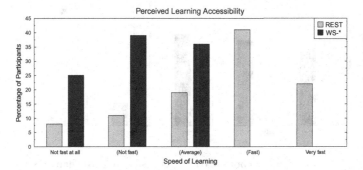

Fig. 2. A majority of participants reported that REST as *fast* or *very fast* to learn and WS-* as *not fast* or *average*

to be statistically significantly easier to learn than WS-* ($M = 2.50, SD = 1.10$): $V = 153, p < 0.001$. Similarly, REST ($M = 3.43, SD = 1.09$) was perceived to be significantly faster to learn than WS-* ($M = 2.21, SD = 0.80$), $V = 53, p < 0.009, N = 14$.

Furthermore, in the feedback form, we collected qualitative data on the challenges of learning both technologies, asking the participants: "What were the challenges you encountered in learning each of the technologies? Which one was faster and easier to learn?". Nine participants explained that REST was easier and faster to learn because RESTful Web services are based on technologies, such as HTTP and HTML, which are well-known to most tech-savvy people: *"Everybody who is using a browser already knows a little about [REST]."*

WS-* was perceived to be overly complicated: *"REST is easy and WS-* is just a complicated mess."* Reasons for such strong statements were the complexity of extracting useful information out of the WSDL and SOAP files (mentioned by 8), as well as the little and poor documentation of parameters for a SOAP call. The lack of clear documentation was perceived as a problem for REST as well: Seven participants said that further request examples, alongside with the traditional documentation (e.g., Javadoc) for both REST and WS-*, would be very useful. Eight participants explicitly mentioned that they had had previous experience with REST during their spare time. This illustrates the accessibility and appeal of RESTful Web services, and it positions them as an ideal candidate for smart things APIs in terms of lowering the entry barrier for creating applications. In the feedback form, 25 participants said that REST made it easier to understand what services the sensor nodes offered. Eight participants explained this by the fact that, for REST, an HTML interface was provided. This emphasizes that RESTful smart things should offer an HTML representation by default. Seven participants found WS-* easier for this matter. They noted that a WSDL file was not necessarily easy to read, but they liked the fact that it was *"standard"*.

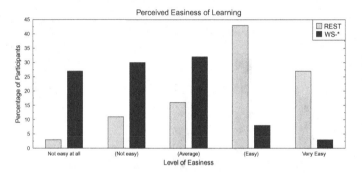

Fig. 3. Participants reported REST as easier to learn than WS-*

3.3   Suitability for Use-Cases

In the feedback form, we asked participants to rate on a Likert scale (1=WS-*, ..., 5=REST) which one of the two technologies they would recommend in specific scenarios. REST was considered more suitable than WS-* for IoT applications running on embedded devices and mobile phones (see Figure 4). The one sample Wilcoxon signed rank test confirmed that the sample average was statistically higher than the neutral 3, and therefore inclined towards REST. This was the case both for embedded devices ($M = 3.86, SD = 1.03, V = 342, p < 0.001$), and for mobile phone applications ($M = 3.51, SD = 1.12, V = 252, p < 0.007$). For business applications, however, a higher preference for WS-* was stated but not statistically significant ($M = 2.67, SD = 1.33, V = 163.5, p = 0.12$).

General Use-Cases. We asked our participants to discuss the general use-cases for which each technology appeared suitable. When asked: "For what kind of applications is REST suitable?", 23 people mentioned that REST was well adapted for simple applications offering limited and atomic functionality: *"for* *applications where you only need create/read/update and delete [operations]"*. 8 participants also advised the use of REST when security is not a core requirement of the application: *"Applications where no higher security level than the one of HTTP[s] is needed"*. This is supported by the fact that the WS-* security specification offers more levels of security than the use of HTTPS and SSL in REST [11]. 6 participants suggested that REST was more adapted for user-targeted applications: *"[...] for applications that present received content directly to the user"*. Along these lines, 14 users said that REST was more adapted for Web applications or applications requiring to integrate Web content: *"[for] Web Mashups, REST services compose easily"*.

We then asked: "For what kind of applications is WS-* more suitable?". 20 participants mentioned that WS-* was more adapted for secure applications: *"applications that require extended security features, where SSL is not enough"*. 16 participants suggested to use WS-* when strong contracts on the message formats were required, often referring to the use of WSDL files: *"with WS-* [...] specifications can easily be written in a standard machine-readable format (WSDL, XSD)"*.

Table 3. REST was perceived to be more suited for simple applications, and WS-* for applications where security is important

REST (N=37)	#
For simple applications, with atomic functionality	23
For Web applications and Mashups	14
If security is not a core requirement	8
For user-centered applications	6
For heterogeneous environments	6
WS-* (N=37)	**#**
For secure applications	20
When contracts on message formats are needed	16

For Smart Things. Both WS-* and RESTful Web Services were not primarily designed to run on embedded devices and mobile phones but rather on business or Web servers. Thus, assessing the suitability of the two approaches for devices with limited capabilities is relevant.

As shown in the first part of Figure 4, for providing services on embedded devices, 66% of the participants suggested that REST was either "adapted" or "very-adapted". When asked to elaborate on their answers, 6 participants suggested that for heterogeneous environments, REST was more suitable: *"for simple application, running on several clients (PC, iPhone, Android) [...]"*. 7 participants said that REST was adapted for embedded and mobile devices because it was more lightweight and better suited for such devices in general: *"the mapping of a sensor network to the REST verbs is natural [...]"*. To confirm this, we investigated the size of the application packages for both approaches. The average footprint of the REST application was 17.46 kB while the WS-* application had a size of 83.27 kB on average. The difference here is mainly due to the necessity to include the *kSoap2* library with every WS-* application. These results confirm earlier performance and footprint evaluations [2,5,13].

For Smart Home Applications. We then went into more specific use cases, asking: *"Imagine you want to deploy a sensor network in your home. Which technology would you use and why?"*. Sixty-two respondents recommended REST to deploy a sensor network in the home, 5 recommended WS-*, and 2 were undecided. Twenty-four participants justified the choice of REST by invoking its simplicity both in terms of use and development: *"REST [...] requires less effort to be set up"*, *"Easier to use REST, especially in connection with a Web interface"*. Eight participants said that REST is more lightweight, which is important in a home environment populated by heterogeneous home appliances. Interestingly, 14 participants mentioned that in home environments there are very little concerns about security and thus, the advanced security features of WS-* were not required: *"I would not care if my neighbor can read these values"*, *"The information isn't really sensitive"*.

For Mobile Phones. Since the mobile phone is a key interaction device for creating IoT applications, we asked the participants to assess the suitability of each platform for creating mobile phone clients to smart things. As shown in the second part of Figure 4, 53% of the participants would use REST, 16% would use WS-* and 32% were undecided. They explained these contrasted results by the fact that mobile phones are getting very powerful. 7 participants explained that the amount of data to be processed was smaller with REST which was perceived as an important fact for mobile clients. Interestingly, some participants considered the customers of mobile platforms to have different requirements: *"I would use REST, since customers prefer speed and fun over security for smaller devices"*. The lack of native WS-* support on Android (which natively supports HTTP) and the required use of external libraries was also mentioned as a decision factor as REST calls can be simply implemented only using the native HTTP libraries.

For Business Applications. The results are much more inclined towards WS-* when considering "business" applications. As shown in the third part of Figure 4, the majority of our participants (52%) would choose WS-* and 24% REST for servicing business applications. Twenty-one (out of 69, see Table 1) justify their decision by the security needs of enterprise applications: *"I would rely on the more secure WS-* technology"*. Eighteen participants talk about the better described service contracts when using WS-*: *"I propose WS-* because we could use WSDL and XSD to agree on a well-specified interface early on [...]"*. Amongst the participants suggesting the use of REST, 10 justify their decision with its simplicity and 10 with its better scalability.

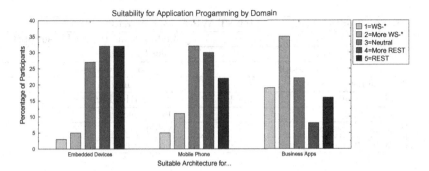

Fig. 4. Participants reported that REST is better suited for Internet of Things applications, involving mobile and embedded devices and WS-* fits better to the requirements of business applications (N = 69)

4   Discussion and Summary

A central concern in the Internet of Things and thus in the Web of Things is the interoperability between smart objects and existing standards and applications. Two service-oriented approaches are currently at the center of research and development: REST and WS-*. Decisions on which approach to adopt have important consequences for an IoT system and should be made carefully. Our contribution is to complement existing studies on performance metrics with an evaluation of the developers' preferences and IoT programming experiences with REST and WS-*. Our results show that, in the context of the conducted study, REST stands out as the favorite service architecture. We summarize the decision criteria used by developers in our study and devise guidelines in Table 4.

Future studies should conduct a long-term assessment of the developers' experience, beyond the initial phase of getting started with the technologies. As an example it would be interesting to address the clear trend (52% for WS-*, 24% for REST) towards choosing a WS-* architecture when considering business applications even if overall the participants favored REST and mentioned its superiority for several important factors in business environments such as scalability or interoperability. Are their decisions solely based on the superior security features of WS-* or is there a perception bias?

Furthermore, some of the participants' remarks (e.g., on the low security requirements in home environments) should be put in the context of relatively novice developers. Hence, future work could be done to compare the experience of advanced developers, possibly within industry projects. However, the more experienced the developers are, the more they are likely to develop a bias towards one or the other technology.

Table 4. Guidelines for choosing a service architecture for IoT platforms

Requirement	REST	WS-*	Justification
Mobile & Embedded	+	-	Lightweight, IP/HTTP support
Ease of use	++	-	Easy to learn
Foster third-party adoption	++	-	Easy to prototype
Scalability	++	+	Web mechanisms
Web integration	+++	+	Web is RESTful
Business	+	++	QoS & security
Service contracts	+	++	WSDL
Adv. security	-	+++	WS-Security

While our results confirm several other research projects that take a more performance-centric approach [2,5,13], they contradict several industry trends. In home and industrial automation, standards such as UPnP, DLNA or DPWS expose their services using WS-* standards. One of the reasons for this, also noted by participants, is the lack of formal service contracts (such as WSDL and SOAP) for RESTful services. This is an arguable point as Web experts [11] already illustrated how a well-designed RESTful interface combined with HTTP content negotiation results in a service contract similar to what WS-* offers [11], with no overhead and more adapted to services of smart things [5]. Yet, this illustrates an important weakness of RESTful Web services: RESTful Web services are a relatively *fuzzy* concept. Even if the basics of REST are very simple, the lack of a clear stakeholder managing "standard" RESTful architectures is subject to many (wrong) interpretations of the concept. Until this is improved, resources such as [3,11] profile themselves as de facto standards.

In cases with strong security requirements, WS-* has a competitive advantage [9,11]. The WS-Security standard offers a greater number of options than HTTPS (TLS/SSL) such as encryption and authentication beyond the communication channel, endpoint-to-endpoint. In theory, these could also be implemented for RESTful Web services. However, the lack of standard HTTP support of these techniques would result in tight coupling between the secured things and their clients. Nevertheless, in the context of smart things, it is also important to realize that WS-Security standards are much more resource intensive than those of HTTPS and, thus, rarely fit resource-constrained devices.

Finally, it is important to consider *how accessible smart things should be*. Participants identified that RESTful Web services represent the most straightforward and simple way of achieving a global network of smart things because RESTful Web services seamlessly integrate with the Web. This goes along the lines of recent developments, such as 6LoWPAN [7] and the IPSO alliance[8], CoRE[9] and CoAP [12], or the Web of Things Architecture [5], where smart things are increasingly becoming part of the Internet and the Web.

---

[8] See `ipso-alliance.org`
[9] See `tools.ietf.org/wg/core`

References

1. Davis, F.D.: Perceived Usefulness, Perceived Ease of Use, and User Acceptance of Information Technology. MIS Quarterly 13(3), 319–340 (1989)
2. Drytkiewicz, W., Radusch, I., Arbanowski, S., Popescu-Zeletin, R.: pREST: a REST-based protocol for pervasive systems. In: Proc. of the IEEE International Conference on Mobile Ad-hoc and Sensor Systems, pp. 340–348. IEEE (2004)
3. Fielding, R.: Architectural styles and the design of network-based software architectures. Phd thesis (2000)
4. Gefen, D., Keil, M.: The impact of developer responsiveness on perceptions of usefulness and ease of use: an extension of the technology acceptance model. SIGMIS Database 29, 35–49 (1998)
5. Guinard, D., Trifa, V., Wilde, E.: A Resource Oriented Architecture for the Web of Things. In: Proc. of the 2nd International Conference on the Internet of Things (IoT 2010), Tokyo, Japan. LNCS, Springer, Heidelberg (2010)
6. Jammes, F., Smit, H.: Service-oriented paradigms in industrial automation. IEEE Transactions on Industrial Informatics 1(1), 62–70 (2005)
7. Mulligan, G.: The 6LoWPAN architecture. In: Proc. of the 4th Workshop on Embedded Networked Sensors (EmNets 2007), Cork, Ireland, pp. 78–82. ACM (2007)
8. Pautasso, C., Wilde, E.: Why is the web loosely coupled?: a multi-faceted metric for service design. In: Proc. of the 18th International Conference on World Wide Web (WWW 2009), Madrid, Spain, pp. 911–920. ACM (April 2009)
9. Pautasso, C., Zimmermann, O., Leymann, F.: Restful web services vs. big web services: making the right architectural decision. In: Proc. of the 17th International Conference on World Wide Web (WWW 2008), pp. 805–814. ACM, New York (2008)
10. Priyantha, N.B., Kansal, A., Goraczko, M., Zhao, F.: Tiny web services: design and implementation of interoperable and evolvable sensor networks. In: Proc. of the 6th ACM conference on Embedded Network Sensor Systems (SenSys 2008), Raleigh, NC, USA, pp. 253–266. ACM (2008)
11. Richardson, L., Ruby, S.: RESTful web services. O'Reilly Media (May 2007)
12. Shelby, Z.: Embedded web services. IEEE Wireless Communications 17(6), 52–57 (2010)
13. Yazar, D., Dunkels, A.: Efficient application integration in IP-based sensor networks. In: Proceedings of the First ACM Workshop on Embedded Sensing Systems for Energy-Efficiency in Buildings, Berkeley, CA, USA, pp. 43–48 (November 2009)

Towards Meeting Assistance: An Integrated Appointment Assistance and Group Pedestrian Navigation System

Bjoern Zenker, Viktor Pyatkovka, and Christian Drabek

University of Erlangen-Nuernberg
Erlangen, Germany
bjoern.zenker@cs.fau.de

Abstract. People often go out with other people, meet friends and prefer covering distances together. 70% of all pedestrians travel in a group according to Moussaïd et al. However, most pedestrian navigation systems are intended for single users only. For closing this gap we built a meeting assistance system for groups of users who want to meet. This paper will present the challenges of building such a system, just as solutions for making appointments, calculating appropriate meeting points and routes using Steiner Trees.

Keywords: appointment assistance, group pedestrian navigation system, Steiner Tree problem.

1 Introduction

People go out together. This was ascertained by Moussaïd et al. who says that 70% of all pedestrians travel in a group. [1] The sizes of pedestrian groups were measured by [2]: 71.07% were groups consisting of two individuals and 28.93% were groups consisting of two to seven individuals. The average group size is 2.41 individuals. However, most pedestrian navigation systems are intended for single users only. For closing this gap we built a mobile Integrated Appointment Assistance and Group Pedestrian Navigation System for users who want to meet. With the help of this system, users can get assistance in making appointments and finding appropriate meeting points and routes to their common destination.

Imagine two first-year fellow students living in two different student dormitories spread across a city. They agree to go to the cinema. On their way they want to talk to each other about their current lectures. But they also have to finish their homework first so they do not want to have too much detour. Thus a compromise between detour and the time walking together is needed. Where should they meet?

This paper we will present our approach to help people solve this everyday problem. First, we will present the state of the art of pedestrian navigation systems and group recommendation systems in Section 2. This Section will also discuss group sizes of pedestrians for motivating the need for multi user and

A. Puiatti et al. (Eds.): MobiQuitous 2011, LNICST 104, pp. 338–349, 2012.
© Institute for Computer Sciences, Social Informatics and Telecommunications Engineering 2012

group pedestrian navigation systems. The integrated appointment assistance and group pedestrian navigation system is presented in section 3. The next Section 4 focuses on the appointment assistance part. We introduce and evaluate different flows of user to user interaction and present our implementations. The group navigation system and a brief overview of the underlying theoretical problem for calculating the meeting points and routes is presented in Section 5. We conclude and give an outlook for further research and development in section 6.

2 State of the Art

2.1 Pedestrian Navigation Systems

To aid people reaching their destination, current pedestrian navigation systems give turn-by-turn instructions and show routes to the destination on detailed maps. Many commercial and freely available systems are in use. However, most to the authors known pedestrian navigation systems are for single users only. Examples of such systems are Google Maps Navigation, ovi maps, MobileNavigator, PECITAS [3], P-Tour [4], RouteCheckr [5], COMPASS [6] and many more. Besides that, most commonly used routing algorithms for street networks or public transport networks (like [7] and [8]) are single source only. They cannot be used to calculate routes for more individuals who want to meet.

There are some exceptions to these single user PNS. One is a prototypical system from [9] which helps people to meet. The system calculates an area which is reachable by all participants in time and calculates direct routes to a single meeting point in this area. There are also commercial systems which assist exactly two users in finding a meeting point. MeetMe (http://aboutmeetme.com) and MeetWays (http://meetways.com) recommend meeting points halfway between the two users. To this point they also find individual routes. This is done by first calculating the shortest path between the two users and second recommending places of interest (POI) which are near to the middle of the calculated path. These two commercial systems indicate, that there is a need for group navigation systems. For further supporting our claim for this need we will have a look at typical group sizes of pedestrians.

2.2 Group Sizes of Pedestrians

While there exist numerous studies about animal group sizes, only few exist for human group sizes. One of the first studies about human group sizes originates in the year 1951, when James measured group sizes in politics and in public places, e.g. pedestrians, in department stores, playgrounds. In [2], he determines a mean group size of 2.41 for people in informal groups. A total of 7405 groups have been studied. 71,07% of all groups consisted of two persons, the other 28,93% have been groups between three and seven persons. In this study, the counting of individuals has not been taken into account. The subsequent paper [10] declares a mean group size of 1,46, if individuals are considered. James also deduced a generalized model of pedestrian group sizes from this data, but this model has been proven incorrect by [11]. From James' data we can calculate, that 34.46% of all groups (including groups of size 1, namely individuals) are groups of two or more people. To a different result comes [1], who observed, that up to 70% of pedestrians in a commercial street walk in groups. Note the difference between the latter two units of measurement. By converting James' result, we find that 55.14% of all pedestrians in James' study are walking in groups. Now one can easily see that the results of the two studies differ about 15%. Further and more detailed studies are needed. These results show that many people go out in groups and support our claim that there is a need for group navigation systems.

2.3   Appointment Assistance

Settling on destinations, good meeting points and routes can be seen as a task for group recommender systems. Jameson and Smyth [12] give an overview of such systems. They structure recommendation in a process of four recommendation subtasks: preference acquisition, generation of recommendations, presentation of recommendation and assistance in achieving consensus. The research on the last subtask "assistance in achieving consensus", which we will call negotiation subtask, is in most publications on group recommenders only rudimentary discussed, as [12] noted. Most systems only present recommended items to their users and leave the choice of a specific item to the users. Examples for such systems are PolyLens [13], Trip.Easy [14] and CATS [15]. In these systems the final choice is achieved by discussions of the users outside of the used system. Travel Decision Forum [16] is a group recommendation system which focuses on the negotiation. In this implementation this phase consists of a discussion which is supported by a visualisation of the user's arguments like people talking in a comic strip.

While group recommendation systems often leave out the negotiation subtask, there is a field of research which addresses the problems which arise here. Group (Decision) Support Systems (GDSS) assist groups in arriving at a final decision. (e.g. [17]). We think, that group recommender systems should also include such a GDSS. We think, that group recommendation is in fact a *process*, in which the subtasks of group recommendation are blend with the subtasks of GDSS. One can not just recommend an item to the group, the item must be narrowed down in a dialog among the group members and with the recommender.

2.4   Steiner Tree Problem

The Steiner Tree Problem will be used to calculate meeting points and corresponding routes. Hence we will give a short introduction to this problem, namely to "Find the shortest network spanning a set of given points..." [18]. A minimal tree for 4 terminals shows the graph in Figure 1.

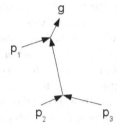

Fig. 1. Meeting tree of three individuals p_1, p_2, p_3 meeting at intermediate points on their way to their common destination

Two similar versions of the Steiner Tree Problem can be found in literature:

Steiner (Tree) Problem in Networks (SPN). Given an undirected network $N = (V, E, c)$ with vertices V, edges E and cost function $c : E \rightarrow \mathbb{R}^+$, and a terminal set $T \subseteq V$ find the subnetwork S of N such that all nodes $t \in T$ are connected and that the total costs $\sum_{x \in E_S} c(x)$ are a minimum. S is called Steiner Minimum Tree (SMT). SPN is NP-complete [19]. An overview of exact and approximative algorithms as well as a introduction to SPN is for example given by [18] and [20].

Euclidian Steiner (Tree) Problem (ESP). Given a set T of n points in the Euclidian plane, find a tree S connecting all $t \in T$ minimizing the length of S. Note that this might introduce new points at which edges of the tree meet. A prominent exact algorithm was given by [21], heuristics e.g. by [22] and [23]. *Geosteiner* [24] implements an exact algorithm with special pruning techniques to rule out implausible SMTs. Detailed information can be found in [25].

3   Integrated Appointment Assistance and Group Pedestrian Navigation System

We have identified two main phases of going out. In a first phase, the appointment phase, the destination and the time to meet have to be agreed upon. In the following meeting phase individuals proceed to the common destination. There exist more phases, but we focus in this paper on the two presented. For appointment phase and meeting phase we built an assistance system each. The meeting assistance system (MAS) consists of two subsystems, the Appointment Assistance System (AAS) and the Group Pedestrian Navigation System (GPNS). AAS helps individuals in the appointment phase to find and agree on a destination. After having settled on a destination, the meeting phase begins: routes for all individuals are calculated by the GPNS. These routes are not only routes directly from each individual to the destination, but routes where individuals meet at intermediate points on their way to the destination. Both systems are presented in the subsequent sections.

Our implementation of the meeting assistance system is built upon the pedestrian navigation system ROSE [26] and is basically structured as follows. Every user is running a client software on her mobile phone. One user can invite other users to a location, e.g. to a certain cinema. After the users have accepted the invitation, their GPS positions are sent to the server. On the server, routes for all users are calculated with appropriate meeting points. The server is implemented in Java EE and communication is done over RESTful webservices using JSON. The server stores user profiles, friends lists and event lists in a database. Also the server offers services such as geocoding, route generation for pedestrians with support of public transport and recommendation of events. These routes are displayed on the users mobile phones and allow turn-by-turn navigation for each user. Due to the fast progress from cellular phones to current smartphones, two versions of the client have been implemented for different platforms. The first one is implemented in Java Mobile Edition and is targeted for older mobile phones. The second one is implemented as an HTML5 web application and can be run with newer browsers and is especially targeted for being run in smartphone browsers. A more detailed description of the workflow of the clients can be found in the subsequent sections.

Currently, AAS and GPNS are coupled loosly. After the destination is settled upon, the result is passed to GPNS as input. For more elaborate systems in the future, characteristics of the routes of the individuals should be considered also in the appointment phase.

4   Appointment Assistance System

The AAS assists groups of individuals settle on a common destination and time. As we cannot rely our design on experienced data we build a flexible system which allows several task flows to be implemented. We then compared task flows to find an appropriate task flow for our scenario.

4.1   Task Flows in Java ME Client

The task flow of the user to user interaction can be modeled in different ways. We implemented different task flows and evaluated them. By using this method, we examined which user to user interaction workflow is best. Several flows have been implemented in the Java Mobile Edition client.[1] The flows are:

Group Rating (GR): The organiser of the group compiles a list of events which he wants to propose. The list is rated by all participants. Afterwards, the system calculates (by an arbitrary algorithm) which suggestion matches the interests of the group best.

Group Criticising (GC): The organiser proposes an event. The participants can accept the proposal or suggest a different event. The process continues until all participants accept the proposal.

---

[1] In all flows, various single user recommender systems can be used to compile lists of events. Using this technique, no group recommender system is needed.

Group Rating after Criticising (GRC): Like GR, but with a more elaborate process for the organiser to compile the list of proposed events.

Individual Search, Merging and Rating (SMR): Organiser and participants
all propose one event and the proposed events are collected in a list. Now, everybody rates the events in this common list and the systems calculates (by an
arbitrary algorithm) which suggestion matches the interests of the group best.

Conjoint Criticising (CC): A list of events is proposed by the organiser. By
criticising events, everybody can change the list. Changes of the list are
propagated to everybody. After some time, the organiser proposes an element
from the list to the participants. If all approve, the process ends. Otherwise,
the process of criticising is continued.

Screenshots of the Java Mobile Edition client displaying various dialogs of the
appointment assistance can be seen in Figure 2.

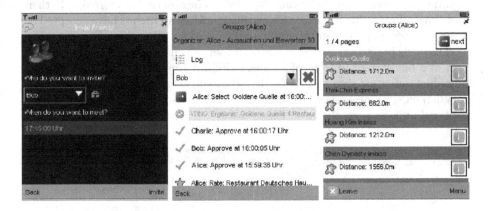

Fig. 2. Screenshots of Java ME client: invitation, approval, list based selection

We conducted a study with nine participants to compare the presented flows
against each other. Groups of participants had to employ each flow to settle on
a destination. Criteria of the evaluation have been the duration of the flow t,
average active time of all users $\bar{t}_U$, user satisfaction with outcome of the flow
SO, user satisfaction with outcome of the process SP (both in relation to [27])
and a subjective voting "Which flow did you like best?" where v counts the votes
the flow received. The results are presented in Table 1.

The fastest flow was GRC, taking 5:24 minutes and also the shortest average
active time $\bar{t}_U = 3 : 00$. The flow SMR was rated the most satisfying by the
organisers (SO_o). Participants are most satisfied with the flow GC concerning the
process (SP_p) and GR concerning the outcome (SO_p). Note, that participants
are overall less satisfied with the flows than organisers are. The subjective vote
shows, that most participants of the study prefer the SMR flow. This might be
to the straightforward nature of the SMR flow.

Table 1. Overview of study results (best results are **highlighted**)

Flow	t	$\bar{t}_U$	SO_o	SP_o	SO_p	SP_p	v
GR	7:01	4:41	4.06	4.00	3.95	**4.35**	1
GC	6:25	3:08	4.25	4.63	**4.25**	4.10	2
GRC	**5:38**	**3:00**	4.19	4.69	4.05	4.20	0
SMR	9:53	8:17	**4.50**	**4.75**	3.55	3.95	**3**
CC	5:24	3:28	4.44	4.69	3.65	3.55	1

4.2 HTML5 Client

In the more up to date client based on HTML5 only one flow is available at the moment: the organiser of the meeting selects a destination and invites his friends. Destinations can be selected from the server's or from Foursquare's database. The Figures 3 through 4 show the flow described above for two users. At the beginning, a user, called the organiser, selects a destination (Figure 3). He then sends invitations to his friend(s) (Figure 3 *left*). After all friends have accepted or declined, meeting points and routes are calculated for all participants. If several good meeting points are available, the organiser can choose, which to take, e.g. to meet at a bus stop or in front of a bakery (Figure 3 *middle*). Finally, calculated individual routes are displayed for each participant (Figure 3 *right*). These routes show amongst others, where to meet the other participants. They can also be displayed on a map, as shown in Figure 5.

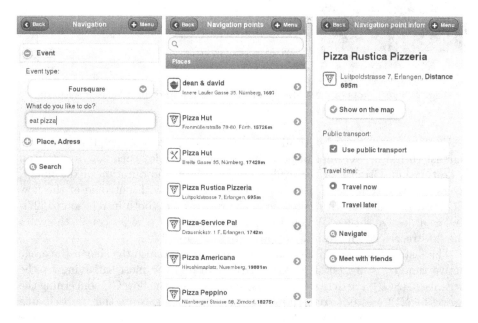

Fig. 3. Screenshots of GroupROSE *(from left to right)*: search for places of interest (POI), overview of POI, POI details and possibility to invite friends

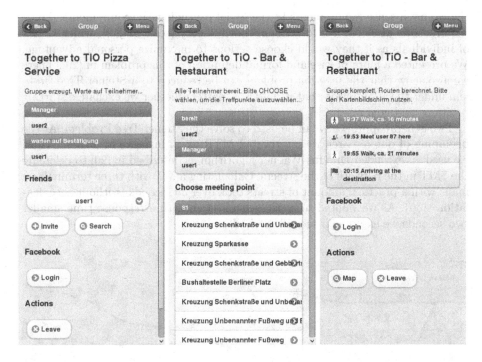

Fig. 4. Screenshots of GroupROSE *(from left to right)*: Dialog to invite friends, select a POI as meeting point, overviews of route for user 1

5   Group Pedestrian Navigation System

After a settlement is achieved our system helps the individuals to navigate to the agreed destination. For this, the current positions of the participants and the destinations are passed to the GPNS. One can easily imagine, where the participants could meet: at the destination, at one of the participants homes or at some dedicated locations in between. Often, the latter is the case: People meet at intermediate locations to yield a good compromise between detour and conjoint travel. To the best of our knowledge there is no literature from other authors about meeting behaviour and especially meeting point finding of individuals. Thus we will give our own definition of the problem.

Given is a map of a city and a set of individuals starting positions and a goal position in that city. For each individual a route has to be found from it's starting positing to the goal position. All these routes together compose a meeting tree (MT). Now, find a MT such that a) the distances travelled together are maximized and b) the detour for doing so is minimized. These requirement correspond to the every day meeting behavior of people as observed by common sense. From a social psychological point of view we can formulate a different requirement: Find a MT such that the costs for all individuals are minimized. By assigning costs for detour and negative costs to distances travelled conjoint we transform the common sense requirements to the social psychological requirements. These requirements also conform to rational choice theory (see e.g. [28]), which thinks of individuals as if they would choose actions to maximize personal advantage. We presented a more precise and formal definition of this problem in [29]. There we also show that the meeting problem can be reduced to a Steiner Tree Problem under the assumption that it does not matter whether we exchange starting positions and goal position.

Two general approaches can be used to solve the Steiner Tree Problem. At the beginning of our research we interpreted MTP as an instance of a SPN. Thus, we used an extended Dreyfus-Wagner algorithm as described in [20] to calculate the SMT in the network of the streets. Calculating a MT with three terminals on maps with a practical amount of streets took over 30 seconds (without precalculation step). As we wanted to construct a system with a response time smaller two seconds we explored a second method.

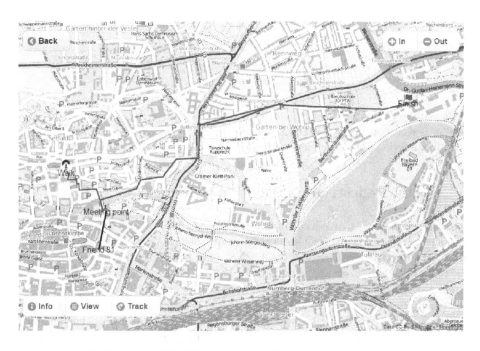

Fig. 5. GroupROSE Routes and meeting point for two people

"Pedestrian navigation [...] is not confined to a network of streets, but includes all passable areas, such as walkways, squares, and open areas, within or out- side buildings." [30]. Thus, pedestrian movement can be seen as largely independent of the street network. Inspired by their observation we neglect the actual structure of the street network in a first step. Now our problem resembles the ESP. Such, we can use e.g. the Melzak algorithm to estimate meeting points on a geometric basis only. For calculating meeting points in the ESP we relied on the program GeoSteiner (see section 2.4). The runtime of GeoSteiner for our limited set of terminals is negligible short. We call meeting points obtained by solving an ESP theoretical meeting points (TMPs). TMPs calculated in the previous step can be situated in unaccessible places like buildings or lakes or unintuitive places. Thus, we move these points to better locations nearby, e.g. restaurants, bars, bus stops, subway stations, some points-of-interest (POIs), public open places or big crossroads. We used OpenStreetMap as source for finding MPOIs. Afterwards routes to these meeting points are calculated in the street network. This is done using OpenRouteService (http://openrouteservice.org/). Also times at which users have to be at specific locations are calculated.

Compared to the optimal solution this method results in an average of 12.5% overall detour [29], which is according to [31] acceptable for pedestrians. In [29] we discuss the calculation of meeting points and routes in more detail. Routes for all individuals can be displayed in the client. An example of a route for two users shows Figure 5.

6   Conclusion

People go out in groups. We built a meeting appointment system which consists of an AAS and GPNS to support people in making appointments, calculating routes to their common destination and navigating there conjoint. We proposed and evaluated several flows of user to user interaction. The flow "Individual Search, Merging and Rating" (SMR) was the best flow under investigation for supporting mobile users in making appointments according to the organiser's satisfaction and the subjective votes. The fastest flow was "Group Rating after Criticising" (GRC). For calculating meeting points and routes we presented two methods which lead back to the Steiner Tree Problem. As the runtime of the method based on Steiner Problem in Networks is (at least when using the exact Dreyfus-Wagner algorithm) too high for our needs, we currently employ a method based on Euclidian Steiner Problem which neglects the street network.

In the future we want to add more flows to the HTML5 client and evaluate them. As meeting assistance systems is a new area of research there are still many open questions to answer and many aspects of meeting behaviour to be researched. At the moment, considering means of public transportation in multi user routing and group navigation is of particular interest to us.

References

1. Moussaïd, M., Perozo, N., Garnier, S., Helbing, D., Theraulaz, G.: The walking behaviour of pedestrian social groups and its impact on crowd dynamics. PLoS ONE 5(4), e10047 (2010)
2. James, J.: A preliminary study of the size determinant in small group interaction. American Sociological Review 16(4), 474–477 (1951)
3. Tumas, G., Ricci, F.: Personalized mobile city transport advisory system. In: EN-TER Conference 2009 (2009)

4. Maruyama, A., Shibata, N., Murata, Y., Yasumoto, K.: P-tour: A personal navigation system for tourism. In: Proc. of 11th World Congress on ITS, pp. 18–21 (2004)
5. Voelkel, T., Weber, G.: Routecheckr: personalized multicriteria routing for mobility impaired pedestrians. In: Proceedings of the 10th International ACM SIGACCESS Conference on Computers and Accessibility, pp. 185–192 (2008)
6. van Setten, M., Pokraev, S., Koolwaaij, J.: Context-Aware Recommendations in the Mobile Tourist Application COMPASS. In: De Bra, P.M.E., Nejdl, W. (eds.) AH 2004. LNCS, vol. 3137, pp. 235–244. Springer, Heidelberg (2004)
7. Huang, R.: A schedule-based pathfinding algorithm for transit networks using pattern first search. Geoinformatica 11, 269–285 (2007)
8. Ding, D., Yu, J.X., Qin, L.: Finding time-dependent shortest paths over large graphs. In: EDBT Proceedings, pp. 697–706 (2008)
9. Martens, J., Treu, G., Küpper, A.: Ortsbezogene community-dienste am beispiel eines mobilen empfehlungsdienstes. Ubiquität, Interaktivität, Konvergenz und die Medienbranche: Ergebnisse des interdisziplinären Forschungsprojektes intermedia (2007)
10. James, J.: The distribution of free-forming small group size. American Sociological Review 18(5), 569–570 (1953)
11. Goodman, L.A.: Mathematical methods for the study of systems of groups. The American Journal of Sociology 70(2), 170–192 (1964)
12. Jameson, A., Smyth, B.: Recommendation to Groups. In: Brusilovsky, P., Kobsa, A., Nejdl, W. (eds.) Adaptive Web 2007. LNCS, vol. 4321, pp. 596–627. Springer, Heidelberg (2007)
13. O'connor, M., Cosley, D., Konstan, J., Riedl, J.: PolyLens: A recommender system for groups of users. In: ECSCW 2001, pp. 199–218. Springer (2001)
14. Touw Ngie Tjouw, K.J.A.: An Intelligent Group Decision Support System for Urban Tourists. Delft University, master thesis (2010)
15. McCarthy, K., Salamó, M., Coyle, L., McGinty, L., Smyth, B., Nixon, P.: Group recommender systems: a critiquing based approach. In: Proceedings of the 11th International Conference on Intelligent User Interfaces, pp. 267–269. ACM (2006)
16. Jameson, A.: More than the sum of its members: challenges for group recommender systems. In: Proceedings of the Working Conference on Advanced Visual Interfaces, pp. 48–54. ACM (2004)
17. Gray, P.: Group decision support systems. Decision Support Systems 3(3), 233–242 (1987)
18. Winter, P.: Steiner problem in networks: a survey. Networks 17(2), 129–167 (1987)
19. Karp, R.: Reducibility Among Combinatorial Problems. In: Complexity of Computer Computations: Proceedings (1972)
20. Proemel, H., Steger, A.: The Steiner tree problem: a tour through graphs, algorithms, and complexity. Friedrick Vieweg & Son (2002)
21. Melzak, Z.: On the problem of Steiner. Canad. Math. Bull 4(2), 143–148 (1961)
22. Smith, J., Lee, D., Liebman, J.: An O (n log n) heuristic for Steiner minimal tree problems on the Euclidean metric. Networks 11(1), 23–39 (1981)
23. Chang, S.: The generation of minimal trees with a Steiner topology. Journal of the ACM (JACM) 19(4), 699–711 (1972)
24. Warme, D., Winter, P., Zachariasen, M.: Exact algorithms for plane Steiner tree problems: A computational study. In: Advances in Steiner Trees, pp. 81–116 (2000)
25. Winter, P.: An algorithm for the Steiner problem in the Euclidean plane. Networks 15(3), 323–345 (1985)

26. Zenker, B., Ludwig, B.: Rose - an intelligent mobile assistant - discovering preferred events and finding comfortable transportation links. In: ICAART (1), pp. 365–370 (2010)

27. Reinig, B.: Toward an Understanding of Satisfaction with the Process and Outcomes of Teamwork. Journal of Management Information Systems 19(4), 65–83 (2003)

28. Becker, G.: The economic approach to human behavior. University of Chicago Press (1976)

29. Zenker, B., Muench, A.: Calculating Meeting Points for Multi User Pedestrian Navigation Systems. In: Bach, J., Edelkamp, S. (eds.) KI 2011. LNCS, vol. 7006, pp. 347–356. Springer, Heidelberg (2011)

30. Wuersch, M., Caduff, D.: Refined Route Instructions Using Topological Stages of Closeness. In: Li, K.-J., Vangenot, C. (eds.) W2GIS 2005. LNCS, vol. 3833, pp. 31–41. Springer, Heidelberg (2005)

31. Helbing, D., Molnar, P., Farkas, I., Bolay, K.: Self-organizing pedestrian movement. Environment and Planning B 28(3), 361–384 (2001)

Recognizing Group Activities
Using Wearable Sensors

Dawud Gordon[1], Jan-Hendrik Hanne[2], Martin Berchtold[2], Takashi Miyaki[1], and Michael Beigl[1]

[1] Karlsruhe Institute of Technology, Kaiserstraße 12
76131 Karlsruhe, Germany
firstname.lastname@kit.edu
[2] Technische Universität Braunschweig, Pockelsstraße 14,
38106 Braunschweig, Germany
{j-h.hanne,m.berchtold}@tu-bs.de

Abstract. Pervasive computing envisions implicit interaction between people and their intelligent environments instead of between individuals and their devices, inevitably leading to groups of individuals interacting with the same intelligent environment. These environments must be aware of user contexts and activities, as well as the contexts and activities of groups of users. Here an application for in-network group activity recognition using only mobile devices and their sensors is presented. Different data abstraction levels for recognition were investigated in terms of recognition rates, power consumption and wireless communication volumes for the devices involved. The results indicate that using locally extracted features for global, multi-user activity recognition is advantageous (10% reduction in energy consumption, theoretically no loss in recognition rates). Using locally classified single-user activities incurred a 47% loss in recognition capabilities, making it unattractive. Local clustering of sensor data indicates potential for group activity recognition with room for improvement (40% reduction in energy consumed, though 20% loss of recognition abilities).

Keywords: group activity recognition, context recognition, distributed systems, multi-user, wearable.

1 Introduction

Context and activity recognition provide intelligent devices in the environment with the ability to act proactively in the interest of users. Many of us now carry around one or more intelligent devices constantly, and the number of intelligent systems in our environment such as entertainment systems, vending machines and informational displays is steadily increasing [2,14]. Implicit pro-active interaction based on situational awareness is increasingly more important in order to prevent us from entering a state of permanent distraction and informational overload. This state is a result of constantly having to administrate and respond to the myriad of intelligent devices in our immediate environment. One vision

A. Puiatti et al. (Eds.): MobiQuitous 2011, LNICST 104, pp. 350–361, 2012.
© Institute for Computer Sciences, Social Informatics and Telecommunications Engineering 2012

within pervasive and ubiquitous computing sees these devices progressing from single-user, private devices to multi-user devices running private applications for those users who are present. A challenge then becomes not only recognizing the context of the single user who is interacting with the device, as is the case with mobile phones [3], but now attempting to recognize the activity of a group of individuals who are in a specific environment or interacting with the system.

The group activity is not necessarily the same as the sum of the activities of the individuals in it [9]. The activity or context of a group is a function of the activity or context of all individuals in the group. Wearable technology has been proven to be effective for human activity recognition (HAR) [3,1,9] and is ever more prevalent, and is therefore an attractive platform for group activity recognition (GAR) as it is already present. Using a distributed wearable platform for both the sensing and processing aspects of activity recognition is advantageous in that it allows the system to operate independent of existing infrastructure and therefore widens the field of applications.

When using wearable technology (badges, mobile phones, coffee cups, etc.) for group activity or context recognition it is inherently a hierarchical problem, where data from wearable sensors on multiple users must be aggregated in order to infer the group context [9]. Preprocessing data locally reduces its volume and therewith the energy required for transmitting that data, but at the same time this process discards information which may be vital for classification [12]. Transmitting unprocessed, raw data guarantees that the maximum amount of information is available for GAR, but is very expensive due to communication.

In this work a system for recognizing group activities using only a distributed network of sensor nodes and mobile phones is presented. A mobile phone is used as a central node for GAR, and wireless sensor nodes are attached to coffee mugs (Smart Mugs) to monitor the activities of the individual user. The Smart Mugs can process measured sensor data locally to different abstraction levels before forwarding that data to the mobile phone for GAR. Different levels of data processing result in different levels of abstraction [12], from low-level raw sensor data to high-level single-user activity information processed using single-user HAR techniques. The later approach introduces the problem of having to doubly-label training data in terms of single-user and group activities in order to train both local single-user classifiers on the Smart Mugs and global GAR classifiers on the mobile phone. Two methods for avoiding the doubly-labeling problem are presented and evaluated here: separate training sessions for local and global activities, and using unsupervised clustering techniques. These different modes of operation are evaluated in terms of distributed energy consumption and GAR rates in a multi-user experiment.

2   Related Work

Activity and context recognition in general are highly researched fields. The majority of all context and activity recognition work is focused on human subjects and concentrates on single user activity and context recognition. Traditionally, this is conducted using body-worn acceleration sensors [1] which forward sampled data to a central server for classification. Other approaches range from embedded recognition approaches [13] to server based approaches which optimize classification results using crowd-sourcing [3].

First attempts at recognizing the activity of a group as a whole were pioneered with the Active Badge [14] and MediaCup [2] projects, which attempted to recognize situations such as meetings and presentations in office spaces. Further work in group activity recognition was conducted using camera-based activity recognition, such as for automatically recognizing group activities in a prison yard [5]. Another approach uses audio classification to recognize group activities, such as concurrent chatting activities [11], or for classifying roles of individuals in conversations and meetings [6]. These methods have proven effective, but rely heavily on infrastructure for recognition (cameras, networks, etc.). Research in GAR using wearable sensors has only recently been introduced to the scientific community. Wirz et al. approach recognition of cluster formations and flow patterns in groups of pedestrians in [15], and outline some of the problems in GAR [16]. Gu et al. [9] combine patterns of individual activities to recognize concurrent multi-user activities using probabilistic methods.

Despite these advances in GAR methods, much is still left to be researched, and in light of the growing number of intelligent objects which we carry with us or wear, the potential of this field has not been fully exploited. Sigg et al. [12] researched the optimal context abstraction level for prediction of future contexts. Since GAR using wearable sensors is inherently a hierarchical problem, these same issues are also present here as well, but with focus on GAR instead of context prediction. Here a case study on GAR to evaluate the optimal context abstraction level for GAR using sensors from wearable devices is presented, as was described in a preliminary poster abstract [8]. The results provide insight into the power-accuracy trade-off for GAR, and uncover several research questions for the field of GAR in general.

3   System Design

The system used here was made up of a wireless sensor network and a mobile phone. Wireless sensor nodes equipped with 3D acceleration sensors were attached to coffee mugs in a university/office setting. The nodes sampled activity and context data at the mugs, processed this data to the desired local abstraction level, and then forwarded this data to the smart-phone for further processing to classify the group activity as demonstrated in Fig. 1. The classifiers used in this paper are the k-Nearest-Neighbors (kNN) (k=10, Euclidean distance, no feature weighting), Decision Tree (DT) (C4.5), and Naive Bayes (nB) (no kernel estimation, single Gaussian, no covariance) algorithms, selected for their simplicity for embedded purposes. A hard K-Means clustering algorithm was used which outputs a single cluster candidate (top-1) for each vector, and uses subtractive clustering to identify the number of clusters present.

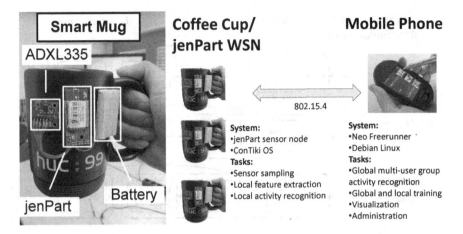

Fig. 1. Left: The Smart Mug with an Acceleration Sensor, jenPart Node and Battery **Right:** Network Topology of the Group Activity Experiment

The wireless sensor nodes used were jenParts from the open-source Jennisense Project[1]. The nodes are based on the JENNIC JN5139 wireless microprocessor, the ConTiki operating system [7], a battery and an analog 3D acceleration sensor[2]. The nodes sample the sensors at a rate of 33 Hz and segment the sample data into windows (1 window $= 16$ samples $\approx 250ms$ with 50% overlap). Based on the operational mode, the windows are then processed and forwarded to the Neo: either the raw sensor data is forwarded (**Raw Data** mode, low-level data [12]), or the sensor signal features average and variance are forwarded (**Feature** and **Training** mode), or single-user activity information from a classifier or clusterer is forwarded (**Classification** mode, high-level data [12]).

A Neo Freerunner[3] was connected to a jenPart bridge in USB host mode for communication with the Smart Mugs. The Neo serves as a mobile platform for classifying the group activity based on the data aggregated from all nodes in the WSN. This involves a training mode and a classification mode for the global classifier. At training time, a vector consisting of data from the local nodes (either raw, features, or classes) and a global group activity label is input into the global classifier. In classification mode, an unlabeled data vector consisting of the local data from the distributed nodes is input into the classifier, which then outputs the classification, or group activity estimation for that vector.

The Neo also serves as a context classifier training platform for the Smart Mugs in the WSN. Following the approach presented by Berchtold et al. [3], after being set in training mode by the Neo, each mug gathers data and forwards it to the Neo along with a local annotation indicated by segmenting activities using the button on the jenParts. Once this process is complete, the Neo trains the

---

[1] The Jennisense Project: https://github.com/teco-kit/Jennisense/wiki
[2] ADXL335 3-Dimensional Acceleration Sensor: http://www.analog.com
[3] http://www.openmoko.org/

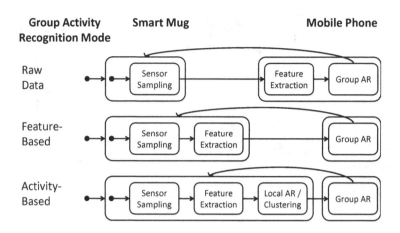

Fig. 2. State Charts for the Three Different System Modes for GAR

selected classifier, segments the trained classifier into packet-sized chunks, and sends these chunks sequentially to the nodes in a JSON format. The Mugs are equipped with a JSON interpreter which then reconstructs the classifiers locally and places them in memory so that they can be executed as a module.

4   Experiment

This experiment was designed to evaluate the different levels of data abstraction carried out by the Smart Mugs in terms of energy consumption and GAR rates. Processing data to the activity abstraction level [12] poses the problem of having to doubly-label the training data in terms of local, single-user activity labels and global, multi-user group activity labels. This must either be done using video recordings and offline annotation (time consuming) or multiple annotators in real time, both of which are too elaborate to allow easy deployment in new scenarios. To counteract this, two methods of skirting the doubly-labeling issue are employed and evaluated. First, local classifiers and global classifiers are trained in two sessions where each session must only be labeled with local or global activities respectively. Second, local activity classifiers are replaced with a hard, top-1, unsupervised k-means clustering [4], which does not require local activity labels, and can therefore be trained on the same data basis as the group activity classifier. Although the system was implemented on the distributed heterogeneous platform, the classification results presented here were generated offline using the WEKA toolkit [10] for analytical purposes but were cross-checked with online results.

4.1   Activity Recognition Experiment

During the course of this experiment, 3 subjects performed 7 different activities, 3 of which were group activities and 4 of which were individual activities involving the Smart Mugs. In total, over 45 minutes of data were collected, making over 22,700 sample windows, although some data was discarded at random to ensure that experimental data was independently and identically distributed (i.i.d.). The experiments were conducted in a meeting room in a university setting over the course of a single day. In the first phase, local classifiers were trained and evaluated, followed by the global classifiers in the second.

Phase 1: Local Classifiers. In the first phase of the evaluation, each user performed a set of activities, each one for a duration from approximately 2 - 15 minutes with the Smart Mug in training mode, meaning features and labels were extracted locally and uploaded to the Neo. The activities were local to the Smart Mugs, and were not performed as part of group activities, as doubly labeling local and group activities in real time is impractical. The local activities were as follows: the subject has placed the mug on the **table** (or other surface), the subject is holding the mug in their **hand**, the subject is **drinking** from the mug, and the subject is **gesticulating**.

After each activity was performed for the specified period of time, a button press on the node updated the label on the feature vector sent to the Neo and the next activity was performed. The first half of the data generated in this phase was used to train the local classifiers, and the second half was used to evaluate their performance. After all local activities were performed, the local classifiers were trained and communicated to the Smart Mug using JSON packets. The procedure of the process conducted in phase 1 is displayed in the upper portion of the sequence diagram in Fig. 3.

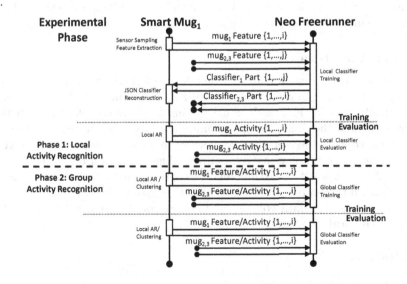

Fig. 3. Sequence Diagram for the Two-Phase Group Activity Recognition Experiment

Phase 2: Global Training and Evaluation. The evaluation of the global classifier was conducted offline using the data generated in this phase, where again half of the data was used for training and the other for performance evaluation. The subjects conducted the following activities together for 4 - 5 minutes each using Smart Mugs trained in the previous phase: **Meeting**, **Presentation** (users 1, 2 and 3) and **Coffee break**. A meeting consists of all subjects either setting their mugs on the table, holding them in their hand or drinking. In a presentation one subject will be gesticulating or holding their mug, and in a coffee break all are either holding, gesticulating with, or drinking from their mugs.

During this period, the nodes transmitted the full locally extracted feature vector, as well as the local classifications of the *local* activities listed previously. The raw sensor data was ignored for reasons which will be explained later. The process flow for phase two is shown in the lower portion of Fig. 3 where feature vectors and local activity classifications are transmitted simultaneously to train global classifiers for each data type respectively.

4.2 Power Measurements

The power consumption of each device was measured by placing the node in serial with a low error tolerance resistor and measuring the drop in voltage across the resistor. For each of the modes (raw sensor data, extracted feature data and classifier/cluster data) the average rate of consumption and the amount of energy consumed was calculated. The amount of energy consumed over the period of time beginning at t_0 and ending at t_1 is then given by $\int_{t_0}^{t_1} V_{supply} \times I_{supply} \, dt = \int_{t_0}^{t_1} V_{supply} \times \frac{V_{meas}}{R_{meas}} \, dt$ where V_{supply} is the supply voltage, I_{supply} is the current drawn by the node, which is given by the voltage drop (V_{meas}) over the measurement resistor with resistance R_{meas}.

4.3 Raw Data Issues

Since the features calculated by the mobile phone and the distributed nodes are identical, the recognition rates for both modes would be identical as well. Theoretically, the Neo is capable of calculating far more complex and extensive feature sets than the Smart Mugs, meaning that recognition rates for the raw data phase could be higher than for locally extracted features. That certain features provide better or worse recognition values is however a known fact, and the field of feature selection is a different area of research, making this comparison out-of-scope in the context of this work. For this reason, the raw data phase was only used to evaluate data volumes and energy consumption rates, and not to compare classification values.

5   Results

5.1 Classification Results

Phase 1: Local Classification. In phase 1 the Smart Mugs were trained using the following four classes: subject has set the mug down, subject is holding the mug, subject is drinking and subject is gesticulating. Tab. 1a displays the results of the evaluation of the local classifiers trained in phase 1 of the experiment. The accuracy, precision, recall and F-measure averaged over the 3 mugs is displayed. The results indicate that all classifiers for local, single-user activities performed at around 95%, where minimal variance across mugs and activities was observed.

Table 1. Classification Rates for Local and Global Classifiers

a) Local Activities (Averaged Over Nodes)

Data	DT		kNN		nB	
Basis	Acc.	F-meas.	Acc.	F-meas.	Acc.	F-meas.
Features	0.958	0.958	0.954	0.955	0.941	0.943

b) Global Activities

Data	DT		kNN		nB	
Basis	Acc.	F-meas.	Acc.	F-meas.	Acc.	F-meas.
Features	0.962	0.962	0.894	0.898	0.565	0.593
Clusters	0.762	0.764	0.597	0.605	0.491	0.494
Activities	0.507	0.524	0.424	0.484	0.491	0.505

Phase 2: Global Classification. Similar to phase 1, the global GAR classifier used half of the data generated in phase 2 for training and the other half for classifier evaluation. Tab. 1b displays the results of the evaluation of the global GAR classifiers from phase 2. Each row of the table represents a different data abstraction level of the Smart Mugs: either feature transmission, transmission of local activities (the local classifier algorithm is always the same as the global one, e.g. the first column is local single-user DT, with a global GAR DT), or transmission of local clustering results. In total 9 global GAR classifiers were trained and tested, 3 classifiers (DT, kNN, nB) for each type of local data abstraction.

Tab. 1b indicates that local classification provided poor results with a accuracies of 51% (DT), 49% (nB) and 42% (kNN). Local clustering provided better GAR results but with greater variance across the different classifiers, with accuracies of 76% (DT), 60% (kNN) and 49% (nB). The best results were achieved using local features and a DT classifier (96%), where the kNN algorithm achieved relatively high recognition rates (89%), while the nB classifier was only able to achieve GAR with an accuracy of 56% (compare with 33% at random).

5.2   Data Transmission and Energy Consumption

In order to analyze the requirements of the three different system modes in terms of resource consumption the nodes were monitored over different modes of operation. The effects of each mode was analyzed in terms of communication time and volume as well as energy consumption. Tab. 2 displays the amount of time required for communication per second (T_{tx}) and the amount of data communicated per second for each node. The results indicate a drop in data volume of 73.5% between transmitting raw data and features, 88.5% between features and

Table 2. Communication Volumes and Power Consumption Results

Mode	T_{tx} (ms)	Data Volume (B/s)	Neo Freerunner Avg(P) (W)	Smart Mug Avg(P) (mW)	E_{Tx} (mJ)
Raw Data	28.79	404.25	1.771	24.574	1.012
Features	24.63	107.25	1.723	24.233	0.909
Classes/Clusters	16.95	12.375	1.700	23.140	0.605

classes/clusters, and a 96.9% drop in the amount of data communicated from raw data mode to local context classification mode.

During the course of these experiments, the energy consumption rates of the different devices were also monitored. Tab. 2 displays the results for the energy measurements for both the Smart Mug hardware and the Neo mobile phone as they carried out the necessary operations. The results indicate a decrease in average energy consumption (Avg(P)) at the Smart Mugs of 1.4% from raw data to feature modes, a decrease of 4.5% from feature mode to classification mode, and a total drop of 5.8% from raw data to classification mode. For the Neo, a drop of 2.7% in average energy consumption was registered from raw data to features, a drop of 1.33% from features to classes, and a total drop of 4.0% from raw data to classification mode.

Due to the difference in the the ratio of operational to transmission power consumptions between the 2 device types, the change in energy consumption due to transmission could only be directly measured accurately at the Smart Mugs, but not at the Neo. The right-most column in Tab. 2 indicates the amount of energy consumed by a node for the purpose of communicating data wirelessly each second (E_{Tx}). This indicates a 10.17% drop in energy consumed when transmitting features as compared to raw data, and a decrease of 33.44% from features to classes, with a total decrease of 40.22% from raw data to classes.

6   Analysis and Discussion

One of the most important issues is selecting local activities relevant to discrimination between the global group activities. Here the experiment was designed to avoid this problem by engineering group activities which can be directly mapped onto the individual activities in order to evaluate the system, rather than the scenario. For real scenarios, either intuitive or experimental knowledge of the relationship between group and individual activities is required for activity selection, otherwise global recognition rates will deteriorate.

In this experiment, global classifiers were trained using the output of the local classifiers in the local classification mode, meaning that local classifier error was present in the training data for global classifiers. Alternatively, doubly-labeling activities would have allowed for training local and global classifiers on the ground truth labels simultaneously. The effects on global rates is unknown; using local labels could allow for the global classifier to account for and correct local errors, though it may also worsen results by distorting global classifier mappings. Furthermore, in this experiment a great deal of the GAR error when using locally classified activities was due to the fact that the data generated in Phase 1 of the experiment differed greatly from the data generated in Phase 2. Although subjects were instructed to conduct local activities as they would in a meeting, they were obviously incapable of reproducing their own behavior under the group activity conditions. This becomes apparent when comparing the average maximum feature values for signal average (812 local vs. 1324 global) and variance (6621 local vs. 148271 global) of the two datasets. Eliminating this discrepancy would involve labeling local activities during group activities which would greatly increase labeling effort.

Tab. 2 indicates that the energy consumed by the nodes for the purpose of transmission dropped by 33% when the nodes only transmit a locally classified situation instead of locally generated features. When compared with Tab. 1b, it becomes clear that these values come at a high price in terms of the recognition rates for global classification. Both the nB and DT classifiers performed comparably locally, but there is a disparity of up to almost 50% for global group activities based on local features. This indicates that GAR presents problems which are not present for single-user AR, and that not every classifier algorithm used for single-user HAR is appropriate for multi-user GAR. Specifically, the nB classifier uses a single Gaussian to model the distribution of each feature given a group activity. Data analysis indicates that often times group activities create multiple clusters in the multi-dimensional feature (18 dimensions) and activity (3 dimensions) space, for instance group activity "Presentation" consists of 3 clusters, one for the activity when each user presents. For GAR, this implies that a probabilistic approach should be combined with clustering and covariance modeling in order to model multiple clusters and dependencies, as the naive Bayes assumption can be detrimental.

Although the results of GAR using local clustering were significantly lower than using local features (76% as opposed to 96%, 20% drop), clustering is quite promising. The approach does not require a separate phase for local training as local labels are not required (unsupervised learning), and reduces the energy consumption due to transmission by 33%. The 20% drop in GAR rates is initially prohibitive for most applications, but the method used (k-means, hard clustering, top-1 class) can be combined with other approaches such as soft clustering and increasing the number of clusters outputted to improve recognition rates [4].

The ratio of how much of the total energy consumption is used for communication can be seen in Tab. 2, and is very much system and implementation dependent, where the volume of data falls by 75%, meaning that a large portion of the energy consumed for communication is in overhead. These values are heavily system and scenario dependent, where factors such as number of sensors and features, as well as window length and sample rate play a large role. Changing these parameters could tip the energy and GAR classification rate trade-off and would require a new evaluation.

7 Conclusion

This paper introduced a system for multi-user group activity recognition using only wearable and mobile devices for both sensing and recognition purposes. Multiple approaches to recognizing these activities were examined, where nodes processed sensor data to different levels of abstraction (raw data, features, local activities or clusters) before combining this information to recognize the group activity on a mobile phone.

An experiment was conducted in an office scenario where nodes attached to mugs were used to monitor user's activities and perform group activity recognition (GAR). Different levels of context preprocessing at the mugs were examined and evaluated in terms of power consumption and activity recognition rates. Specifically, using raw data, signal features, locally classified single-user activities and local clustering were examined as the basis for GAR and evaluated in terms of the cost of transmission incurred as well as GAR rates.

The results indicate that the optimal recognition was achieved using locally extracted features, with GAR accuracy of 96% and a 10% drop in the amount of energy consumed for the purpose of wireless communication. Locally classifying activities and using these to classify the global group activity reduced power consumption by a further 33%, but incurred a 47% drop in global multi-user GAR rates due to subjects' inability to recreate their own behavior under different conditions. Using local clustering showed potential by reducing power consumption by 40%. The recognition drop of 20% is severe, but can be improved upon by using more advanced clustering methods, indicating that this approach represents a topic for further research into reducing power consumption while avoiding the doubly-labeling issue.

Acknowledgments. The authors would like to acknowledge funding by the European Commission under the ICT project "CHOSeN" (Project No. 224327, FP7-ICT-2007-2).

References

1. Bao, L., Intille, S.S.: Activity Recognition from User-Annotated Acceleration Data. In: Ferscha, A., Mattern, F. (eds.) PERVASIVE 2004. LNCS, vol. 3001, pp. 1–17. Springer, Heidelberg (2004)
2. Beigl, M., Gellersen, H.-W., Schmidt, A.: Mediacups: experience with design and use of computer-augmented everyday artefacts. Comput. Netw. 35, 401–409 (2001)
3. Berchtold, M., Budde, M., Gordon, D., Schmidtke, H., Beigl, M.: ActiServ: Activity recognition service for mobile phones. In: ISWC 2010: Proceedings of the Fourteenth International Symposium on Wearable Computers, pp. 83–90. IEEE Computer Society, Seoul (2010)
4. Blanke, U., Schiele, B.: Daily Routine Recognition through Activity Spotting. In: Choudhury, T., Quigley, A., Strang, T., Suginuma, K. (eds.) LoCA 2009. LNCS, vol. 5561, pp. 192–206. Springer, Heidelberg (2009)

5. Chang, M.-C., Krahnstoever, N., Lim, S., Yu, T.: Group level activity recognition in crowded environments across multiple cameras. In: IEEE Conference on Advanced Video and Signal Based Surveillance, pp. 56–63 (2010)

6. Dong, W., Lepri, B., Cappelletti, A., Pentland, A.S., Pianesi, F., Zancanaro, M.: Using the influence model to recognize functional roles in meetings. In: Proceedings of the 9th International Conference on Multimodal Interfaces, ICMI 2007, pp. 271–278. ACM, New York (2007)

7. Dunkels, A., Grönvall, B., Voigt, T.: Contiki - a lightweight and flexible operating system for tiny networked sensors. In: Proceedings of the First IEEE Workshop on Embedded Networked Sensors (Emnets-I), Tampa, Florida, USA (November 2004)

8. Gordon, D., Hanne, J.-H., Berchtold, M., Miyaki, T., Beigl, M.: An Experiment in Hierarchical Recognition of Group Activities Using Wearable Sensors. In: Beigl, M., Christiansen, H., Roth-Berghofer, T.R., Kofod-Petersen, A., Coventry, K.R., Schmidtke, H.R. (eds.) CONTEXT 2011. LNCS, vol. 6967, pp. 104–107. Springer, Heidelberg (2011)

9. Gu, T., Wu, Z., Wang, L., Tao, X., Lu, J.: Mining emerging patterns for recognizing activities of multiple users in pervasive computing. In: 6th Annual International Mobile and Ubiquitous Systems: Networking Services, MobiQuitous 2009, pp. 1–10 (July 2009)

10. Hall, M., Frank, E., Holmes, G., Pfahringer, B., Reutemann, P., Witten, I.H.: The weka data mining software: an update. SIGKDD Explor. Newsl. 11, 10–18 (2009)

11. Hsu, J.Y.-J., Lian, C.-C., Jih, W.-R.: Probabilistic models for concurrent chatting activity recognition. ACM Trans. Intell. Syst. Technol. 2, 4:1–4:20 (2011)

12. Sigg, S., Gordon, D., von Zengen, G., Beigl, M., Haseloff, S., David, K.: Investigation of context prediction accuracy for different context abstraction levels. In: IEEE Transactions on Mobile Computing (2011)

13. Stäger, M., Lukowicz, P., Tröster, G.: Power and accuracy trade-offs in sound-based context recognition systems. Pervasive and Mobile Computing 3, 300–327 (2007)

14. Want, R., Hopper, A., Falcão, V., Gibbons, J.: The active badge location system. ACM Trans. Inf. Syst. 10, 91–102 (1992)

15. Wirz, M., Roggen, D., Tröster, G.: Decentralized detection of group formations from wearable acceleration sensors. In: Proceedings of the 2009 International Conference on Computational Science and Engineering, vol. 4, pp. 952–959. IEEE Computer Society, Washington, DC (2009)

16. Wirz, M., Roggen, D., Tröster, G.: A methodology towards the detection of collective behavior patterns by means of body-worn sensors. In: Workshop at the 8th International Conference on Pervasive Computing (2010)

Author Index

Printed in the United States
By Bookmasters